Architecting Intelligent Agents in Azure

Building Agentic Systems with Python and the Microsoft Agent Framework

Hari Narayn

Apress®

Architecting Intelligent Agents in Azure: Building Agentic Systems with Python and the Microsoft Agent Framework

Hari Narayn
Melbourne, VIC, Australia

ISBN-13 (pbk): 979-8-8688-2432-6   ISBN-13 (electronic): 979-8-8688-2433-3
https://doi.org/10.1007/979-8-8688-2433-3

Managing Director, Apress Media LLC: Welmoed Spahr
Acquisitions Editor: Smriti Srivastava
Editorial Assistant: Marina Engler

Cover designed by eStudioCalamar

Distributed to the book trade worldwide by Springer Science+Business Media New York, 1 New York Plaza, New York, NY 10004. Phone 1-800-SPRINGER, fax (201) 348-4505, e-mail orders-ny@springer-sbm.com, or visit www.springeronline.com. Apress Media, LLC is a Delaware LLC and the sole member (owner) is Springer Science + Business Media Finance Inc (SSBM Finance Inc). SSBM Finance Inc is a **Delaware** corporation.

For information on translations, please e-mail booktranslations@springernature.com; for reprint, paperback, or audio rights, please e-mail bookpermissions@springernature.com.

Apress titles may be purchased in bulk for academic, corporate, or promotional use. eBook versions and licenses are also available for most titles. For more information, reference our Print and eBook Bulk Sales web page at http://www.apress.com/bulk-sales.

Any source code or other supplementary material referenced by the author in this book is available to readers on GitHub. For more detailed information, please visit https://www.apress.com/gp/services/source-code.

If disposing of this product, please recycle the paper

To my children, Ithal and Rain.

You are the brightest parts of my life.

Stay curious, stay kind,

and always believe in yourselves.

You are my inspiration, today and always.

Table of Contents

About the Author

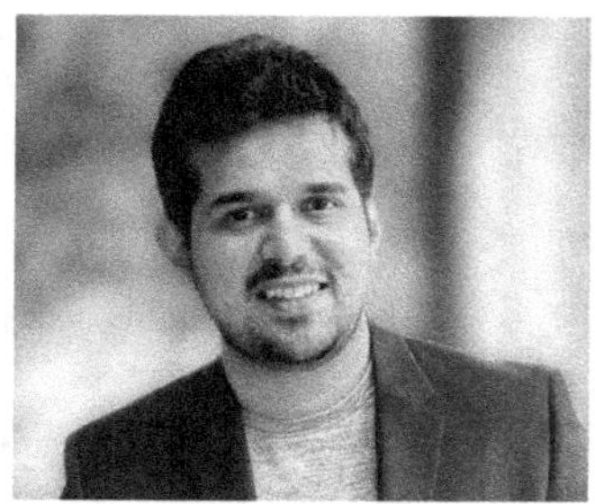

Hari Narayn is an AI architect and technology author specializing in enterprise-grade agentic systems and cloud-native AI platforms. With over 15 years of experience, he designed and delivered scalable, production-ready solutions across the public and private sectors, with a strong focus on Microsoft Azure.

Based in Melbourne, Hari architects and engineers intelligent systems within the Victorian public sector, that combine large language models, semantic retrieval, multi-agent orchestration, and governed execution. His work spans agentic systems, Retrieval-Augmented Generation (RAG), vector search, and responsible AI, with a focus on building systems that are reliable, observable, and secure by design.

He has led the development of enterprise AI platforms on Azure, helping organizations move from experimentation to scalable, production-grade adoption. His recent work focuses on multi-agent architectures using the Microsoft Agent Framework, integrating reasoning, memory, and tool-driven automation into cohesive systems. He also designs sytems around standardized interfaces such as the Model Context Protocol (MCP).

Hari holds multiple Microsoft certifications, including Azure Solutions Architect Expert and Azure AI Engineer Associate. He is a published author with titles spanning enterprise platforms, modern web architectures, and intelligent agent systems. Hari is passionate about bridging architecture and hands-on engineering. Through his writing and mentoring, he helps developers and architects build practical AI systems that scale in real-world environments.

About the Technical Reviewer

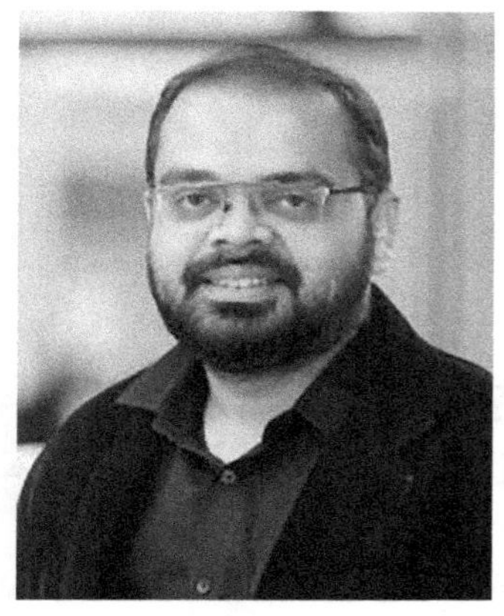 **Kasam Shaikh** is a prominent figure in India's artificial intelligence landscape, holding the distinction of being one of the country's first four Microsoft Most Valuable Professionals (MVPs) in AI. Currently serving as a Chief Architect, Kasam boasts an impressive track record as an author, having authored five best-selling books dedicated to Azure and AI technologies. Beyond his writing endeavors, Kasam is recognized as a Microsoft Certified Trainer (MCT) and influential tech YouTuber (@mekasamshaikh). He also leads the largest online Azure AI community, known as DearAzure | Azure INDIA, and is a globally renowned AI speaker. His commitment to knowledge sharing extends to contributions to Microsoft Learn, where he plays a pivotal role.

Within the realm of AI, Kasam is a respected Subject Matter Expert (SME) in Generative AI for the Cloud, complementing his role as a Chief Cloud Architect. He actively promotes the adoption of No Code and Azure OpenAI solutions and possesses a strong foundation in Hybrid and Cross-Cloud practices. Kasam Shaikh's versatility and expertise make him an invaluable asset in the rapidly evolving landscape of technology, contributing significantly to the advancement of Azure and AI.

In summary, Kasam Shaikh is a multifaceted professional who excels in both technical expertise and knowledge dissemination. His contributions span writing, training, community leadership, public speaking, and architecture, establishing him as a true luminary in the world of Azure and AI. Kasam was recently awarded as top voice in AI by LinkedIn, making him the sole exclusive Indian professional acknowledged by both Microsoft and LinkedIn for his contributions to the world of artificial intelligence!

Acknowledgments

Writing this book has been both a technical and personal journey. I am grateful to those who stood beside me through every chapter and every moment of doubt and clarity.

To my wife, Divya, your patience, encouragement, and love made space for this book to exist.

To my mentors, colleagues, and everyone I've worked with over the years, thank you for the conversations, challenges, and experiences that shaped my understanding of engineering and problem-solving. The lessons drawn from real systems and real teams form the foundation of this book.

Thank you to the Apress editorial team and the technical reviewer for their careful and professional guidance throughout this project.

To the engineering community at large, your curiosity and willingness to explore new ideas inspire me to give back.

Finally, to every reader exploring the world of agentic systems, thank you. I hope this book gives you the foundation to build agents that reason with purpose, remember what matters, and earn the trust of the systems they operate in.

Introduction

Artificial intelligence has moved beyond simple question-and-answer interactions. We now have systems that can weigh context, draw on memory, take action, use tools, and work together as coordinated agents. These agentic capabilities are already powering real products, from coding assistants to enterprise workflows.

Yet building one that holds up in production is a different challenge entirely.

This book explores that question through a hands-on journey of building an agentic system on Azure. Across the chapters, we create Thain, a support-triage agent that starts with simple conversational behavior and gradually grows into a system that can retrieve information, coordinate tasks, and support real enterprise workflows. As the chapters progress, Thain develops new capabilities, including reasoning, memory, tools, semantic recall, and collaboration, while we design the cloud environment needed to deploy and operate it.

A key part of this journey is the Microsoft Agent Framework, which provides the foundation for reasoning loops, memory, and tool integration. Along the way, we work with Azure AI services, Python, and familiar cloud-architecture patterns to design intelligent systems with practical purpose. We explore how memory shapes an agent's behavior, how tools guide its decisions, how agents communicate, and what's required to keep these systems safe, reliable, and observable in production.

If you're an AI engineer, Azure developer, or architect curious about agentic systems, this book aims to make the path clear and approachable. By the final chapter, you'll understand how these systems think and operate and how to design them with care and intention. With that foundation, you'll be ready to build agents of your own, systems that can reason, remember, collaborate, and grow.

How to Read This Book

This book presents an architectural journey through the design and evolution of a production-grade agentic system on Azure. It follows a single system, Thain, from conceptual prototype to governed, observable, enterprise-ready service. Each chapter introduces a new capability layer, and each layer is integrated without weakening the system's existing invariants.

The implementation is real and executable, but the primary focus is architectural. The book demonstrates how reasoning, memory, orchestration, governance, evaluation, and operational discipline form a cohesive system.

Who This Book Is For

This book is intended for AI engineers, Azure developers, and solution architects seeking to build durable agentic systems rather than isolated prompt experiments.

Readers should be comfortable with Python and familiar with core Azure services. Prior experience with agent frameworks is not required, as key abstractions are introduced progressively in the early chapters.

What You Will Need

The system described in this book is implemented and deployed on Azure. To reproduce it, you will need

- An Azure subscription with Azure OpenAI access, and a supported model deployment

- Python 3.11 or later

- Docker Desktop (required from Chapter 8 onward)

- Azure CLI

- The book's GitHub repository (`https://github.com/Apress/Architecting-Intelligent-Agents-in-Azure`)

The repository is structured by chapter, with the code base at each chapter boundary available as a starting point. The companion repository includes two runnable code paths: the original beta listings that match the book, and Microsoft Agent Framework 1.5.0 General Availability (GA) code with chapter-by-chapter migration notes. The beta path preserves the book's architectural learning journey, while the GA path reflects the framework's stable release. DevUI is used in the book as a learning aid to make agent behavior, tool calls, and traces more visible than the command line; treat it as a development companion, not a production interface.

Azure resources are provisioned with cost awareness throughout the book. Early chapters operate within near-free development tiers, allowing experimentation without material expense. Azure AI Search, introduced in Chapter 4, incurs ongoing service costs. In Chapter 8, Thain is deployed as a managed service in Azure Container Apps, introducing sustained runtime compute costs consistent with production environments.

Resources can be scaled down or stopped between development sessions to keep costs controlled. Cost management and optimization are addressed explicitly in later chapters.

How the Book Is Structured

The book follows a single narrative arc, with each chapter sequential. Each chapter concludes with a validated system version, and the next begins from that state.

Chapter 1 establishes Thain's architectural vision and provisions the Microsoft Foundry workspace and GPT-4o model deployment required from Chapter 2 onward.

Chapters 2 through 8 establish Thain v1.0, a deployed, multi-agent service with governance, observability, and safety controls. Thain goes fully live as a containerized service in Chapter 8, completing the first release cycle.

Chapters 9 and 10 extend v1.0 with formal evaluation, human feedback integration, operational hardening, and scale readiness, resulting in Thain v2.0.

If You Are Joining Mid-book

Each chapter begins with a scope definition and ends with validation steps. Readers interested in specific architectural topics, such as multi-agent orchestration in Chapter 7 or reliability hardening in Chapter 10, may start there if they are comfortable with the earlier abstractions. The companion repository contains the code base at each chapter boundary.

A Note on the Code

Chapters 2 through 5 present complete inline implementations to establish core mechanics. From Chapter 6 onward, the emphasis shifts to architectural structure. Key patterns are illustrated through representative excerpts, with full implementations available in the companion repository.

This progression mirrors the system's evolution. As Thain matures, the focus moves from basic behavior to systemic properties: determinism, safety, observability, failure isolation, and operational discipline. Microsoft Agent Framework is evolving quickly. The companion repository includes Architectural Notes for each chapter and a note named MAF-Evolving-Capabilities.md that maps newer framework features such as workflows, middleware, checkpointing, built-in evaluation, hosted agents, and more to each chapter's architecture.

Thain: The Beginning

Introduction

Thain begins as a simple idea: a single agent that reads a customer complaint, reasons about its meaning, and returns a structured response. It starts with this foundational capability and does not stay there. Across the chapters that follow, Thain evolves, gaining memory, retrieval, action tools, collaborative agents, governance, and production-grade reliability, with each capability layered deliberately on top of the last.

Ahead of the implementation, this chapter establishes two foundations. The first is architectural: it maps the full journey Thain will take, the capabilities it will acquire, and the patterns that will shape its design. Understanding the destination early ensures that every chapter that follows has a clear purpose, not just a task.

The second is practical. Thain's reasoning is powered by GPT-4o, hosted in Microsoft Foundry (formerly Azure AI Foundry). This chapter sets up that workspace and deploys the model. It is the only infrastructure required to begin, and everything else is built incrementally as the system evolves.

Architectural clarity, combined with a working Azure foundation, sets the tone for the rest of the book.

The Agent Runtime: From Responses to Systems

Most interactions with a large language model (LLM) follow the same pattern: a message is sent, the model generates a response, and the exchange ends. The model does not retain memory across calls unless context is explicitly provided, has no inherent ability to take action, and cannot revise its response once generated. It is effectively stateless, reactive, and single shot.

H. Narayn, *Architecting Intelligent Agents in Azure*, https://doi.org/10.1007/979-8-8688-2433-3_1

1

An agent changes that model fundamentally. Instead of generating one response and stopping, it operates within a reasoning loop. The agent observes the input; decides what to do; takes an action such as calling a tool, retrieving a document, or writing to a database; then observes the result; and decides what to do next. This loop continues until the agent has enough information to produce a final response or determines that human input is required.

Three properties emerge from this loop that a plain LLM call cannot replicate. First, memory. An agent can carry context across turns and sessions, building a picture of what it has seen before. Second, tool use. An agent can interact with external systems, not just describe what should happen but make it happen. Third, judgment. Because the agent sees the results of its own actions, it can adjust its approach mid-task rather than committing to a single answer.

These properties make agents valuable in enterprise contexts, but they also introduce architectural demands. A system that takes actions must be observable. You need to understand what the agent did, why it did it, and what it cost. A system that handles sensitive data must be governable, with behavior that is bounded, auditable, and safe. A system that runs in production must be resilient, able to degrade gracefully when dependencies fail, and recover without manual intervention.

These are not optional concerns. They are the constraints that separate a working prototype from a system that can be trusted at scale. Thain is built with all of them in mind.

Thain's Architecture: Capability Evolution

Thain's capabilities are introduced layer by layer, each grounded in a real architectural pattern. The system evolves through three phases: building the core agent, making it trustworthy and deployable, and hardening it for production scale.

Building the Core Agent

The foundation is a reasoning loop. GPT-4o processes input, selects tools, and returns a structured response through the Microsoft Agent Framework. On top of this, Thain gains short-term memory, an in-session buffer that keeps recent context available across a multi-turn conversation.

Persistence is the next layer. Thain connects to Azure Cosmos DB, storing every complaint as a retrievable record. What Thain encounters in one session becomes available in the next. The memory boundary moves from process lifetime to database lifetime.

Semantic retrieval extends this further. By integrating Azure AI Search and vector embeddings, Thain can find related complaints even when the wording differs significantly. This is the Retrieval-Augmented Generation (RAG) pattern, implemented as part of the reasoning loop rather than added afterward.

Action tools complete the core. Thain gains the ability not just to analyze but to act, writing records, triggering workflows, and surfacing decisions for human review through an approval gate. This human-in-the-loop control for consequential actions becomes a recurring pattern throughout the production chapters.

From Capable to Production-Ready

With a capable core in place, the focus shifts to safe operation. Content safety scanning protects against harmful inputs and outputs. Application Insights provides end-to-end observability, capturing tool calls, token usage, and latency as queryable telemetry. Policy controls ensure consistent behavior across environments.

A second agent is then introduced through the Blackboard pattern, forming a multi-agent system where specialized agents share context, challenge conclusions, and coordinate toward outcomes no single agent could achieve alone.

Azure Container Apps, CI/CD scripts, and infrastructure as code transition Thain from a development project to a versioned, production-grade service.

Learning and Scaling

The final phase closes the feedback loop and addresses production realities. An LLM-as-judge evaluation pipeline continuously assesses response quality, while a policy hardening layer applies improvements based on those results.

Streaming responses, cost optimization, caching strategies, and a reliability layer based on timeouts, retries, and circuit breakers ensure the system remains efficient and resilient under load.

These layers culminate in a reference production architecture: a three-plane system spanning data acquisition, knowledge preparation, and agent execution. Running on Azure Container Apps with full observability and governance controls, it is the architectural destination every chapter builds toward.

Thain's Capability Arc Diagram

Figure 1-1 maps Thain's evolution across the three phases.

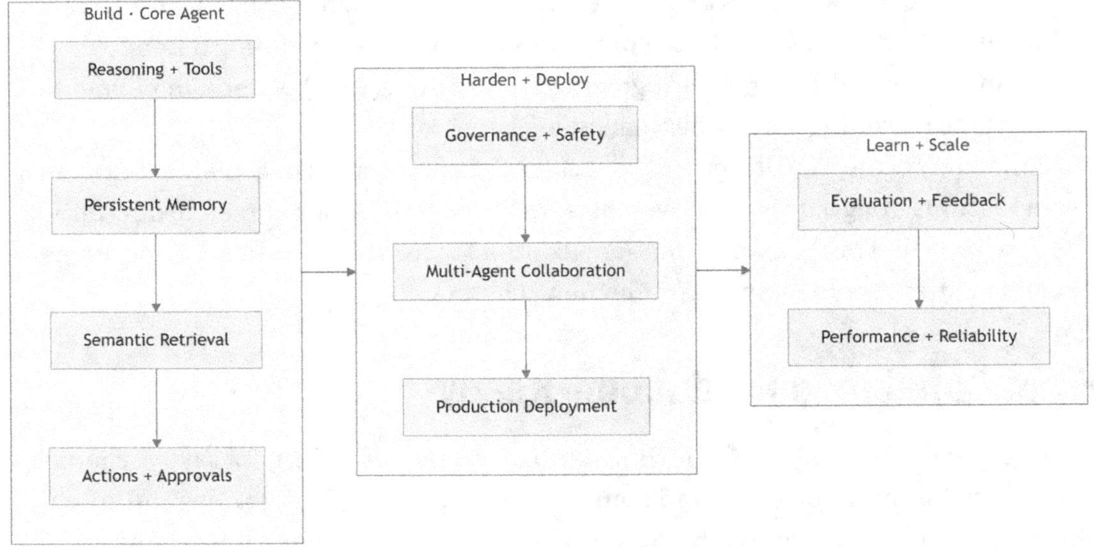

Figure 1-1. *Thain's capability arc: from first agent to production system*

Provisioning the Microsoft Foundry Environment

With the architectural foundation established, the remaining task is practical: provision the Microsoft Foundry workspace and deploy the GPT-4o model that Thain will use from Chapter 2 onward. **Note**: Microsoft Foundry is an actively evolving platform. The portal layout, menu structure, and deployment steps shown in this chapter reflect the experience at the time of writing. If the interface differs when you follow along, the underlying concepts and resource names remain the same. Treat the steps as guidance rather than an exact script.

Setting Up Azure

Azure typically offers $200 in free credits for the first month, which is ideal for our early stages.

Note   Use a region where your subscription has quota for the model you deploy. The screenshots use East US 2, but model availability and quota vary by subscription and change over time.

- Go to `https://azure.microsoft.com/free`.

- Sign in with your Microsoft account or create one if needed.

- Complete the signup steps.

These steps are standard Azure setup and are included here only to ensure a consistent starting point.

Create Your Foundry Workspace

Once you are in the Azure Portal, click Create a resource, and search for `Microsoft Foundry`. Select `Create` to start setting up the Foundry resource. In the form that appears, fill in the following details:

- **Resource group**: `rg-aiaa-book` (create a new one, as this doesn't exist yet.)

- **Foundry name**: `foundryThain`

- **Region**: `East US 2`

- **Default project name**: `projectThain`

Leave defaults for the rest and click `Review + Create`.
Check out Figure 1-2.

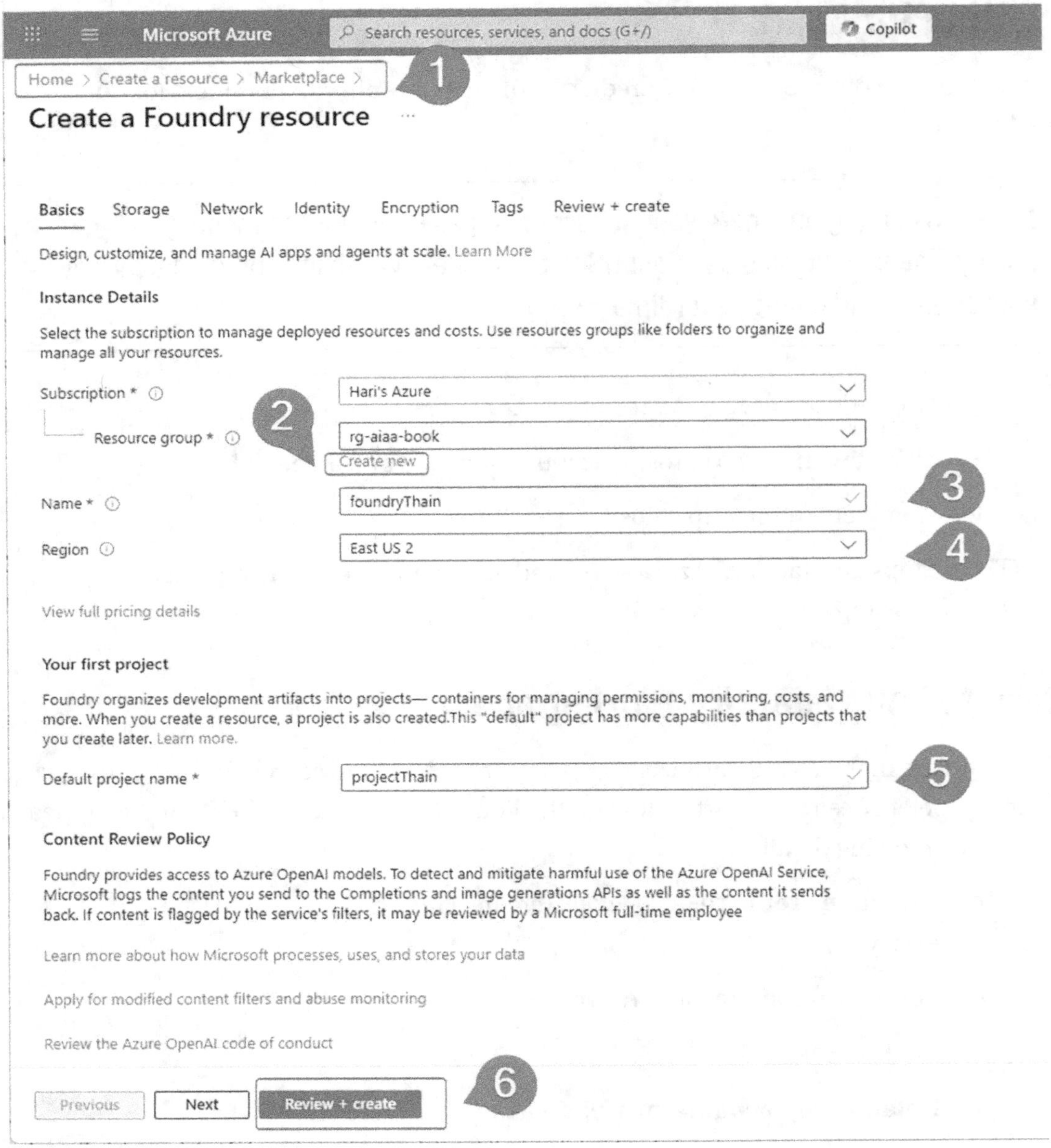

Figure 1-2. *Create Foundry resource*

Launch the Project Space

Once the deployment is completed, select `Go to resource` to open the `foundryThain` resource page in the Azure Portal.

After opening the Foundry resource, click `Go to Foundry portal` to open the project space. If the New Foundry toggle appears in the top-right corner and is enabled by default, turn it off to use the classic experience.

Note   We will use the classic experience for this chapter to maintain consistency in the walkthrough. You are welcome to explore the new experience later once you're comfortable with the core concepts.

You will arrive at the `project-thain` landing page. You will notice things like Project Endpoints, API keys, and other settings – don't worry about those just yet. We will unpack all of that in later chapters when we start wiring up external tools and deploying custom logic.

Look at Figure 1-3. In the left-hand sidebar, notice menu items like `Models + endpoints` and `Agents`; we will use this in the next section.

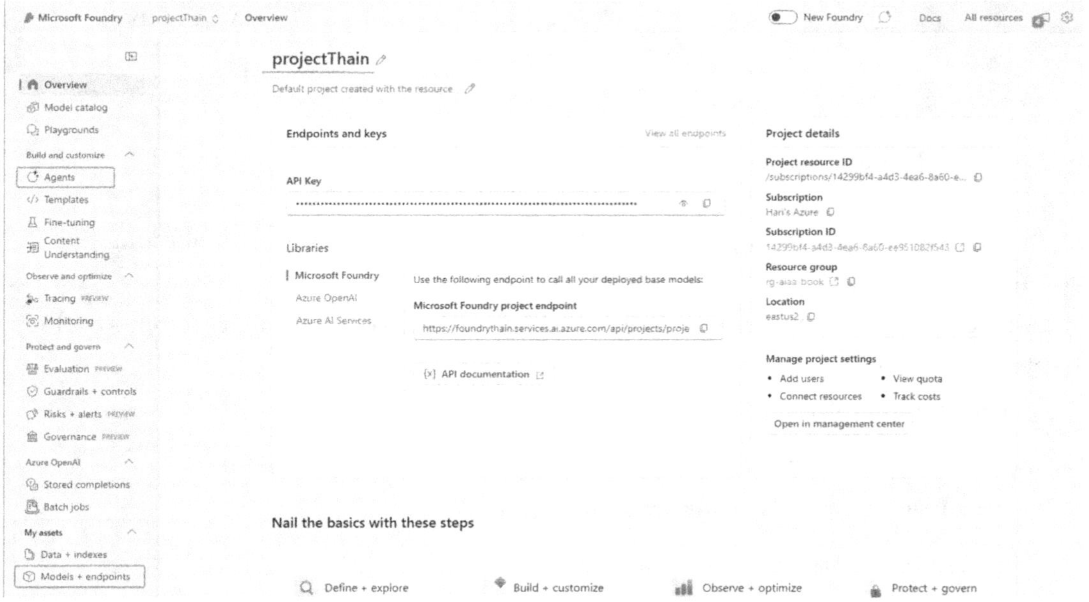

Figure 1-3. *Foundry project space*

Deploy the Language Model

First, let us deploy the model that powers Thain's intelligence. We'll use GPT-4o for this book. It's fast, cost-effective, and more than capable of handling the workloads we're using in this book. Select GPT-4o and click Confirm to deploy the model.

Click `Models + endpoints` in the left-hand sidebar under `My assets`. Then click `Deploy model` ➤ `Deploy base model`. A pop-up window will appear. Search and select `gpt-4o`. Refer to Figure 1-4.

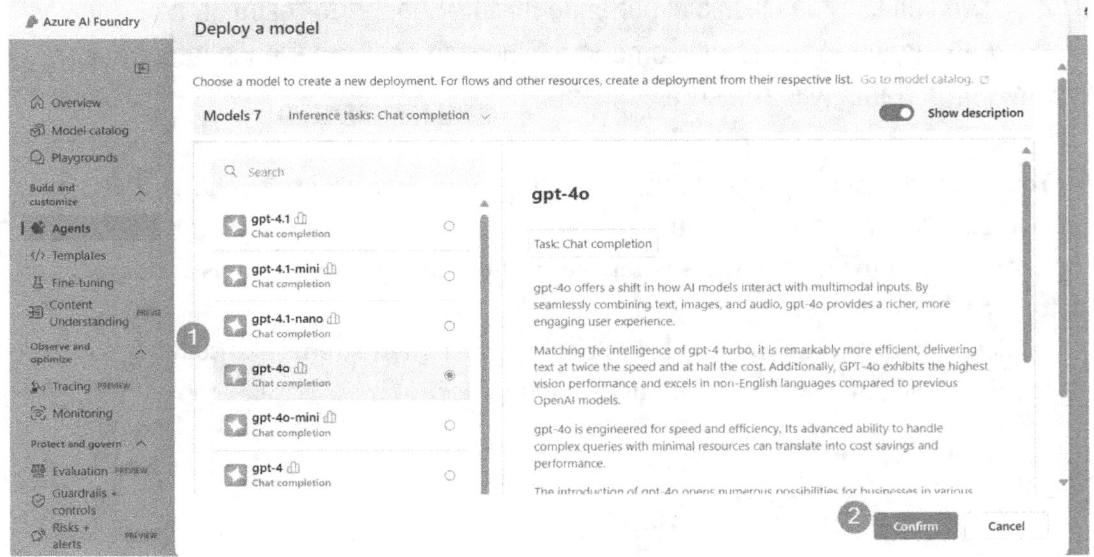

Figure 1-4. *Deploy a model-1*

In the new pop-up that appears, you can keep the default deployment name (gpt-4o).

For Deployment type, select Standard. This is appropriate for the workloads in this chapter.

Leave all other options as the defaults:

- **Model version upgrade policy**: Upgrade once the new default version becomes available.

- **Model version**: Whatever is pre-selected (e.g., 2024-11-20).

- **Resource location**: Select the East US.

- **Tokens per minute**: Keep the default slider (the included quota is more than enough).

- **Dynamic quota**: Keep enabled.

Once everything is set, click Create resource and deploy. Observe Figure 1-5.

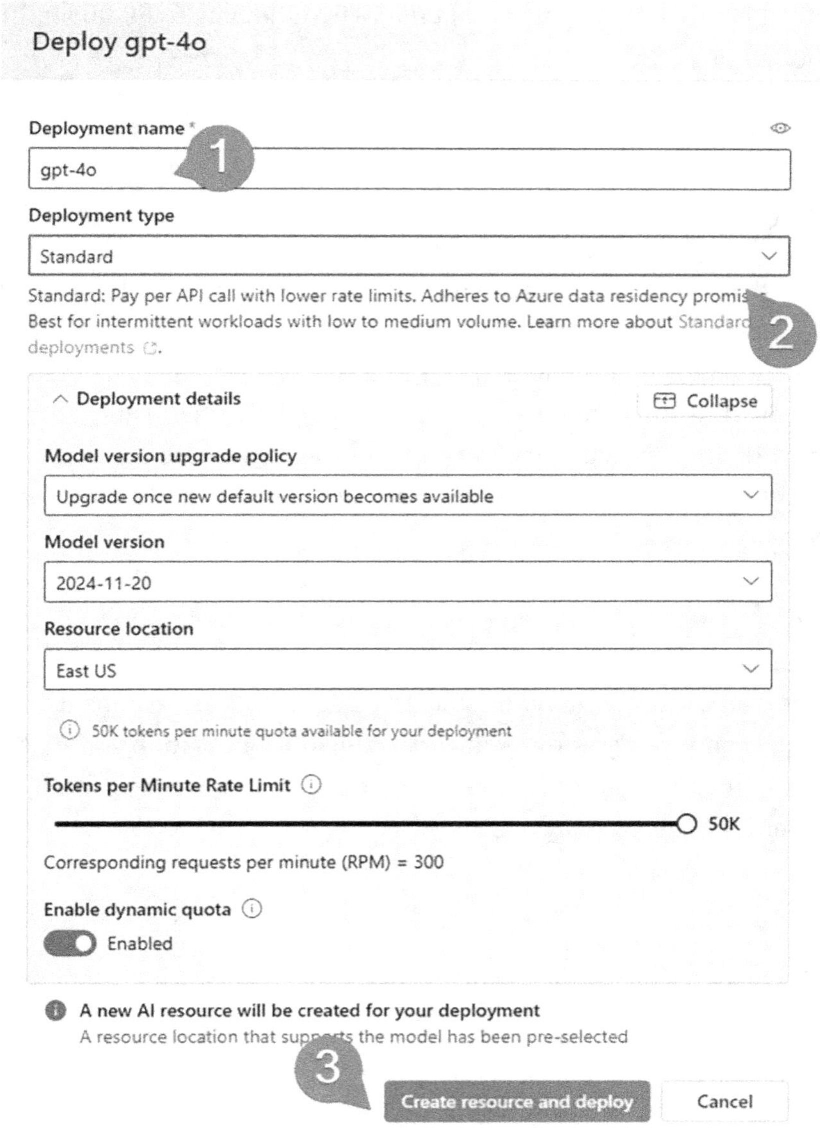

Figure 1-5. *Deploy a model-2*

> **Note**   You can view all deployed models by clicking Models + Endpoints on the left menu.
>
> We'll continue using this same model deployment when we start building Thain in code in Chapter 2. If you'd like to experiment, you can always deploy a newer model (like GPT-5.4 or GPT-5.5) and switch models in the environment configuration at any stage.

Summary

In this chapter, the foundation for everything that follows was established, both conceptually and practically.

The distinction between a plain language model call and an agent was introduced through the reasoning loop, tool use, and memory, along with the enterprise properties required for production systems. Thain's capability arc was mapped, from a single reasoning agent to a governed, multi-agent production system, with each layer aligned to a concrete architectural pattern.

The Microsoft Foundry workspace was provisioned and the GPT-4o model deployed to power Thain's reasoning. This deployment is the only infrastructure required for Chapter 2. Everything else is built in code, one layer at a time.

In the next chapter, implementation begins. Thain v0.1 takes shape using the Microsoft Agent Framework, introducing a working reasoning loop, a classification tool, and a short-term memory buffer. By the end of it, the system will be running in a local development environment, ready to evolve.

Thain Meets the Agent Framework

Introduction

In Chapter 1, Thain's architectural journey was mapped and the Microsoft Foundry workspace was prepared. The reasoning loop, tool use, and enterprise properties that shape every design decision were established as the foundation. Now the implementation begins.

This chapter moves into engineering mode, building Thain's first working version using the Microsoft Agent Framework. Thain takes shape not as a concept but as a running Python system: reasoning, invoking tools, and maintaining short-term memory in a single coordinated loop.

The Microsoft Agent Framework is a unified layer that connects large language models such as GPT-4o with tools, workflows, and memory, enabling them to operate as a single coherent system. Think of it as an operating system for agents: it manages context, coordinates tool use, and maintains data flow while giving you full visibility and control.

In this chapter, Thain plugs into the framework using an async runtime, tool decorators, and the built-in Dev UI for live tracing. You'll see how reasoning, tools, and short-term memory come together in a clean, testable Python project you can run locally.

We'll start with a keyword classifier as Thain's first tool, pair it with a lightweight in-memory context buffer, and tie everything together with an async agent loop that returns structured JSON. By the end, Thain v0.1 runs from your editor in two modes: a single-message CLI and an interactive session that preserves short-term memory. You'll also use the Dev UI to observe how Thain reasons and which tools it calls.

© Hari Narayn 2026
H. Narayn, *Architecting Intelligent Agents in Azure*, https://doi.org/10.1007/979-8-8688-2433-3_2

With this build, Thain works through the Agent Framework: reasoning, recalling, and improving. In the next chapter, we add persistent memory with Cosmos DB and Azure AI Search so Thain can recognize patterns across sessions.

Note   Throughout this book, we'll mostly use GPT-4o for the demonstrations. However, you're welcome to use GPT-5.5 or any of the latest available models instead. The Microsoft Agent Framework works in the same way, and you may even notice faster reasoning or better contextual understanding with the latest versions.

Thain v0.1: The First Working Agent

By the end of this chapter, Thain reaches version 0.1 – its first working implementation as a real agent built in Python using the Microsoft Agent Framework.

You will build

- **A configuration layer**: Typed environment loading with validation, ensuring the agent fails fast and clearly if Azure credentials are missing

- **A memory layer**: A bounded in-memory buffer that maintains short-term context across turns within a session

- **A classification tool**: A keyword-based classifier exposed to the agent through the native MAF tool decorator, giving Thain its first callable skill

- **An async agent runtime**: The core orchestration loop that connects reasoning, tools, and memory through the Microsoft Agent Framework

- **Three execution modes**: Single-message CLI, interactive session, and Dev UI for live observability

Note   The complete project for this chapter is available in the Chapter 2 folder of the companion repository at `https://github.com/Apress/Architecting-Intelligent-Agents-in-Azure`. While all code listings are included in this chapter, the repository is the single source of truth for runnable, up-to-date code. The repository also includes a Microsoft Agent Framework 1.5.0 General Availability version of this chapter's code in the Code GA folder. The GA version uses the current agent class, Foundry chat client, tool decorator, and context-provider lifecycle while preserving the chapter's architecture and behavior. A detailed migration note is also available in the repository.

Designing Thain v0.1

Thain begins as a single agent with one focused responsibility: read a customer complaint, understand the issue, and return a clear structured insight. Just as every organization starts with a defined role before growing into a team, Thain's architecture follows the same principle.

This first agent becomes the foundation for everything that follows: the logic, structure, and reasoning you design here will scale seamlessly into the broader feedback-analysis ecosystem in later chapters.

At a high level, Thain v0.1 listens to a single customer message, reasons through it with GPT-4o, optionally calls a helper tool for classification, and responds with a concise JSON object that includes both the detected issue category and a summary.

For instance, imagine a customer reporting a recurring hardware issue:

```
Input: "The phone battery started swelling again after the last update."
Output: { "category": "Battery Issue", "summary": "Customer reports
repeated battery swelling after the recent software update." }
```

Behind the scenes, the Microsoft Agent Framework (MAF) coordinates three essential components:

1. **Reasoning**: Acts as Thain's brain, powered by GPT-4o through the Azure OpenAI endpoint

2. **Tool**: A lightweight Python function that classifies text by keywords or patterns

3. **Memory**: A short-term in-memory list that stores recent complaints, allowing Thain to maintain context during a session

You'll implement these parts using the same MAF packages we'll rely on throughout the book. This continuity ensures that what you build here will naturally evolve into a multi-agent workflow, and the same design patterns will carry forward as Thain becomes more capable.

Setting Up Your Workspace in VS Code

Before we write a single line of code, let's prepare the environment where Thain will come to life.

You'll need Visual Studio Code, Python 3.11 or later, and the Azure CLI installed.

In Chapter 1, we explored the Azure Portal and Microsoft Foundry, and we created a project that connects to an Azure OpenAI resource. We'll now build directly on top of that setup, and everything we do in code will connect to the same environment you already configured.

If you don't have the Azure CLI yet, download it from Microsoft's official page:

https://learn.microsoft.com/en-us/cli/azure/install-azure-cli

Once installed, sign in to your Azure account from the terminal inside VS Code:

```
az login
```

If the login window doesn't open or you're running in a restricted or remote environment, use the device-code option instead:

```
az login --use-device-code
```

This will display a short code and a link you can open in any browser to complete the sign-in process. Once you authenticate, the Azure CLI caches your credentials for subsequent commands.

To confirm which subscription is active:

```
az account show
```

If you have multiple subscriptions, set the one you'll use for this project:

```
az account set --subscription "<SUBSCRIPTION_NAME_OR_ID>"
```

You're now connected to Azure and ready to start building.

Creating the Project Structure

We'll now create the local workspace for Thain's first version, a small, modular Python project you can run directly from VS Code.

Open a terminal in VS Code (the default is PowerShell on Windows) and create a new folder:

```
mkdir thain
cd thain
```

Inside it, create a virtual environment to isolate dependencies and activate it:

```
python -m venv .venv
# Windows (PowerShell in VS Code)
.venv\Scripts\Activate.ps1
```

Note   If PowerShell prevents the activation script from running and shows a policy warning, you can temporarily allow scripts for this session by running

```
Set-ExecutionPolicy -Scope Process -ExecutionPolicy Bypass
```

This change applies only to the current terminal window and reverts automatically when you close it.

Project Layout

Next, create the following folders and files:

```
thain/
  main.py
  config/
    settings.py
  tools/
    classifier.py
  memory/
    buffer.py
  .env
  README.md
  requirements.txt
```

Each part of the project has a focused role:

- `main.py`: Coordinates everything; it loads the configuration, connects tools, and manages the agent's flow.

- `config/`: Stores environment settings and Azure configuration logic.

- `tools/`: Contain helper functions that the agent can call, starting with a simple keyword classifier.

- `memory/`: Holds a small, in-memory buffer that gives Thain short-term context.

- `.env`: Keeps local environment variables so you don't have to re-enter them each time.

- `requirements.txt`: Tracks all Python dependencies for easy setup on any machine.

- `README.md`: Explains how to install, configure, and run the agent.

Installing Dependencies

With your virtual environment active, the next step is to add the packages that Thain will rely on.

We'll list them inside a file called `requirements.txt`, which keeps all project dependencies in one place.

Create the file in the project root and add the following lines:

```
azure-ai-agents==1.2.0b5
azure-identity==1.17.0
python-dotenv==1.0.0
agent-framework-azure-ai==1.0.0b251016
agent-framework-devui==1.0.0b251016
```

Each of these libraries has a specific role:

- `azure-ai-agents`: Provides Azure AI Foundry project and agent service client support used by the framework integration

- `azure-identity`: Provides secure authentication through Microsoft Entra ID (so no API keys are needed)

- `python-dotenv`: Loads configuration values from the local .env file, keeping setup clean and consistent

- `agent-framework-azure-ai`: Connects the Microsoft Agent Framework runtime to Azure AI Foundry and the deployed model

- `agent-framework-devui`: Local Dev UI for live visualization

Once you've saved the file, install everything in one step:

```
pip install -r requirements.txt
```

The `-r` flag stands for requirements file. It tells pip to read the list from the file and install each package (and its dependencies) automatically.

When the installation completes, your environment will include all the tools Thain needs to connect to Azure, authenticate securely, and load configuration data. Your workspace is now fully equipped. In the next section, we'll add the .env file and load these values into Python. Note that these versions match the code listings in this chapter; the companion repository also includes a Microsoft Agent Framework 1.5.0 GA version with updated package versions.

Adding the .env File

To make configuration easier, we'll store Thain's connection details in a .env file at the project root. This file keeps your environment variables in one place, so you don't have to set them manually every time you open VS Code.

Inside your thain directory, create a file named .env to store environment variables, and insert the lines below:

```
AZURE_AI_PROJECT_ENDPOINT=https://<your-foundry-project-endpoint>/api/
projects/<project-name>
AZURE_AI_MODEL_DEPLOYMENT_NAME=gpt-4o
```

You can copy this endpoint directly from your Azure Portal:

1. Go to `https://portal.azure.com` and open the Microsoft Foundry project (the same one you created in Chapter 1).

2. Under the libraries section, copy the URL against the Foundry project endpoint. It will look like the endpoint I showed above.

3. Paste that full URL into your .env file for `AZURE_AI_PROJECT_ENDPOINT`.

See Figure 2-1 for a visual reference showing where to locate the *project endpoint* section in the Azure Portal.

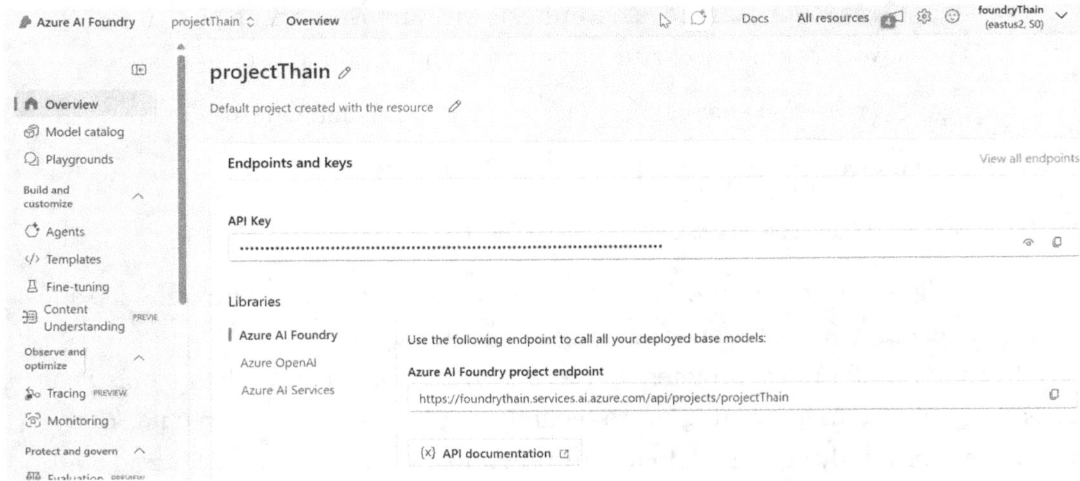

Figure 2-1. *Copying the project endpoint*

The second variable, `AZURE_AI_MODEL_DEPLOYMENT_NAME`, specifies which deployed model the agent should use. If you deployed GPT-4o in Chapter 1, use `gpt-4o` here.

If your workspace already includes GPT-5, you can safely replace the model name; the Microsoft Agent Framework works identically with either version.

Note   Python is indentation sensitive. When copying code from this book, ensure indentation is preserved exactly. If you encounter indentation errors, refer to the corresponding source file in the book's GitHub repository for a clean copy.

The Configuration Layer

With the .env file in place, the next step is to load those values into Python so your code can use them.

The `settings.py` file inside the config folder handles this. It reads your environment variables, validates them, and makes them available as a simple, typed configuration object.

This file has four primary responsibilities:

1. **Load environment variables**: Using python-dotenv, it automatically reads your .env file when the project starts.

2. **Provide structure**: The AzureAgentConfig dataclass defines the fields your agent will rely on (endpoint and model).

3. **Validate configuration**: If a required value like the endpoint is missing, it raises a clear error before anything runs.

4. **Expose a helper function**: load_config() gives other parts of the code a single, safe way to retrieve configuration.

The complete implementation is shown in Listing 2-1. Copy this code into your config/settings.py file inside the config folder.

Listing 2-1. config/settings.py

```python
import os
from dataclasses import dataclass
from dotenv import load_dotenv

# Load environment variables from a local .env file if present.
load_dotenv(override=True)

class MissingConfigError(RuntimeError):
    """Raised when required Azure configuration values are not provided."""

@dataclass(frozen=True)
class AzureAgentConfig:
    """Typed container for Azure OpenAI Agent settings."""

    endpoint: str
    model: str

    @classmethod
    def from_env(cls) -> "AzureAgentConfig":
        """Create configuration from environment variables."""
        endpoint = os.getenv("AZURE_AI_PROJECT_ENDPOINT", "").strip()
```

```python
        model = os.getenv("AZURE_AI_MODEL_DEPLOYMENT_NAME", "").strip()

        if not endpoint:
            raise MissingConfigError(
                "Missing Azure configuration value: endpoint. Set AZURE_AI_
                PROJECT_ENDPOINT environment variable."
            )

        if not model:
            raise MissingConfigError(
                "Missing model deployment name. Set AZURE_AI_MODEL_
                DEPLOYMENT_NAME in your .env file "
                "to match your deployed model (e.g., gpt-4o)."
            )

        return cls(endpoint=endpoint, model=model)
def load_config() -> AzureAgentConfig:
    """Helper to load Azure configuration from the environment."""

    return AzureAgentConfig.from_env()
```

When you call `load_config()`, Python loads your `.env` file (via `load_dotenv()`), reads the endpoint and model deployment name, and returns them as a neatly packaged AzureAgentConfig object.

If the `.env` file is missing or the endpoint isn't set, you'll see a clear, actionable error instead of a vague authentication failure later. This settings file acts as Thain's configuration checkpoint; nothing else in the project runs until the essentials are in place.

With configuration handled, you're ready to give Thain its first skill: a simple, keyword-based classifier that can recognize what type of issue a user is reporting.

Building the Memory Layer

In real conversations, context matters even for an AI agent. Earlier, we introduced the three core components that make Thain work: reasoning, tools, and memory.

In this section, we'll bring the third part, *memory*, to life by building a simple in-memory store that helps Thain retain short-term context.

If a customer reports "battery swelling again," Thain should remember that a similar issue appeared earlier.

To make this possible, we'll give Thain a small, short-term memory module that stores the last few complaints and summaries in local memory. This section creates a helper class that mimics how an agent recalls recent context, allowing it to learn from the flow of conversation.

The `memory/buffer.py` module gives Thain three core abilities:

1. **Record recent complaints**: Thain stores each complaint as a structured `ComplaintRecord` object containing message, category, and summary.

2. **Limit memory size**: The system keeps only the latest few entries (by default, five).

3. **Feed context back into the agent**: Thain uses `contextual_instructions()` to turn stored summaries into a short text block that helps the model maintain consistency between runs.

Think of it as a rolling window of memory – like how we recall the last few topics of a conversation without remembering everything we ever said. The complete implementation is shown in Listing 2-2.

Copy this code into your `memory/buffer.py` file.

Listing 2-2. memory/buffer.py

```python
from collections import deque
from dataclasses import dataclass
from typing import Deque, Iterable, Optional

@dataclass
class ComplaintRecord:
    """Represents a single customer complaint captured by Thain."""

    message: str
    category: str
    summary: str

class ConversationMemory:
    """Simple bounded in-memory store for recent complaints."""
```

```python
    def __init__(self, capacity: int = 5) -> None:
        if capacity <= 0:
            raise ValueError("Memory capacity must be greater than zero.")
        self._records: Deque[ComplaintRecord] = deque(maxlen=capacity)

    def add(self, record: ComplaintRecord) -> None:
        """Append a complaint to memory."""

        self._records.append(record)

    def records(self) -> Iterable[ComplaintRecord]:
        """Return an iterable view over stored complaints."""

        return tuple(self._records)

    def contextual_instructions(self) -> Optional[str]:
        """Render memory into a string the agent can consume as extra
        guidance."""

        if not self._records:
            return None

        lines = [
            "- {category}: {summary}".format(category=entry.category,
            summary=entry.summary)
            for entry in self._records
        ]
        return "Recent customer complaints to keep in mind:\n" + "\n".
        join(lines)
```

deque(maxlen=5): A double-ended queue that automatically discards the oldest
ComplaintRecord when a new one is added beyond the limit. This ensures the memory
always contains only the most recent complaints and keeps the agent's context
lightweight. The default size of five is a practical balance: enough to preserve short-term
context without overloading the agent or cluttering its reasoning.

ComplaintRecord: A @dataclass that neatly packages each message, category, and
summary into an object instead of loose strings.

`contextual_instructions()`: This method compiles these recent complaints into a text block such as

```
Recent customer complaints to keep in mind:
- Battery Issue: Swelling after update
- Screen Issue: Touch not responding
```

The agent will later attach this string to its system prompt to keep it consistent across runs.

In the next section, we'll give Thain its first skill: a simple classifier tool that can recognize what type of issue a user is reporting.

Building the Classification Tool

In the previous section, Thain gained a short-term memory to remember recent complaints.

Next, we'll give Thain its first tool, a lightweight classifier exposed directly through the Microsoft Agent Framework using the `@ai_function` decorator. It helps the agent identify the type of issue described in each complaint. This is Thain's first working skill. It doesn't rely on machine learning yet; instead, it uses a straightforward keyword-based approach, allowing you to focus on how tools integrate into the Microsoft Agent Framework.

Later in the book, you'll enhance this with more advanced, AI-driven classifiers, but the core principle remains the same, giving Thain modular tools it can invoke as part of its reasoning process.

The `tools/classifier.py` module gives Thain three core capabilities, implemented as a native Agent Framework tool using the `@ai_function` decorator:

1. **Recognize common complaint patterns**: By matching customer messages against a list of domain-specific keywords.

2. Estimate confidence by counting how many of the defined keywords occur in the message.

3. **Return structured results**: Producing a JSON object that the framework can read, validate, or refine during reasoning.

The complete implementation is shown in Listing 2-3. Copy this code into your `tools/classifier.py` file inside the tools folder.

Listing 2-3. tools/classifier.py

```python
import re
from typing import Annotated, Dict, Union
from agent_framework import ai_function

CATEGORY_KEYWORDS: Dict[str, tuple[str, ...]] = {
    "Battery Issue": ("battery", "charge", "swelling", "overheat",
    "power"),
    "Screen Issue": ("screen", "display", "pixel", "glass", "lcd",
    "touch"),
    "Connectivity Issue": ("wifi", "bluetooth", "lte", "signal", "network",
    "connection", "connectivity"),
    "Performance Issue": ("slow", "lag", "freeze", "crash", "performance"),
    "Software Update": ("update", "patch", "firmware", "install"),
    "Audio Issue": ("speaker", "microphone", "audio", "sound", "volume"),
}

def classify_issue(customer_message: str) -> Dict[str, Union[str, float]]:
    """

    Lightweight classifier that maps a complaint to an issue category.

    :param customer_message: Raw customer complaint text to classify.
    :return: Mapping with ``category`` and ``confidence`` keys derived from
    keyword matches.
    """

    normalized = customer_message.lower()
    category = "General Inquiry"
    confidence = 0.1

    for label, keywords in CATEGORY_KEYWORDS.items():
        hits = sum(1 for keyword in keywords if re.search(rf"\b{re.
        escape(keyword)}\b", normalized))
        if hits > 0 and hits / len(keywords) > confidence:
            category = label
```

```python
        confidence = min(0.9, hits / len(keywords) + 0.3)

    return {"category": category, "confidence": round(confidence, 2)}


@ai_function(
    name="classify_issue",
    description="Classify a customer complaint into a support category and
    return a confidence percentage.",
)
def classify_issue_tool(
    customer_message: Annotated[str, "The customer complaint text to
    triage."]
) -> Dict[str, Union[str, float]]:
    """Expose the lightweight classifier as an Agent Framework tool."""

    return classify_issue(customer_message)


__all__ = ["classify_issue", "classify_issue_tool"]
```

Inside the Classifier

1. **Keyword mapping**: The CATEGORY_KEYWORDS dictionary defines a
   simple taxonomy for the feedback domain. Each key represents an
   issue category, and each tuple lists the keywords that commonly
   appear in that kind of complaint.

2. **Pattern matching**: The core classify_issue() function
   normalizes text to lowercase and uses regular expressions to
   detect category keywords. Confidence rises as more matches
   are found.

3. **Tool exposure**: The @ai_function decorator wraps this
   logic in classify_issue_tool, making it available to the
   Agent Framework. From this point on, MAF can call the tool
   autonomously whenever classification is needed.

The agent can use this value later to decide whether to accept the classification or override it. The result is returned as a JSON string like the example below:

```
{"category": "Battery Issue", "confidence": 0.78}
```

Starting with a rule-based approach keeps the behavior transparent and easy to debug. When you later introduce LLM-powered or embedding-based tools, you'll be able to swap them in without changing the overall architecture.

Orchestrating Thain with the Agent Framework

So far, you've created the configuration loader, a short-term memory helper, and a classifier tool decorated with `@ai_function`.

In this section, you'll connect them through the Microsoft Agent Framework's async runtime to form Thain v0.1, a working agent that can read a complaint, reason about it, classify it, and respond with a structured summary.

The `main.py` file acts as the orchestrator. It initializes the async Agent Framework client, wires in configuration and memory, registers the tool, and then runs Thain either once or interactively.

You'll also see how to launch the Dev UI, a local debugging dashboard that visualizes agent runs and tool calls.

Here's what happens inside:

1. Load configuration from `.env` through `settings.py`.

2. Authenticate with Azure AD via `DefaultAzureCredential (aio)` and initialize `AzureAIAgentClient`.

3. Register Thain's tools using the Agent Framework's native decorator model and require tool execution during reasoning (via `ToolMode.REQUIRED`).

4. Build a `ChatAgent` object with base instructions, tool list, and the `MemoryContextProvider` for short-term context.

5. Execute a run using `AzureAIAgentClient` (via a Chat Completions call) and parse the JSON payload returned in the assistant message.

6. Update the short-term memory buffer after each turn so the
   `MemoryContextProvider` can supply context in follow-up requests.

7. Expose optional Dev UI flags (`--devui`, `--devui-open`) to launch
   the framework's visual dashboard.

8. Handle errors cleanly through `MissingConfigError` and
   `HttpResponseError`.

This structure mirrors how production-grade MAF agents operate, but it is simplified so you can see each part clearly.

Now that you've seen how each part fits together, add the following code to your project's root-level `main.py` file. The complete listing is shown in Listing 2-4.

Listing 2-4. main.py

```python
import argparse
import asyncio
import json
import sys
from contextlib import AsyncExitStack
from typing import Any, Dict, Optional, Tuple
from azure.core.exceptions import HttpResponseError
from azure.identity.aio import DefaultAzureCredential

from agent_framework import (
    AgentRunResponse,
    ChatAgent,
    ChatMessage,
    Context,
    ContextProvider,
    ToolMode,
)
from agent_framework.azure import AzureAIAgentClient
from agent_framework.devui import serve as serve_devui  # DevUI server
launcher

from config.settings import AzureAgentConfig, MissingConfigError,
load_config
```

```python
from memory.buffer import ComplaintRecord, ConversationMemory
from tools.classifier import classify_issue, classify_issue_tool

memory_store = ConversationMemory(capacity=5)

BASE_INSTRUCTIONS = (
    "You are Thain, a concise customer support triage assistant. "
    "Listen to a single customer complaint, reason about the likely issue, "
    "and respond with a JSON "
    "object that includes `category` and `summary` keys. "
    "Call the `classify_issue` tool to validate the category you return. "
    "If the tool's confidence is low, silently choose the best category "
    "yourself; do not mention the confidence or the fallback step. "
    "Keep the summary brief (one sentence). "
    "When you are given a list of recent complaints, explicitly consider "
    "how the new problem relates to them "
    "and mention any meaningful connections or contrasts in your summary."
)

def parse_args() -> argparse.Namespace:
    parser = argparse.ArgumentParser(description="Thain support
    triage agent")
    parser.add_argument(
        "-m",
        "--message",
        help="Customer complaint to triage. If omitted, the script reads
        from stdin.",
    )
    parser.add_argument(
        "-i",
        "--interactive",
        action="store_true",
        help="Run Thain in interactive REPL mode to preserve short-term
        memory during the session.",
    )
    # DevUI CLI options
    parser.add_argument(
```

```python
        "--devui",
        action="store_true",
        help="Launch the Agent Framework DevUI to explore and interact with
        Thain.",
    )
    parser.add_argument(
        "--devui-host",
        default="127.0.0.1",
        help="Host interface for the DevUI server (default: 127.0.0.1).",
    )
    parser.add_argument(
        "--devui-port",
        type=int,
        default=8080,
        help="Port for the DevUI server (default: 8080).",
    )
    parser.add_argument(
        "--devui-open",
        action="store_true",
        help="Automatically open the DevUI in the browser when the server
        starts.",
    )
    parser.add_argument(
        "--devui-tracing",
        action="store_true",
        help="Enable OpenTelemetry tracing when launching the DevUI.",
    )
    return parser.parse_args()

def read_customer_message(args: argparse.Namespace) -> str:
    if args.message:
        return args.message.strip()

    if not sys.stdin.isatty():
        piped = sys.stdin.read().strip()
        if piped:
```

```python
            return piped

    raise SystemExit("No customer message supplied. Use --message or pipe
    text into stdin.")


class MemoryContextProvider(ContextProvider):
    """Context provider that surfaces recent complaints to the agent."""

    def __init__(self, memory: ConversationMemory) -> None:
        self._memory = memory

    async def invoking(self, messages: Any, **kwargs: Any) -> Context:   #
    type: ignore[override]
        instructions = self._memory.contextual_instructions()
        return Context(instructions=instructions) if instructions else
        Context()


def parse_structured_response(raw_text: str) -> Dict[str, Any]:
    cleaned = raw_text.strip()
    if cleaned.startswith("```"):
        segments = cleaned.split("```")
        if len(segments) >= 2:
            cleaned = segments[1]
            if cleaned.startswith("json"):
                cleaned = cleaned[4:]
            cleaned = cleaned.strip()
    candidates = [cleaned]
    if "{" in cleaned and "}" in cleaned:
        first = cleaned.find("{")
        last = cleaned.rfind("}") + 1
        if last > first:
            candidates.append(cleaned[first:last])
    for candidate in candidates:
        try:
            return json.loads(candidate)
        except json.JSONDecodeError:
            continue
```

```python
    raise ValueError(f"Agent response was not valid JSON: {cleaned}")
def update_memory(customer_message: str, payload: Dict[str, Any]) -> None:
    category = str(payload.get("category", "General Inquiry"))
    summary = str(payload.get("summary", customer_message[:120]))
    memory_store.add(ComplaintRecord(message=customer_message,
    category=category, summary=summary))

async def run_thain_agent(
    customer_message: str, config: AzureAgentConfig
) -> Tuple[Dict[str, Any], AgentRunResponse]:
    """Execute the Thain agent and return both structured payload and raw
    Agent Framework response."""

    memory_provider = MemoryContextProvider(memory_store)
    async with AsyncExitStack() as stack:
        credential = DefaultAzureCredential(exclude_interactive_browser_
        credential=False)
        stack.push_async_callback(credential.close)

        chat_client = AzureAIAgentClient(
            project_endpoint=config.endpoint,
            model_deployment_name=config.model,
            async_credential=credential,
        )
        await stack.enter_async_context(chat_client)

        agent = ChatAgent(
            chat_client=chat_client,
            name="Thain",
            instructions=BASE_INSTRUCTIONS,
            tools=[classify_issue_tool],
            context_providers=memory_provider,
            tool_choice=ToolMode.REQUIRED(classify_issue_tool.name),
            store=True,
        )
        await stack.enter_async_context(agent)

        response = await agent.run(customer_message)
```

```python
    raw_text = response.text.strip()
    if not raw_text:
        raise RuntimeError("Agent run completed but produced no assistant
        message.")

    try:
        payload = parse_structured_response(raw_text)
    except ValueError:
        fallback = classify_issue(customer_message)
        payload = {
            "category": fallback.get("category", "General Inquiry"),
            "summary": customer_message,
        }

    if "category" not in payload:
        fallback = classify_issue(customer_message)
        payload["category"] = fallback["category"]
    if "summary" not in payload:
        payload["summary"] = customer_message

    update_memory(customer_message, payload)
    normalized = {"category": payload["category"], "summary":
    payload["summary"]}
    response.value = normalized
    return normalized, response

async def run_thain_async(customer_message: str, config: AzureAgentConfig)
-> Dict[str, Any]:
    """Async triage routine built on the Microsoft Agent Framework."""

    payload, _ = await run_thain_agent(customer_message, config)
    return payload

def run_thain(customer_message: str, config: Optional[AzureAgentConfig] =
None) -> Dict[str, Any]:
    """Synchronous facade used by CLI, REPL, and DevUI integrations."""

    resolved_config = config or load_config()
    return asyncio.run(run_thain_async(customer_message, resolved_config))
```

```python
def _extract_latest_role_text(messages: Any, role: str) -> Optional[str]:
    """Helper to pull the latest message text for a given role from Agent
    Framework structures."""

    if messages is None:
        return None

    if isinstance(messages, ChatMessage):
        message_role = getattr(messages.role, "value", None)
        if message_role == role:
            return messages.text
        return None

    if isinstance(messages, (list, tuple)):
        for item in reversed(messages):
            text = _extract_latest_role_text(item, role)
            if text:
                return text
        return None

    if isinstance(messages, str):
        return messages if role == "user" else None

    return None

# --- DevUI helper classes/functions ---
class ThainDevAgent:
    """Thin wrapper that adapts run_thain for the Agent Framework DevUI."""

    def __init__(self, config: AzureAgentConfig) -> None:
        self._config = config
        self.name = "Thain"
        self.description = "Customer support triage assistant that
        classifies complaints and generates summaries."
        self.instructions = BASE_INSTRUCTIONS
        self.tools = [classify_issue_tool]

    async def run(self, messages: Any, **kwargs: Any) -> AgentRunResponse:
        user_text = _extract_latest_role_text(messages, "user")
```

```python
        if not user_text:
            raise ValueError("ThainDevAgent requires a user message to
            operate.")

        _, agent_response = await run_thain_agent(user_text, self._config)
        return agent_response

def launch_devui(host: str, port: int, auto_open: bool, tracing_enabled:
bool) -> None:
    """Launch the Agent Framework DevUI with the Thain agent registered."""

    config = load_config()
    agent_entity = ThainDevAgent(config)
    serve_devui(entities=[agent_entity], host=host, port=port, auto_
    open=auto_open, tracing_enabled=tracing_enabled)
# --- End DevUI helper classes/functions ---

def main() -> None:
    args = parse_args()
    if args.devui and args.interactive:
        sys.exit("Choose either --devui or --interactive, not both.")
    if args.devui and args.message:
        sys.exit("The --devui option cannot be combined with --message.")

    if args.devui:
        try:
            launch_devui(args.devui_host, args.devui_port, args.devui_open,
            args.devui_tracing)
        except MissingConfigError as config_error:
            sys.exit(f"Configuration error: {config_error}")
        except Exception as unexpected:
            sys.exit(f"Failed to launch DevUI: {unexpected}")
        return

    if args.interactive:
        print("Entering interactive Thain session. Type 'exit' or 'quit' to
        leave.\n")
        while True:
            try:
```

```python
        user_input = input("Customer message> ").strip()
    except KeyboardInterrupt:
        print("\nExiting.")
        break

    if not user_input:
        continue
    if user_input.lower() in {"exit", "quit"}:
        break

    try:
        response = run_thain(user_input)
    except MissingConfigError as config_error:
        print(f"Configuration error: {config_error}")
        break
    except HttpResponseError as azure_error:
        print(f"Azure request failed: {azure_error}")
        break
    except Exception as unexpected:
        print(f"Unexpected failure: {unexpected}")
        break

    print(json.dumps(response, ensure_ascii=False))
    return

customer_message = read_customer_message(args)

try:
    response = run_thain(customer_message)
except MissingConfigError as config_error:
    sys.exit(f"Configuration error: {config_error}")
except HttpResponseError as azure_error:
    sys.exit(f"Azure request failed: {azure_error}")
except Exception as unexpected:
    sys.exit(f"Unexpected failure: {unexpected}")

print(json.dumps(response, ensure_ascii=False))

if __name__ == "__main__":
    main()
```

The `main.py` file ties every subsystem together through the Microsoft Agent Framework. When Thain runs, the Agent Framework client sends your message to GPT-4o along with memory context, decides when to call the `classify_issue_tool`, and composes a structured JSON response.

The `MemoryContextProvider` maintains a short, rolling history in RAM, allowing Thain to link related complaints within a session. If you start the agent with `--devui`, the Dev UI visualizes this reasoning process in real time, showing model traces, tool usage, context injection, and JSON reasoning.

By keeping the architecture asynchronous and modular, you're now following the same runtime pattern that multi-agent systems use, just scaled down for a single-agent example.

Running and Testing Thain v0.1

At this point, your agent is complete; configuration, memory, tool, and reasoning are all connected. Now it's time to run Thain v0.1, the first working version of your single-agent system.

Thain v0.1 now supports three execution modes:

- **Single-message mode (`--message`)**: Processes one complaint and exits

- **Interactive mode (`--interactive`)**: Keeps short-term memory in RAM for multi-turn sessions

- **Dev UI mode (`--devui`)**: Launches a visual debug dashboard on localhost

This mirrors how production systems keep session context alive without persisting data to the cloud.

Start with a single-message test to confirm your configuration works, and then switch to interactive mode to see Thain hold a live conversation.

You've already prepared your virtual environment and logged in with Azure CLI earlier in this chapter. From the project root, run the following command to test Thain v0.1:

```
python main.py --message "The phone battery started swelling again after
the last update."
```

Expected Output:

Your terminal should display a clean JSON response like this:

```
{
    "category": "Battery Issue",
    "summary": "The phone battery appears to be swelling, potentially
    linked to a recent update."
}
```

The exact wording may vary slightly since GPT-4o's reasoning is probabilistic, but the structure will remain the same: a concise category and one-sentence summary. The agent may choose its own category wording (e.g., Connectivity vs. Connection Issue). The keyword classifier only steps in if the model fails to include a category or the JSON needs repair.

Each response you see in JSON is the structured payload returned by ChatAgent. run(), parsed and printed to the console.

```
python main.py --interactive
```

You'll see the responses similar to below:

```
Entering interactive Thain session. Type 'exit' or 'quit' to leave.
Customer message> My phone keeps losing Wi-Fi connection
{"category": "Connectivity", "summary": "The phone frequently disconnects
from Wi-Fi, indicating a possible network or device issue."}
Customer message> Now it's also losing 5G; could these issues be related?
{"category": "Connectivity", "summary": "The phone is losing both 5G and
Wi-Fi connections, suggesting a broader network issue likely linked to
earlier complaints."}
```

Refer to Figure 2-2.

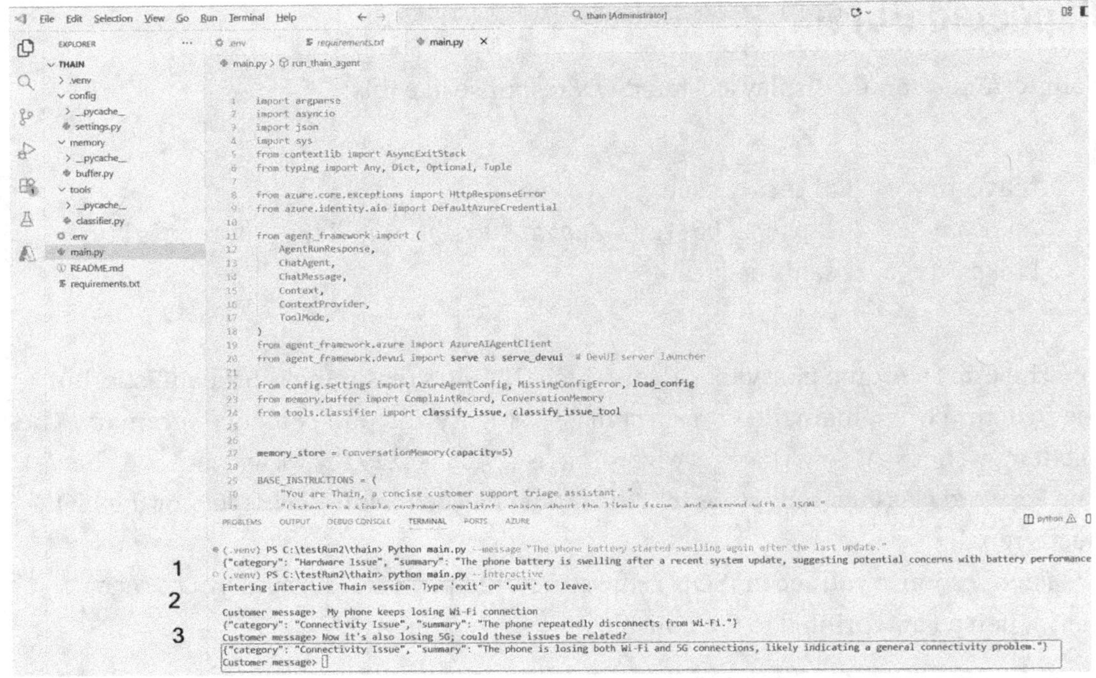

Figure 2-2. *Thain v0.1 interactive mode*

In interactive mode, Thain keeps its short-term memory in RAM. Each new message is processed in the context of the previous ones so that it can link related complaints naturally. Here, Thain recognized that both Wi-Fi and 5G failures belong to the same connectivity problem. This demonstrates session-level memory.

Type exit or quit or press Ctrl + C to end the session.

Running Thain in Dev UI Mode

Interactive mode lets you run multiple messages in a single session, but to truly understand how Thain thinks, we can visualize its reasoning using the Microsoft Agent Framework's Dev UI.

This is the third and most insightful way to run Thain v0.1. Run the below command from your VS Code terminal:

```
python main.py --devui --devui-tracing --devui-open
```

--devui enables the dashboard.

--devui-open automatically launches it in your browser.

--devui-tracing adds deeper diagnostic logs called traces.

(You won't need --devui-tracing for everyday development.)

Once launched, you can test Thain exactly as you did in interactive mode: example below. Refer to Figure 2-3 as well.

```
You:
My phone keeps losing Wi-Fi connection
Thain:
{
  "category": "Connectivity",
  "summary": "The customer's phone consistently drops its Wi-Fi
  connection."
}
You:
Now it's also losing 5G. Could these be related?
Thain:
{
  "category": "Connectivity",
  "summary": "The issue with losing 5G may be related to the Wi-Fi dropping
  problem..."
}
```

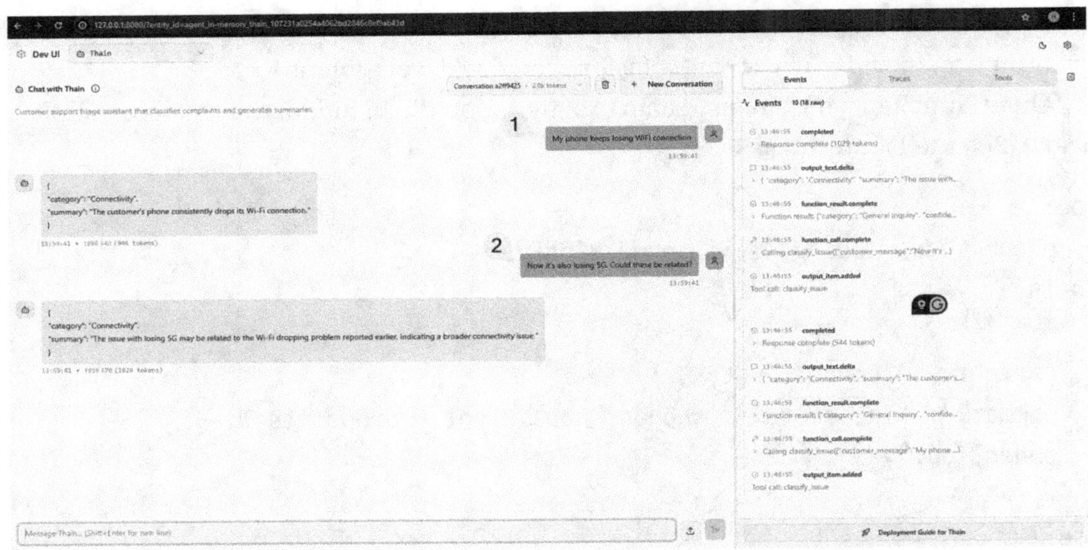

Figure 2-3. *Thain v0.1 Dev UI Chat and Events*

The same features from interactive mode apply. Thain remembers short-term context and uses tools during reasoning, but now you can see it all happening live.

Dev UI Tabs

Chat (left): The messages between you and Thain. This helps you test the agent in a natural, user-driven way. Refer to Figure 2-3.

Events (right): Play-by-play timeline for the run. Every partial chunk the model emits shows up here in order, so you can see the conversation unfold step by step. See the same Figure 2-3.

Traces (right): Think of this as the telemetry log. When tracing is enabled, it records spans of what the agent framework is doing under the hood, which helps debug latency or see which services were called behind the scenes. Look at Figure 2-4.

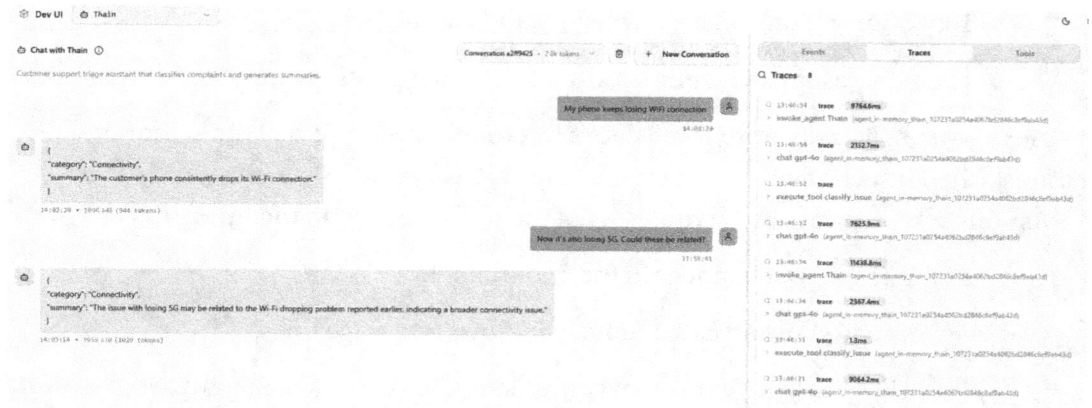

Figure 2-4. *Thain v0.1 Dev UI – Traces*

Tools (right): List every tool the agent invokes (like the `classify_issue` helper). For each call, it captures the arguments sent in and the result returned so that you can audit the agent's function usage alongside the conversation. Refer to Figure 2-5.

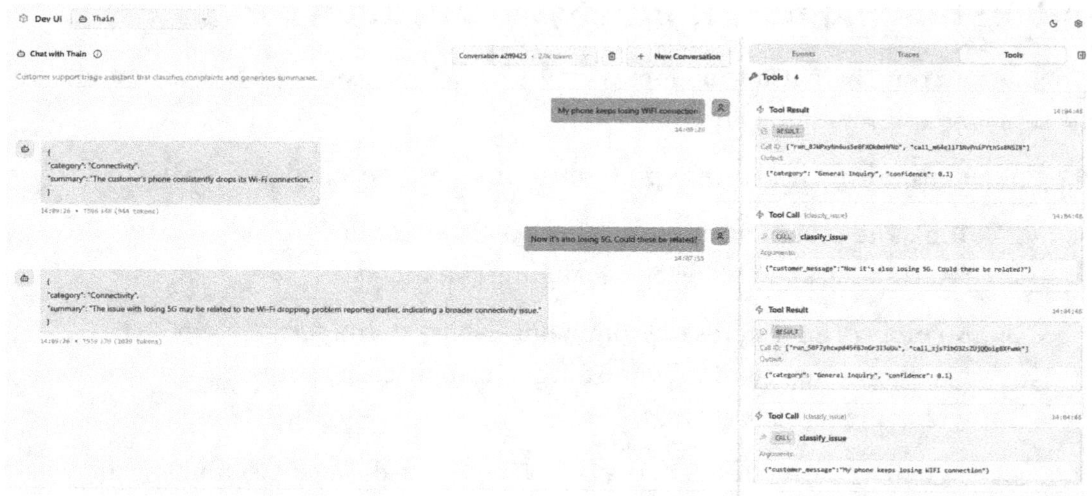

Figure 2-5. *Thain v0.1 Dev UI – Tools*

If you inspect these tabs after your conversation, you'll notice key insights:

- Thain decides when to call the `classify_issue` tool.

- Tool inputs show the exact customer message passed in.

- Tool outputs confirm both category and confidence.

- The final response is generated after the tool results return.

Here, you are literally watching Thain's internal workflow in real time – how it reasons, when it seeks help from a tool, and how it arrives at its conclusion.

As your system grows into a multi-agent architecture later in the book

- Multiple tools will appear in the Tools panel.

- Agents will show up as separate workflows and trace lines.

- You will visually confirm tool coordination and message passing.

By mastering the Dev UI now, you'll be more confident when debugging later, even as things get more complex.

With Dev UI support fully enabled, Thain is now a transparent, traceable agent with live diagnostics.

Understanding the Three-Layer Execution

Whether you run Thain using interactive or the Dev UI, all execution flows demonstrate the same three-layer interaction:

1. **Reasoning**: GPT-4o interprets the user's message and decides what to do.

2. **Tool**: The `classify_issue` runs as a real tool inside MAF, returning structured insights including confidence.

3. **Memory**: Thain stores the complaint, category, and summary in a rolling buffer, guiding context-aware responses in later turns within the same session.

Seeing the tool call and result in the Dev UI confirms the agent is thinking and deciding, not just generating generic text.

Troubleshooting

If something doesn't work as expected, check the following:

```
MissingConfigError - Ensure your .env file includes both AZURE_AI_PROJECT_
ENDPOINT and AZURE_AI_MODEL_DEPLOYMENT_NAME
```

Authentication failures – rerun `az login` and verify you're signed in to the correct Azure tenant.

Empty or missing responses – confirm that your AZURE_AI_PROJECT_ENDPOINT and AZURE_AI_MODEL_DEPLOYMENT_NAME values match those in Microsoft Foundry project.

Dev UI does not open automatically. Add the `--devui-open` flag, or open the local URL shown in the console manually. If you see tool calls appearing in the Dev UI, your setup is correct.

You've now built and tested Thain v0.1, a fully functional single agent powered by the Microsoft Agent Framework, complete with reasoning, tools, memory, async execution, and real-time visibility through the Dev UI.

Note   The current state of Thain's code for this chapter is available in the book's GitHub repository at `https://github.com/Apress/Architecting-Intelligent-Agents-in-Azure`.

You can clone the repository and set it up locally with the following commands:

```
git clone https://github.com/Apress/Architecting-Intelligent-
Agents-in-Azure.git
```

```
cd Architecting-Intelligent-Agents-in-Azure
```

For the manuscript code, open the Chapter 2/thain folder. For the GA code, open Code GA/Chapter 2/thain. The repository version also includes a constraints.txt file to keep package resolution consistent across chapters. After cloning, create and activate a virtual environment, and then install the dependencies by running

```
python -m venv .venv
```

```
.\.venv\Scripts\activate
```

```
pip install -r requirements.txt -c constraints.txt
```

Finally, create your own .env file with the required Azure settings before running the project. Also, ensure you have authenticated, else run `az login` or `az login --use-device-code` as mentioned in the "Setting Up Your Workspace in VS Code" section earlier.

You can also browse the repository online to review the reference implementation.

Note on SDK Versions and Compatibility

For current Microsoft Agent Framework usage, refer to the GA code path in the companion repository and the Chapter 2 migration notes. The main changes are `ChatAgent` to `Agent`, `AzureAIAgentClient` to `FoundryChatClient`, `@ai_function` to `@tool`, and the context provider hook from `invoking()` to `before_run()`.

These changes do not affect the underlying architecture, the concepts demonstrated in this chapter, or the chapters that follow.

If you run into a compatibility issue with a newer SDK version, please raise a GitHub issue and include

- The SDK versions you are using (you can get this via python -m pip list)

- The error message or stack trace

- The chapter and file involved

I actively monitor these issues and will provide guidance or updated examples where appropriate.

Thain v0.1 Architecture

Figure 2-6 brings together the components built in this chapter, showing how reasoning, tool invocation, and memory connect at runtime through the Microsoft Agent Framework.

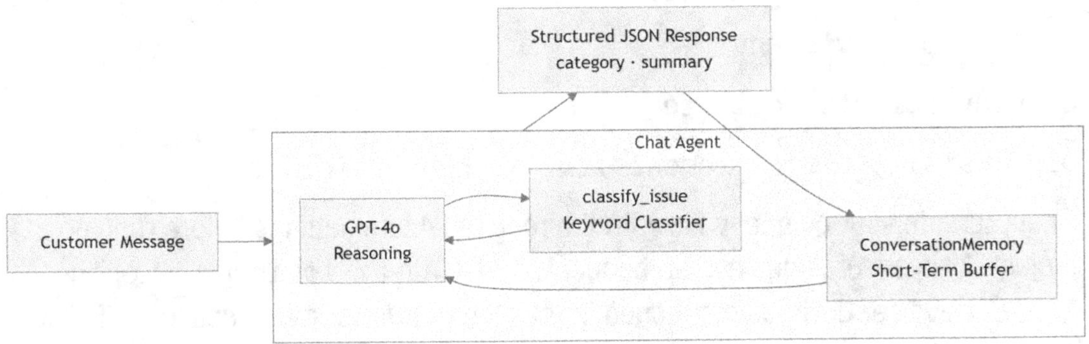

Figure 2-6. *Thain v0.1 Architecture*

Summary

In this chapter, you moved from exploring Thain's capabilities to building its intelligence in code. You introduced Thain to the Microsoft Agent Framework, giving it an authentic agentic architecture with core components working together: reasoning powered by GPT-4o, a Python-based classification tool, and a lightweight memory buffer for short-term context.

You created a clean Python project with a modular structure: config, tools, memory, and a fully asynchronous agent loop. By wiring everything through the Agent Framework, Thain can now call tools automatically when needed and return structured JSON responses. This foundation will scale directly into multi-agent workflows later in the book.

You also enabled two different execution modes, single-message and interactive, allowing Thain to either respond once or engage in a short conversation while remembering recent issues. Finally, you connected Thain to the Dev UI, gaining real-time visibility into how it reasons, when it invokes tools, and how its internal workflow evolves with context. This makes debugging and learning much easier as the system grows more intelligent.

By the end of this chapter, Thain has taken its first fundamental steps:

- It can reason.

- It can classify complaints using a real tool.

- It can remember short-term context.

- It can show you how it thinks through the Dev UI.

Thain v0.1 is officially alive, running directly in your development environment, ready to evolve.

In the next chapter, we'll teach Thain how to remember what it has seen before. By adding persistent storage using Cosmos DB and search capabilities with Azure AI Search, Thain will be able to recognize recurring issues and build on past insights, even when feedback arrives days or weeks apart.

Architectural Outcomes

By the end of this chapter, Thain's architecture supports the following:

- A functional agent runtime based on the Microsoft Agent Framework, offering integrated reasoning, tool invocation, and memory within a unified system

- An asynchronous execution model that mirrors production-grade agent operations, enabling non-blocking reasoning and tool calls

- A tool integration pattern using the MAF's native decorator, allowing the agent to invoke domain-specific logic during reasoning

- A session-scoped memory buffer that maintains conversational context across multiple turns without persisting data beyond the session

- A modular project structure that separates configuration, tools, memory, and orchestration, supporting incremental system evolution in later chapters

- Multiple execution modes (single-message, interactive, and Dev UI) that present consistent agent logic across different interfaces

- End-to-end observability through the Dev UI, ensuring agent reasoning, tool usage, and context injection are transparent and easily debuggable from the outset

CHAPTER 3

Thain Learns to Remember

Introduction

With in-session reasoning established, the next step is to introduce persistence, enabling Thain to retain memory beyond a single session.

In the last chapter, we provided Thain, a reasoning core through the Microsoft Agent Framework, one that could analyze, classify, and respond intelligently to feedback. However, when we stopped the process and restarted, Thain began anew, with no recollection, no context, and no sense of what had come before.

That's a limitation every real-world agent must overcome. Human teams don't restart every morning forgetting yesterday's issues; they retain what matters and discard what doesn't. Thain needs the same ability to remember what it has already seen, relate new messages to old ones, and recognize when a pattern is forming. Without that, it's reactive. With memory, it becomes insightful.

In this chapter, we'll give Thain a durable memory: its own long-term store of experience. We'll connect it to Azure Cosmos DB, turning feedback conversations into retrievable records. Once this layer is in place, Thain will be able to recall related complaints across sessions, summarize recurring problems, and even continue a conversation days later with full awareness of its history.

Think of it as upgrading Thain from conversation mode to continuity mode.

47

© Hari Narayn 2026

H. Narayn, *Architecting Intelligent Agents in Azure*, https://doi.org/10.1007/979-8-8688-2433-3_3

Thain v0.2 at a Glance

This chapter extends Thain with a two-tier memory architecture. By the end of the build, Thain v0.2 will have

- **A persistent data model**: Typed complaint records stored in Azure Cosmos DB, scoped by conversation and customer ID, with configurable TTL.

- **A persistent context provider**: Surfaces the most relevant past records into every new message, giving Thain recall across sessions.

- **Blended memory**: Short-term RAM buffer from v0.1 working alongside long-term Cosmos DB retrieval; each tier serving a different horizon.

- **Cross-session continuity**: Thain recognizes recurring issues even after a full restart, because memory lives in the database, not the process.

Seeing Thain Forget

Before we add persistence, let's watch the problem firsthand.

- Launch your Thain Dev UI from Chapter 2 and start a new conversation.

- Send: `My phone battery gets hot during charging.`

- Wait for Thain's response, and then click New Conversation in the toolbar.

- Send another message: `Now the phone shuts down suddenly at 60 percent. Could these be related?`

- Notice what happens; Thain treats this as a brand-new issue.

It has no recollection of the earlier complaint because its memory is currently limited to short-term RAM.

Once you click New Conversation, the entire context vanishes.

In this chapter, we'll address this by integrating Azure Cosmos DB, allowing Thain to recall what it has seen before, even across sessions.

Note   The complete project for this chapter is available in the Chapter 3 folder of the companion repository at `https://github.com/Apress/Architecting-Intelligent-Agents-in-Azure`. While all code listings are included in this chapter, the repository is the single source of truth for runnable, up-to-date code. The repository also includes a Microsoft Agent Framework 1.5.0 General Availability version of this chapter's code in the Code GA folder. The GA version updates the context-provider lifecycle and provider-chaining interface while preserving the chapter's Cosmos DB persistent memory architecture and behavior. A detailed migration note is also available in the repository.

Setting Up Cosmos DB in Azure

Before bringing memory into Thain's code, we need a place for Thain's memories to live.

Azure Cosmos DB is a fully managed NoSQL database that stores data as JSON documents. It scales automatically and responds in milliseconds, making it an excellent choice for Thain, which needs to save flexible, structured records without worrying about performance or schema limits.

We'll now walk through creating the Cosmos DB account, database, and container that will hold Thain's long-term memory.

Provisioning the Cosmos DB Account

1. In the Azure Portal, go to Create a resource and search for Azure Cosmos DB. When the results appear, click Azure Cosmos DB to open the creation page. On the next screen, choose Azure Cosmos DB for NoSQL.

2. **Workload environment**: select Development/Test. This keeps cost and throughput low while still exposing every feature.

3. Choose your Subscription and select the same Resource Group that holds your Azure AI Foundry resources.

4. Keeping everything in one group makes it easier to manage and clean up later.

5. **Account name**: `cosmos-thain`. For Availability Zones, keep the setting Disabled. We don't need zone redundancy for this small development setup and turning it off helps keep costs lower.

6. **Location**: Select East US or another region that best suits your needs. It's a good idea to keep this in the same region as your AI Foundry resource to reduce latency.

7. **Capacity mode**: select Serverless. This mode removes the need for capacity planning: you pay only for the Request Units (RUs) you consume.

8. Leave all other defaults unchanged and click Review + Create. Deployment typically takes 1–2 minutes.

Refer to Figure 3-1 for an example of these selections.

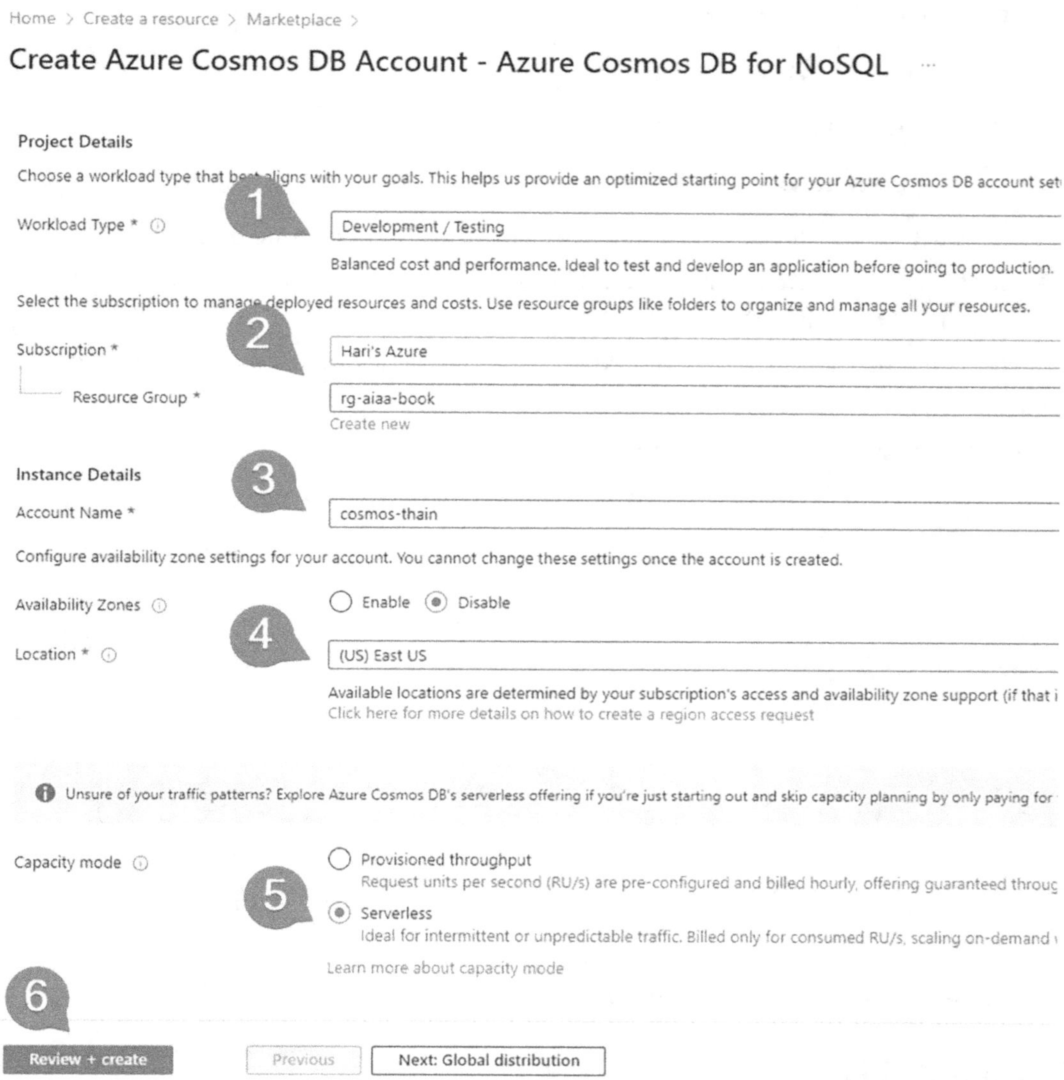

Figure 3-1. *Creating a new Cosmos DB for NoSQL account*

Configuring the Database and Container

Once deployment is complete, click Go to resource. You'll be taken to the newly created Cosmos DB account. From here, click Add Container in the top-right corner, or open Data Explorer from the left menu and choose New Container.

Enter the following details:

Database ID: `db-thain`

Container ID: `Complaints`

Partition Key: `/customerId`

The partition key tells Cosmos DB how to group and distribute data internally for fast reads and writes. At this stage of the book, we'll store every record under a fixed customer ID (`thain-demo`).

Leave all other settings unchanged and click OK. The database and container will be created.

Refer to Figure 3-2 for an example of the configuration.

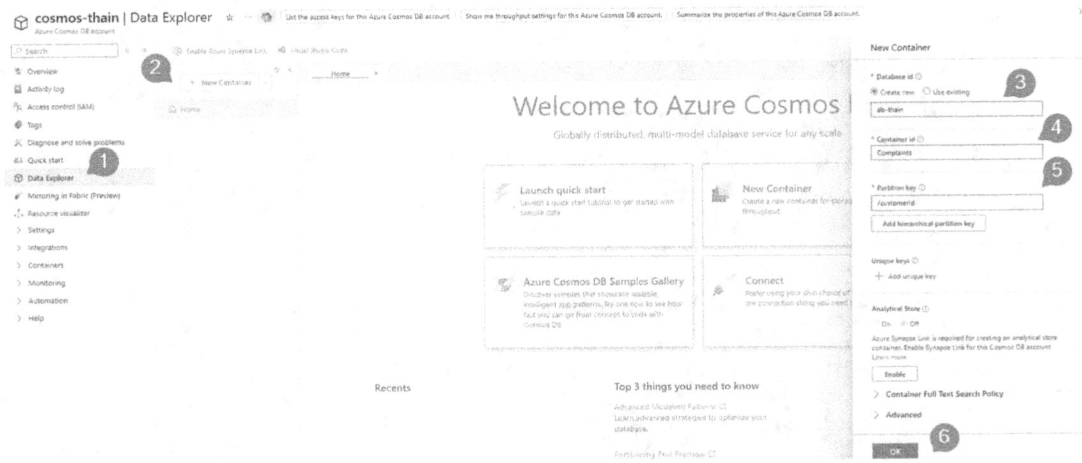

Figure 3-2. *Creating the Complaints container with /customerId partition key*

Configure TTL

Once the container is created, you'll be taken to the `Data Explorer`, where you can see your database and container listed in the left panel.

To enable automatic record expiry, configure the Time to Live (TTL) setting for your container:

1. In the left panel, expand your database (`db-thain`) and select the `Complaints` container.

2. Click Settings under the container name.

3. Under Time to Live, choose On (no default).

4. Click Save at the top of the screen.

Refer to Figure 3-3 for an example.

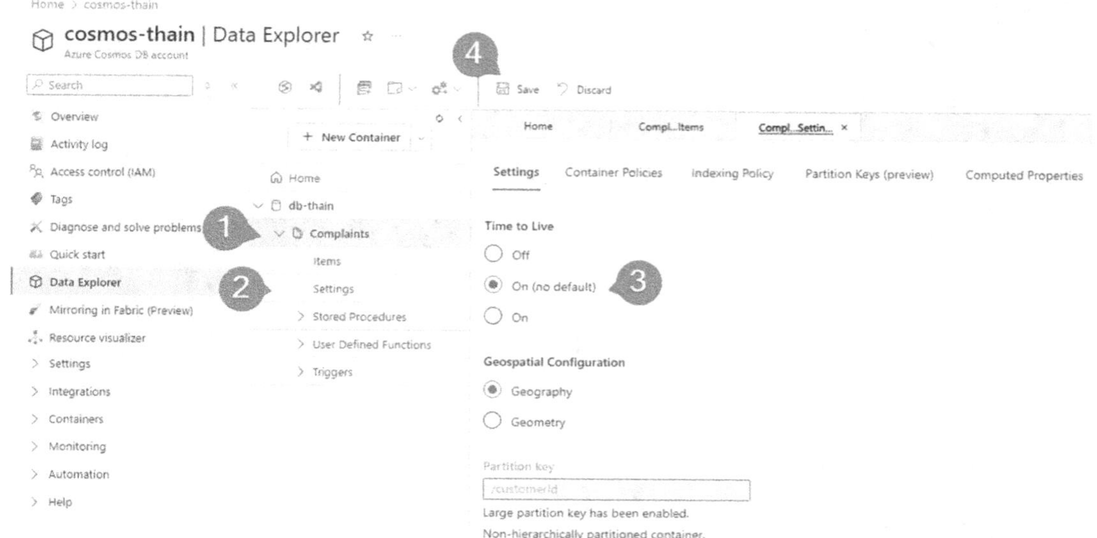

Figure 3-3. *Configuring TTL on the Complaints container*

TTL defines how long documents stay in the container before Cosmos DB automatically deletes them.

In Thain's case, this ensures that older complaint records are cleaned up after the number of days specified in your .env file, keeping memory relevant without allowing the database to grow indefinitely.

Update the . env File and Dependencies

Record the endpoint and key values you'll need for your environment configuration.

In the left panel of your Cosmos DB account, expand Settings and select Keys.

Refer to Figure 3-4 for an example.

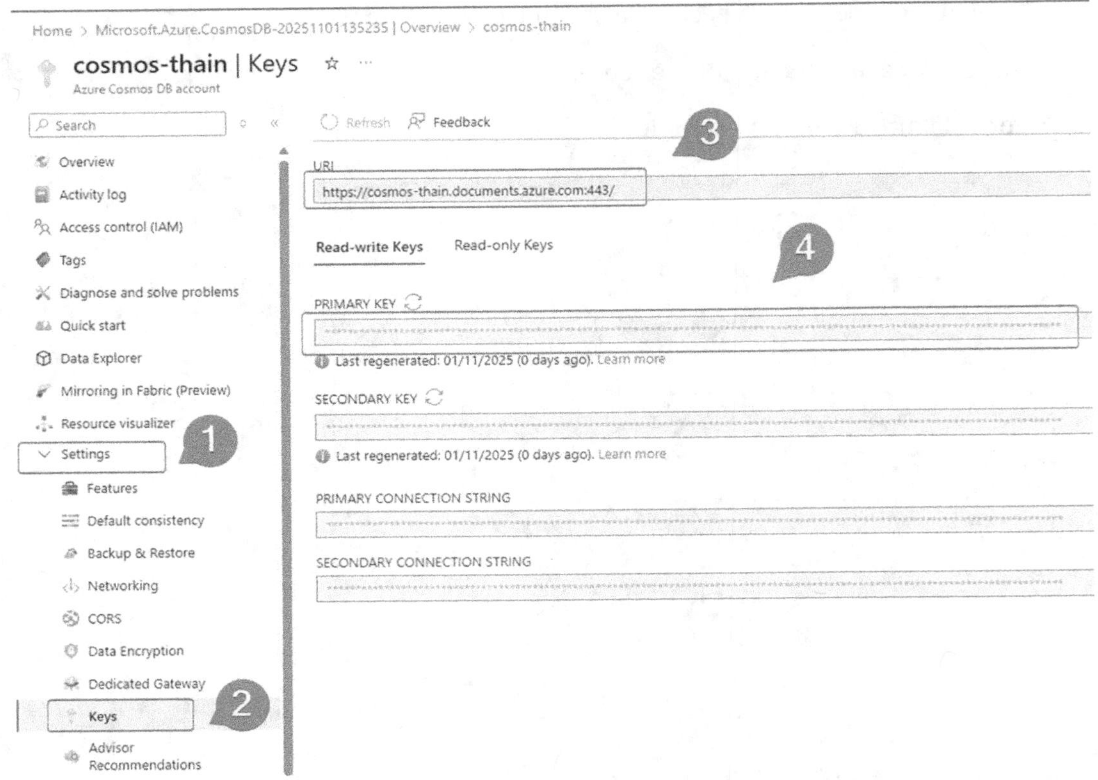

Figure 3-4. *Cosmos DB URI and Key*

Copy URI and Primary Key. Also note your database and container names. From the project folder, open the `.env` file, and update it with the following six entries:

```
COSMOS_ENDPOINT= <URI>
COSMOS_KEY=<your_primary_key>
COSMOS_DATABASE=db-thain
COSMOS_CONTAINER=Complaints
COSMOS_TTL_DAYS=30
THAIN_CUSTOMER_ID=thain-demo
```

The `COSMOS_TTL_DAYS` setting determines the duration each record remains in the database before it's automatically deleted. In this example, we're keeping data for 30 days, which helps Thain remember recent context without growing endlessly over time.

These settings allow Thain to connect securely to the Cosmos DB container and store persistent memory records.

At this stage, you've completed the setup for Thain's persistent memory:

- A Cosmos DB for NoSQL account running in Development/ Test mode

- A database (`db-thain`) and container (`Complaints`) using the partition key `/customerId`

- Endpoint, key, and configuration values saved securely in your .env file

Update Dependencies

Implementing persistent memory will need a few additional SDK dependencies. Add the new Azure Cosmos and Pydantic packages listed below to your requirements.txt:

```
azure-cosmos==4.6.0
pydantic==2.13.4
```

And then install them:

```
pip install -r requirements.txt
```

That completes the update of the environment and the installation of dependencies.

With this infrastructure in place, Thain now has the foundation it needs to remember what it learns.

In the next section, we'll integrate this database with the agent's code, enabling every conversation to be stored, retrieved, and used as context in future sessions.

Implementing Persistent Memory in Code

Now that Thain has a place to store its experiences, we need to decide what to store and how to represent it in code.

We'll begin by defining a durable complaint model and then add a repository, service, and context provider. This approach reflects the typical introduction of persistent memory in production agent systems: schema first, storage second, and reasoning last.

Defining the Data Model

Before Thain can persist memory, it needs a stable, explicit representation of a complaint, one that can survive beyond a single reasoning cycle.

This structure lives in `models/complaint.py` and is implemented using `Pydantic`, which provides validation, defaults, and seamless JSON conversion.

This file has three primary responsibilities:

- **Define a durable schema**: Every complaint Thain stores in Cosmos DB follows a consistent structure (ID, category, summary, message, confidence, timestamp, and TTL).

- **Bridge agent output and storage**: Pydantic maps Python-friendly field names (such as `customer_id`) to Cosmos DB JSON fields (such as `customerId`) without leaking storage concerns into agent logic.

- **Support controlled recall**: Helper models like `ComplaintQuery` define how earlier complaints can be retrieved without exposing raw database queries to the agent.

- At the root of the project, create a new folder named `models` and add a file called `complaint.py` inside it. Copy the code shown in Listing 3-1 into that file.

We will review the code in detail below after the listing. As you read through the model, notice the following three points:

- How storage-specific concerns (IDs, timestamps, and TTL) are handled inside the model rather than the agent

- How field aliases keep Cosmos DB naming out of the rest of the code base

- How record creation is centralized through a single factory method

Listing 3-1. models/complaint.py

```
from __future__ import annotations
from datetime import datetime, timezone
from typing import Optional
from uuid import uuid4
```

```python
from pydantic import BaseModel, Field
class ComplaintRecordModel(BaseModel):
    """Pydantic model describing a stored complaint record."""
    id: str = Field(default_factory=lambda: str(uuid4()))
    customer_id: str = Field(alias="customerId")
    issue_category: str = Field(alias="issueCategory")
    summary: str
    raw_message: str = Field(alias="rawMessage")
    confidence: float = 1.0
    created_at: datetime = Field(default_factory=lambda: datetime.
    now(timezone.utc), alias="createdAt")
    source: str = "thain"
    embedding_id: Optional[str] = Field(default=None, alias="embeddingId")
    ttl_seconds: Optional[int] = Field(default=None, alias="ttl")

    model_config = {
        "populate_by_name": True,
        "str_strip_whitespace": True,
        "json_encoders": {datetime: lambda dt: dt.isoformat()},
    }
    @classmethod
    def from_agent_payload(
        cls,
        *,
        customer_id: str,
        category: str,
        summary: str,
        message: str,
        confidence: float = 1.0,
        ttl_seconds: Optional[int] = None,
    ) -> "ComplaintRecordModel":
        return cls(
            customerId=customer_id,
            issueCategory=category,
            summary=summary,
            rawMessage=message,
```

```
            confidence=confidence,
            ttl=ttl_seconds,
        )
class ComplaintQuery(BaseModel):
    """Query parameters for retrieving previously stored complaints."""

    customer_id: str = Field(alias="customerId")
    category: Optional[str] = Field(default=None, alias="category")
    limit: int = 5
    model_config = {"populate_by_name": True}
```

How This Model Supports Persistent Memory

Each `ComplaintRecordModel` represents a single durable memory entry, a normalized snapshot of what Thain understood from a complaint at the time it was processed.

When the agent classifies a complaint, its result is passed to `from_agent_payload()`, which converts the model's output into a ready-to-store record: complete with a UUID, timestamp, and optional TTL for expiry.

The model configuration allows Thain to work entirely with Python-friendly names, while Cosmos DB receives documents in its expected JSON shape. This keeps persistence concerns isolated from the agent's reasoning logic.

`ComplaintQuery` defines a lightweight structure for reading data back from Cosmos DB. By passing a `customer_id`, an optional `issue_category`, and a result limit, Thain can recall earlier complaints that match the current situation.

Together, these models form the contract for Thain's long-term memory. With a stable schema in place, we can now introduce a repository layer that handles storage and retrieval without entangling persistence logic with reasoning.

Repository Layer

Once the data model is defined, Thain needs a dedicated persistence boundary, a layer responsible for talking to Cosmos DB without leaking database concerns into the agent or memory logic.

The repository layer fulfills this role. It encapsulates all Cosmos DB operations behind a clean, asynchronous interface.

This repository is responsible for

- **Managing Cosmos DB connectivity**: Initializing the client using the endpoint and credentials supplied via configuration

- **Ensuring storage primitives exist**: Creating the database and container if they do not already exist

- **Persisting complaint records**: Upserting validated complaint documents in a partition-aware manner

- **Retrieving recent memory**: Executing scoped, parameterized queries to fetch the most relevant prior complaints

- **Failing safely**: Isolating Cosmos DB failures so the agent can continue operating in a degraded mode

Notably, this layer does not perform any business logic, caching, or agent-specific reasoning. Its sole responsibility is reliable data access. This keeps persistence concerns isolated and allows higher layers to evolve independently.

Inside your memory folder, create a new file named `repositories.py` and copy the code shown in Listing 3-2.

As you read through the repository implementation below, focus on three design choices:

- Container creation is idempotent and safe to call repeatedly.

- All Cosmos interactions are asynchronous and parameterized.

- Storage failures are surfaced as a single, explicit error type.

Listing 3-2. memory/repositories.py

```
from __future__ import annotations
import logging
from typing import Any, Iterable, Optional
from azure.cosmos import PartitionKey
from azure.cosmos.aio import CosmosClient
from azure.cosmos.exceptions import CosmosResourceExistsError
from config.settings import PersistentMemoryConfig
from models.complaint import ComplaintQuery, ComplaintRecordModel
```

```python
logger = logging.getLogger(__name__)
class PersistentStoreError(RuntimeError):
    """Raised when the persistent store cannot be reached."""
class CosmosRepository:
    """Async Cosmos DB repository for complaint records."""

    def __init__(self, config: PersistentMemoryConfig) -> None:
        self._config = config
        self._client = CosmosClient(self._config.endpoint,
        credential=self._config.key)
        self._database = None
        self._container = None
    async def _ensure_container(self) -> Any:
        if self._container:
            return self._container
        try:
            self._database = await self._client.create_database_if_not_
            exists(id=self._config.database)
        except Exception as exc:
            logger.error("Failed to access Cosmos database '%s': %s",
            self._config.database, exc, exc_info=True)
            raise PersistentStoreError("Unable to access Cosmos DB
            database.") from exc

        try:
            kwargs: dict[str, Any] = {}
            if self._config.ttl_seconds:
                kwargs["default_ttl"] = self._config.ttl_seconds
            self._container = await self._database.create_container_if_
            not_exists(
                id=self._config.container,
                partition_key=PartitionKey(path="/customerId"),
                offer_throughput=400,
                **kwargs,
            )
        except CosmosResourceExistsError:
```

```
        self._container = await self._database.get_container_
        client(self._config.container)
    except Exception as exc:
        logger.error("Failed to access Cosmos container '%s': %s",
        self._config.container, exc, exc_info=True)
        raise PersistentStoreError("Unable to access Cosmos DB
        container.") from exc
    return self._container
async def upsert_complaint(self, record: ComplaintRecordModel) -> None:
    container = await self._ensure_container()
    try:
        payload = record.model_dump(by_alias=True)
        payload["createdAt"] = record.created_at.isoformat()
        if payload.get("ttl") is None and self._config.ttl_seconds:
            payload["ttl"] = self._config.ttl_seconds
        await container.upsert_item(payload)
    except Exception as exc:
        logger.warning("Failed to upsert complaint record to Cosmos DB:
        %s", exc, exc_info=True)
        raise PersistentStoreError("Unable to write to Cosmos DB.")
        from exc
async def fetch_recent(self, query: ComplaintQuery) ->
list[ComplaintRecordModel]:
    container = await self._ensure_container()
    parameters = [
        {"name": "@limit", "value": query.limit},
        {"name": "@partitionKey", "value": query.customer_id},
    ]
    where_clause = "c.customerId = @partitionKey"
    if query.category:
        where_clause += " AND c.issueCategory = @category"
        parameters.append({"name": "@category", "value": query.
        category})
    cosmos_query = (
        f"SELECT TOP @limit * FROM c "
```

```python
        f"WHERE {where_clause} "
        f"ORDER BY c.createdAt DESC"
    )
    try:
        items = container.query_items(
            query=cosmos_query,
            parameters=parameters,
            partition_key=query.customer_id,
            max_item_count=query.limit,
        )
        results: list[ComplaintRecordModel] = []
        async for item in items:
            results.append(ComplaintRecordModel.model_validate(item))
        return results
    except Exception as exc:
        logger.warning("Failed to fetch complaints from Cosmos DB: %s",
        exc, exc_info=True)
        raise PersistentStoreError("Unable to read from Cosmos DB.")
        from exc
async def close(self) -> None:
    await self._client.close()
```

Repository Layer: Storage and Retrieval Flow

When the repository is first accessed, `_ensure_container()` establishes the physical storage boundary by verifying that the database and container exist, creating them only if required.

It also sets the default TTL to match your `.env` configuration, so records automatically expire after the defined number of days.

When Thain saves a new record, `upsert_complaint()` converts the ComplaintRecordModel into a JSON payload using field aliases (so `customer_id` becomes `customerId`).

If TTL isn't set on the record, it's added automatically.

When retrieving context, `fetch_recent()` runs a parameterized query to fetch the most recent complaints for a customer or category.

This method streams results asynchronously and validates each result against a `ComplaintRecordModel` before returning them to the service layer.

All Cosmos-related failures are normalized into `PersistentStoreError`, allowing higher layers to treat persistence as optional rather than fatal. If the database is temporarily unavailable, Thain logs a warning and continues to operate in a degraded mode rather than failing.

With the repository in place, Thain now has a reliable persistence primitive. The next step is to introduce a service layer that coordinates when persistence happens, applies caching, and shields the agent from transient storage concerns.

Service Layer

With the repository established, Thain requires a coordination layer to determine when to write or read memory and to manage failures without disrupting reasoning. That responsibility belongs to the service layer.

The service layer has four primary responsibilities:

- **Orchestrate persistence**: Convert agent output into validated complaint records and persist them using the repository.

- **Control recall**: Fetch recent complaints based on customer and category without exposing query logic to the agent.

- **Reduce storage pressure**: Apply short-lived in-memory caching to avoid repeated database reads during active sessions.

- **Fail gracefully**: Ensure that transient Cosmos DB issues do not interrupt the agent's reasoning loop.

The service layer is also the natural place to introduce caching. By keeping this concern out of the repository, we preserve a clean separation between data access and memory policy.

Inside the memory folder, create a new file named `persistence.py` and copy the code from Listing 3-3.

As you read through the implementation below, note how the service layer deliberately stays thin: it delegates storage mechanics to the repository, keeps caching local and short-lived, and exposes a minimal API to the rest of the system.

Listing 3-3. memory/persistence.py

```python
from __future__ import annotations
import logging
from collections import OrderedDict
from datetime import datetime, timezone
from typing import Optional
from config.settings import PersistentMemoryConfig
from memory.repositories import CosmosRepository, PersistentStoreError
from models.complaint import ComplaintQuery, ComplaintRecordModel
logger = logging.getLogger(__name__)
class _LRUCache:
    """Simple TTL-aware LRU cache for query results."""
    def __init__(self, capacity: int = 32, ttl_seconds: int = 30) -> None:
        self.capacity = capacity
        self.ttl_seconds = ttl_seconds
        self._store: OrderedDict[str, tuple[datetime,
        list[ComplaintRecordModel]]] = OrderedDict()
    def _now(self) -> datetime:
        return datetime.now(timezone.utc)
    def get(self, key: str) -> Optional[list[ComplaintRecordModel]]:
        entry = self._store.get(key)
        if not entry:
            return None
        timestamp, value = entry
        if (self._now() - timestamp).total_seconds() > self.ttl_seconds:
            self._store.pop(key, None)
            return None
        self._store.move_to_end(key)
        return value
    def set(self, key: str, value: list[ComplaintRecordModel]) -> None:
        self._store[key] = (self._now(), value)
        self._store.move_to_end(key)
        if len(self._store) > self.capacity:
            self._store.popitem(last=False)
    def clear(self) -> None:
```

```python
        self._store.clear()
class PersistentMemoryService:
    """Coordinates storing and retrieving complaints from Cosmos DB."""
    def __init__(self, config: PersistentMemoryConfig, repository:
    CosmosRepository | None = None) -> None:
        self._config = config
        self._repository = repository or CosmosRepository(config)
        self._cache = _LRUCache()
    async def persist(
        self,
        *,
        customer_id: str,
        category: str,
        summary: str,
        message: str,
        confidence: float = 1.0,
        embedding_id: str | None = None,
    ) -> None:
        record = ComplaintRecordModel.from_agent_payload(
            customer_id=customer_id,
            category=category,
            summary=summary,
            message=message,
            confidence=confidence,
            ttl_seconds=self._config.ttl_seconds or None,
        )
        if embedding_id:
            record.embedding_id = embedding_id
        try:
            await self._repository.upsert_complaint(record)
        except PersistentStoreError:
            raise
        except Exception as exc:
            logger.warning("Unexpected failure while persisting complaint:
            %s", exc, exc_info=True)
```

```python
            raise PersistentStoreError("Persistent memory write failed.")
            from exc
        finally:
            self._cache.clear()
    async def fetch_recent(
        self,
        *,
        customer_id: str,
        category: str | None = None,
        limit: int = 5,
    ) -> list[ComplaintRecordModel]:
        cache_key = f"{customer_id}:{category}:{limit}"
        cached = self._cache.get(cache_key)
        if cached is not None:
            return cached
        query = ComplaintQuery(customerId=customer_id, category=category,
        limit=limit)
        try:
            results = await self._repository.fetch_recent(query)
            self._cache.set(cache_key, results)
            return results
        except PersistentStoreError:
            raise
        except Exception as exc:
            logger.warning("Unexpected error fetching persistent context:
            %s", exc, exc_info=True)
            raise PersistentStoreError("Persistent memory read failed.")
            from exc
    async def close(self) -> None:
        await self._repository.close()
        self._cache.clear()
```

How the Service Layer Coordinates Persistent Memory

The _LRUCache class provides a deliberately small, TTL-aware cache that exists solely to smooth rapid, repeated recall during development and testing. Each entry is timestamped and automatically expires after a short period (default 30 seconds).

This helps reduce repeated reads from Cosmos DB when the same context is requested multiple times during testing or rapid conversation loops.

- `PersistentMemoryService` wraps all persistence logic.

- `persist()` converts an agent's output into a `ComplaintRecordModel`, applies TTL and metadata, writes it to Cosmos DB, and clears the cache so that subsequent recalls always reflect the latest persisted state.

- `fetch_recent()` retrieves the latest complaints for a given customer or category. If the same query is made within the cache window, the results are served directly from memory rather than being retrieved from Cosmos again.

- Error handling: All persistence-related failures are normalized into `PersistentStoreError`, allowing the agent to treat long-term memory as an enhancement rather than a dependency.

- `close()` cleans up the repository connection and clears any cached entries.

This service layer completes Thain's durable memory pipeline. What remains is to surface these stored memories at the right moment during reasoning, which is the role of the persistent context provider.

Persistent Context Provider

With the service layer complete, the next step is to connect Thain's stored memories to its reasoning process.

The persistent context provider manages this process, acting as the bridge between Cosmos-stored memory and the Microsoft Agent Framework's reasoning context.

The `PersistentContextProvider` class extends MAF's built-in `ContextProvider` to surface long-term memory as ephemeral contextual instructions before each reasoning cycle.

If persistent memory is unavailable, it silently falls back to an empty context, ensuring that memory enhances reasoning but never becomes a dependency.

Its responsibilities are simple and focused:

- **Retrieve historical context**: Fetches recent complaints from Cosmos DB through the `PersistentMemoryService`

- **Format memory for reasoning**: Converts the retrieved complaints into concise, readable bullet points for model consumption

- **Handle degraded mode**: If the storage or connectivity is unavailable, logs diagnostic information and allows the session to continue uninterrupted

Inside the memory folder, create a new file named `persistent_provider.py` and copy the code from Listing 3-4.

Listing 3-4. memory/persistent_provider.py

```python
from __future__ import annotations
import logging
from datetime import datetime
from typing import Any, Iterable, Optional
from agent_framework import ChatMessage, Context, ContextProvider
from memory.persistence import PersistentMemoryService,
PersistentStoreError
logger = logging.getLogger(__name__)
class PersistentContextProvider(ContextProvider):
    """Loads long-term memories from Cosmos DB and surfaces them as context
    instructions."""
    def __init__(
        self,
        *,
        memory_service: PersistentMemoryService,
```

```
    default_customer_id: str,
    lookup_limit: int = 5,
) -> None:
    self._memory_service = memory_service
    self._default_customer_id = default_customer_id
    self._lookup_limit = lookup_limit
async def invoking(self, messages: Any, **kwargs: Any) -> Context:  #
type: ignore[override]
    customer_id = kwargs.get("customer_id") or self._default_
    customer_id
    try:
        records = await self._memory_service.fetch_recent(customer_
        id=customer_id, limit=self._lookup_limit)
    except PersistentStoreError:
        logger.debug("Persistent memory unavailable; continuing without
        durable context.", exc_info=True)
        return Context()
    if not records:
        return Context()
    formatted = [
        f"- [{record.issue_category}] {record.summary} ({record.
        created_at.strftime('%Y-%m-%d %H:%M UTC')})"
        for record in records
    ]
    instructions = (
        "Consider the following recent complaints from persistent
        memory:\n"
        + "\n".join(formatted)
    )
    return Context(instructions=instructions)
```

How Persistent Memory Is Injected into Reasoning

The provider is registered with the Agent Framework's runtime and participates in the invocation phase of each agent turn.

Before each agent call, MAF invokes the `invoking()` method, which performs three deliberate steps:

- **Identify the customer**: Checks whether the current request includes a `customer_id`; if not, falls back to a default (e.g., `thain-demo`)

- **Retrieve records**: Fetches the latest complaint entries using `fetch_recent()` from the memory service

- **Format for context**: Converts each complaint into a line like `[Connectivity] Wi-Fi keeps dropping (2025-10-31 11:45 UTC)`

All retrieved items are then joined into a formatted instruction block, which is injected as ephemeral context for the upcoming reasoning step.

Consider the following recent complaints from persistent memory:

This instruction is passed as a Context object back into the agent loop, giving Thain immediate access to recent history before generating its following response.

If Cosmos DB is unreachable or empty, the provider logs a debug message and returns an empty context, allowing the reasoning chain to proceed without delay or failure.

With the context provider in place, Thain's memory becomes actionable. Past complaints are no longer just stored; they actively shape how new problems are interpreted during reasoning.

Next, we'll update `settings.py` to make this persistent layer configurable and connect all components in the main orchestration flow.

Updating Configuration

In Chapter 2, `config/settings.py` was responsible only for loading Microsoft Foundry configuration through `AzureAgentConfig`. That code remains unchanged.

To support persistent memory, we extend `settings.py` with additional configuration, allowing the memory layer to read Cosmos DB settings without affecting the existing agent setup.

Configuration Changes for Persistent Memory

We added two new elements:

1. PersistentMemoryConfig, a dedicated dataclass that captures all Cosmos DB–specific settings required by the memory layer

2. load_persistent_config(), a helper that reads these values from the environment and returns a configuration object only when persistent memory is explicitly configured

In config/settings.py, update the code in two steps:

Step 1: Insert the code from Listing 3-5a immediately after the existing AzureAgentConfig dataclass definition.

Listing 3-5a. Adding PersistentMemoryConfig to config/settings.py

```python
@dataclass(frozen=True)
class PersistentMemoryConfig:
    """Configuration for Cosmos DB-backed persistent memory."""
    endpoint: str
    database: str
    container: str
    ttl_days: int = 30
    key: str | None = None
    customer_id: str = "thain-demo"
    @property
    def ttl_seconds(self) -> int:
        return max(self.ttl_days, 0) * 24 * 60 * 60
    @classmethod
    def from_env(cls) -> "PersistentMemoryConfig | None":
        endpoint = os.getenv("COSMOS_ENDPOINT", "").strip()
        database = os.getenv("COSMOS_DATABASE", "").strip()
        container = os.getenv("COSMOS_CONTAINER", "").strip()
        if not endpoint or not database or not container:
            return None
        key = os.getenv("COSMOS_KEY", "").strip() or None
        ttl_days_raw = os.getenv("COSMOS_TTL_DAYS", "").strip()
```

```python
    customer_id = os.getenv("THAIN_CUSTOMER_ID", "").strip() or
"thain-demo"
    ttl_days = 30
    if ttl_days_raw:
        try:
            ttl_days = max(int(ttl_days_raw), 0)
        except ValueError:
            ttl_days = 30
    return cls(
        endpoint=endpoint,
        database=database,
        container=container,
        key=key,
        ttl_days=ttl_days,
        customer_id=customer_id,
    )
```

Step 2: Insert the code from Listing 3-5b immediately after the existing load_
config() function.

Listing 3-5b. Adding load_persistent_config() helper

```python
def load_persistent_config() -> PersistentMemoryConfig | None:
    """Helper to load persistent memory configuration if available."""
    return PersistentMemoryConfig.from_env()
```

Configuration Loading and Validation

The PersistentMemoryConfig follows the same pattern as AzureAgentConfig but
encapsulates the configuration required for Cosmos DB–backed persistent memory.

- endpoint, database, and container tell Thain where the
  complaints container lives.

- The key is optional for future-proofing the configuration. In this
  chapter's implementation, the persistence layer still requires a
  Cosmos DB key to be provided.

- ttl_days is the same value you set in COSMOS_TTL_DAYS in your .env.

- `customer_id` defaults to `thain-demo`, which is used as the partition key value for the Cosmos DB container.

- The `ttl_seconds` property converts days into the number of seconds Cosmos DB expects for TTL.

- If `ttl_days` is set to 0, the computed TTL is 0 seconds, which effectively disables record expiry in Cosmos DB.

- `load_persistent_config()` reads the Cosmos DB settings from the environment. If any required settings are missing (endpoint, database, or container), it simply returns None, allowing Thain to run without persistent memory.

- When all required settings are present, the loader parses `COSMOS_TTL_DAYS`, reads the optional `COSMOS_KEY`, and builds a `PersistentMemoryConfig` instance.

Elsewhere in the project (such as in `main.py`), `load_persistent_config()` is called once at startup to determine whether persistent memory should be enabled. If it returns a config object, Thain will enable persistent memory. If it returns None, Thain behaves exactly like Chapter 2, running without Cosmos, but still fully functional.

Integrating Persistent Memory

In Chapter 2, the `main.py` file built and ran Thain's core logic using a single short-term memory provider. Persistent memory extends that design, allowing conversations to be durably stored in Cosmos DB and recalled across sessions.

This version of `main.py` adds long-term memory support without changing how we run Thain from the CLI or Dev UI.

Extending the Agent Entry Point

Everything from Chapter 2 (Listing 2-4) remains intact:

- Command-line options (`--message, --interactive, --devui`, etc.)

- The `MemoryContextProvider`, `ConversationMemory`, and Dev UI integration

- The same reasoning, instructions, and short-term context behavior

We're adding four significant enhancements:

- **Persistent memory setup**: Loads the Cosmos DB configuration and creates a `PersistentMemoryService`.

- Provider chaining merges both short-term and persistent contexts via the `AggregateContextProvider`.

- **Automatic persistence**: Writes every conversation result into Cosmos DB after each run.

- **Graceful fallback**: If Cosmos DB isn't configured or available, Thain runs exactly as before.

The following listings show only the changes introduced in Chapter 3, each annotated with its placement in `main.py`.

Add these imports in Listing 3-6a into the existing import section at the top of `main.py`.

Listing 3-6a. New imports for persistent memory

```python
import logging
from agent_framework import AggregateContextProvider
from config.settings import (
    PersistentMemoryConfig,
    load_persistent_config,
)
from memory.persistence import PersistentMemoryService,
PersistentStoreError
from memory.persistent_provider import PersistentContextProvider
```

These imports introduce the building blocks required for persistent memory: a composite context provider, a dedicated persistence service, and a provider that can surface long-term memory during reasoning. We also add logging to safely record persistence failures without breaking execution.

Note   This listing will work as shown if the imports are placed at the top of
`main.py`.

For a cleaner final implementation, you may later merge these imports into the
existing import section, positioning them according to standard Python conventions
(stdlib, third-party, and then local modules).

Persistent Memory Initialization

Insert code from Listing 3-6b above the existing `memory_store =`
`ConversationMemory(capacity=5)` line.

Listing 3-6b. Persistent memory initialization

```
persistent_memory_config: PersistentMemoryConfig | None = load_persistent_
config()
persistent_memory_service: PersistentMemoryService | None = (
    PersistentMemoryService(persistent_memory_config)
    if persistent_memory_config
    else None
)
logger = logging.getLogger(__name__)
```

At startup, Thain attempts to load persistent memory configuration
from the environment. If the required Cosmos DB settings are present, a
`PersistentMemoryService` is created. If not, the service remains None, allowing the
application to run exactly as it did in Chapter 2.

Provider Chaining

In `run_thain_agent()`, replace `memory_provider = MemoryContextProvider(memory_`
`store)` with the following block as provided in Listing 3-6c.

Listing 3-6c. Provider chaining in run_thain_agent()

```
provider_chain: list[ContextProvider] =
[MemoryContextProvider(memory_store)]
    if persistent_memory_service and persistent_memory_config:
        provider_chain.append(
            PersistentContextProvider(
                memory_service=persistent_memory_service,
                default_customer_id=persistent_memory_config.customer_id,
            )
        )
    context_provider: ContextProvider | AggregateContextProvider
    if len(provider_chain) == 1:
        context_provider = provider_chain[0]
    else:
        context_provider = AggregateContextProvider(provider_chain)
```

Rather than replacing the existing short-term memory provider, this approach composes multiple providers using AggregateContextProvider. When persistent memory is enabled, both short-term and durable contexts are supplied to the agent. When it is not, the agent continues to use only in-memory context.

Also locate the ChatAgent(...) call and replace memory_provider with context_provider:

```
context_providers=context_provider
```

Automatic Persistence

Insert code from Listing 3-6d immediately after the below existing line:

```
normalized = {"category": payload["category"], "summary":
payload["summary"]}
```

Listing 3-6d. Automatic persistence after each run

```
if persistent_memory_service and persistent_memory_config:
        try:
```

```
        await persistent_memory_service.persist(
            customer_id=persistent_memory_config.customer_id,
            category=normalized["category"],
            summary=normalized["summary"],
            message=customer_message,
            confidence=float(payload.get("confidence", 1.0)),
        )
    except PersistentStoreError:
        logger.debug("Persistent memory write failed; continuing
        without durable storage.", exc_info=True)
response.value = normalized
return normalized, response
```

After each successful agent run, Thain attempts to persist the normalized output to Cosmos DB. Any storage failures are logged and ignored, ensuring that durable memory enhances the system without ever becoming a hard dependency.

How Persistent Memory Is Integrated

When Thain starts, it first tries to load `PersistentMemoryConfig` from `.env`.

If the Cosmos DB endpoint and container are defined, the agent initializes a `PersistentMemoryService`.

At runtime, each agent invocation follows a consistent flow:

1. **Context assembly**: The `AggregateContextProvider` requests both recent in-memory complaints and stored ones from Cosmos DB.

2. **Reasoning**: The Microsoft Agent Framework combines these contexts and invokes the configured Microsoft Foundry model (GPT-4o in this implementation) to classify and summarize the complaint.

3. **Persistence**: The normalized output is stored asynchronously in Cosmos DB for future reference.

4. **Fallback**: If Cosmos DB is unreachable, Thain logs a debug message and continues normally.

This unified design allows Thain to reason across sessions while preserving its original simplicity, blending short-term session awareness with durable, cross-session recall.

How It All Comes Together

At this point, every part of Thain's memory stack works in harmony:

- `models/complaint.py` defines the structure of each record stored in Cosmos DB.

- `memory/repositories.py` handles low-level communication with Cosmos DB: creating the container, writing documents, and fetching recent complaints.

- `memory/persistence.py` orchestrates these operations and adds a lightweight cache for quick lookups.

- `memory/persistent_provider.py` bridges the stored records into the Agent Framework's reasoning loop, turning past complaints into contextual hints.

- `config/settings.py` loads both the Azure AI and Cosmos DB configurations, allowing the agent to connect securely at startup.

- Finally, `main.py` brings it all together by loading the configuration, chaining context providers, and persisting each result for future recall.

Together, these files transform Thain into an agent that can retain and reuse knowledge across conversations.

Seeing Thain Remember

Now that Thain can persist memory, let's watch it in action inside the Dev UI.

If you paused development since Chapter 2, reactivate your virtual environment before launching Thain:

```
.venv\Scripts\Activate.ps1
```

Demo Conversations

Run the following command to start the Dev UI and open it automatically in your browser:

```
python main.py --devui --devui-open
```

You'll see Thain listed as the active agent.

Convo 1 – Starting a New Conversation

Type and press Enter:

```
The battery keeps swelling after the last firmware update.
```

Thain categorizes it as Hardware and stores it. That's Thain's first persistent memory entry (Figure 3-5).

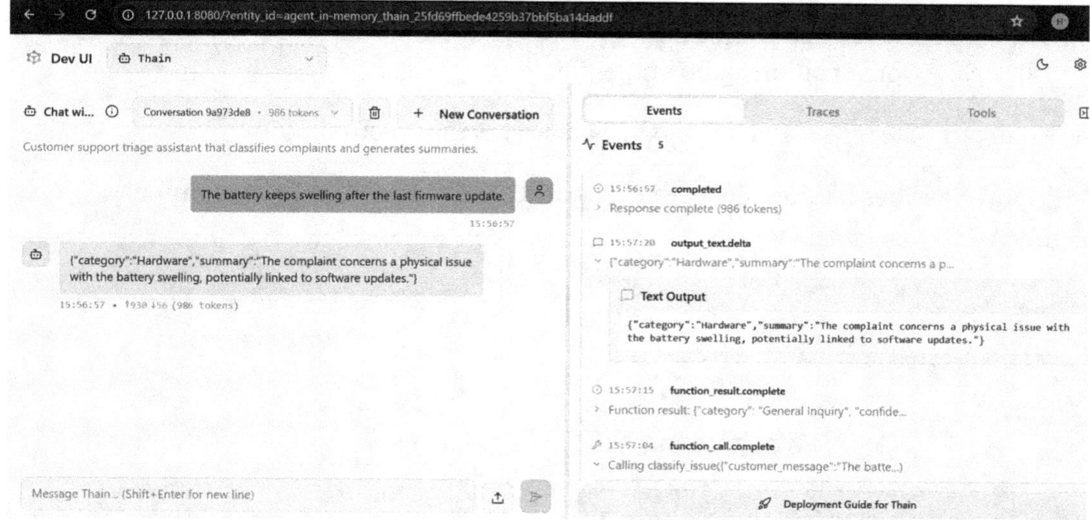

Figure 3-5. *Convo 1 – Starting a New Conversation*

Convo 2 – Persistent Memory in a New Conversation

Click the New Conversation button at the top.

Notice that the Conversation ID changes; each session is unique.

Now enter

```
Replacement battery bloated overnight.
```

Notice that Thain links this to earlier Hardware issues, showing memory recall across sessions (as shown in Figure 3-6).

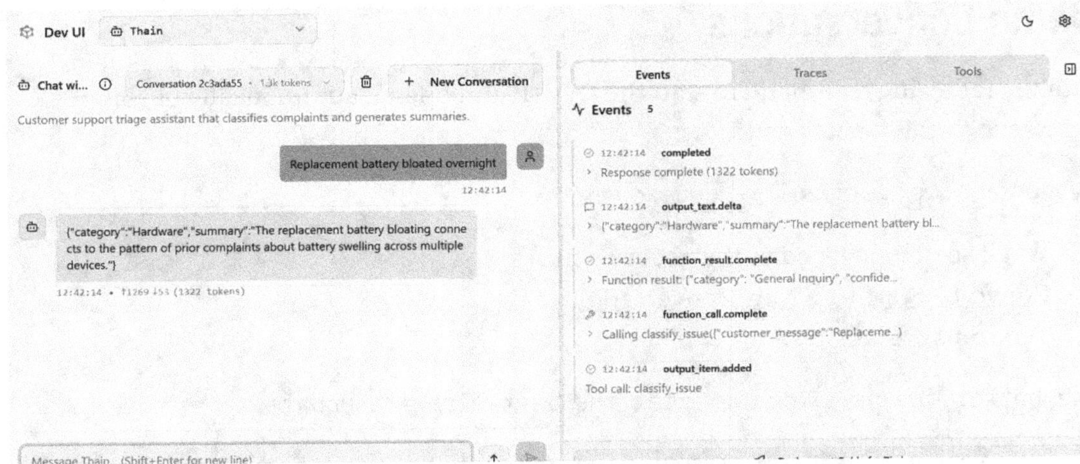

Figure 3-6. *Convo 2 – Persistent Memory in a New Conversation*

Convo 3 – Different Complaint

Click New Conversation again and enter

```
Wi-Fi drops whenever I step outside the living room.
```

Thain classifies it under `Connectivity` and produces a short JSON summary (Figure 3-7).

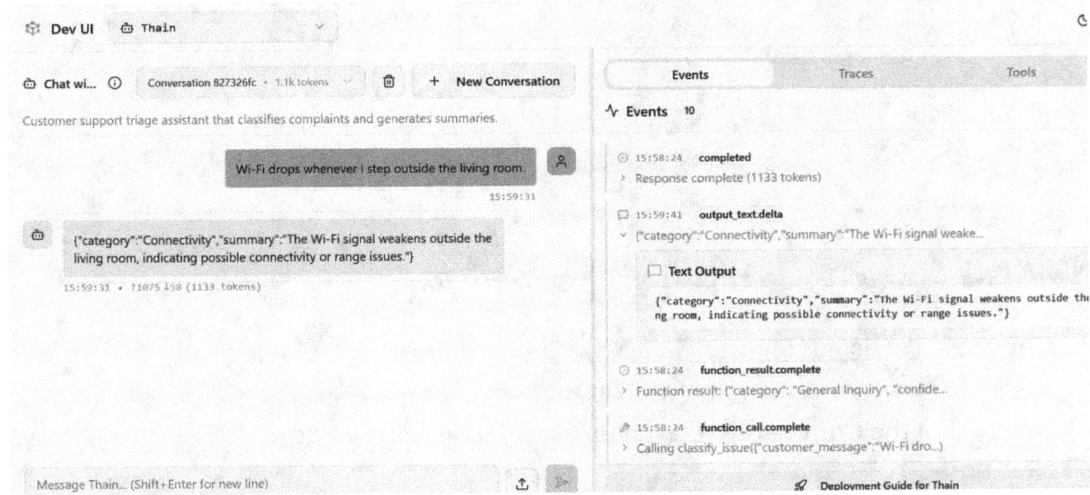

Figure 3-7. *Convo 3 – Different Complaint*

<u>Convo 4 – Persistent Memory After Restart</u>

Stop Thain (Ctrl + C) and relaunch it using the same command:

```
python main.py --devui --devui-open
```

Start a new conversation and enter

```
Signal collapsed again on the patio this morning.
```

Thain recognizes the earlier `Connectivity` complaint and references it, demonstrating persistent memory even after a restart (Figure 3-8).

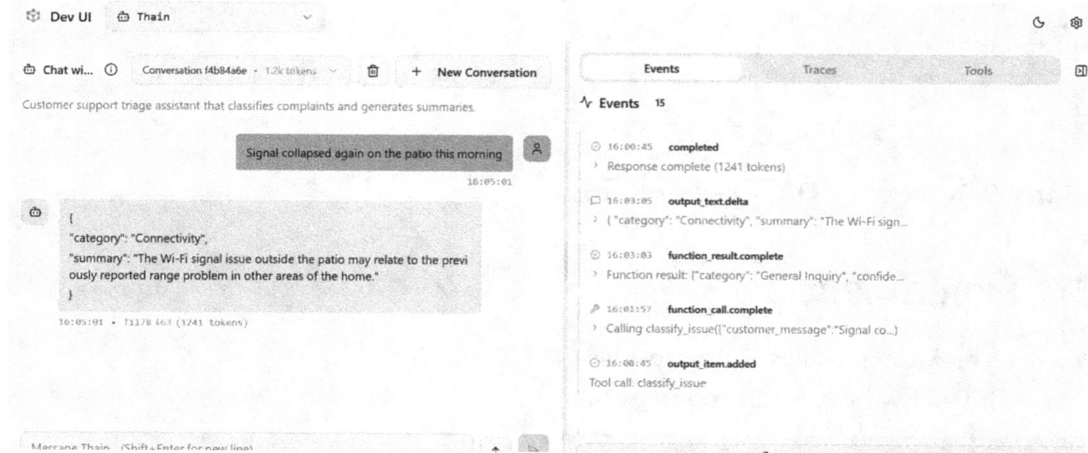

Figure 3-8. *Convo 4 – Persistent Memory After Restart*

These examples demonstrate the chapter's main point: Thain's memory now extends beyond a single session or process lifetime.

By storing complaints in Cosmos DB and accessing them through a persistent context provider, Thain can identify related issues across separate conversations and after a restart. Each Dev UI session remains isolated, while long-term memory is securely shared in the background.

This distinction between ephemeral session context and durable system memory is foundational to everything that follows.

Verify in Azure Cosmos DB

Open your Cosmos DB account in the Azure Portal, select Data Explorer → Complaints → Items, and you'll see each conversation stored as a JSON document. Look at Figure 3-9 for an example for our last conversation record.

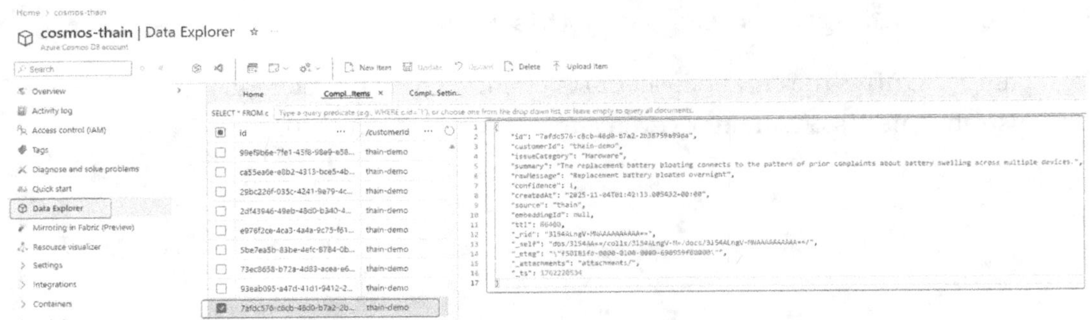

Figure 3-9. *Cosmos DB persists records*

TTL Experiment

You can verify Cosmos DB's Time-to-Live (TTL) behavior.

Set the following value in your .env file:

```
COSMOS_TTL_DAYS=1
```

Run a few conversations, and then return the next day. Those items will have expired automatically, and Thain will no longer be able to recall them. This confirms that the TTL cleanup works precisely as expected.

Note   The current state of the project at the end of this chapter is available in the book's GitHub repository: https://github.com/Apress/Architecting-Intelligent-Agents-in-Azure. You can clone the repository and set it up locally with the following commands:

```
git clone https://github.com/Apress/Architecting-Intelligent-
Agents-in-Azure.git

cd Architecting-Intelligent-Agents-in-Azure
```

For the manuscript code, open the Chapter 3/thain folder. For the GA code, open Code GA/Chapter 3/thain. After cloning, create and activate a virtual environment, and then install the dependencies by running the below commands in order:

```
python -m venv .venv
```

```
.\.venv\Scripts\activate
```

```
pip install -r requirements.txt -c constraints.txt
```

Finally, create your own `.env` file with the required Azure settings before running the project.

You can also browse the repository online to review the reference implementation.

As a best practice, this chapter includes a simple unit-test module that validates Thain's persistent memory layer: `tests/test_persistent_memory.py`

Run it from your project root using

```
python -m unittest tests.test_persistent_memory.
```

These tests confirm that Thain can safely store, retrieve, and handle context data. You're welcome to expand these tests further; for example, to simulate failures, add mock Cosmos DB responses, or verify that the TTL cleanup behaves as expected.

Thain v0.2 Architecture

Figure 3-10 shows how Thain's two memory tiers connect at runtime: the short-term buffer for within-session context and Cosmos DB for persistence across sessions.

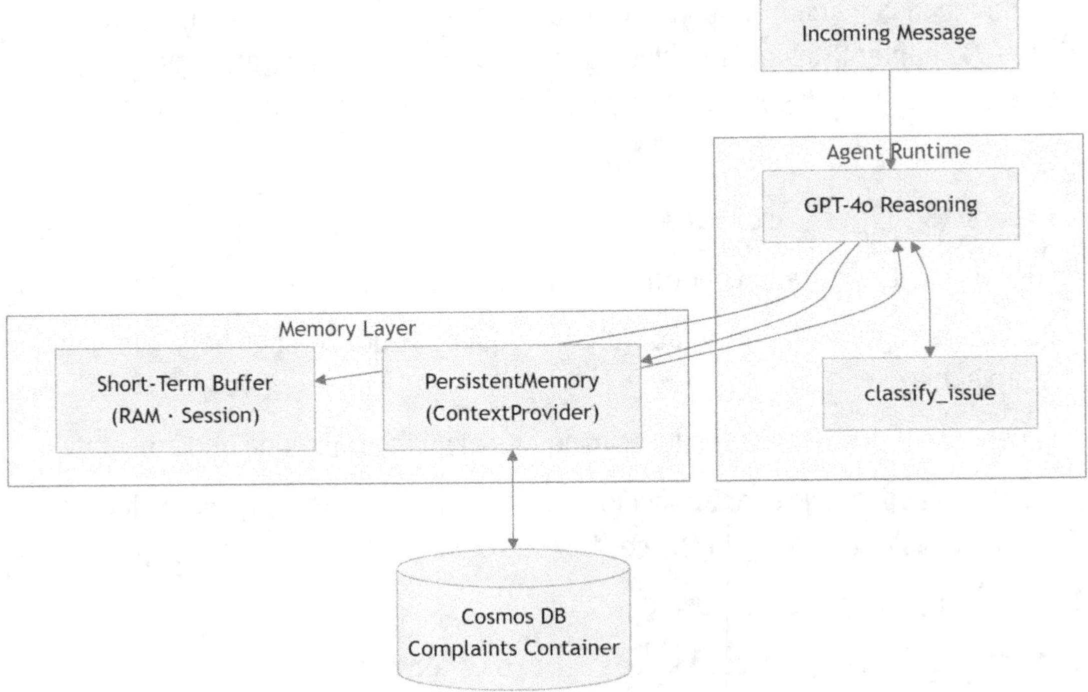

Figure 3-10. *Thain v0.2 Architecture*

Summary

In this chapter, Thain learned how to remember.

We built a durable memory layer powered by Azure Cosmos DB, allowing every conversation to be stored, retrieved, and reused as context in future sessions. Throughout the design, we ensured that everything was aligned with the Microsoft Agent Framework, allowing memory to integrate naturally with reasoning and tools.

You built the data models that define a complaint record, wrote the repository and service layers that handle Cosmos operations, and connected everything through a new persistent context provider. Then, inside the Dev UI, you watched Thain recall past issues, proof that its short-term and long-term memories now work together.

Thain v0.2 is officially alive. It has taken its first real step toward intelligence: remembering what it learns and using that knowledge to guide future responses.

In Chapter 4, we'll move on to Thain v0.3, where it gains semantic memory: the ability to recall not just exact complaints but related ones using vector search and embeddings. With Azure AI Search, Thain's understanding will evolve from memory to true insight, the point at which its intelligence begins to scale.

Architectural Outcomes

By the end of this chapter, Thain's architecture supports the following:

- Durable, user-scoped memory integrated into the agent architecture, with Azure Cosmos DB serving as the persistence boundary for long-term recall

- A stable memory schema defined using Pydantic that separates agent reasoning output from storage concerns while ensuring validation and consistency

- A persistence layer that manages storage and retrieval, allowing the agent to evolve independently of the database implementation

- A persistent context provider that surfaces long-term memory as ephemeral reasoning context within the Microsoft Agent Framework, without making memory a strict dependency

- Short-term session context and long-term memory composed within the agent execution flow and observable directly through the Dev UI

- TTL policies that govern memory relevance over time, preventing unbounded growth while keeping recent experience available for reasoning

## CHAPTER 4

Thain Connects the Dots Azure AI Search

Introduction

Before Thain can reason beyond a single user, it needs access to a broader knowledge base.

In Chapter 3, we taught Thain how to remember. By storing prior complaints in Cosmos DB, it gained continuity within a single user conversation scope. It could recall what a user had said before and build on that context. That was an important milestone, but it also revealed a rigid boundary: Thain's memory stopped at the customer edge.

Real-world support systems do not work that way. Issues repeat across users, patterns surface in different forms, and problems evolve. Without a way to recognize those similarities, Thain is forced to treat each new complaint as if it were the first of its kind.

This chapter addresses that limitation by introducing semantic retrieval. Instead of retrieving everything and asking the model to reason across it all, semantic retrieval searches by meaning, retrieves only what matters, and gives the LLM just enough context to think clearly.

We begin by examining the limits of persistent, user-scoped memory and showing why it cannot surface insights across users. From there, we wire Thain into Azure AI Search and Azure OpenAI embeddings, enabling it to retrieve past complaints based on semantic similarity rather than exact wording. We introduce a semantic context provider that injects relevant historical complaints into the agent's reasoning context, grounding its responses in prior evidence.

Before giving Thain more knowledge to reason over, however, we first improve how it presents its answers. We upgrade its output from raw JSON to structured triage summaries, making insights easier to read, compare, and trust.

H. Narayn, *Architecting Intelligent Agents in Azure*, https://doi.org/10.1007/979-8-8688-2433-3_4

By the end of this chapter, Thain no longer relies solely on user-scoped memory. It now includes a semantic retrieval layer that can connect the dots across its knowledge base, surface relevant insights from past cases, and use those connections to reason more effectively about new problems.

Structuring Thain's Responses

In Chapter 3, Thain returned a plain JSON object. In this chapter, we replace those instructions with a structured Markdown template that produces a triage summary card. Earlier, Thain responded with a plain JSON structure:

For example,

```
{"category": "Hardware Issues", "summary": "Sensor calibration failure..."}
```

It was minimal, but it did not read like something we would hand off to a support team.

Now let us transition to a structured triage summary card, a more readable format that simulates what a real assistant might report back to a team. It includes

- A generated complaint ID

- Category (issue type)

- A timestamped summary line

- A reference to past complaints (Insight)

- A suggested next step (Suggest)

To enable this new format, we updated the base instructions passed to the agent. Locate the BASE_INSTRUCTIONS part and make this change in main.py. Refer to Listing 4-1.

Listing 4-1. main.py updates for base instructions

```
BASE_INSTRUCTIONS = (
    "You are Thain, an enterprise customer support triage assistant. "
    "Always call the `classify_issue` tool to validate the category you "
    "return. "
    "If the tool's confidence is low, silently choose the best category
```

```
yourself; do not mention the confidence or the fallback step. "
    "When you are given a list of recent complaints, explicitly consider
    how the new problem relates to them "
    "and mention any meaningful connections or contrasts in the Insight
    section. "
    "Produce ONE triage summary card in Markdown using this template (do
    NOT emit JSON):\n"
    "**Triage Summary for Complaint ID #C-<YYYYMMDD><RAND4>**\n"
    "---\n"
    "**Issue Type**\n"
    "<Category Path>\n"
    "---\n"
    "**Summary**\n"
    "<One-sentence summary on the next line (no timestamps required).>\n"
    "---\n"
    "**Insight**\n"
    "<Reference prior complaints/context. If none apply, state 'No prior
    insight available.'>\n"
    "---\n"
    "**Suggest**\n"
    "<Concrete next action or investigation step>\n"
)
```

With the new format in place, Thain's responses are easier to read, more informative, and better suited for operational handoff. Each card clearly states the issue, how it connects to past cases, and what should happen next. It is a slight change in output but a significant improvement in how we observe and debug Thain's evolving reasoning.

To see it in action, run Thain in the Dev UI. Submit a new complaint, like `My WiFi keeps dropping`, and watch how the response now appears as a clear triage card. Figure 4-1 shows an example of the new layout.

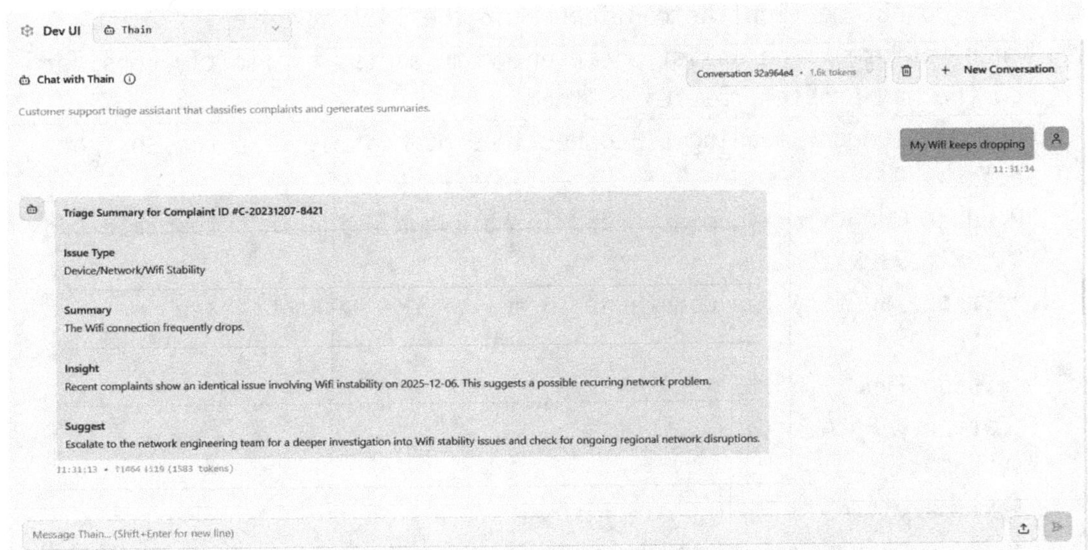

Figure 4-1. *Triage summary card generated by Thain*

Although Thain now presents its response as a Markdown triage summary card, this change affects only how results are displayed to humans.

The underlying data captured by the system remains unchanged. Thain still invokes the `classify_issue` tool during reasoning to determine the issue category and extract a structured summary. These values are recorded internally and used for persistence, indexing, and retrieval, precisely as in Chapter 3.

The Markdown output is generated after these structured values are available and serves purely as a presentation layer.

Now that Thain's output is more readable, we turn to the main challenge: giving Thain a broader memory through semantic retrieval.

The Limits of Persistent Memory

Before we add semantic retrieval, let's test what our current version of Thain can already do with its built-in persistent memory and LLM.

In this experiment, we'll use two different customers: `ray-harkins` and `john-smith`, representing separate support sessions. Each session is launched with a scoped customer ID using the environment variable THAIN_CUSTOMER_ID. This ensures Thain retrieves only that customer's prior complaints from Cosmos DB, keeping memory strictly scoped to the active session.

We'll walk through four runs to show how Thain behaves with scoped memory, paraphrased inputs, and completely reworded complaints.

Run 1: Ray Harkins Creates the First Complaint

Launch Thain using

```
$env:THAIN_CUSTOMER_ID="ray-harkins"; python main.py --devui --devui-open
```

Send the following message:

```
Since the last patch, the headset reboots whenever the motion
sensor spikes.
```

Thain classifies and stores this complaint under the customer ID ray-harkins. You can verify this by checking Cosmos DB.

See Figure 4-2 for the triage card output.

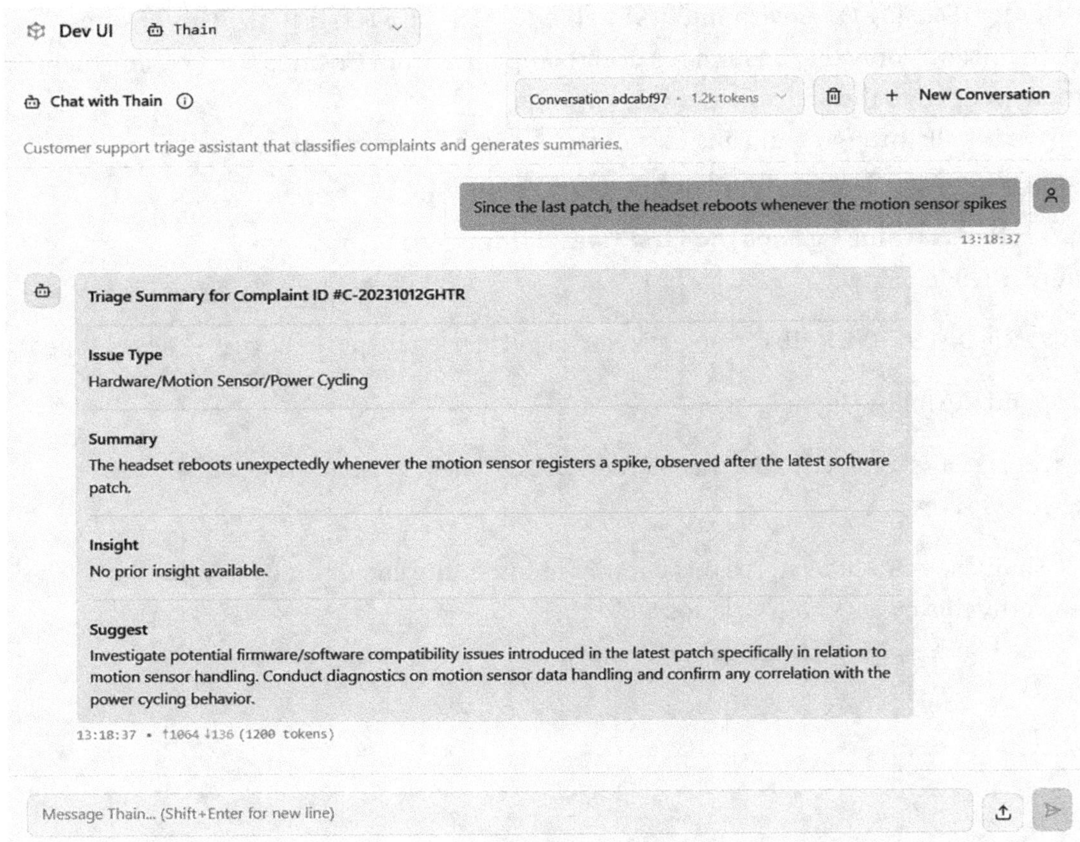

Figure 4-2. *Run 1: Thain's response to Ray Harkins initial complaint*

Run 2: Same User, Different Phrasing

Relaunch Dev UI with the same customer ID or open a new conversation, since the app is already running under the same customer ID:

```
$env:THAIN_CUSTOMER_ID="ray-harkins"; python main.py --devui --devui-open
```

Send

```
The headset keeps shutting off when I turn my head fast.
```

This time, persistent memory retrieves the prior complaint. Thain's LLM interprets the similarity between the issues and correctly surfaces the link in the Insight section.

Even though the phrasing changed, Thain remembered the past because the memory was there. See Figure 4-3 for the triage card output.

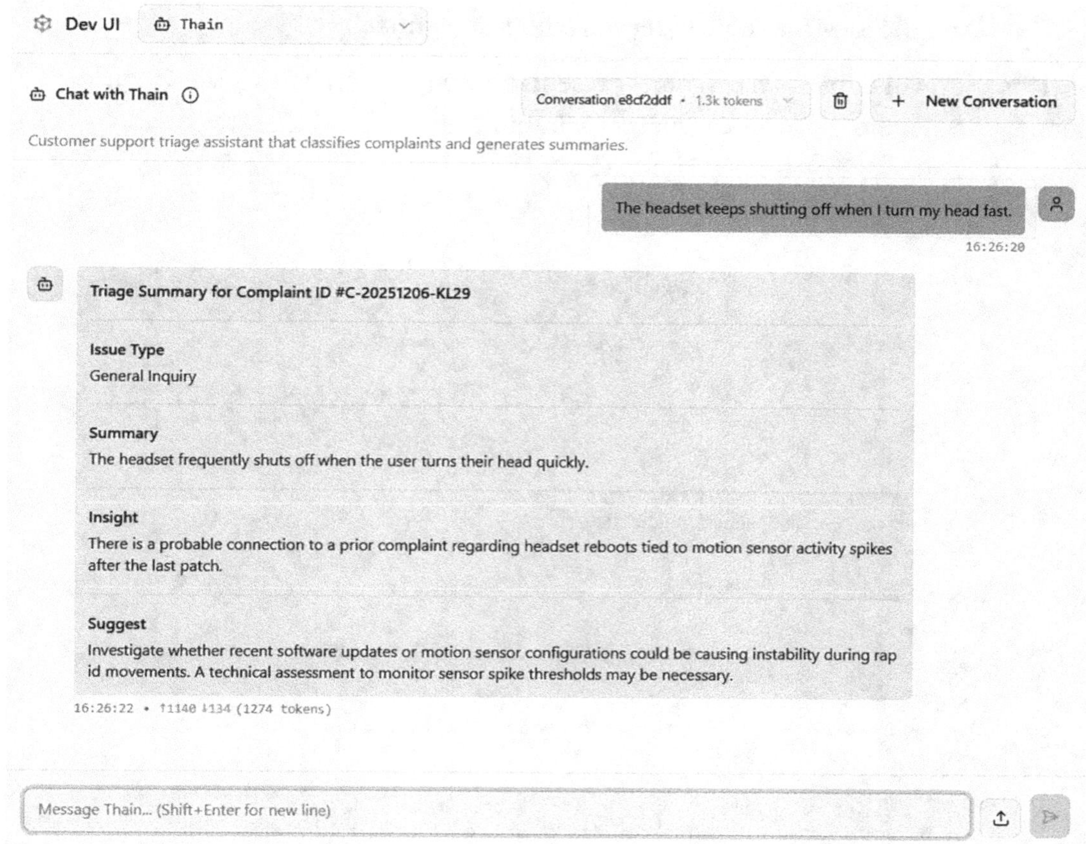

Figure 4-3. Run 2: Thain connects input to memory

Run 3: Same User, Entirely Abstract Phrasing

Again, relaunch Dev UI or open a new conversation (with the same customer ID, `ray-harkins.`

Send

```
The goggles go dark whenever I run.
```

Now the wording is entirely different, no mention of headset, reboot, or motion spikes.

Yet Thain still returns the correct insight:

- Because it retrieved the prior record from Cosmos.

- And the LLM was able to reason with it semantically.

This shows that the LLM can perform semantic work when it has access to prior memory. See Figure 4-4 for the triage card output.

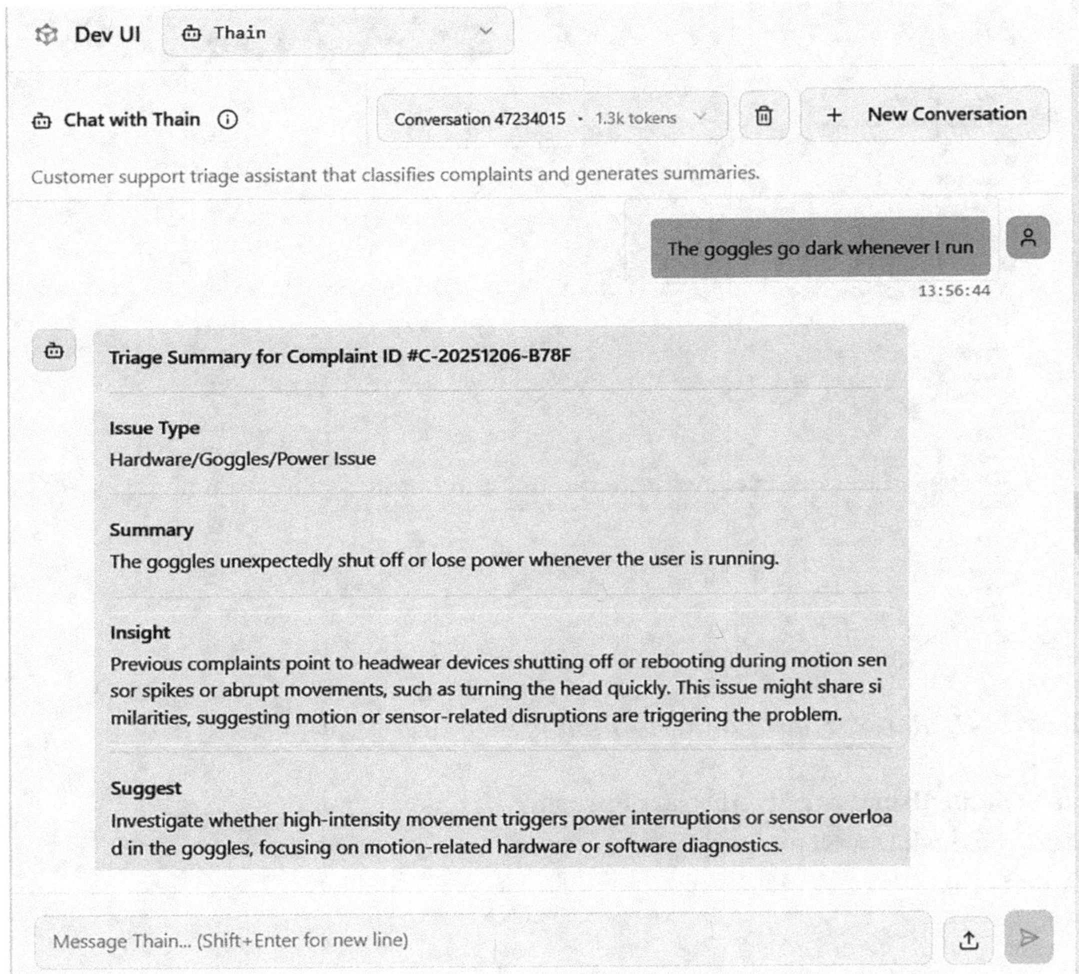

Figure 4-4. *Run 3: Thain surfaces insights from abstract phrasing*

Run 4: New User, Same Message

Now relaunch Dev UI by switching to a different customer:

```
$env:THAIN_CUSTOMER_ID="john-smith"; python main.py --devui
```

Send the exact message as Run 2:

```
The headset keeps shutting off when I turn my head fast.
```

This time, there's no prior record in memory. Thain has no previous complaints for john-smith, even though similar complaints exist for ray-harkins.

The result

- Insight is empty.

- The model responds in isolation.

See Figure 4-5 for the triage summary.

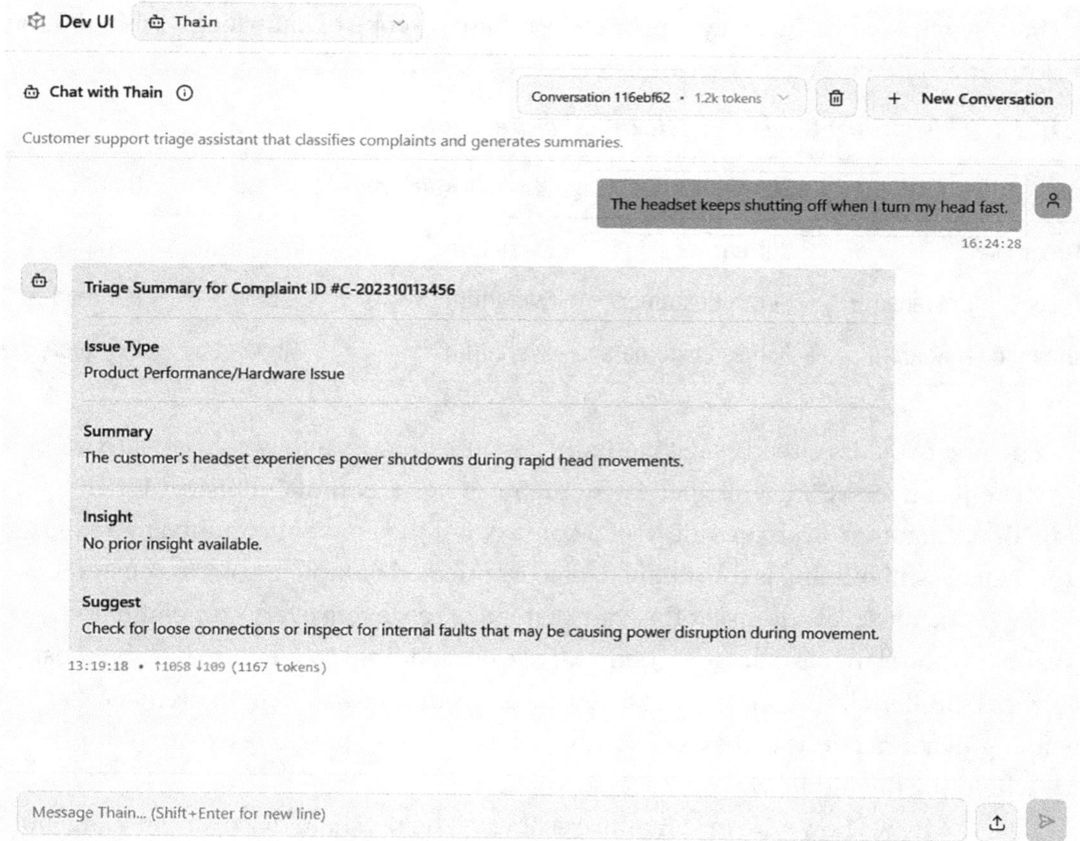

Figure 4-5. *Run 4: No insight retrieved for John Smith*

The Limits of User-Scoped Memory

In our scenario, persistent memory is tied to the individual user, so it can only surface what that person has said before. The model can still recognize patterns and interpret meaning, but it relies on that stored context to do so. Without something to refer to, even the smartest model is essentially starting from zero.

Technically, we could remove the user-level filtering and pull every complaint from Cosmos DB, but that would mean feeding the entire dataset to the LLM and asking it to reason across every record. This is inefficient and expensive and breaks the principle of customer-level isolation and privacy.

Before we add semantic retrieval, it helps to understand the memory layers emerging in Thain's architecture. Each layer provides a different scope of knowledge, with different performance and cost characteristics. Refer to Table 4-1.

Table 4-1. *Memory Layers in Thain's Architecture*

Tier	Scope	When It Retrieves	Speed	Cost
In-memory	Current session	Every turn	Immediate	None
Persistent (Cosmos DB)	Single customer	Every turn	Fast	Per read
Semantic (AI Search)	Across customers	Every turn	Moderate	Per query

The first two tiers already exist in Thain. Session memory allows the agent to track the current conversation, while persistent memory stores complaint history for an individual customer. Both provide useful context, but they remain confined to a single user. What is still missing is the ability to discover related complaints across customers.

Semantic retrieval addresses this gap. Instead of retrieving every complaint and asking the model to reason across them, we use embeddings to identify only the most relevant complaints and retrieve those few results. This allows Thain to discover meaningful connections across its knowledge base without breaking isolation or overwhelming the model with unnecessary data.

That is why we now wire in semantic retrieval; it helps Thain discover meaning, not just remember text.

Azure AI Search and Embedding Model

Before Thain can perform semantic retrieval, it needs two foundational pieces:

1. A vector-capable search engine to store and query embeddings

2. An embedding model to convert complaint text into vector form

Azure AI Search provides the first, and Azure OpenAI provides the second. Together, they create the semantic retrieval pipeline that Thain v0.3 relies on.

In earlier versions, Thain retrieved only a customer's own complaints from Cosmos DB. But semantic retrieval requires something broader: the ability to embed every complaint across all customers and quickly retrieve the most relevant matches regardless of who reported them. Azure AI Search is the engine that makes this possible.

Provisioning Azure AI Search

Navigate to Azure Portal → Create a Resource, and search and create Azure AI Search. Choose the same subscription, Resource group:

- **Resource name**: `ai-search-thain`.

- **Region**: Same region as Azure OpenAI and Cosmos DB (East US2).

- **Pricing tier**: Click `Change Pricing Tier` and change to Basic (sufficient for development, supports vector search).

- After selecting the tier, click Review + Create. Azure displays a summary of the configuration and the estimated cost before you confirm resource creation.

Refer to Figure 4-6.

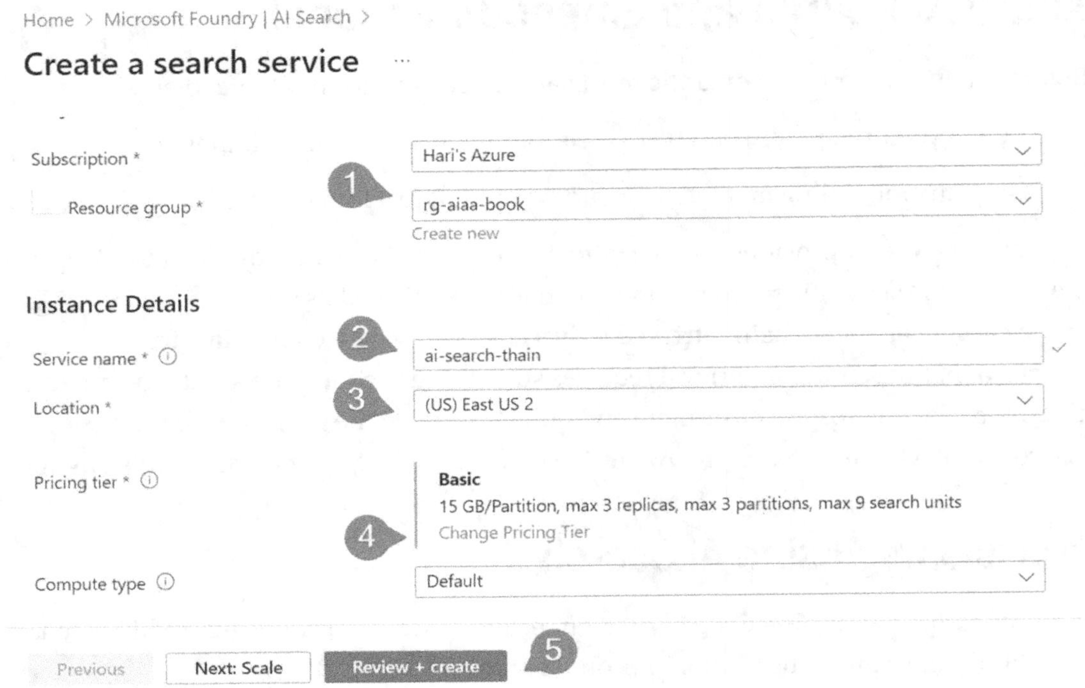

Figure 4-6. *Create Azure AI Search*

Once the resource is deployed, open the Azure AI Search service and copy the endpoint URL from the Overview page. Refer to Figure 4-7.

Then navigate to Settings → Keys and copy one of the admin API keys.

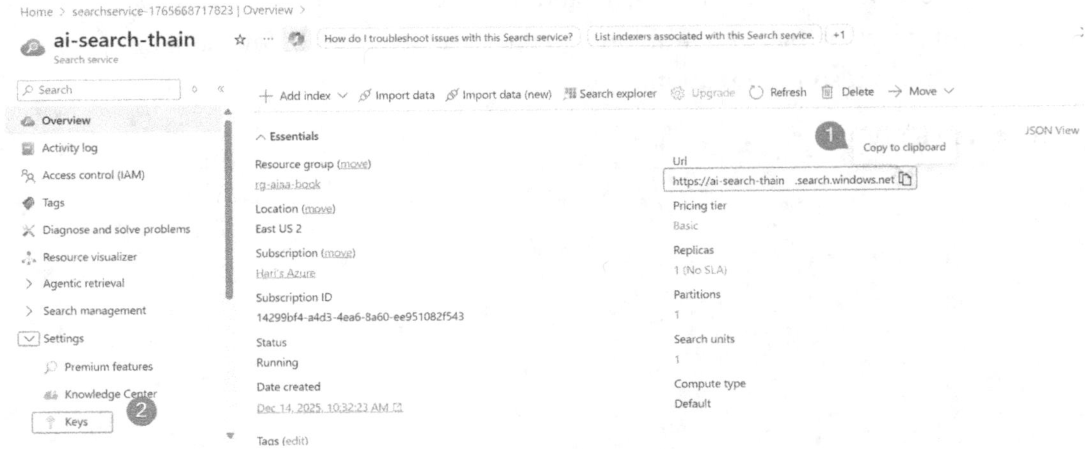

Figure 4-7. *Azure AI Search endpoint and key*

Later in this section, we'll add these values to the .env file. Thain uses the search endpoint and key when creating the index and executing vector-based queries.

Deploying the Embedding Model

Semantic recall requires that each complaint be converted into an embedding vector. For this, we deploy a lightweight but high-quality embedding model.

Navigate to

Azure OpenAI → ProjectThain → Foundry → Models + endpoints

Deploy the base model text-embedding-3-small. The deployment steps are identical to the model deployment process covered in Chapter 1.

This model provides strong semantic similarity performance while keeping token costs low, making it a good fit for Thain v0.3.

After deployment, note the Embedding endpoint and key as marked in Figure 4-8. We'll add these values to the .env file shortly.

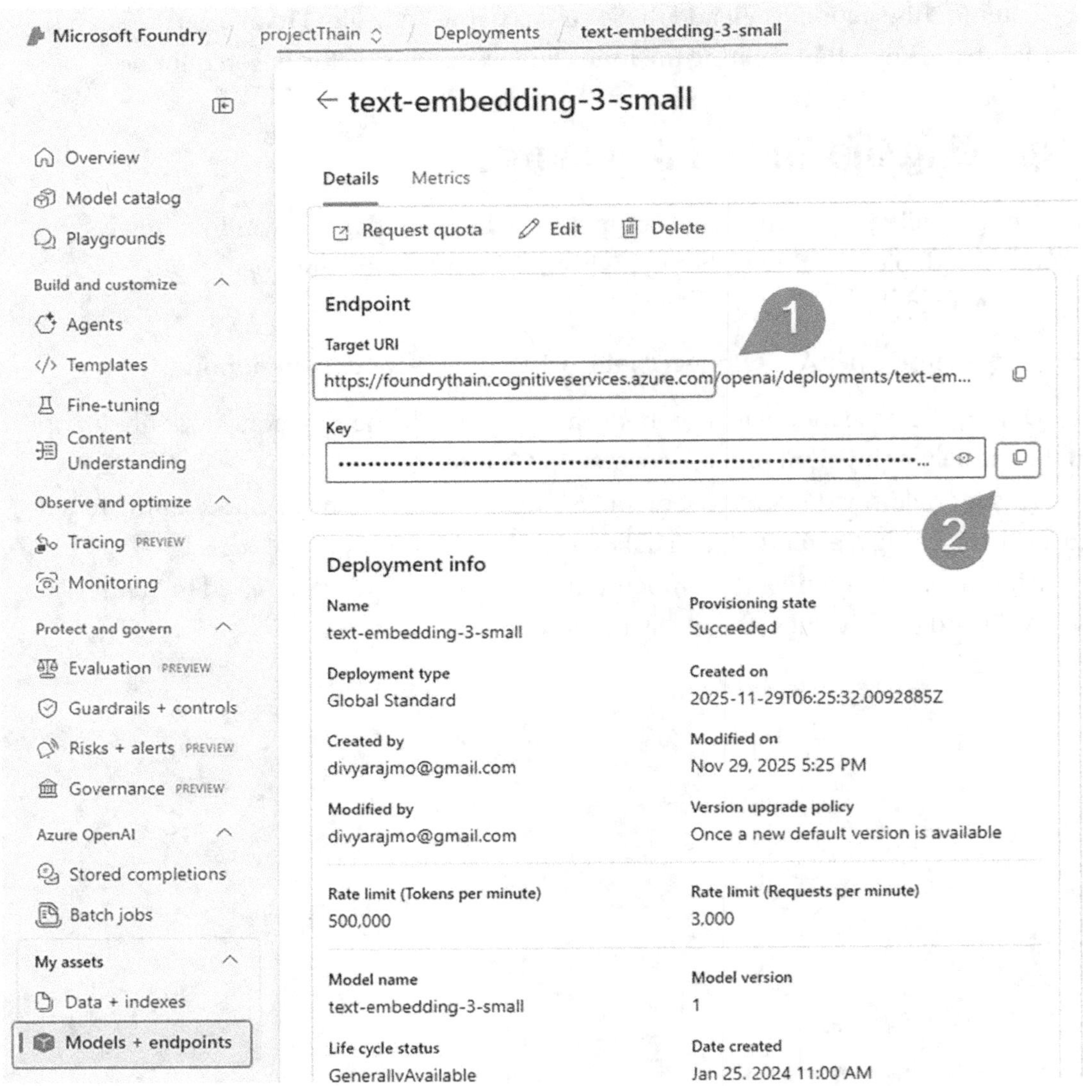

Figure 4-8. Embedding model endpoint and key

Configuring Semantic Retrieval in .env

With both Azure services now available, Thain must be configured to use them.

Add the following entries in your project's `.env` file:

```
# AI Search for Semantic recall

AZURE_SEARCH_ENDPOINT=https://<your-search-service>.search.windows.net
AZURE_SEARCH_INDEX_NAME=thain-complaints
```

```
AZURE_SEARCH_API_KEY=<your-search-api-key>
AZURE_SEARCH_MODE=semantic
AZURE_SEARCH_TOP_K=3
```

Embedding model for semantic retrieval

```
AZURE_OPENAI_EMBEDDING_ENDPOINT=<your-embedding-api-endpoint>
AZURE_OPENAI_EMBEDDING_DEPLOYMENT=text-embedding-3-small
AZURE_OPENAI_EMBEDDING_API_KEY=<your-embedding-api-key>
AZURE_OPENAI_EMBEDDING_API_VERSION=2024-02-15-preview
```

Explanation on the variables

- `AZURE_SEARCH_MODE` allows us to toggle semantic retrieval on/off during experiments.

- `TOP_K=3` returns the top 3 closest matches. A value of 3 is a good starting point: wide enough to surface meaningfully similar complaints without overwhelming the LLM.

Note   At the time of writing, the embedding configuration in this chapter uses the Azure OpenAI API version 2024-02-15-preview, which supports the text-embedding-3-small model used throughout the examples.

Azure OpenAI API versions evolve over time. When following this chapter, always verify the latest recommended API version for embeddings in the Microsoft Foundry or Azure OpenAI documentation and update the .env configuration accordingly.

The complete project for this chapter is available in the Chapter 4 folder of the book's GitHub repository, `https://github.com/Apress/Architecting-Intelligent-Agents-in-Azure`. While all code listings are included in this chapter, the repository is the single source of truth for runnable, up-to-date code. The repository also includes a Microsoft Agent Framework 1.5.0 General Availability version of this chapter's code in the Code GA folder. The GA version updates the lifecycle interface used by the persistent and semantic context providers, and simplifies how provider chains are assembled, while preserving the chapter's two-layer memory architecture built on Cosmos DB and Azure AI Search. A detailed migration note is also available in the repository.

This section completes the infrastructure prerequisites. Thain v0.3 dynamically creates its search index on startup and stores embeddings as users submit complaints. But none of this is possible until both Azure AI Search and the embedding model exist.

Before we enable Thain to use these resources, let's install the new dependencies.

Note   Azure AI Search is a paid resource, and even the Basic tier incurs cost while the service is running. If you are following this chapter over multiple days or are not actively testing semantic retrieval, it's a good practice to delete the Azure AI Search resource when you're done and recreate it later when needed.

After recreation, update the corresponding endpoint and API key values in your .env file accordingly.

Azure OpenAI deployments, such as the embedding model, are billed based on usage rather than uptime. It is fine to keep the embedding model deployed, as you are charged only when embeddings are generated.

Installing Required Dependencies

Semantic retrieval introduces a few additional Azure SDK dependencies. Add the following packages to `requirements.txt`:

```
openai==1.0.0
azure-search-documents==11.6.0
```

Note   The book repository includes a `constraints.txt` file under Chapter 4 -> `thain` project folder, that pins the Microsoft Agent Framework packages to the exact versions used in this book. Use it during installation to avoid version conflicts. The GA code path with its own pinned dependency files.

After updating `requirements.txt` and adding `constraints.txt`, update dependencies by running the below command:

```
pip install -r requirements.txt -c constraints.txt
```

Everything else in this file remains unchanged from Chapter 3.

Configuring Semantic Retrieval

Persistent memory (introduced in Chapter 3) required only Cosmos DB configuration. Semantic retrieval expands this layer by adding two new Azure components:

- Azure AI Search, which stores and retrieves complaint vectors

- Azure OpenAI embeddings, which generate the vectors used for similarity search

Everything else in `settings.py` remains unchanged from Chapter 3. Let's do this in five steps.

1. Adding the Semantic Retrieval Dataclass

To support these new services, we introduce an additional configuration class in `settings.py`. Add the following `dataclass` below the existing Persistent Memory Configuration definition. Refer to Listing 4-2.

Listing 4-2. AzureAISearchConfig (dataclass definition)

```
@dataclass(frozen=True)
class AzureAISearchConfig:
    """Configuration for Azure AI Search semantic retrieval."""

    endpoint: str
    index_name: str
    api_key: str | None
    embedding_endpoint: str
    embedding_deployment: str
    embedding_api_key: str | None
    embedding_api_version: str = "2024-02-15-preview"
    mode: str = "semantic"
    default_top_k: int = 3
    customer_id: str = "thain-demo"
```

What This Class Captures (field-accurate)

`endpoint`: Azure AI Search endpoint

`index_name`: where vector embeddings are stored

`api_key`: required for search (AAD not wired in this version)

`embedding_endpoint`: Azure OpenAI endpoint used for embeddings

`embedding_deployment`: e.g., `text-embedding-3-small`

`embedding_api_key`: optional; we fall back to AAD if missing

`embedding_api_version`: defaults to `2024-02-15-preview`

If the environment variable `AZURE_OPENAI_EMBEDDING_API_VERSION` is not provided

`mode`: defaults to `semantic` if `AZURE_SEARCH_MODE` is missing from `.env`

`default_top_k`: floors at 1

`customer_id`: consistent indexing/tagging

We do include a `customer_id` field in each indexed document, but Thain never surfaces this value in its responses. The customer ID is used only for internal grouping, logging, and test isolation.

In our scenario, `customer_id` is simply a label written into the search index to identify which session a record came from. How sensitive that value is depends entirely on what we choose to store there.

In Thain v0.3, semantic retrieval does not actively filter on `customer_id`. This is intentional. Semantic recall is designed to operate across scoped boundaries so that meaningfully similar issues can be discovered regardless of who originally reported them. The `customer_id` remains in the index only to support auditing, debugging, and basic traceability, reflecting patterns commonly required in real enterprise systems.

In practice, this field would not contain a real customer identity. Teams usually store a neutral internal identifier instead, keeping personal data out of the index while still retaining enough visibility to manage and audit the system.

2. Environment Variable Rules

Before semantic retrieval can be enabled, Thain must be able to load its Azure AI Search and embedding settings from the environment variables. The logic for this lives in the `from_env()` class method.

Listing 4-3 shows the full `from_env()` implementation, which controls when semantic retrieval is enabled and how environment variables are interpreted.

Listing 4-3. AzureAISearchConfig.from_env() (loading from environment variables)

```
@classmethod
```

```python
def from_env(cls) -> "AzureAISearchConfig | None":
    endpoint = os.getenv("AZURE_SEARCH_ENDPOINT", "").strip()
    index_name = os.getenv("AZURE_SEARCH_INDEX_NAME", "").strip()
    embedding_deployment = os.getenv("AZURE_OPENAI_EMBEDDING_DEPLOYMENT",
    "").strip()
    embedding_endpoint = os.getenv("AZURE_OPENAI_EMBEDDING_ENDPOINT",
    "").strip()

    if not endpoint or not index_name or not embedding_deployment or not
    embedding_endpoint:
        return None

    api_key = os.getenv("AZURE_SEARCH_API_KEY", "").strip() or None
    embedding_api_key = os.getenv("AZURE_OPENAI_EMBEDDING_API_KEY", "").
    strip() or None
    api_version = os.getenv("AZURE_OPENAI_EMBEDDING_API_VERSION", "").
    strip() or "2024-02-15-preview"
    mode = (os.getenv("AZURE_SEARCH_MODE", "semantic").strip() or
    "semantic").lower()
    default_top_k_raw = os.getenv("AZURE_SEARCH_TOP_K", "").strip()
    customer_id = os.getenv("THAIN_CUSTOMER_ID", "").strip() or
    "thain-demo"

    default_top_k = 3
    if default_top_k_raw:
        try:
            default_top_k = max(int(default_top_k_raw), 1)
        except ValueError:
            default_top_k = 3

    return cls(
        endpoint=endpoint,
        index_name=index_name,
        api_key=api_key,
        embedding_endpoint=embedding_endpoint,
        embedding_deployment=embedding_deployment,
        embedding_api_key=embedding_api_key,
```

```
        embedding_api_version=api_version,
        mode=mode,
        default_top_k=default_top_k,
        customer_id=customer_id,
    )
```

The class method AzureAISearchConfig.from_env() requires all four of these to be present before semantic retrieval is enabled:

```
AZURE_SEARCH_ENDPOINT
AZURE_SEARCH_INDEX_NAME
AZURE_OPENAI_EMBEDDING_DEPLOYMENT
AZURE_OPENAI_EMBEDDING_ENDPOINT
```

If any of these are missing, the method returns None, and Thain runs without semantic retrieval, falling back to persistent memory only.

3. Loader for Semantic Retrieval

Add the following loader to the end of settings.py. Refer to Listing 4-4.

Listing 4-4. load_search_config()

```
def load_search_config() -> AzureAISearchConfig | None:
    """Helper to load Azure AI Search configuration if available."""
    return AzureAISearchConfig.from_env()
```

If required values are present, semantic retrieval becomes active; if not, the entire semantic layer is skipped safely.

4. Mapping the .env Variables

The variables defined in the .env configuration above map directly into this configuration. These provide everything needed to index, embed, and retrieve complaints semantically.

5. Integration in main.py

At this point in the chapter, we have not yet built the semantic retrieval service or provider, but we can already define the hook in main.py where these components will be attached later.

Semantic retrieval becomes active only when load_search_config() returns a valid configuration. That function reads your Azure AI Search and embedding environment variables; if any required value is missing, it returns None and the semantic layer stays inactive.

These three module-level lines perform all startup setup: load the configuration, determine the active mode, and create the service object once for the lifetime of the process. Placing this code at module level means the service is constructed once when Python loads main.py, not once per request. The _search_mode guard prevents instantiation even when a config object exists, but AZURE_SEARCH_MODE is set to off, which lets you disable semantic retrieval without removing environment variables.

Add the new lines in main.py below the persistent memory service setup. Refer to Listing 4-5.

Listing 4-5. Loading semantic retrieval configuration

```
semantic_search_config: AzureAISearchConfig | None = load_search_config()
_search_mode = (semantic_search_config.mode if semantic_search_config else
"off").strip().lower()
semantic_service: SemanticRecallService | None = (
    SemanticRecallService(semantic_search_config) if semantic_search_config
    and _search_mode != "off" else None
)
```

With the service ready at startup, the final wiring step adds SemanticContextProvider to Thain's context provider chain inside run_thain_agent(). The Agent Framework evaluates providers in the order they appear in provider_chain, so the semantic provider is appended after the persistent memory provider. Thain sees user-scoped history first, and then cross-user semantic matches. The semantic_service and semantic_search_config guard ensures both are valid before the provider is registered; if either is None, the semantic layer is simply absent with no error.

Append the provider in run_thain_agent() beneath the persistent memory provider, as listed in Listing 4-6.

Listing 4-6. Adding the SemanticContextProvider

```
if semantic_service and semantic_search_config:
    provider_chain.append(
        SemanticContextProvider(
            service=semantic_service,
            customer_id=semantic_search_config.customer_id,
            lookup_limit=semantic_search_config.default_top_k,
            mode=semantic_search_config.mode,
        )
    )
```

Semantic Retrieval Behavior

- If the .env is fully populated, semantic retrieval turns on.

- If required values are missing, semantic retrieval stays off, and nothing breaks.

We will implement both the service and the provider later in this chapter. For now, this wiring establishes where semantic retrieval will attach itself in the agent pipeline.

Building the Embedding Service

Before Thain can store or retrieve similar complaints, it needs a reliable way to generate embeddings. Every complaint is ultimately compared in vector space, so the first step in the semantic retrieval pipeline is converting raw text into numerical vectors. To keep this independent and reusable, we introduce a new EmbeddingService class under a new folder named services. This service wraps Azure OpenAI embeddings using the OpenAI Python SDK for generating embeddings.

Create a new folder and file:

```
services/embedding.py
```

Copy the code from Listing 4-7 into this file.

The following sections explain the implementation in detail.

Listing 4-7. services/embedding.py

```python
from __future__ import annotations

import logging
from typing import Sequence

try:
    from openai import AsyncAzureOpenAI
except ImportError:  # pragma: no cover - dependency missing
    AsyncAzureOpenAI = None  # type: ignore[assignment]

logger = logging.getLogger(__name__)

class EmbeddingService:
    """Thin wrapper around Azure OpenAI embeddings via the OpenAI SDK."""

    def __init__(
        self,
        *,
        endpoint: str,
        deployment: str,
        api_version: str,
        api_key: str | None = None,
    ) -> None:
        if AsyncAzureOpenAI is None:
            raise RuntimeError("The openai package is required for
            embeddings. Install openai>=1.0.")
        if not api_key:
            raise RuntimeError("An embedding API key is required when using
            the OpenAI SDK path.")

        self._deployment = deployment
        self._client = AsyncAzureOpenAI(
            api_key=api_key,
            azure_endpoint=endpoint,
            api_version=api_version,
        )
```

```python
async def embed(self, text: str) -> list[float]:
    """Generate an embedding vector for the provided text."""

    response = await self._client.embeddings.create(model=self._
    deployment, input=text)
    vector: Sequence[float] = response.data[0].embedding
    return list(vector)

async def close(self) -> None:
    close_method = getattr(self._client, "close", None)
    if callable(close_method):
        maybe_await = close_method()
        if hasattr(maybe_await, "__await__"):
            await maybe_await
```

Understanding the Embedding Service

Constructor and Client Setup

The constructor accepts the embedding endpoint, deployment name, API version, and an API key. These values are passed directly into the OpenAI SDK's `AsyncAzureOpenAI` client, configured for Azure-hosted models.

Generating an Embedding

The core of the service is the `embed()` method:

```python
response = await self._client.embeddings.create(model=self._deployment,
input=text)
vector = response.data[0].embedding
```

This method

1. Sends the input text to the deployed embedding model

2. Retrieves the embedding vector

3. Returns it as a plain Python list

These vectors are what Azure AI Search uses later to perform similarity queries.

At this point in the chapter, the service is not yet used directly; subsequent sections will integrate it into the semantic indexing and retrieval pipeline.

Cleaning Up

The embedding client may maintain open network resources. The `close()` method safely releases them if supported by the underlying SDK.

Concurrency and Async Execution

All semantic retrieval components in this chapter use asynchronous Azure SDKs and the async Azure OpenAI client. Embedding generation, search indexing, and similarity queries are all network-bound operations. By executing these calls asynchronously, the agent does not have to pause its reasoning while it waits for Azure services to respond.

Using async clients also allows Thain to handle multiple complaints concurrently and fit naturally into modern Azure workloads, such as async web APIs, background processors, and event-driven pipelines.

Where This Fits in Thain

Embedding service is the foundation of semantic retrieval. Its responsibility is intentionally narrow: accept text and return the embedding vector produced by Azure OpenAI. Later components – index creation, document upsert, and similarity search – will build on top of this service, but its role remains focused and self-contained.

Upcoming sections will show how Azure AI Search stores these vectors and how they are used to retrieve similar complaints. For now, this standalone service gives Thain a clean, reliable way to generate embeddings whenever they are needed.

Creating the Semantic Search Client

With the embedding service in place, the next step in the semantic retrieval pipeline is to store embeddings so that Thain can efficiently retrieve similar complaints. Azure AI Search provides a vector-capable index that supports querying by "meaning" rather than exact text. To interact with this index, we introduce a new module called `AzureSemanticSearchClient`.

This client encapsulates all Azure Search responsibilities:

- Creating the semantic index (if it does not already exist)

- Upserting complaint documents with their embeddings

- Running vector-based similarity searches

- Managing Azure Search authentication and indexing operations

By isolating these operations, Thain keeps its semantic retrieval logic clean while giving Azure Search its own dedicated abstraction layer.

Create a new file:

`memory/search_client.py`

Copy the contents from Listing 4-8 into this file.

The sections below explain the implementation in detail.

Listing 4-8. memory/search_client.py

```
from __future__ import annotations
import logging
from typing import Any
from azure.core.credentials import AzureKeyCredential
from azure.identity.aio import DefaultAzureCredential
from azure.search.documents.aio import SearchClient
from azure.search.documents.indexes.aio import SearchIndexClient
from azure.search.documents.indexes.models import (
    HnswAlgorithmConfiguration,
    SearchField,
    SearchFieldDataType,
    SearchIndex,
    SearchableField,
    SimpleField,
    VectorSearch,
    VectorSearchProfile,
)
```

```python
from azure.search.documents.models import VectorizedQuery

from config.settings import AzureAISearchConfig
from models.complaint import ComplaintRecordModel
logger = logging.getLogger(__name__)
class SemanticSearchError(RuntimeError):
    """Raised when the Azure AI Search layer is unavailable."""

class AzureSemanticSearchClient:
    """Manages Azure AI Search index creation and querying."""

    def __init__(self, config: AzureAISearchConfig) -> None:
        self._config = config
        self._index_name = config.index_name
        self._credential: AzureKeyCredential | DefaultAzureCredential
        if config.api_key:
            self._credential = AzureKeyCredential(config.api_key)
            self._aad_credential = None
        else:
            self._aad_credential = DefaultAzureCredential(exclude_
            interactive_browser_credential=False)
            self._credential = self._aad_credential
        self._index_client = SearchIndexClient(endpoint=config.endpoint,
        credential=self._credential)
        self._search_client: SearchClient | None = None
        self._vector_dimensions: int | None = None

    async def close(self) -> None:
        if self._search_client:
            await self._search_client.close()
        await self._index_client.close()
        if isinstance(self._credential, DefaultAzureCredential):
            await self._credential.close()

    async def ensure_index(self, vector_dimensions: int) -> None:
        if self._search_client:
            return
```

```python
    try:
        await self._index_client.get_index(self._index_name)
        self._vector_dimensions = vector_dimensions
        logger.debug("Using existing Azure AI Search index '%s'.",
        self._index_name)
    except Exception:
        logger.info("Creating Azure AI Search index '%s'.", self._
        index_name)
        await self._create_index(vector_dimensions)

    self._search_client = SearchClient(
        endpoint=self._config.endpoint,
        index_name=self._index_name,
        credential=self._credential,
    )

async def _create_index(self, vector_dimensions: int) -> None:
    fields = [
        SimpleField(name="id", type=SearchFieldDataType.String,
        key=True),
        SimpleField(name="customerId", type=SearchFieldDataType.String,
        filterable=True, facetable=True),
        SimpleField(name="issueCategory", type=SearchFieldDataType.
        String, filterable=True, facetable=True),
        SearchableField(name="summary"),
        SearchableField(name="rawMessage"),
        SimpleField(name="createdAt", type=SearchFieldDataType.
        DateTimeOffset, filterable=True, sortable=True),
        SearchField(
            name="vector",
            type=SearchFieldDataType.Collection(SearchFieldDataType.
            Single),
            vector_search_dimensions=vector_dimensions,
            vector_search_profile_name="thain-vector-profile",
        ),
    ]
```

```python
        vector_search = VectorSearch(
            algorithms=[
                HnswAlgorithmConfiguration(name="thain-hnsw"),
            ],
            profiles=[
                VectorSearchProfile(name="thain-vector-profile", algorithm_
                configuration_name="thain-hnsw"),
            ],
        )

        index = SearchIndex(name=self._index_name, fields=fields, vector_
        search=vector_search)
        await self._index_client.create_index(index)
        self._vector_dimensions = vector_dimensions

    async def upsert_document(self, record: ComplaintRecordModel,
    embedding: list[float]) -> None:
        if not self._search_client or not self._vector_dimensions:
            await self.ensure_index(len(embedding))
        if not self._search_client:
            raise SemanticSearchError("Search client unavailable.")

        document = {
            "id": record.id,
            "customerId": record.customer_id,
            "issueCategory": record.issue_category,
            "summary": record.summary,
            "rawMessage": record.raw_message,
            "createdAt": record.created_at,
            "vector": embedding,
        }

        try:
            await self._search_client.upload_documents(documents=[
            document])
        except Exception as exc:
            logger.warning("Failed to upsert document into Azure AI Search:
            %s", exc)
```

```python
            raise SemanticSearchError("Unable to upsert search document.")
            from exc

    async def search_similar(
        self,
        *,
        customer_id: str,
        embedding: list[float],
        category: str | None = None,
        top_k: int = 3,
    ) -> list[dict[str, Any]]:
        if not self._search_client or not self._vector_dimensions:
            await self.ensure_index(len(embedding))
        if not self._search_client:
            raise SemanticSearchError("Search client unavailable.")

        filter_expression = None
        if category:
            sanitized_category = category.replace("'", "''")
            filter_expression = f"issueCategory eq '{sanitized_category}'"

        vector_query = VectorizedQuery(
            vector=embedding,
            k_nearest_neighbors=top_k,
            fields="vector",
            kind="vector",
        )

        try:
            results_iter = await self._search_client.search(
                search_text="",
                filter=filter_expression,
                vector_queries=[vector_query],
                select=["id", "customerId", "issueCategory", "summary",
                "rawMessage", "createdAt"],
                top=top_k,
            )
```

```python
    results: list[dict[str, Any]] = []
    async for doc in results_iter:
        results.append(
            {
                "id": doc["id"],
                "customerId": doc.get("customerId", ""),
                "issueCategory": doc.get("issueCategory", ""),
                "summary": doc.get("summary", ""),
                "rawMessage": doc.get("rawMessage", ""),
                "createdAt": doc.get("createdAt"),
            }
        )
    return results
except Exception as exc:
    logger.warning("Failed to query Azure AI Search: %s", exc)
    raise SemanticSearchError("Unable to query search index.")
    from exc
```

Index Creation and Schema

Before storing any embeddings, the client must ensure that the Azure AI Search
index exists.

The ensure_index() method performs this initialization.

If an index already exists, it is reused. Otherwise, _create_index() constructs a new
one using the schema defined in the client.

Fields in the Index

The index includes

- id: Unique key

- customerId: Grouping/logging metadata; filterable

- issueCategory: Category metadata; filterable and facetable

- summary: A searchable summary of the complaint

- `rawMessage`: The full complaint text

- `createdAt`: Timestamp; filterable and sortable

- `vector`: The embedding vector (`Collection[Single]`)

Azure Search requires the vector field to specify

- The vector dimension count

- The vector type

- The name of the vector search profile to use

Vector Search Configuration

The index defines

- One HNSW algorithm configuration (`thain-hnsw`)

- One vector search profile (`thain-vector-profile`)

These settings allow Azure AI Search to perform fast approximate similarity search as the index grows.

Upserting Complaint Documents

Once the index exists, documents can be written into it.

The client exposes an `upsert_document()` method that accepts

- A `ComplaintRecordModel`

- The embedding generated by the `EmbeddingService`

The upsert operation writes a document containing the same fields defined in the index schema, including the embedding vector. Upserting is idempotent: if a document with the same ID already exists, it is overwritten. This makes the operation safe to call during reindexing or repeated ingestion.

Any errors from Azure Search are wrapped in a `SemanticSearchError` so that higher layers can handle failures consistently.

Vector-Based Retrieval

To retrieve semantically similar complaints, Thain uses the `search_similar()` method.
This method

- Accepts an embedding representing the user's query

- Optionally applies a category filter (`issueCategory`)

- Runs a vector search through Azure AI Search

- Returns the `top-K` most similar documents

Azure Search compares vectors and returns the closest matches in meaning,
allowing Thain to find related complaints even when the wording differs completely.

The search results return the stored schema fields. Higher layers of the system will
later interpret these results and pass them to the agent as semantic context. No sensitive
information is surfaced to the user.

Where This Fits in Thain

The search client is the storage engine for vector-based recall. Its responsibilities are
deliberately low level:

- Define the index schema.

- Manage index creation.

- Store complaint documents with embeddings.

- Retrieve semantically similar documents on demand.

This client is focused purely on indexing and searching. It does not know how
embeddings are produced or how the results will be interpreted; those responsibilities
belong to the components built in the following sections. For now, this client gives Thain
a clean, reliable foundation for vector indexing and semantic search.

Building the Semantic Retrieval Service

With both the embedding generator and the search client in place, we now combine
them into a single semantic retrieval workflow. The `SemanticRecallService` sits
between these two components and provides a clean orchestration layer: it embeds text,

indexes complaints, and performs on-demand similarity searches. This is the point at which semantic retrieval becomes a usable capability within Thain.

Create a new file:

```
memory/semantic_service.py
```

Copy the code from Listing 4-9 into this file. The explanation below will walk through how this service works and why it exists.

Listing 4-9. memory/semantic_service.py

```python
from __future__ import annotations
import logging
from typing import Any, List

from config.settings import AzureAISearchConfig
from models.complaint import ComplaintRecordModel
from services.embedding import EmbeddingService
from .search_client import AzureSemanticSearchClient, SemanticSearchError
logger = logging.getLogger(__name__)
class SemanticRecallService:
    """Coordinates embedding generation and Azure AI Search queries."""

    def __init__(self, config: AzureAISearchConfig) -> None:
        self._config = config
        self._search_client = AzureSemanticSearchClient(config)
        self._embedding_service = EmbeddingService(
            endpoint=config.embedding_endpoint,
            deployment=config.embedding_deployment,
            api_version=config.embedding_api_version,
            api_key=config.embedding_api_key,
        )
        self._default_top_k = config.default_top_k

    async def close(self) -> None:
        await self._embedding_service.close()
        await self._search_client.close()

    async def index_record(self, record: ComplaintRecordModel) -> None:
```

```python
    """Store the complaint embedding inside Azure AI Search."""

    try:
        embedding = await self._embedding_service.embed(record.raw_
        message)
        await self._search_client.upsert_document(record, embedding)
    except SemanticSearchError:
        raise
    except Exception as exc:
        logger.warning("Failed to index complaint for semantic
        retrieval: %s", exc, exc_info=True)
        raise SemanticSearchError("Semantic indexing failed.") from exc

async def find_similar(
    self,
    *,
    customer_id: str,
    text: str,
    category: str | None = None,
    top_k: int | None = None,
) -> list[dict[str, Any]]:
    try:
        embedding = await self._embedding_service.embed(text)
        return await self._search_client.search_similar(
            customer_id=customer_id,
            embedding=embedding,
            category=category,
            top_k=top_k or self._default_top_k,
        )
    except SemanticSearchError:
        raise
    except Exception as exc:
        logger.warning("Semantic search failed: %s", exc, exc_
        info=True)
        raise SemanticSearchError("Semantic search failed.") from exc
```

Purpose of the SemanticRecallService

Neither the embedding module nor the search client knows anything about complaints, users, or Thain's retrieval semantics.

They perform narrow, low-level jobs:

- The embedding service turns text into vectors.

- The search client stores and retrieves documents from Azure AI Search.

The semantic retrieval service ties these pieces together. Its job is to

- Generate embeddings for new complaints

- Store those embeddings in Azure Search

- Generate embeddings for queries

- Retrieve the closest-matching complaints

It acts as the semantic memory engine that Thain uses throughout this chapter.

Constructor and Dependencies

The constructor receives an `AzureAISearchConfig` and initializes

- An internal `AzureSemanticSearchClient` (for indexing and querying)

- An internal `EmbeddingService` (for generating vectors)

- The default `top_k` value used for search

Both dependencies are created directly inside the service. This keeps the interface simple for callers: if a semantic search configuration exists, the service is ready to use.

Indexing Complaints

The `index_record()` method adds a new complaint to semantic memory.

The workflow is

1. Generate an embedding from the complaint's raw_message.

2. Pass both the complaint record and the embedding to the search client.

3. The search client writes the combined document into the Azure Search index.

Under the hood, this operation is idempotent – if the record already exists, it is overwritten.

Any Azure Search failure is wrapped and rethrown as a `SemanticSearchError` to maintain consistent error handling across the rest of the system.

This method is called whenever new complaint data enters Thain. By indexing records at ingestion time, we ensure that future similarity searches have rich data to work with.

Retrieving Similar Complaints

When Thain needs to look up related complaints, it calls `find_similar()`. This method

1. Embeds the input text using the same embedding model used during indexing

2. Sends that vector to Azure AI Search along with

   - The customer ID

   - The optional issue category filter

   - The desired number of results (`top_k`)

3. Returns the most semantically similar documents that match the filters

The search client performs the actual vector lookup and returns the final documents.

The service does not interpret or transform results; it simply retrieves and returns them to callers.

This keeps the service focused on coordinating embedding + search rather than performing business logic.

Error Handling and Service Cleanup

Both indexing and search operations wrap failures in `SemanticSearchError`, providing a consistent failure path for higher layers. The `close()` method ensures that both the embedding client and the search client release their resources (HTTP connections, credentials) when the service shuts down.

Where This Fits in Thain

The semantic retrieval service provides Thain with a usable, high-level capability: indexing and retrieving information by meaning. It does not determine how the results will be incorporated into the agent's reasoning; that responsibility lies with the context provider introduced in the next section.

For now, this service acts as the orchestration layer that joins embeddings and search into a single semantic memory workflow.

Injecting Semantic Context into the Agent

With the semantic retrieval service now able to index and retrieve similar complaints, the final step is to make those results available to the agent during its reasoning loop. The Microsoft Agent Framework accomplishes this through context providers. Context providers are lightweight components that add extra instructions to the agent before it generates a response.

To enable semantic retrieval in Thain, we add a new provider called `SemanticContextProvider`.

Create a new file:

`memory/semantic_provider.py`

Copy the code from Listing 4-10 into this file.

The sections below walk through how this provider works.

Listing 4-10. memory/semantic_provider.py

```python
from __future__ import annotations
import logging
from datetime import datetime, timezone, timedelta
from typing import Any
from agent_framework import ChatMessage, Context, ContextProvider
from memory.semantic_service import SemanticRecallService,
SemanticSearchError
logger = logging.getLogger(__name__)
AEST_TZ = timezone(timedelta(hours=10))
class SemanticContextProvider(ContextProvider):
    """Context provider that surfaces semantically similar complaints from
    Azure AI Search."""

    def __init__(
        self,
        *,
        service: SemanticRecallService,
        customer_id: str,
        lookup_limit: int = 3,
        mode: str = "semantic",
    ) -> None:
        self._service = service
        self._customer_id = customer_id
        self._lookup_limit = lookup_limit
        self._mode = mode

    async def invoking(self, messages: Any, **kwargs: Any) -> Context:
    # type: ignore[override]
        if self._mode != "semantic":
            logger.info("SemanticContextProvider: semantic retrieval
            disabled (mode=%s).", self._mode)
            return Context()

        query_text = _extract_user_text(messages)
        if not query_text:
```

```python
        return Context()

    try:
        records = await self._service.find_similar(
            customer_id=self._customer_id,
            text=query_text,
            category=None,
            top_k=self._lookup_limit,
        )
    except SemanticSearchError:
        logger.debug("Semantic recall unavailable; continuing without
        semantic context.", exc_info=True)
        return Context()

    if not records:
        logger.info("SemanticContextProvider: no semantic matches for
        query '%s'.", query_text[:80])
        return Context()

    top = records[0]
    logger.info(
        "SemanticContextProvider: surfaced %d semantic match(es); top
        summary='%s'.",
        len(records),
        top.get('summary', '(no summary)'),
    )

    formatted = []
    for record in records:
        created_at = record.get("createdAt")
        if isinstance(created_at, datetime):
            timestamp = created_at.astimezone(AEST_TZ).
            strftime("%d/%m/%y %H:%M AEST")
        else:
            timestamp = str(created_at or "unknown time")
        formatted.append(
            f"- [{record.get('issueCategory','Unknown')}] at
```

```
{timestamp}] {record.get('summary','(no summary)')}"
            )

        instructions = "Consider related complaints found via semantic
        retrieval:\n" + "\n".join(formatted)
        return Context(instructions=instructions)
def _extract_user_text(messages: Any) -> str | None:
    if isinstance(messages, ChatMessage):
        role_value = getattr(messages.role, "value", None)
        if role_value == "user":
            return messages.text
        return None

    if isinstance(messages, str):
        return messages

    if isinstance(messages, (list, tuple)):
        for item in reversed(messages):
            text = _extract_user_text(item)
            if text:
                return text
    return None
```

Purpose of the Semantic Context Provider

This provider acts as the bridge between semantic search and the agent. Its job is

- Look at the user's latest message.

- Use the semantic retrieval service to find similar past complaints.

- Format those results into short, readable instructions.

- Attach them to the agent's context for the current turn.

In other words, it injects additional understanding before the LLM thinks.

This allows Thain to reference trends, similar issues, and related complaints without hard coding any rules.

Initialization and Configuration

The provider receives

- The `SemanticRecallService` instance

- The `customer_id` used for filtering/grouping

- A lookup limit (default: 3 results)

- A mode flag (semantic or off)

The `.env` file controls this mode flag.

If semantic retrieval is disabled, the provider returns no context.

Extracting the User Message

The provider's `invoking()` method is called by the framework before the agent reasons. The first step is to extract the actual user message from the incoming structure. The helper `_extract_user_text()` handles different shapes of messages:

- Single `ChatMessage`

- Raw strings

- Nested arrays of messages

If no user text is found, the provider contributes no additional context.

Performing the Semantic Lookup

If semantic retrieval is enabled and the user text was found, the provider calls

```
records = await self._service.find_similar(...)
```

This retrieves the most semantically similar complaints or an empty list if none are found.

If Azure Search is unavailable, misconfigured, or returns an error, the provider logs the issue and continues gracefully. Thain never breaks because semantic retrieval failed.

Formatting the Context Instructions

When matches are found, the provider formats them into a short list with

- Issue category

- Timestamp (converted to AEST)

- Summary text

These lines are wrapped inside a single instruction block. The provider then returns a `Context(instructions=...)` object, which the Agent Framework merges with all other context providers.

This keeps the formatting simple, readable, and easy for the LLM to incorporate into its triage summary.

Semantic-On/Semantic-Off Mode

If `AZURE_SEARCH_MODE` is not set to `semantic` in the .env file, the provider logs semantic retrieval as disabled and returns an empty context.

This allows us to run Thain locally without Azure Search while keeping all components intact.

Integration with main.py

This provider attaches to the semantic retrieval hook we defined earlier in `main.py` (see Listings 4-5 and 4-6). With this, Thain can now surface semantic matches during reasoning.

Where This Fits in Thain

This provider is the final piece that connects semantic retrieval to Thain's reasoning. It does not index data, perform searches, or interpret results; that work is delegated to the service layer. Its role is to surface the right context at the right moment.

Together with indexing, embedding, and search orchestration, the context provider completes Thain's semantic retrieval capability.

Validating Semantic Retrieval

Now that semantic retrieval is fully wired into Thain v0.3, let's test it end to end and see how it improves over persistent memory alone.

Rather than introducing a new scenario, we'll reuse the same experimental style from earlier in this chapter (refer to section "The Limits of Persistent Memory").

The difference is that, this time, semantic retrieval is enabled and backed by Azure AI Search.

To keep the results unambiguous, we'll use new customer IDs so that no prior persistent memory exists in Cosmos DB.

Prerequisites

Before running the tests, ensure that the following prerequisites are met (as outlined earlier in the Azure AI Search and Embedding Model section of this chapter):

- Azure AI Search is created and running.

- The embedding model (`text-embedding-3-small`) is deployed.

- Your `.env` file is updated with all required Azure AI Search and embedding variables.

- `AZURE_SEARCH_MODE` is set to `semantic`.

Test Setup

We'll use two new users for this test:

```
alen-starc
lucas-chen
```

This guarantees that persistent memory is empty for both users, and any insights surfaced must come from semantic retrieval.

Run 1: Alen Starc Creates the First Complaint

Launch Dev UI using

```
$env:THAIN_CUSTOMER_ID="alen-starc"; python main.py --devui --devui-open
```

Send the following message:

```
Since the last patch, the headset reboots whenever the motion
sensor spikes.
```

Review Thain's response in the Dev UI. No prior insight is shown.
What happens behind the scenes:

- The complaint is stored in Cosmos DB under `alen-starc`.

- An embedding is generated for the complaint.

- The complaint and its embedding are indexed into Azure AI Search
  (we'll inspect this later in this section).

- No semantic insight is shown yet, as this is the first related complaint.

Run 2: New User, Semantically Similar Complaint

Now relaunch Dev UI by switching to a different customer:

```
$env:THAIN_CUSTOMER_ID="lucas-chen"; python main.py --devui --devui-open
```

Send the following message:

```
The goggles go dark whenever I make fast movements.
```

Review Thain's response in the Dev UI. An insight is shown.
What happens behind the scenes:

- No prior complaints exist in Cosmos DB for `lucas-chen`, so persistent
  memory returns no results.

- An embedding is generated for the new complaint.

- Azure AI Search is queried using semantic similarity.

- A related complaint reported earlier by another user is discovered.

- Thain surfaces a semantic insight, even though the user is new and
  the wording is entirely different.

At this point, Thain is no longer relying on user-scoped memory. Instead, it connects the new complaint with an earlier one based purely on meaning.

Figure 4-9 shows the Dev UI output for this run, highlighting the populated Insight section.

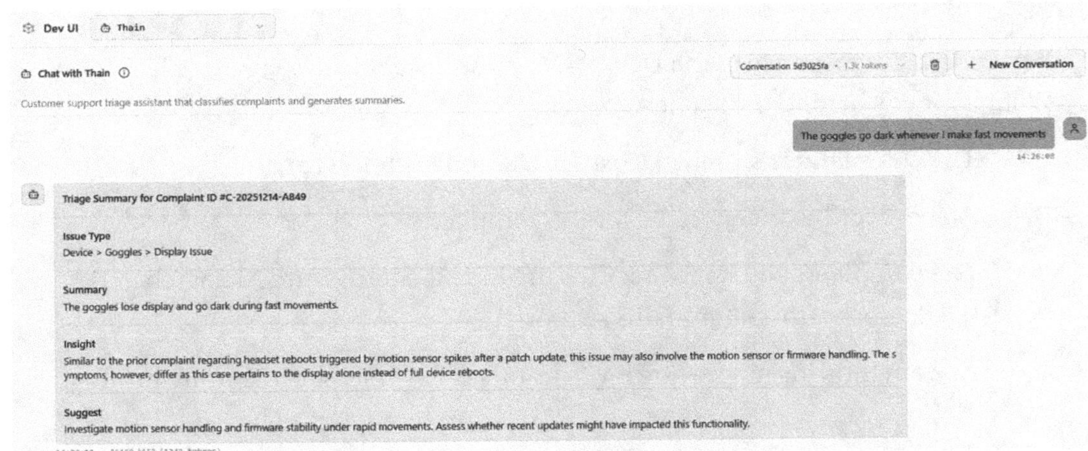

Figure 4-9. *Run 2: Semantic recall succeeds where persistent memory alone would not*

This run demonstrates the core value of semantic retrieval:

- Persistent memory remains empty for the new user.

- Semantic recall operates across users without exposing identities.

- Similar issues are discovered even when no keywords overlap.

Notice that Alen's complaint and Lucas's complaint sound very different, yet both involve a device failing during sudden movements. A human triage agent might not catch that relation from keywords alone, but semantic retrieval does.

Inspecting the Azure AI Search Index

After completing the semantic retrieval test, we can inspect how complaints are stored internally.

Navigate to the Azure portal and open your Azure AI Search resource (`ai-search-thain`). From the left-hand menu, select Indexes, and then click `thain-complaints`.

Figure 4-10 shows the index schema created by Thain.

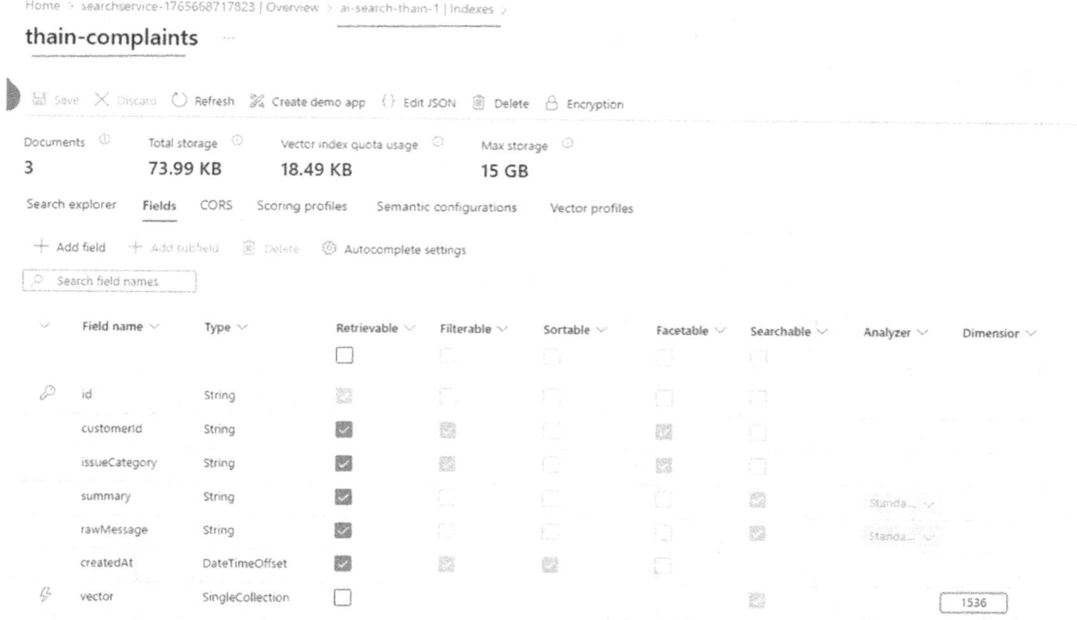

Figure 4-10. *Azure AI Search index storing complaint embeddings*

This view confirms that

- Each complaint is stored as a document.

- Text fields (`summary`, `rawMessage`) are indexed for diagnostics.

- Metadata fields (`customerId`, `issueCategory`, `createdAt`) support filtering and auditing.

- The vector field stores the embedding generated by Azure OpenAI.

The vector field shows a dimension of 1536, which matches the output size of the text-embedding-3-small model. Azure AI Search manages these vectors internally using its vector search engine; raw vector values are not displayed in the portal UI.

This index is what allows Thain to retrieve semantically similar complaints without relying on keyword matching or user-specific memory.

Embeddings and Vectors

When we say embedding, we're referring to the process of converting text into numbers. When we say vector, we're referring to the result of that process.

In other words

- Embedding is the act of encoding meaning.
- Vector is the numeric representation of that meaning.

An embedding model reads a piece of text and produces a long list of numbers that captures its meaning. In Thain's case, each complaint becomes a vector with 1536 numeric values.

You can think of this vector as a coordinate in a very high-dimensional space, where

- Complaints with similar meaning end up close together.
- Complaints describing different issues end up far apart.

Azure AI Search compares these vectors to find complaints that are close in meaning, even when the wording is entirely different.

Where Azure AI Search Stores the Vectors

The vectors are stored inside the Azure AI Search index itself, alongside the textual and metadata fields.

Internally, Azure AI Search

- Stores vectors in a highly optimized binary format
- Builds a specialized vector index for fast similarity lookup
- Manages all distance calculations and performance optimizations automatically

For this reason

- Raw vector values are not shown in the Azure Portal.
- We interact with vectors only through queries, not direct inspection.

This abstraction allows Thain to use semantic search without worrying about low-level vector math or storage mechanics.

Why This Matters for Thain

By storing embeddings as vectors inside Azure AI Search, Thain gains the ability to

- Compare complaints by meaning instead of keywords

- Retrieve relevant historical issues across users

- Scale semantic retrieval efficiently as data grows

At this point, Thain is no longer just remembering complaints; it is connecting them based on meaning.

Unit Tests Included in This Chapter

This chapter introduces a test suite that validates the new semantic-recall provider:

- `tests/test_semantic_provider.py` – verifies that semantic matches are converted into context instructions and that the provider fails gracefully when Azure Search is offline

The persistent memory test from Chapter 3 is also kept:

- `tests/test_persistent_memory.py` – continues to validate user-scoped memory behavior

Run both tests from the project root:

```
python -m unittest tests.test_semantic_provider
python -m unittest tests.test_persistent_memory
```

These tests confirm that Thain can

- Surface semantic matches correctly.

- Handle semantic-off mode or retrieval failures safely.

- Maintain persistent and semantic memory as independent, testable layers.

Feel free to expand these tests, for example, by mocking different semantic-recall responses, simulating empty results, or verifying that category filters work as expected.

Semantic Retrieval Thain's Processing Pipeline

Figure 4-11 summarizes how semantic retrieval fits into Thain's processing pipeline. Relevant complaints are retrieved before the agent reasons about the message, and newly generated summaries are indexed afterward so they can inform future interactions.

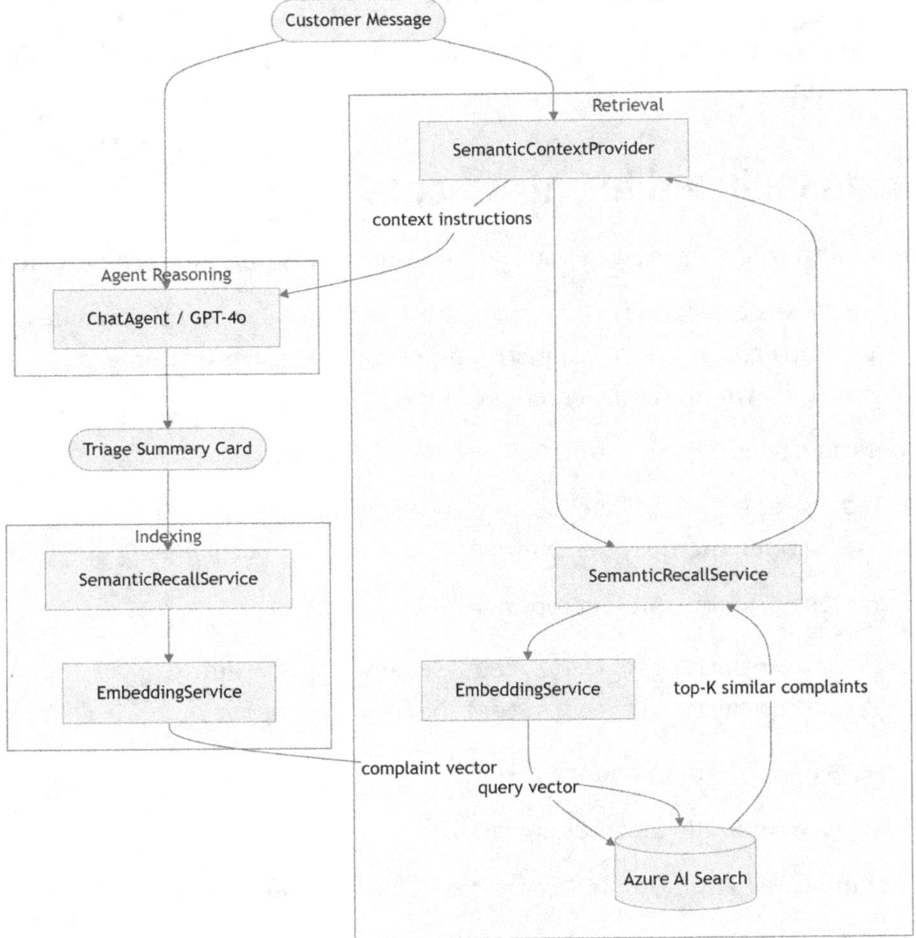

Figure 4-11. *Semantic retrieval in Thain*

Note   The current state of the project at the end of this chapter is available in the book's GitHub repository: `https://github.com/Apress/Architecting-Intelligent-Agents-in-Azure`. You can clone the repository and set it up locally with the following commands:

```
git clone https://github.com/Apress/Architecting-Intelligent-
Agents-in-Azure.git
```

```
cd Architecting-Intelligent-Agents-in-Azure
```

For the manuscript code, open the Chapter 4/thain folder. For the GA code, open Code GA/Chapter 4/thain. After cloning, create and activate a virtual environment, and then install the dependencies:

```
python -m venv .venv && .\.venv\Scripts\activate
```

```
pip install -r requirements.txt -c constraints.txt
```

Finally, create your own `.env` file with the required Azure AI Search and embedding settings before running the project. You can also browse the repository online to review the reference implementation.

Looking Ahead: Managed Retrieval Services

As this chapter was written, Microsoft Foundry is introducing higher-level agent capabilities, such as Foundry IQ, that aim to provide managed retrieval and grounding for agent applications.

These capabilities are expected to reduce the amount of custom code teams need to write when adding semantic retrieval. That said, the underlying ideas remain unchanged. Semantic retrieval is still about representing meaning with embeddings, comparing it using vector similarity, injecting only the most relevant context, and keeping memory concerns clearly separated from the agent's reasoning process.

In parallel, the Microsoft Agent Framework is evolving its memory layer to support pluggable connectors for external vector stores and retrieval providers. This follows the same pattern demonstrated in this chapter, where retrieval and storage are treated as distinct concerns and introduced into the agent through explicit context injection.

For that reason, this chapter builds semantic retrieval from the ground up. The goal is to help you understand what is happening beneath platform abstractions so that you can reason about behavior, cost, performance, and failure modes. As Azure's agent ecosystem continues to mature, future editions of this book will incorporate new capabilities while continuing to build on the same architectural principles introduced here.

Summary

In this chapter, we transformed Thain from a memory-aware assistant into a system capable of discovering meaning across its knowledge base through a semantic retrieval layer.

We began by refining how Thain presents its responses, introducing structured triage summary cards. We then explored the limits of persistent, user-scoped memory. Persistent memory supports conversational continuity, but it remains confined to a defined operational scope.

To handle this, we added semantic retrieval. At this point, Azure AI Search and Azure OpenAI embeddings are in place. By embedding complaints and storing them in a vector-capable index, Thain can now retrieve relevant historical issues based on semantic similarity rather than keyword matching, without breaking customer isolation or privacy boundaries.

Finally, we integrated semantic retrieval into Thain's reasoning loop through a semantic context provider. This allows related complaints to be surfaced dynamically during response generation, grounding the agent's reasoning in relevant historical evidence, even when the current user has no prior history.

Together, these changes move Thain beyond simply recalling past messages toward recognizing patterns across related complaints. This marks Thain's transition from a memory-bound assistant to a knowledge-aware agent capable of reasoning over historic patterns. In the next chapter, we build on this foundation by giving Thain explicit tools and decision-making control, allowing it to decide when and how to act on retrieved information.

Architectural Outcomes

By completing Chapter 4, you now know how to

- Recognize the architectural limits of scoped persistent memory in real-world systems.

- Use Azure OpenAI embedding models to encode textual meaning for semantic retrieval.

- Configure Azure AI Search as a vector-capable engine for semantic retrieval.

- Store embeddings alongside metadata to support efficient semantic search and filtering.

- Build a semantic retrieval service that coordinates embedding generation and search operations.

- Create a semantic context provider that injects relevant evidence into the agent's reasoning loop.

- Validate semantic retrieval through end-to-end testing, index inspection, and unit tests.

- Design semantic retrieval that operates across scoped boundaries while preserving isolation and preventing identity leakage.

## CHAPTER 5

Thain Builds Its Toolkit

Introduction

To date, Thain has learned to understand problems, retain memory across conversations, and connect related information through semantic retrieval. It can reason with context, identify patterns, and present structured insights in a consistent and transparent way.

However, real-world agent systems are rarely valuable if they only observe and explain. In enterprise environments, insight is usually just the first step. What matters next is action: the ability to invoke external systems, trigger downstream processes, retrieve supporting context, and do so in a manner that is deliberate, auditable, and safe.

In this chapter, we move to the next stage by shifting the focus from enhancing Thain's intelligence to enabling its practical use in real systems. Thain is extended with tools that allow it to interact with external services, suggest follow-up actions based on its reasoning, and pause for confirmation before executing changes that have an impact. Retrieval is no longer performed automatically in the background. Instead, the agent can determine when additional context is required and when it has enough information to proceed.

Autonomy in enterprise systems is most effective when applied thoughtfully and with restraint. As Thain's capabilities expand, we introduce simple approval steps, clear behavioral rules, and explicit, traceable outcomes to make agent actions transparent and easy to reason about. Human oversight remains essential where context and judgment are required.

© Hari Narayn 2026
H. Narayn, *Architecting Intelligent Agents in Azure*, https://doi.org/10.1007/979-8-8688-2433-3_5

Thain v0.4 at a Glance

By the end of this chapter, Thain reaches version 0.4. It evolves beyond an insight engine to become an agent capable of operating within defined boundaries, interacting with real systems through integrated tools, and behaving in ways that align with enterprise expectations around safety, transparency, and trust.

You will build

- **Agentic retrieval**: Complaint history search exposed as an explicit tool, making evidence gathering intentional and traceable rather than a background side effect

- **Core action tools**: Ticket creation and team notification (write tools) and document retrieval (read tool), controlled by feature flags per environment

- **A read/write tool split**: A tool registry that cleanly separates unrestricted read operations from governed write operations

- **An approval gate**: An approval service that intercepts write-tool execution and requires explicit human authorization before any external action takes effect

---

Note   The full code for this chapter is in the Chapter 5/thain folder of the book's companion repository at `https://github.com/Apress/Architecting-Intelligent-Agents-in-Azure`. The repository also includes a Microsoft Agent Framework 1.5.0 General Availability version of this chapter's code in the Code GA/Chapter 5/thain folder. The GA version renames the tool-registration decorator used across all four tool definitions introduced in this chapter, and carries forward the agent client, context-provider lifecycle, and provider-chaining updates from earlier chapters, while preserving the agentic retrieval, action tool, and approval-gate architecture. A detailed migration note is also available in the repository.

Extending the Complaint Record for Agentic Outcomes

Before introducing agent-driven retrieval and action tools, we prepare the data model to capture the outcomes of future actions. In Chapter 4, a complaint record represented what happened and how it was classified. In Chapter 5, the same record must also answer a new question:

```
What did we do about it?
```

As Thain begins to reason about escalation and next steps, it becomes important to record not only the incident itself but also the decisions made in response. To support this, we add a small set of outcome-related fields to the complaint model. These fields do not yet drive behavior. Instead, they provide a place to persist decisions, such as ticket creation or team notifications, so that they can be retrieved, inspected, and audited later.

File location

```
models/complaint.py
```

Code changes

Add the following fields to `ComplaintRecordModel` just above the `model_config` definition. See Listing 5-1.

Listing 5-1. complaint.py updates for outcome fields

```python
ticket_created: bool = Field(default=False, alias="ticketCreated")
notified_team: Optional[str] = Field(default=None, alias="notifiedTeam")
outcome: Optional[str] = None
```

Next, extend the factory method, so these values can be persisted when a complaint is created from an agent response. Replace the existing `from_agent_payload` method with the version shown in Listing 5-2.

Listing 5-2. complaint.py updates for persisting outcomes

```python
def from_agent_payload(
    cls,
    *,
    customer_id: str,
    category: str,
    summary: str,
    message: str,
    confidence: float = 1.0,
    ttl_seconds: Optional[int] = None,
    ticket_created: bool = False,
```

```
    notified_team: Optional[str] = None,
    outcome: Optional[str] = None,
) -> "ComplaintRecordModel":
    return cls(
        customerId=customer_id,
        issueCategory=category,
        summary=summary,
        rawMessage=message,
        confidence=confidence,
        ttl=ttl_seconds,
        ticketCreated=ticket_created,
        notifiedTeam=notified_team,
        outcome=outcome,
    )
```

At this stage of the chapter, these fields default to `no action taken`. Their presence ensures that when Thain later opens tickets or notifies teams, the outcomes of those actions can be stored alongside the original complaint, rather than being lost as transient agent behavior.

Preparing the Search Index for Agentic Retrieval

Extending the index schema is only part of the preparation required for agentic retrieval. Once the index can store outcome-related fields, the write and read paths must also be updated so those fields are consistently persisted and returned during search.

In addition, agent-driven retrieval often needs tighter control over when prior incidents occurred. For that reason, we also extend the search interface to support time-scoped queries, which becomes particularly useful when the agent explicitly asks for "recent" incidents.

All the following changes are made in the same file:

File location

```
memory/search_client.py
```

Extending the Index Schema

Locate the _create_index method, where the Azure AI Search index schema is defined. Inside this method, find the field array that defines the index structure.

In Chapter 4, this array already includes core fields such as createdAt, which is defined as follows:

```
SimpleField(name="createdAt", type=SearchFieldDataType.DateTimeOffset,
filterable=True, sortable=True),
```

Immediately below this existing createdAt field, add the following entries shown in Listing 5-3.

Listing 5-3. Extending the index schema

```
SimpleField(name="ticketCreated", type=SearchFieldDataType.Boolean,
filterable=True),
SimpleField(name="notifiedTeam", type=SearchFieldDataType.String,
filterable=True, facetable=True),
SearchableField(name="outcome"),
```

These additions allow the recall layer to track whether previous incidents resulted in specific actions, such as ticket creation or team notification.

Although these fields do not yet influence behavior, they prepare the index for agentic queries that consider past outcomes instead of only past descriptions. If you reused an Azure AI Search index from Chapter 4, recreate the index or use a new index name before running this chapter. Chapter 5 adds action-related fields such as ticketCreated, notifiedTeam, and outcome; an older index schema will not accept or return those fields.

Persisting Outcome Fields During Upsert

Locate the upsert_document method, which is responsible for writing complaint records into the Azure AI Search index. In Chapter 4, this method only persisted the core complaint fields and the embedding vector.

Replace the document payload to include the newly added outcome fields, as shown in Listing 5-4.

Listing 5-4. Updating the search document payload

```
document = {
        "id": record.id,
        "customerId": record.customer_id,
        "issueCategory": record.issue_category,
```

```
        "summary": record.summary,
        "rawMessage": record.raw_message,
        "createdAt": record.created_at,
        "ticketCreated": record.ticket_created,
        "notifiedTeam": record.notified_team,
        "outcome": record.outcome,
        "vector": embedding,
    }
```

This approach keeps the recall layer aligned with the persistent memory model. As Thain takes action later in the chapter, those outcomes are recorded once and are immediately available for future retrieval.

Supporting Time-Scoped Agentic Queries

Explicit retrieval requires more precise control than passive semantic retrieval. For instance, when searching for similar incidents, it may be appropriate to consider only recent complaints rather than the entire history.

To address this, update the search_similar method signature to include an optional created_after parameter.

Replace the method signature with the version shown in Listing 5-5.

Listing 5-5. Extending the search interface with a time filter

```
async def search_similar(
    self,
    *,
    customer_id: str,
    embedding: list[float],
    category: str | None = None,
    top_k: int = 3,
    created_after: Optional[datetime] = None,
) -> list[dict[str, Any]]:
```

Inside the method, replace the single-filter logic with a composable filter list. Replace the following code with the one in Listing 5-6. This is located at the top of the method, just before the VectorizedQuery is created.

```
filter_expression = None
        if category:
            sanitized_category = category.replace("'", "''")
            filter_expression = f"issueCategory eq '{sanitized_category}'"
```

Listing 5-6. Building a safe, composable filter expression

```
filters = []
        if category:
            sanitized_category = category.replace("'", "''")
            filters.append(f"issueCategory eq '{sanitized_category}'")
        if created_after:
            dt = created_after
            if created_after.tzinfo is None:
                dt = created_after.replace(tzinfo=timezone.utc)
            else:
                dt = created_after.astimezone(timezone.utc)
            filters.append(f"createdAt ge {dt.strftime('%Y-%m-
            %dT%H:%M:%SZ')}")
        filter_expression = " and ".join(filters) if filters else None
```

Normalizing all timestamps to UTC and building the filter centrally ensures that time-based logic remains within the search layer, rather than being distributed across agent tools or prompts.

Returning Outcome Fields in Search Results

Finally, update the search query to return the new fields to the caller. Locate the select list passed to the search call and replace it with the version shown in Listing 5-7.

Listing 5-7. Returning outcome fields from search

```
select=[
    "id",
    "customerId",
    "issueCategory",
    "summary",
    "rawMessage",
```

```
    "createdAt",
    "ticketCreated",
    "notifiedTeam",
    "outcome",
]
```

Then extend the result-mapping logic so these fields are included in each returned item. See Listing 5-8.

Listing 5-8. Mapping outcome fields into search results

```
results.append(
    {
        "id": doc["id"],
        "customerId": doc.get("customerId", ""),
        "issueCategory": doc.get("issueCategory", ""),
        "summary": doc.get("summary", ""),
        "rawMessage": doc.get("rawMessage", ""),
        "createdAt": doc.get("createdAt"),
        "ticketCreated": doc.get("ticketCreated", False),
        "notifiedTeam": doc.get("notifiedTeam"),
        "outcome": doc.get("outcome"),
    }
)
```

With these changes, agentic retrieval can provide similar complaints as well as evidence of how they were previously addressed.

Making Retrieval Agent Directed

These updates ensure that retrieval can function as an explicit agent decision:

- Search results now include action outcomes in addition to descriptions.

- Queries can be scoped by time, which is essential for operational reasoning.

- Retrieval remains auditable and explainable, rather than implicit.

With the storage and search layers established, the next step is to refine semantic retrieval to support targeted, agent-driven queries.

Refining Semantic Retrieval for Deliberate Use

Earlier, semantic retrieval functioned as a basic similarity lookup: the input text was embedded, the search index was queried, and the top matches were returned. As retrieval becomes an explicit agent decision, the requirements for the semantic retrieval layer change as well. Two additional considerations become important:

1. **Time scoping**: Agentic queries often require recent history instead of the entire archive.

2. **Outcome awareness**: The same retrieval call may be used in different contexts. In some cases, only incident summaries are required. In others, it becomes useful to include information about how similar incidents were handled, such as ticket creation or notifications.

To support these needs, we extend `SemanticRecallService.find_similar` to accept a time window parameter and an option to include or exclude outcome fields.

File location

```
memory/semantic_service.py
```

Add Imports for Time Scoping

At the top of the file, locate the imports. Immediately below the existing import logging line, add the following import, as shown in Listing 5-9.

Listing 5-9. Imports for time-scoped recall

```
from datetime import datetime, timedelta, timezone
```

This enables the service to compute a `created_after` timestamp when a query is limited to recent history.

Enhancing Semantic Retrieval with Time and Outcome Awareness

Locate the existing `find_similar` method in `SemanticRecallService`. Replace the entire method with the version shown in Listing 5-10.

Listing 5-10. Updating find_similar method

```python
async def find_similar(
        self,
        *,
        customer_id: str,
        text: str,
        category: str | None = None,
        top_k: int | None = None,
        time_window_days: int | None = None,
        include_outcomes: bool = False,
    ) -> list[dict[str, Any]]:
        try:
            embedding = await self._embedding_service.embed(text)
            created_after = None
            if time_window_days and time_window_days > 0:
                created_after = datetime.now(timezone.utc) - \
                timedelta(days=time_window_days)

            results = await self._search_client.search_similar(
                customer_id=customer_id,
                embedding=embedding,
                category=category,
                top_k=top_k or self._default_top_k,
                created_after=created_after,
            )

            if not include_outcomes:
                for item in results:
                    item.pop("ticketCreated", None)
                    item.pop("notifiedTeam", None)
```

```
            item.pop("outcome", None)

        return results
    except SemanticSearchError:
        raise
    except Exception as exc:
        logger.warning("Semantic search failed: %s", exc,
        exc_info=True)
        raise SemanticSearchError("Semantic search failed.") from exc
```

Design Implications of the Retrieval Update

The updated retrieval method maintains original behavior by default. Without a specified time window, the search covers the entire history. Outcome fields are excluded from results unless explicitly requested, even if present in the index.

This design is intentional. It ensures the retrieval layer remains broadly reusable while supporting targeted retrieval when necessary. The same method can handle both simple similarity lookups and more evidence-based queries without imposing additional requirements on every call.

As Thain's capabilities grow, retrieval can focus solely on context or incorporate detailed information about how similar incidents were previously managed. This flexibility is essential when retrieval becomes a deliberate part of the agent's reasoning process.

With these refinements, the retrieval layer is prepared to support agent-driven retrieval. The next step is to offer this capability as a tool that the agent can choose to use.

Exposing Semantic Retrieval As an Explicit Tool

To date, semantic retrieval has functioned primarily as infrastructure: text is embedded, the search index is queried, and similar complaints are returned. The next step is to make retrieval a deliberate action initiated by the agent, rather than an automatic background step.

To achieve this, we introduce a dedicated tool: `search_similar_complaints`. The tool is intentionally focused. Its sole purpose is to retrieve semantically similar past complaints based on the current customer message. The agent can then decide whether that evidence should influence its recommendation, such as determining whether an issue warrants escalation.

The tool wraps the semantic retrieval service behind a stable, audit-friendly interface. The agent provides the current message and may include optional constraints such as category, time window, or result count. In response, the system returns a concise set of relevant prior incidents. When necessary, the tool also supplies outcome metadata, allowing the agent to reason using decision-grade evidence instead of relying solely on raw similarity.

Designing the Tool Contract

The tool provides a clear and straightforward contract:

- **Input**: The most recent customer message, with optional constraints such as `top_k`, `category`, and `time_window_days`.

- **Output**: A list of similar complaints, each with core fields (`id`, `category`, `summary`, `createdAt`), and optionally outcome fields.

- **Failure behavior**: If retrieval fails, the tool returns an empty list and logs the error without interrupting the process.

This approach maintains the robustness of the agent's reasoning loop and supports evidence-based decisions when retrieval is successful.

Creating the Search Tool

Create a folder named `tools`, and then add a file called `search.py` to it. Insert the contents from Listing 5-11 into this file.

Listing 5-11. tools/search.py – the agentic retrieval tool

```
from __future__ import annotations
import logging
from typing import Any, Dict, Annotated
from agent_framework import ai_function
```

```python
logger = logging.getLogger(__name__)
def create_search_tool(semantic_service, semantic_search_config):
    """Factory to build the agentic search tool bound to the current
    semantic service/config."""

    @ai_function(
        name="search_similar_complaints",
        description="Retrieve semantically similar past complaints using
        Azure AI Search embeddings.",
    )
    async def search_similar_complaints(
        customer_message: Annotated[str, "The latest customer message to
        match for similarity."],
        top_k: Annotated[int, "Maximum number of similar complaints to
        return."] = 3,
        category: Annotated[str | None, "Optional issue category
        filter."] = None,
        time_window_days: Annotated[int, "Restrict to complaints created
        within the last N days."] = 90,
        include_outcomes: Annotated[bool, "If true, include decision-grade
        metadata like ticket/notification/outcome."] = False,
    ) -> list[Dict[str, Any]]:
        if not semantic_service or not semantic_search_config:
            return []
        if semantic_search_config.mode != "agentic":
            return []

        try:
            k = max(1, top_k) if top_k else semantic_search_config.
            default_top_k
            results = await semantic_service.find_similar(
                customer_id=semantic_search_config.customer_id,
                text=customer_message,
                category=category,
                top_k=k,
                time_window_days=time_window_days,
```

```
            include_outcomes=include_outcomes,
        )
    except Exception as exc:  # avoid raising into the agent;
    surface empty
        logger.warning("Agentic search tool failed: %s", exc, exc_
        info=True)
        return []

    return results

return search_similar_complaints
```

Design Principles Behind the Retrieval Tool

- **Factory pattern**: The tool is created by `create_search_tool(...)`, allowing it to bind to the appropriate semantic retrieval service instance and current configuration. This approach avoids global state and enables conditional registration.

- **Guard clauses**: If retrieval is disabled (`mode != "agentic"`) or dependencies are missing, the tool returns an empty list rather than raising errors.

- **Controlled outputs**: The tool returns a concise set of matches that serve as evidence. The agent can review the retrieved information and determine its impact on the response.

- **Safe failure behavior**: Retrieval failures are logged and the tool returns an empty list. This ensures Thain remains responsive even if the search back end is temporarily unavailable.

Currently, the tool is read-only. It collects evidence but does not create tickets or send notifications to teams.

Integrating Agentic Retrieval into Thain

Now that semantic retrieval can be invoked explicitly through `search_similar_complaints`, Thain needs a clear way to control when retrieval is implicit and when it is deliberate. The design uses a small set of retrieval modes to determine whether context is injected automatically, retrieved explicitly, or disabled entirely.

All changes are made in `main.py`.

Import the Search Tool Factory

At the top of `main.py`, add the tool import alongside the existing classifier import. See Listing 5-12.

Listing 5-12. Importing the agentic search tool

```
from tools.search import create_search_tool
```

This is the only new import required for tool registration.

Wiring Semantic Context Injection by Mode

Semantic retrieval is no longer always injected automatically. Instead, it is enabled only when semantic mode is active.

Locate the block that appends `SemanticContextProvider` to the provider chain and guard it with a semantic-only condition by extending the existing if statement. See Listing 5-13.

Listing 5-13. Semantic context injection (semantic mode only)

```
if semantic_service and semantic_search_config and search_mode ==
"semantic":
    provider_chain.append(
        SemanticContextProvider(
            service=semantic_service,
            customer_id=semantic_search_config.customer_id,
            lookup_limit=semantic_search_config.default_top_k,
            mode=semantic_search_config.mode,
        )
    )
```

This ensures that, in agentic mode, the agent receives no background semantic context. If historical evidence is required, it must be retrieved intentionally using a tool.

Registering the Agentic Search Tool

Next, register the retrieval tool itself, but only when the configuration calls for it. Unlike `classify_issue_tool`, which is always available and invoked as part of every request, the search tool represents an optional reasoning step. It is registered conditionally and called only when the agent decides that additional historical evidence is required.

Create a tools list that includes `classify_issue_tool` by default. Append the search tool if agentic mode is active. Insert the code from Listing 5-14 directly above the following line in `main.py`.

Listing 5-14. Conditional tool registration

```
tools_list = [classify_issue_tool]
if semantic_service and semantic_search_config and search_mode ==
"agentic":
    tools_list.append(create_search_tool(semantic_service, semantic_search_
    config))
```

Finally, update the ChatAgent construction to use this `tools_list`. Locate the existing `ChatAgent(...)` block and replace `tools=[classify_issue_tool]` with `tools=tools_list`, as shown in Listing 5-15.

Listing 5-15. Wiring the conditional tools list into ChatAgent

```
agent = ChatAgent(
        chat_client=chat_client,
        name="Thain",
        instructions=instructions,
        tools=tools_list,
        context_providers=context_provider,
        tool_choice=ToolMode.REQUIRED(classify_issue_tool.name),
        store=True,
    )
```

How Retrieval Modes Shape Agent Behavior

With these changes, retrieval is now a visible and explicit part of the system. The use and source of historical context are clearly integrated into the agent's reasoning.

When semantic retrieval is enabled, relevant history is automatically provided as background context. With agentic retrieval, this context is removed, and the agent must actively retrieve evidence using search_similar_complaints. If both are disabled, the agent operates without access to prior incidents.

This separation clarifies the agent's knowledge sources. Evidence obtained through tool calls can be inspected, logged, and audited, while decisions made without retrieval are evident by the lack of such calls.

With the integration complete, we can now run Thain in different modes to observe how these configurations affect its behavior. The next section presents test runs that demonstrate the practical impact of agentic retrieval compared to semantic retrieval.

Observing Agentic Retrieval in Practice

With agentic retrieval integrated into Thain, we can observe how its behavior changes across different retrieval modes. For consistency, each run uses the same complaint scenario and persisted data. The only variable is the retrieval method.

The following three runs demonstrate this progression.

Seed Run: Establishing the Baseline

Start Thain in semantic mode. Set AZURE_SEARCH_MODE to semantic and launch the application. Then, submit an initial complaint.

Run the following commands:

```
$Env:AZURE_SEARCH_MODE = "semantic"
python main.py --devui --devui-open
```

In the Dev UI, submit an initial complaint about an unexpected equipment shutdown during routine operations. See Figure 5-1.

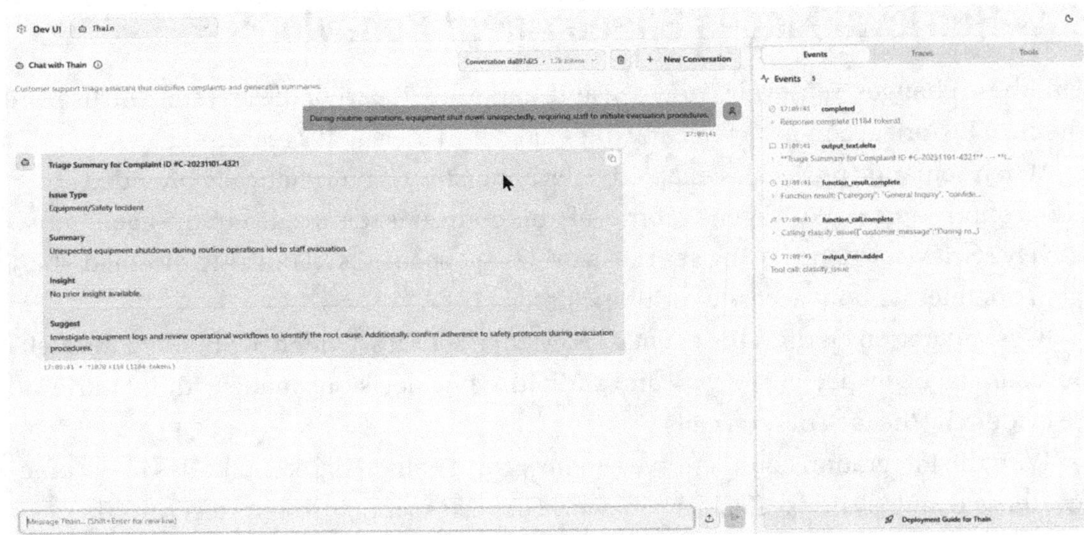

Figure 5-1. *Seed message submitted to Thain*

This run is intended solely to populate persistent storage and the search index with a baseline complaint record.

At this stage, there is no prior history to retrieve. The Insight section correctly indicates that no prior insight is available, confirming that Thain does not infer historical context when none exists.

This seed run provides a reliable starting point for subsequent runs.

Semantic Mode: Passive Recall

Next, restart the application in semantic mode:

Stop the application using `Ctrl+C`, and then restart it.

```
python main.py --devui --devui-open
```

Ask the escalation question:

```
During yesterday's shift, the equipment shut down twice without warning and
caused a brief evacuation. Should we open a ticket or notify someone?
```

See Figure 5-2.

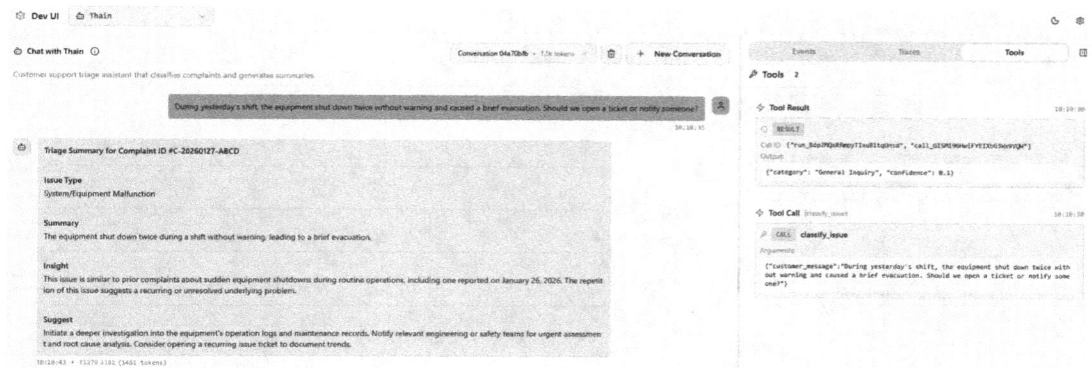

Figure 5-2. *Semantic mode response with passive recall*

In this run, Thain accesses the same indexed complaint history created during the seed step. Semantic retrieval operates passively, so relevant historical context may be injected automatically into the agent's prompt, but no explicit retrieval step is visible.

This behavior is reflected in the execution trace shown in Figure 5-2. Only the classification tool is invoked. No search tool is registered or called, and no retrieval parameters or results appear in the tool panel.

Despite this, Thain can still reference similar past incidents in the Insight section and recommend escalation in the Suggest section. The system functions as designed, but the retrieval step remains implicit and opaque.

Agentic Mode: Explicit, Evidence-Driven Retrieval

Switch Thain to agentic mode, and then restart the application.

Run the following commands:

```
$Env:AZURE_SEARCH_MODE = "agentic"
python main.py --devui --devui-open
```

Repeat the escalation question.

See Figure 5-3.

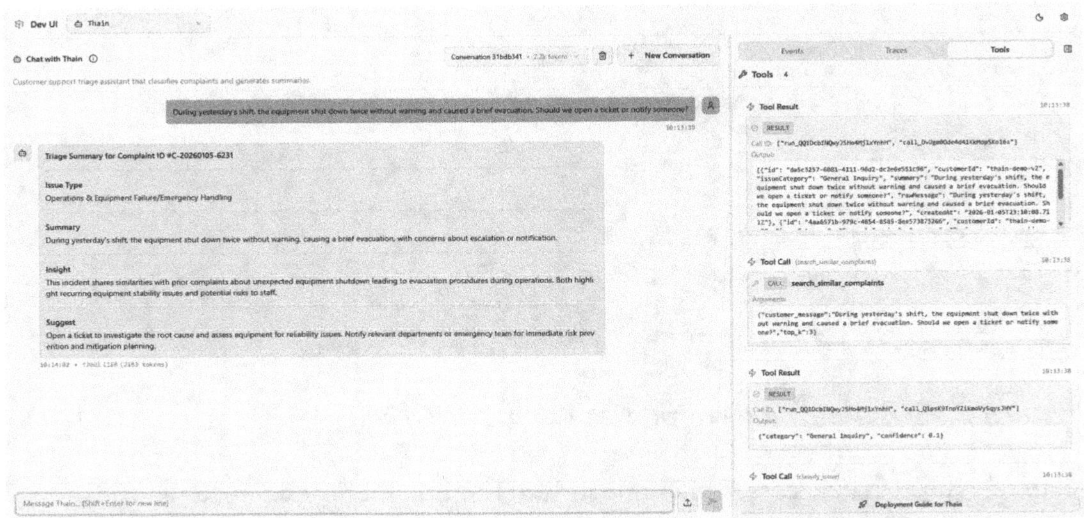

Figure 5-3. *Agentic mode with explicit retrieval via search_similar_complaints*

In this run, passive semantic injection is disabled. The agent must actively retrieve historical evidence if needed.

This decision is transparent. Thain explicitly invokes the `search_similar_complaints` tool, providing the current message and retrieval parameters. The tool returns a concise set of similar past complaints, which the agent uses to support its assessment and recommendation.

The resulting Insight and Suggest sections are based on retrieved evidence. The entire decision path is observable, including when retrieval occurred, what was retrieved, and how it influenced the response.

Note   After completing the test, run `Remove-Item Env:AZURE_SEARCH_MODE` to ensure the environment value matches your .env file.

Why Explicit Retrieval Matters

Thain may provide similar recommendations in both semantic and agentic modes when the available evidence is identical. This outcome is expected.

Agentic retrieval does not ensure different answers, but it does ensure a distinct decision path.

In semantic mode, retrieval occurs automatically in the background. In agentic mode, retrieval is a deliberate and inspectable step in the agent's reasoning process. This distinction is important in enterprise environments, where understanding the rationale behind a recommendation is as critical as the recommendation itself.

With agentic retrieval, evidence gathering is no longer an implicit result of prompt construction. It becomes an explicit action the agent chooses to take, which can be audited, logged, and governed.

With this foundation, Thain moves beyond generating insights. It now supports decisions with traceable evidence, enabling a shift from analysis to action.

The next section presents core action tools that allow Thain to take controlled steps, such as creating tickets, notifying stakeholders, or retrieving supporting documents, rather than only suggesting escalation.

Introducing Core Action Tools

Agentic retrieval ensures Thain's evidence gathering is deliberate and observable. The next step is to enable Thain to perform controlled actions. In enterprise systems, this typically involves interacting with external systems, such as opening tickets, notifying teams, or retrieving procedural guidance.

This section introduces three tools that support these capabilities:

- `create_ticket` (write tool)

- `notify_team` (write tool)

- `retrieve_docs` (read tool)

Currently, these tools are implemented as safe stubs. They provide realistic, deterministic outputs and generate clear tool traces in the Dev UI. This approach maintains focus on agent design and orchestration without adding external system dependencies.

Adding the Action Tools Module

All three tools are included in one new module.

This module

- Contains tool contracts defined using `@ai_function`

- Includes straightforward, deterministic stub logic

- Provides structured return payloads for downstream use, such as links, IDs, and status fields

This design establishes a clear separation between read tools, which are safe by default, and write tools, which will be governed by future approval and policy.

The tools are created through a factory function that registers each capability only when it is enabled in the configuration. This allows Thain's action surface to expand or contract without changing the core agent logic. Each tool logs its execution to simplify debugging and traceability during development.

The initial version of this module focuses only on deterministic tool behavior. Approval gates and policy checks will be added later in the chapter.

Create a new file at *tools/action_tools.py* and add the contents shown in Listing 5-16.

Listing 5-16. tools/action_tools.py (action tools module)

```python
from __future__ import annotations
import hashlib
import logging
from typing import Annotated, Any, Dict
from agent_framework import ai_function
logger = logging.getLogger(__name__)
def _stable_id(prefix: str, seed: str) -> str:
    digest = hashlib.sha256(seed.encode("utf-8")).hexdigest()[:8].upper()
    return f"{prefix}-{digest}"

def _clip_items(items: list[str] | None, limit: int = 3) -> list[str]:
    if not items:
        return []
    return list(items)[:limit]

def create_action_tools(action_config) -> list[Any]:
    tools: list[Any] = []

    if action_config.enable_tickets:

        @ai_function(
            name="create_ticket",
```

```python
        description="Create an incident ticket for follow-up.",
    )
    async def create_ticket(
        summary: Annotated[str, "Short ticket summary."],
        severity: Annotated[str, "Severity label (e.g., low, medium,
        high, critical)."],
        customer_id: Annotated[str, "Customer or tenant identifier."],
        evidence_summary: Annotated[str, "Short evidence summary used
        to justify the ticket."],
        evidence_items: Annotated[list[str] | None, "Up to three short
        evidence bullet points."] = None,
    ) -> Dict[str, Any]:
        ticket_id = _stable_id("TCK", f"{customer_id}:{summary}")
        result = {
            "ticket_id": ticket_id,
            "status": "created",
            "url": f"https://tickets.thain.local/{ticket_id}",
            "summary": summary,
            "severity": severity,
            "evidence_summary": evidence_summary,
            "evidence_items": _clip_items(evidence_items),
        }
        logger.info("Ticket stub created: %s", ticket_id)
        return result

    tools.append(create_ticket)

if action_config.enable_notifications:

    @ai_function(
        name="notify_team",
        description="Send a notification to a team or channel.",
    )
    async def notify_team(
        channel: Annotated[str, "Target channel or team."],
        message: Annotated[str, "Notification message."],
```

```python
            priority: Annotated[str, "Priority label (e.g., low, medium,
            high)."],
            related_ticket_id: Annotated[str | None, "Optional related
            ticket ID."] = None,
        ) -> Dict[str, Any]:
            seed = f"{channel}:{message}:{related_ticket_id or ''}"
            message_id = _stable_id("MSG", seed)
            result = {
                "message_id": message_id,
                "status": "sent",
                "channel": channel,
                "priority": priority,
                "related_ticket_id": related_ticket_id,
            }
            logger.info("Notification stub sent: %s", message_id)
            return result

        tools.append(notify_team)

    if action_config.enable_docs:

        @ai_function(
            name="retrieve_docs",
            description="Retrieve relevant knowledge-base documents for a
            query.",
        )
        async def retrieve_docs(
            query: Annotated[str, "Search query for documents."],
            top_k: Annotated[int, "Maximum number of documents to
            return."] = 3,
            tags: Annotated[list[str] | None, "Optional tag
            filters."] = None,
        ) -> list[dict[str, Any]]:
            corpus = [
                {
                    "title": "Equipment shutdown response checklist",
```

```
            "snippet": "Steps to follow after an unexpected
        shutdown and evacuation.",
            "url": "https://kb.thain.local/shutdown-checklist",
            "source": "kb",
            "tags": ["shutdown", "safety", "evacuation"],
        },
        {

            "title": "Recurring incident escalation playbook",
            "snippet": "When to open tickets and notify safety
        teams for repeat incidents.",
            "url": "https://kb.thain.local/escalation-playbook",
            "source": "kb",
            "tags": ["escalation", "incident"],
        },
        {

            "title": "Sensor calibration troubleshooting",
            "snippet": "Diagnosing sensor faults that lead to
        operational disruptions.",
            "url": "https://kb.thain.local/sensor-calibration",
            "source": "kb",
            "tags": ["sensor", "hardware"],
        },
    ]

query_lower = query.lower()
matches = [
    doc
    for doc in corpus
    if query_lower in doc["title"].lower() or query_lower in
    doc["snippet"].lower()
]

if tags:
    tag_set = {tag.lower() for tag in tags}
    matches = [
        doc
```

```
                        for doc in matches
                        if tag_set.intersection({tag.lower() for tag in doc.
                        get("tags", [])})
                    ]

                limit = max(1, top_k) if top_k else 3
                results = list(matches)
                if len(results) < limit:
                    for doc in corpus:
                        if doc not in results:
                            results.append(doc)
                            if len(results) >= limit:
                                break
                return results[:limit]

        tools.append(retrieve_docs)

    return tools
```

Controlling Tool Availability via Feature Flags

Action tools are powerful, and in production systems, you often need to enable or disable them by environment. To simplify this process, this chapter uses feature flags controlled by environment variables.

Add the following values to the .env file as shown in Listing 5-17.

Listing 5-17. .env (feature flags for action tools)

```
ENABLE_TICKETS=true
ENABLE_NOTIFICATIONS=true
ENABLE_DOCS=true
```

Wiring Feature Flags into Settings

We have enabled the action tool feature flags in .env, but we need a clear way to access these values in the application.

We extend settings.py with a small, typed configuration object for action tools. This keeps tool availability centralized, explicit, and testable.

In `settings.py`, we will add three items:

- `_env_flag()`: A small helper that parses common boolean values consistently (true, 1, yes, on)

- `ActionToolsConfig`: A typed container that represents which tool groups are enabled

- `load_action_tools_config()`: A single helper function that loads this configuration from the environment

1. Adding a Helper for Boolean Environment Flags

Insert this block in Listing 5-18 after the existing load_search_config() function.

Listing 5-18. settings.py (add _env_flag() helper)

```python
def _env_flag(name: str, default: bool = False) -> bool:
    raw = os.getenv(name, "").strip().lower()
    if not raw:
        return default
    return raw in {"1", "true", "yes", "y", "on"}
```

2. Defining Configuration for Action Tools

Immediately below the _env_flag() helper you just added, add the code block in Listing 5-19.

Listing 5-19. settings.py (add ActionToolsConfig)

```python
@dataclass(frozen=True)
class ActionToolsConfig:
    """Configuration for optional action tools (tickets, notifications, docs)."""

    enable_tickets: bool = False
    enable_notifications: bool = False
    enable_docs: bool = False

    @classmethod
```

```
    def from_env(cls) -> "ActionToolsConfig":
        return cls(
            enable_tickets=_env_flag("ENABLE_TICKETS", False),
            enable_notifications=_env_flag("ENABLE_NOTIFICATIONS", False),
            enable_docs=_env_flag("ENABLE_DOCS", False),
        )
```

3. Loading Action Tool Configuration

Insert code block listed in Listing 5-20 immediately below `ActionToolsConfig`.

Listing 5-20. settings.py (add load_action_tools_config())

```
def load_action_tools_config() -> ActionToolsConfig:
    """Helper to load action tool configuration from the environment."""
    return ActionToolsConfig.from_env()
```

Wiring Action Tools into the Agent Runtime

With action tools defined and their availability controlled through configuration, the final step is to wire them into Thain's runtime. This is done centrally in `main.py`, where the agent is assembled, instructed, and registered with the Dev UI.

The `main.py` now treats action tools as optional capabilities, loaded and registered based on the current environment.

1. Import Action Tool Helpers

At the top of `main.py`, extend the existing imports. Refer to Listing 5-21.

Listing 5-21. main.py (import action tool helpers)

```
from config.settings import load_action_tools_config
from tools.action_tools import create_action_tools
```

This allows the application to load action tool flags from configuration and construct the enabled tools dynamically.

2. Load the Action Tools Configuration

Insert code block in Listing 5-22 immediately after the existing semantic and persistent configuration loading.

Listing 5-22. main.py (load action tool configuration)

```
action_tools_config = load_action_tools_config()
```

This mirrors how search and memory configuration are handled, keeping all environment-driven behavior centralized and predictable.

3. Register Action Tools with the Agent

Place the code in Listing 5-23 inside the method run_thain_agent where the tool list is assembled.

Listing 5-23. main.py (register action tools)

```
action_tools = create_action_tools(action_tools_config)
if action_tools:
    tools_list.extend(action_tools)
```

Only tools enabled by the current configuration are registered. If all flags are disabled, Thain runs exactly as before, with no action capabilities available.

4. Add Agentic-Only Guidance for Document Retrieval

Inside the run_thain_agent function in main.py, locate the conditional that checks the search mode:

```
if search_mode != "agentic":
    ...
else:
    ...
```

The else branch executes when Thain operates in agentic retrieval mode. Previously, this section instructed the agent to retrieve historical complaints before escalation.

In this update, this same else block is extended with an additional instruction that allows Thain to retrieve procedural knowledge. When users ask for playbooks, SOPs, or known procedures, the agent is now guided to call the `retrieve_docs` tool before responding.

Add the code shown in Listing 5-24 to the existing `else` block.

Listing 5-24. main.py (agentic instruction for retrieve_docs)

```
instructions += (
    " If the user asks for known procedures, playbooks, or SOPs, "
    "call the `retrieve_docs` tool before responding."
)
```

5. Surface Tool Availability in Agent Instructions

The next update will explicitly inform the agent of the currently available action tools. This will reduce ambiguity during reasoning and prevent attempts to use tools that are disabled by configuration.

Insert code shown in Listing 5-25 inside the `run_thain_agent` function in `main.py` immediately after the agentic-only guidance added in step 4 and before the `ChatAgent` is instantiated.

Listing 5-25. main.py (append action tool availability notes)

```
action_notes = []
if action_tools_config.enable_tickets:
    action_notes.append("create_ticket (write)")
if action_tools_config.enable_notifications:
    action_notes.append("notify_team (write)")
if action_tools_config.enable_docs:
    action_notes.append("retrieve_docs (read)")

if action_notes:
    instructions += (
        " You may use the following tools when appropriate: "
        + ", ".join(action_notes)
        + "."
    )
```

6. Wire Action Tools into the Dev UI Agent

Refer to Listing 5-26 and add the specified line to the __init__ method of
ThainDevAgent.

Place this line outside of the if block that checks for agentic retrieval mode and
immediately above the line.

In other words, the action tools should be registered after the conditional search-tool
logic, not inside it.

Listing 5-26. main.py (register action tools in Dev UI)

```
tools.extend(create_action_tools(action_tools_config))
```

This ensures that action tools are available in the Dev UI regardless of search mode,
while retrieval tools remain gated by AZURE_SEARCH_MODE=agentic.

Separating Agentic Retrieval from Agentic Actions

Action tools are registered regardless of search mode. This allows Thain to operate as an
action-capable agent even when historical retrieval is disabled. Only the semantic search
tool is gated by AZURE_SEARCH_MODE=agentic. This distinction is intentional.

The search_similar_complaints tool is a retrieval tool that expands the agent's
evidence base via external search. Because it can be higher cost and broader in scope, it
is enabled only when agentic retrieval is explicitly turned on.

By contrast, create_ticket and notify_team are action tools that produce side
effects, while retrieve_docs is a read/knowledge tool that fetches procedural guidance.
These tools can be enabled independently of retrieval mode, allowing different agents in
a multi-agent system to expose only the capabilities they require.

Although retrieval, read, and action tools all follow the same agentic pattern, the
model decides when to call them; they serve different purposes:

- Retrieval tools gather additional evidence.

- Read tools fetch guidance or reference material.

- Action tools execute operational changes.

Keeping these concerns separate gives Thain flexibility across roles and establishes
clear governance boundaries as the system scales to multiple agents.

Validating Action Tools in the Dev UI

With the core action tools integrated into Thain and configured, we can now validate the end-to-end flow using the Agent Framework Dev UI. This enables us to observe both the final response and the intermediate tool calls that produce it.

To start Thain in Dev UI mode, run the following command from the project root:

```
python main.py --devui --devui-open
```

This launches the Dev UI server and opens the interface in your browser. Ensure that the action tool feature flags are enabled in your `.env` file before proceeding.

After the UI loads, select the Tools panel on the right to view tool execution in real time.

Initial Query: Requesting Known Procedures

In the chat panel, submit the following message:

```
During yesterday's shift, the equipment shut down twice and caused a brief
evacuation. Do we have any known procedure for this, and what should we
do next?
```

Thain begins by executing its standard triage process:

- The complaint is classified.

- A structured triage summary is generated.

Because the question explicitly asks for known procedures, Thain operates in agentic mode and calls the `retrieve_docs` tool. This is visible in the Tools panel, where the tool invocation and returned results are shown. See Figure 5-4.

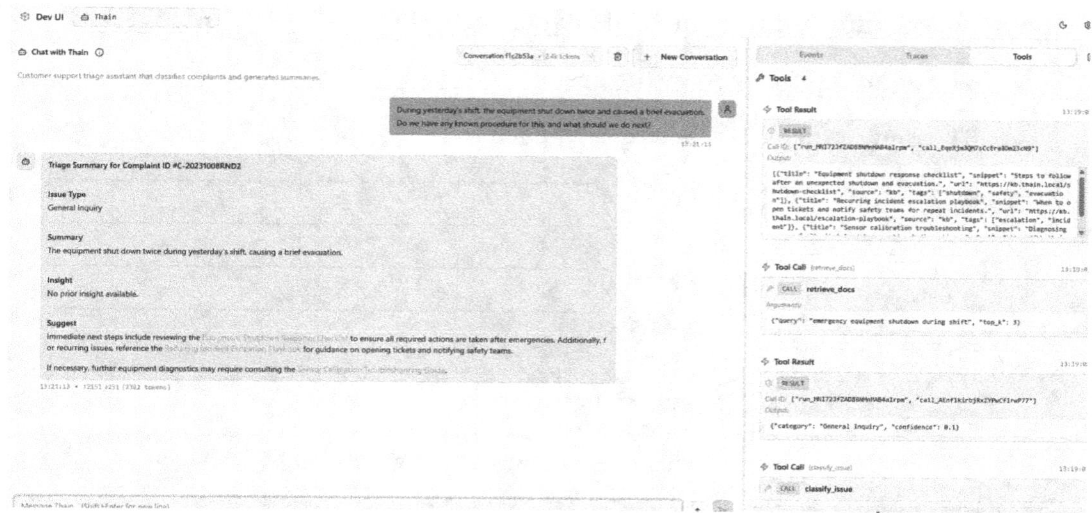

Figure 5-4. *Thain retrieving procedural documents using the retrieve_docs tool*

The final response incorporates the retrieved documents directly into the Suggest section of the triage summary, referencing items such as

- An equipment shutdown response checklist

- A recurring incident escalation playbook

- Relevant troubleshooting guidance

At this stage, Thain is still operating in a read-only advisory role. It supports its recommendation with evidence but has not yet taken any action.

Follow-Up Query: Requesting Action

Next, submit a follow-up message in the same conversation:

```
Okay, please create a ticket and notify the safety team.
```

This time, Thain's behavior changes from advisory to operational. Because action tools are enabled and registered for this environment

- Thain calls the `notify_team` tool to send a high-priority message to the safety channel.

- Thain calls the `create_ticket` tool to open a follow-up incident ticket.

Both tool calls are visible in the `Tools` panel, including

- The arguments passed by the agent

- The deterministic IDs returned by each tool

See Figure 5-5.

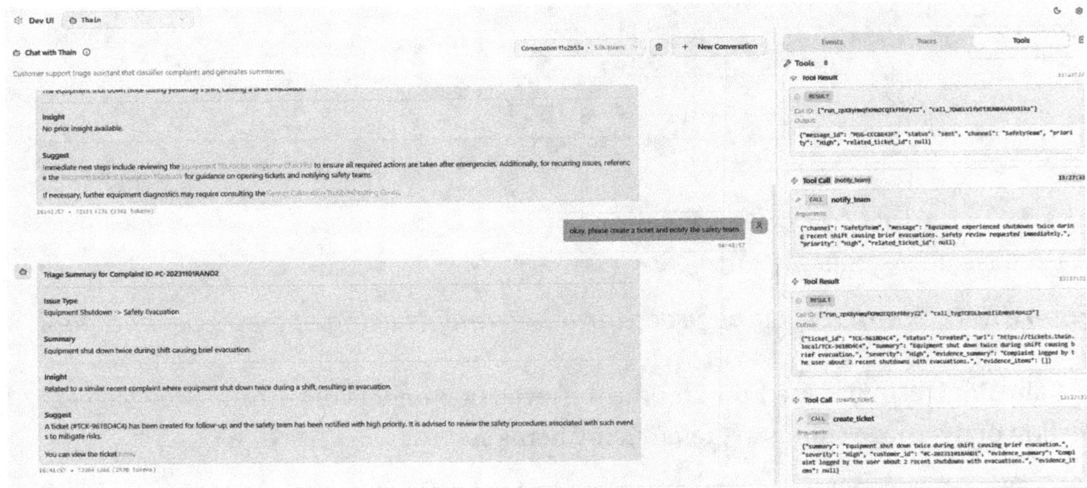

Figure 5-5. *Thain executing follow-up actions using notify_team and create_ticket*

The final triage summary is updated to reflect these actions. The `Suggest` section now confirms that

- A ticket has been created.

- The safety team has been notified.

- Further review is recommended.

This demonstrates a complete progression from analysis to evidence to action within a single, traceable agent run. While this end-to-end flow highlights Thain's ability to move from reasoning to action, it also prompts an important consideration: when should these actions be permitted to execute?

Approval Gates for Agentic Actions

In enterprise environments, write operations such as creating tickets, sending notifications, or updating systems require stricter governance than read operations like retrieving documents or similar complaints. Retrieval can often remain unrestricted, while actions that modify downstream systems typically require explicit approval.

Here, we introduce a single approval switch that applies only to write tools:

- Write tools (gated): `create_ticket, notify_team`

- Read tools (ungated): `retrieve_docs, search_similar_complaints`

When approvals are enabled, Thain may still plan to use write tools as part of its reasoning. However, execution pauses until explicit approval is granted. If approval is denied, the tool returns a clear denial response, and the agent must explicitly confirm that the action did not occur.

Enable Write Approvals via Configuration

We are introducing a new environment flag. Update the .env file as follows:

```
ENABLE_WRITE_APPROVALS=true
```

This flag is loaded from settings.py using a helper function, allowing the rest of the code to treat approvals as a simple boolean capability.

Add the code block from Listing 5-27 to `settings.py` near the bottom with your other `_env_flag`-based loaders.

Listing 5-27. settings.py – adding a write-approvals flag loader

```
def load_write_approvals_enabled() -> bool:
    return _env_flag("ENABLE_WRITE_APPROVALS", default=False)
```

Introducing an Approval Service

Next, add an approval service that performs two functions:

- Determine whether approval is required based on the tool type.

- Request approval through a console prompt.

Implement this functionality in a new file to keep approval logic separate from the tool code. Create *services/approvals.py* and add the code from Listing 5-28.

Listing 5-28. services/approvals.py

```python
from __future__ import annotations
from typing import Any, Callable

def requires_approval(tool_type: str, enabled: bool) -> bool:
    return enabled and tool_type == "write"

class ApprovalService:
    def __init__(self, enabled: bool, prompt: Callable[[str], str] | None =
    None) -> None:
        self._enabled = enabled
        self._prompt = prompt

    @property
    def enabled(self) -> bool:
        return self._enabled

    async def request_approval(self, tool_name: str, payload: dict[str,
    Any]) -> bool:
        if not self._enabled:
            return True

        prompt_text = (
            f"Approve write action '{tool_name}'? (y/n): "
        )
        if self._prompt:
            response = self._prompt(prompt_text)
        else:
            response = input(prompt_text)
        approved = str(response).strip().lower() in {"y", "yes"}
        if approved:
            print(f"Approval granted for write action: {tool_name}")
        else:
            print(f"Approval denied for write action: {tool_name}")
        return approved
```

A few intentional design choices

- The service is framework agnostic and does not rely on development UI dependencies.

- It accepts a prompt function, allowing unit testing of approval flows without requiring interactive input.

- It clearly logs granted or denied actions in the terminal.

Implement a Tool Registry and Restrict Access to Write Tools

Now we integrate approvals inside the action tools layer. First, add the following import to the top of `action_tools.py`:

```
from services.approvals import ApprovalService, requires_approval
```

Next, proceed with the below updates.

1. Creating an Explicit Tool Registry

Introduce a registry that designates each tool as read or write, serving as the single source of truth for approval requirements.

Insert the code from Listing 5-29 near the top of `action_tools.py` immediately following the import statements.

Listing 5-29. tools/action_tools.py – adding tool registry

```
TOOL_REGISTRY = {
    "create_ticket": "write",
    "notify_team": "write",
    "retrieve_docs": "read",
}
```

2. Providing Approval Controls to Action Tools

Locate the `create_action_tools` method and update the factory to accept `ApprovalService` as an optional parameter. See Listing 5-30.

Listing 5-30. tools/action_tools.py – passing approval service

```
def create_action_tools(action_config, approval_service: ApprovalService |
None = None):
```

3. Implementing Gating for the Write Tools

Both write tools now enforce the same approval checks at execution:

- Are approvals enabled?

- Is this tool type `write`?

If both conditions are met, prompt the user for approval.

- If approval is denied, return a consistent denial payload.

- If approved, proceed and return approved: true with standard status.

Insert the code block from Listing 5-31 at the start of `async def create_ticket(...)`.

Listing 5-31. tools/action_tools.py – approval gate inside create_ticket

```
if approval_service and requires_approval(TOOL_REGISTRY["create_ticket"],
approval_service.enabled):
    approved = await approval_service.request_approval("create_ticket", {
        "summary": summary,
        "severity": severity,
        "customer_id": customer_id,
        "evidence_summary": evidence_summary,
        "evidence_items": evidence_items
    })
    if not approved:
        return {"status": "denied", "approved": False, "reason": "approval_
        not_provided"}
```

Insert the code block from Listing 5-32 at the start of `async def notify_team(...)`.

Listing 5-32. tools/action_tools.py – approval gate inside notify_team

```python
if approval_service and requires_approval(TOOL_REGISTRY["notify_team"],
approval_service.enabled):
    approved = await approval_service.request_approval("notify_team", {
        "channel": channel,
        "message": message,
        "priority": priority,
        "related_ticket_id": related_ticket_id
    })

    if not approved:
        return {"status": "denied", "approved": False, "reason": "approval_
        not_provided"}
```

To display approvals in the Dev UI Tools panel:
Approved path now includes

- **Approved**: true.

- The existing success status (created for create_ticket, sent for notify_team) is preserved.

Denied path now includes

- **Status**: denied

- **Approved**: false

- **Reason**: approval_not_provided

Integrating Approval into the Agent Runtime

Finally, main.py needs to load the new flag, create the approval service, and pass it into create_action_tools(...).

1. Importing the Approval Service

Import ApprovalService at the top of the file with the other imports. Refer to Listing 5-33. Also extend the config.settings import with load_write_approvals_enabled.

Listing 5-33. main.py – importing approval service

```
from services.approvals import ApprovalService
```

2. Initializing the Approval Service

Add the code from Listing 5-34 in the same config bootstrapping area where other feature flags and config are loaded. Place it just below `action_tools_config = load_action_tools_config()`.

Listing 5-34. main.py – loading approval flag and constructing approval service

```
write_approvals_enabled = load_write_approvals_enabled()
approval_service = ApprovalService(enabled=write_approvals_enabled)
```

3. Providing the Approval Service to Action Tools

Locate the `create_action_tools(...)` used for runtime agent setup and replace

```
action_tools = create_action_tools(action_tools_config)
```

with the code shown in Listing 5-35.

Listing 5-35. main.py – passing approval service (runtime agent setup)

```
action_tools = create_action_tools(action_tools_config, approval_service)
```

For the Dev UI agent, replace

```
tools.extend(create_action_tools(action_tools_config))
```

with the code shown in Listing 5-36.

Listing 5-36. main.py – passing approval service (Dev UI agent setup)

```
tools.extend(create_action_tools(action_tools_config, approval_service))
```

With this wiring, approval behavior is managed entirely at the environment level, allowing write actions to be governed without modifying agent logic or tool implementations.

Testing the Approval Gate in the Dev UI

With approval gating enabled, we can validate Thain's behavior when executing write actions under various approval outcomes. All tests use the Agent Framework Dev UI for transparency and observability.

Before you begin, ensure the following environment flags are set:

```
ENABLE_TICKETS=true
ENABLE_NOTIFICATIONS=true
ENABLE_DOCS=true
ENABLE_WRITE_APPROVALS=true
```

For these tests, set AZURE_SEARCH_MODE=agentic so Thain can invoke read tools explicitly as part of its reasoning; the tool call and result will appear in the Tools panel. Start Thain in Dev UI mode from the project root:

```
python main.py --devui --devui-open
```

Keep the terminal visible, since approval prompts will appear there.

Step 1: Read Tools Remain Unblocked

Prompt:

```
During yesterday's shift, the equipment shut down twice and caused a brief
evacuation.
Do we have any known procedure for this?
```

What to observe:

Thain calls the `retrieve_docs` tool.

No approval prompt appears in the terminal.

The response references procedural guidance.

The Tools panel shows the `retrieve_docs` invocation and result.

Refer to Figure 5-6.

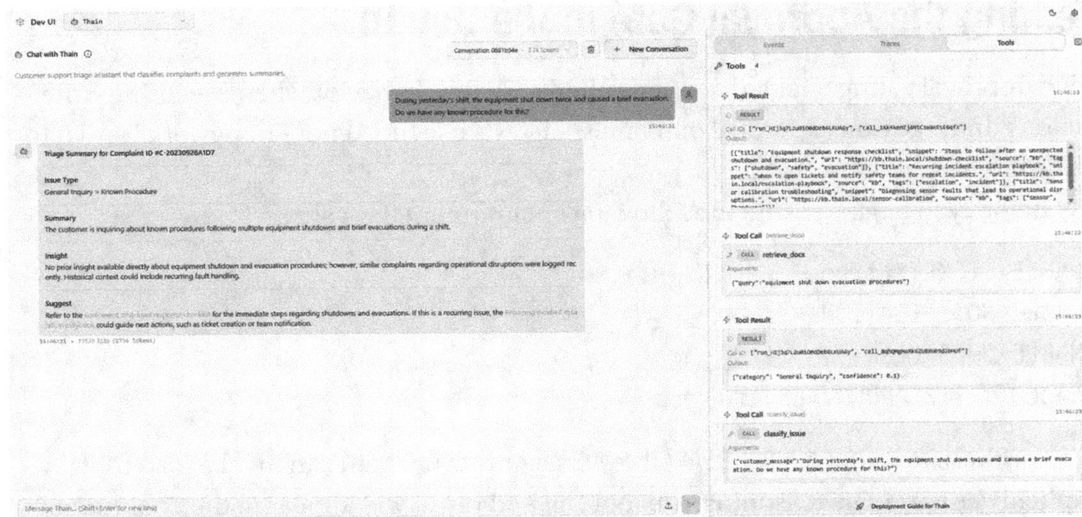

Figure 5-6. *Read Tools execution without approval*

This confirms that read tools bypass approvals.

Step 2: Write Action Approved (Yes)

Prompt:

```
Create a ticket for now for this incident and confirm once it is done.
```

What to observe:

The terminal prompts for approval (for `create_ticket`).

Enter y to approve. The terminal will display a message confirming approval.

See Figure 5-7. If the agent asks for clarification, provide the missing ticket details such as severity, and supporting evidence; the approval gate is triggered once the ticket request contains enough information for the write action.

```
PROBLEMS    OUTPUT    DEBUG CONSOLE    TERMINAL    PORTS    AZURE

 INFO:       Started server process [24660]
 INFO:       Waiting for application startup.
 INFO:       Application startup complete.
 INFO:       Uvicorn running on http://127.0.0.1:8080 (Press CTRL+C to quit)
 INFO:       127.0.0.1:61319 - "GET /health HTTP/1.1" 200 OK
 INFO:       127.0.0.1:63219 - "GET /v1/entities HTTP/1.1" 200 OK
 INFO:       127.0.0.1:63219 - "GET /v1/conversations?agent_id=agent_in-memory_thain_0319dde435be40d9971302435f4b5
 INFO:       127.0.0.1:63219 - "POST /v1/conversations HTTP/1.1" 200 OK
 INFO:       127.0.0.1:64155 - "POST /v1/responses HTTP/1.1" 200 OK
[2026-01-09 15:46:00 - C:\AIAA\thain\memory\persistent_provider.py:42 - INFO] PersistentContextProvider: return
 INFO:       127.0.0.1:53781 - "POST /v1/responses HTTP/1.1" 200 OK
[2026-01-09 15:46:54 - C:\AIAA\thain\memory\persistent_provider.py:42 - INFO] PersistentContextProvider: return
Approve write action 'create_ticket'? (y/n): y
Approval granted for write action: create_ticket
```

Figure 5-7. *Approval prompt for write action*

After approval is granted, the tool executes successfully. The Dev UI displays the tool result with `approved: true` and a created ticket ID.

See Figure 5-8.

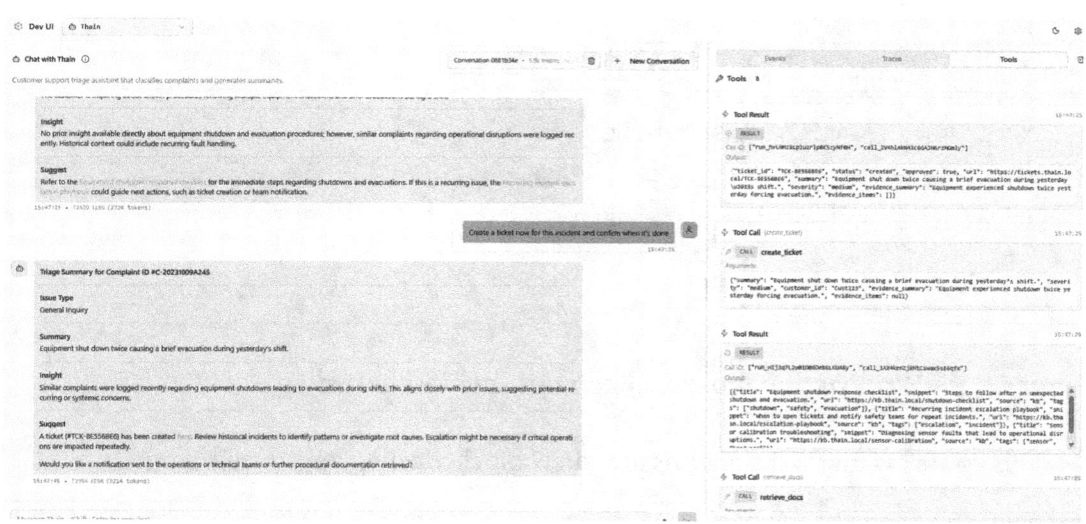

Figure 5-8. *Write action executed after approval*

This confirms that write actions execute when approval is granted.

Step 3: Write Action Denied (No)

Create a new conversation and repeat Steps 1 and 2.

During Step 2, observe the terminal. The approval prompt will appear.

Enter "n" to deny approval.

Expected outcome:

The create_ticket tool returns a denied status:

```
{ "status": "denied", "approved": false, "reason": "approval_not_provided" }
```

No ticket is created.

Thain explicitly states that the ticket was not created, explains that approval is required, and offers safe alternatives such as retrying with approval or notifying the appropriate team.

Refer to Figure 5-9.

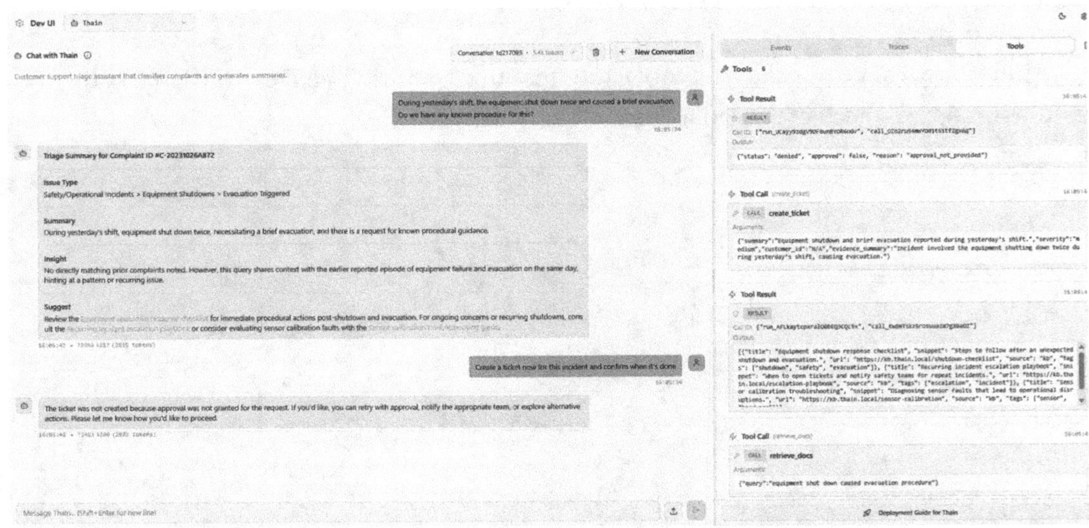

Figure 5-9. *Write action blocked when approval is denied*

This confirms that write actions are safely blocked when approval is denied.

The Role of Approval Gates in Agentic Systems

Together, these scenarios validate a comprehensive, enterprise-ready approval model:

- Read actions remain fast and unrestricted.

- Write actions are explicitly governed.

- Approval outcomes are transparent and traceable.

- Agent behavior remains predictable under policy constraints.

While this walkthrough focused on the `create_ticket` tool, the same approval-gated process applies to other write tools, such as `notify_team`. The approval mechanism is generic and consistent across all write actions.

These scenarios confirm that Thain's agentic capabilities go beyond reasoning and retrieval. They show how intent, evidence, policy, and action are integrated into a controlled execution flow. As the system matures, this approval boundary can be backed by durable workflow state, checkpointing, or MAF-native approval mechanisms, but the architectural principle remains the same: the agent may propose an action, while the system governs when that action is allowed to execute.

Thain's Tool Architecture

Now that Thain has a complete toolkit, it is useful to step back and examine how the pieces fit together. Figure 5-10 illustrates the three structural forces shaping Thain v0.4: the context provider chain (carried forward from Chapters 3 and 4) prepares the reasoning context before the agent begins reasoning, the tool layer separates read tools from write tools through an explicit registry, and the approval interceptor governs write-tool execution without coupling approval logic to any individual tool implementation.

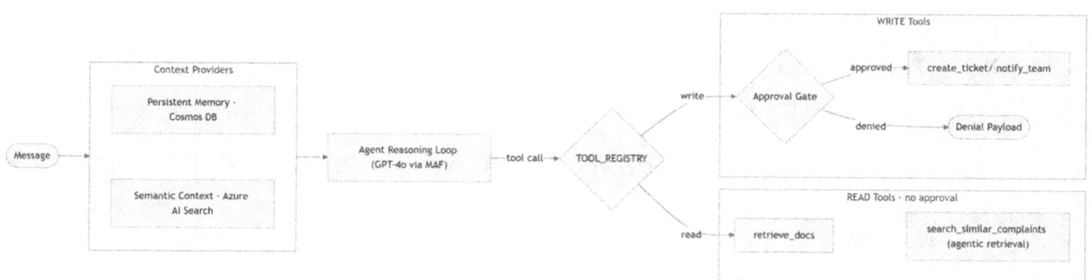

Figure 5-10. *Thain v0.4 tool architecture: context providers, read/write tool split, and approval gate*

Figure 5-10 shows how these elements interact during a single reasoning cycle.

The approval gate is the only point in the system where a write action can be blocked. All other tool calls including agentic search and document retrieval proceed without human intervention. This separation of concerns keeps individual tool implementations clean and allows approval behavior to be configured entirely through the environment settings.

Note on Stubbed Integrations and Governance

The ticketing, notification, document retrieval, and approval mechanisms introduced in this chapter are implemented as deterministic stubs. This is a deliberate design choice.

The focus of this chapter is on agent decision-making, orchestration, and control boundaries rather than on external system integration or deployment-specific workflows. Using stubs ensures the agent's behavior, intent, approval flow, and action semantics remain clear, testable, and reproducible without introducing unnecessary infrastructure complexity.

In real-world Azure deployments, these capabilities are typically backed by services such as Azure Functions, Logic Apps, Azure AI Search, or other enterprise platforms. Chapter 8 discusses how the action tools and governance patterns established here map to production-ready Azure architectures and best practices without implementing the integrations themselves.

Note   Unit tests covering agentic retrieval, action tools, and approval behavior are included in the book's GitHub repository at `https://github.com/Apress/Architecting-Intelligent-Agents-in-Azure`. These tests are not listed in the chapter to maintain focus on agent behavior, system design, and architecture.

The final project state for this chapter is in the repository. To set up the repository locally, use the following commands:

```
git clone https://github.com/Apress/Architecting-Intelligent-
Agents-in-Azure.git
```

```
cd Architecting-Intelligent-Agents-in-Azure
```

For the manuscript code, open the Chapter 5/thain folder. For the GA code, open Code GA/Chapter 5/thain. After cloning, create and activate a virtual environment, and then install the dependencies:

```
python -m venv .venv
```

```
.\.venv\Scripts\activate
```

```
pip install -r requirements.txt -c constraints.txt
```

Before running the project, update your `.env` file with the necessary Azure settings and feature flags.

You may also browse the repository online to review the reference implementation.

Summary

In this chapter, Thain advanced to version 0.4, shifting from a system focused on analysis and explanation to one capable of deliberate action under real-world constraints. Instead of introducing autonomy all at once, we incrementally added structures to ensure agentic behavior is observable, controllable, and trustworthy.

We began by exposing semantic and document retrieval as explicit tools, allowing Thain to decide when additional context was required instead of retrieving information automatically. This made evidence gathering intentional and traceable, laying the groundwork for responsible decision-making.

Next, we introduced core action tools that enabled Thain to interact with downstream systems. These tools allowed the agent to move beyond recommendations and begin proposing concrete operational steps while still operating in a controlled, deterministic environment.

Finally, we added approval gates for write actions, ensuring that operations with external impact cannot execute without explicit authorization. This establishes a clear separation between reasoning, intent, and execution with human judgment remaining in the loop at critical moments. Approval outcomes were made visible through both tool results and the Dev UI, reinforcing transparency and auditability.

Thain v0.4 demonstrates a full progression from analysis to evidence to action, governed by straightforward and effective controls. It retrieves context as needed, suggests and executes actions responsibly, and clearly communicates its actions at every step. This balance of autonomy and restraint makes agentic systems viable in enterprise settings.

With controlled action execution established, the next chapter will evaluate Thain not only on its capabilities but on how reliably and safely those capabilities operate over time.

Architectural Outcomes

Thain's architecture now supports the following core capabilities:

- **Explicit tool-based interaction with external systems**: Retrieval, notification, and ticket creation appear as primary agent tools rather than hidden implementation details.

- **Agent-directed retrieval**: Thain determines when additional context is required rather than relying on automatic background searches. This approach ensures evidence gathering is intentional and traceable.

- **Clear separation between read and write operations**: Read tools remain unrestricted and write tools are explicitly controlled to prevent unintended downstream effects.

- **Approval-gated write actions**: Operations with external side effects require explicit authorization while maintaining the agent's ability to reason and plan independently.

- **Deterministic action outcomes**: Every write attempt produces a clear, structured response indicating approval, denial, or execution and preventing ambiguous or partial outcomes.

- **Human-in-the-loop control embedded in the execution flow**: Human judgment can intervene at critical points without disrupting the agent's reasoning.

- **Traceable agent behavior through explicit tool calls and results**: Each action attempt, approval decision, and executed operation can be clearly observed during a run.

Thain Earns Trust

Introduction

In previous chapters, Thain learned to reason, remember, retrieve context, and act using tools. While the agent is now capable, engineering demands more than capability alone.

As systems become more autonomous, trust becomes a first-class architectural concern. In production environments, we must be able to observe what the agent did, understand what information it captured or excluded, control its permissions, and explain its behavior, especially when issues arise.

This chapter presents the architectural layers that enable Thain to earn trust.

Traditional application logging is not sufficient for agentic systems. An agent's execution spans multiple decisions, tools, approvals, and external dependencies, often within a single turn. Without structured visibility and explicit control boundaries, debugging becomes guesswork, and governance is often an afterthought.

Rather than starting with policies or safety rules, we begin with observability. Clear visibility is a prerequisite for meaningful control. The chapter is structured in three parts:

- Part A establishes a tracing foundation that records every agent interaction as a deterministic, structured event stream.

- Part B introduces governance rules that define Thain's permissions and specify what the system may and may not record.

- Part C completes the trust loop by standardizing failure responses, ensuring trace emission, and providing audit tools for post-incident analysis.

By the end of this chapter, Thain is no longer a black box. Its actions are visible, its boundaries are explicit, and its behavior is auditable. This foundation supports the secure, reliable deployment of autonomous agents in production environments.

189

© Hari Narayn 2026
H. Narayn, *Architecting Intelligent Agents in Azure*, https://doi.org/10.1007/979-8-8688-2433-3_6

Working with This Chapter's Code

From this chapter onward, code is presented as focused excerpts rather than complete file listings. As Thain's architecture grows, full listings become too long to serve as learning aids, the patterns and enforcement mechanics matter more than boilerplate.

Complete implementations of all referenced files are available in the book's companion GitHub repository `https://github.com/Apress/Architecting-Intelligent-Agents-in-Azure` under the folder:

Chapter 6 → {Part} → thain

These reference implementations serve as the definitive source for the code discussed in this chapter. The repository also includes a Microsoft Agent Framework 1.5.0 General Availability version of this chapter's code in the Code GA/Chapter 6 folder. The GA version updates the tool decorator used across all three tool files in each part, and replaces the internal type check in the tool-wrapping helper that enables trace interception. The short-term memory provider wired directly in the main agent loop also adopts the lifecycle pattern introduced in Chapters 3 and 4. All governance, policy, and audit modules introduced in this chapter have no Agent Framework dependency and carry over without modification. A detailed migration note is also available in the repository.

Code Reference Convention

Each code section specifies its source using the following format:

Source   Chapter 6 → {Part} → thain → {folder} → {filename} (action)

This notation shows

- Where the complete reference implementation is in the repository

- Whether the file should be **created** or **updated** in your local project

As you follow along, replicate the folder structure in your local workspace and create or update the referenced files as indicated.

Part A: Tracing Foundations

So far, Thain has demonstrated reasoning, memory, and the ability to act through tools. However, one critical question remains: how do we know what Thain actually did?

In enterprise systems, intelligence without visibility poses a risk. Before implementing governance, policy enforcement, or safety constraints, we need a reliable method to observe an agent's behavior deterministically and consistently without altering its decision logic.

This section introduces a foundational tracing layer for Thain with a focused scope: to record what occurred, in what order, and within which execution context.

By the end of Part A, every agent interaction generates a single structured JSON trace that provides a clear, auditable account of the agent's actions during that turn.

Design Goals for Tracing

Before writing any code, it is important to clearly define what this tracing system is and what it is not. The tracing layer introduced in this part is designed to be

- **Deterministic**: Events are recorded in strict sequence order.

- **Append-only**: No mutation and no rewriting of history.

- **Safe by construction**: Payloads are redacted and truncated by default.

- **Non-intrusive**: No changes to tool implementations or agent logic.

- **Forward compatible**: Ready to support governance, auditing, and replay.

At this stage, the focus is solely on observability.

Stable Identity: Run, Trace, and Turn IDs

Each trace starts with identity. Thain operates across several conceptual layers: the lifetime of a running process, the flow of a conversation, and individual agent turns. To ensure traces are meaningful and can be correlated, we introduce three explicit identifiers:

- `run_id`: Identifies the lifetime of a Thain process

- `trace_id`: Identifies a logical interaction trace

- `turn_id`: Identifies an individual agent turn within a run

Currently, these identifiers serve a structural purpose only. No behavior depends on them yet. Their separation allows flexibility: runs may include multiple turns, traces can be grouped or replayed, and individual turns can be audited independently.

Source   Chapter 6 → Part A → thain → observability → trace_ids.py (create)

Core Enforcement Mechanics (Key Excerpts)

1. UUID-Based Run and Trace Identity

Run and trace identifiers use UUID4 to ensure global uniqueness across processes and restarts. The run ID persists for the lifetime of the process; the trace ID is unique per interaction. See Listing 6-1a for the implementation.

Listing 6-1a. Run and trace ID generators (observability/trace_ids.py).

```
def new_run_id() -> str:
    return uuid.uuid4().hex
def new_trace_id() -> str:
    return uuid.uuid4().hex
```

2. Monotonic Turn Sequencing

Turn identity uses a process-scoped counter rather than a UUID. This ensures turns within a run are strictly ordered and can be correlated by sequence number. See Listing 6-1b.

Listing 6-1b. Monotonic turn counter (observability/trace_ids.py)

```
_TURN_COUNTER = itertools.count(1)
def new_turn_id() -> int:
    return next(_TURN_COUNTER)
```

Architectural Results

- Run IDs are globally unique across sessions, while turn IDs increase sequentially within each process.

- All IDs are generated at a single point and then propagated. IDs are not regenerated during a turn.

- Restarting the process resets the turn counter, so turn IDs are relative to the process lifetime rather than global.

Safe Payload Handling by Default

Tracing is only valuable when it can be safely retained. Instead of aiming for perfect redaction rules initially, Part A sets a defensive baseline: every payload in the trace is guaranteed to be JSON serializable and size limited. The `redaction.py` module provides the following guarantees:

- All values are JSON serializable.

- Long strings are truncated to a fixed maximum length.

- Nested structures are recursively processed.

- Unknown or complex objects are converted to strings and truncated.

This module is not a security policy engine. It acts as a safety measure to prevent tracing from inadvertently logging large payloads, raw prompts, or unexpected objects.

In Part B, this approach will develop into explicit must-log and must-not-log rules. For now, it provides a safe foundation.

Source   Chapter 6 → Part A → thain → observability → redaction.py (create)

Core Enforcement Mechanics (Key Excerpts)

1. Truncation Primitive

All strings captured in trace payloads are passed through a fixed-length truncation before they leave the recorder. See Listing 6-2a.

Listing 6-2a. String truncation primitive (observability/redaction.py)

```python
_MAX_STR_LEN = 200
def _truncate(text: str, limit: int = _MAX_STR_LEN) -> str:
    if len(text) <= limit:
        return text
    return text[:limit] + "..."
```

2. Recursive Safe Payload Reduction

Truncation is applied recursively to all structures, including dicts, lists, and scalars, ensuring no nested content exceeds the size limit. See Listing 6-2b.

Listing 6-2b. Recursive payload reduction (observability/redaction.py)

```python
def redact_payload(value: Any) -> Any:
    if value is None:
        return None
    if isinstance(value, (int, float, bool)):
        return value
    if isinstance(value, str):
        return _truncate(value)
    if isinstance(value, dict):
        return {str(key): redact_payload(val) for key, val in value.
        items()}
    if isinstance(value, (list, tuple)):
        return [redact_payload(item) for item in value]
    return _truncate(str(value))
```

Architectural Results

- All string values are bounded before emission, ensuring no unbounded payloads reach the trace sink.

- Recursive processing ensures all nested structures, such as dicts and lists, are fully sanitized.

- Primitive types, including int, float, and bool, pass through unchanged, preventing unnecessary truncation of numeric data.

Event Model and Recorder

With identity and safe payload handling in place, we can now define the core tracing abstraction. The TraceRecorder is a lightweight, in-memory event collector that captures a deterministic sequence of events during a single agent turn.

Each recorded event is immutable. Events include a strictly increasing sequence number, a UTC timestamp, the event type, and execution identifiers that link them to a specific run, trace, and turn. Recording and emission are intentionally decoupled; the recorder collects events during the turn and emits the completed trace as structured JSON at the end.

Source   Chapter 6 → Part A → thain → observability → tracing.py (create)

Core Enforcement Mechanics (Key Excerpts)

1. Immutable Event Contract

TraceEvent is a frozen dataclass. Once created, it cannot be modified. The seq field enforces strict ordering; no two events share the same sequence number within a turn. See Listing 6-3a.

Listing 6-3a. Immutable trace event model (observability/tracing.py)

```python
@dataclass(frozen=True)
class TraceEvent:
    seq: int
    ts: str
    type: str
    run_id: str
    trace_id: str
    turn_id: int
    data: dict[str, Any]
```

2. Strictly Sequenced, Append-Only Capture

record() increments the sequence counter before constructing the event, ensuring ordering is determined at the point of capture, not at emission. Events are appended to an in-memory list and never mutated. See Listing 6-3b.

Listing 6-3b. Append-only event recorder (observability/tracing.py)

```python
def record(self, event_type: str, data: dict[str, Any]) -> None:
    self._seq += 1
    event = TraceEvent(
        seq=self._seq,
        ts=datetime.now(timezone.utc).isoformat(),
        type=event_type,
        run_id=self.run_id,
        trace_id=self.trace_id,
        turn_id=self.turn_id,
        data=data,
    )
    self._events.append(event)
```

3. Decoupled Emission

emit() serializes the collected events to JSON and optionally writes to a file path. Emission is independent of recording; the recorder continues to accept events after an emit call. See Listing 6-3c.

Listing 6-3c. Decoupled trace emission (observability/tracing.py)

```python
def emit(self, path: str | None = None) -> str:
    payload = json.dumps(self.to_dict(), ensure_ascii=False, indent=2)
    if path:
        target = Path(path)
        target.parent.mkdir(parents=True, exist_ok=True)
        target.write_text(payload, encoding="utf-8")
    return payload
```

Architectural Results

- Events are immutable once recorded. No post-hoc modification is possible.

- Sequence numbers are assigned at record time. Event ordering reflects the sequence of agent decisions.

- Serialization is decoupled from recording. The event log can be exported at any point without affecting the recorded sequence.

Emitting Traces via Pluggable Sinks

Recording events is only part of the tracing life cycle; traces must also be emitted to a destination. A sink receives a completed trace and determines how it is persisted or forwarded. By isolating emission behind a protocol, tracing can later target Azure Storage, Application Insights, or other platforms without modifying the recorder.

The initial implementation uses a file-based sink. Traces are grouped by run, with one JSON file written per agent turn. File names are deterministic to simplify inspection and correlation.

Source   Chapter 6 → Part A → thain → observability → trace_sinks.py (create)

Core Enforcement Mechanics (Key Excerpts)

1. Pluggable Sink Protocol

The TraceSink Protocol defines the emission contract. Any object with a matching emit() signature satisfies the protocol; inheritance is not required. See Listing 6-4a.

Listing 6-4a. Pluggable sink protocol (observability/trace_sinks.py)

```
class TraceSink(Protocol):
    def emit(self, trace: dict[str, Any]) -> str:
        ...
```

2. Deterministic File Path Construction

`FileTraceSink.emit()` derives the output path directly from the trace context, ensuring each file is uniquely and predictably named. A failed or replayed turn always resolves to the same path. See Listing 6-4b.

Listing 6-4b. Deterministic trace file output (observability/trace_sinks.py)

```python
def emit(self, trace: dict[str, Any]) -> str:
    context = trace.get("context", {})
    run_id = context.get("run_id", "run")
    trace_id = context.get("trace_id", "trace")
    turn_id = context.get("turn_id", "turn")
    target_dir = self._output_dir / f"run_{run_id}"
    target_dir.mkdir(parents=True, exist_ok=True)
    path = target_dir / f"trace_{trace_id}_turn_{turn_id}.json"
    path.write_text(
        __import__("json").dumps(trace, ensure_ascii=False, indent=2),
        encoding="utf-8"
    )
    return str(path)
```

Architectural Results

- The sink interface is defined as a structural contract rather than a base class. Any object that conforms to the expected signature qualifies, no explicit inheritance required.

- File paths are deterministic given the same context IDs, allowing traces to be located without a registry.

- Switching from a file-based to a remote sink requires no changes to the recorder or agent loop.

Integrating Tracing

With the tracing foundation in place, the next step is to integrate it into Thain's execution flow.

Tracing is intentionally non-invasive. We do not modify individual tools or agent logic. Instead, tracing is applied at the two most critical boundaries:

- The interaction life cycle (`request -> response`)

- The tool boundary (`tool.call -> tool.result`)

Source   Chapter 6 → Part A → thain → main.py (update)

Core Enforcement Mechanics (Key Excerpts)

1. Create a Stable Run Identifier

Each trace must be linked to a broader execution context. RUN_ID is generated once at module load and shared across all turns during the process lifetime. All per-turn recorders reference this ID, allowing the entire session to be traced as a single run without requiring coordination between turns. See Listing 6-5a.

Listing 6-5a. Global RUN_ID (main.py)

```
RUN_ID = new_run_id()
```

2. Tool-Wrapping Helpers

To trace tool usage without modifying individual tool implementations, two helpers wrap tools at the registration boundary. `_tool_name()` provides a stable, human-readable identifier for each tool. `_wrap_tool()` intercepts only `AIFunction` tools by replacing `tool.func` with a `traced()` closure that records a `tool.call` event before execution and a `tool.result` event after, capturing execution duration for both success and error paths.

Before recording, `customer_message` and `summary` arguments are replaced with their lengths to prevent customer content from entering the trace. The wrapper also detects failures signaled by return values, recording them as structured error events and returning an empty result to the agent.

Key enforcement mechanics of the `traced()` closure are shown in Listing 6-5b. The `search.py` update in the next section demonstrates how tools produce the failure signal detected by the wrapper.

Listing 6-5b. Tool intercept (main.py)

```python
@functools.wraps(original)
async def traced(*args: Any, **kwargs: Any) -> Any:
    redacted_args = redact_payload(kwargs)
    recorder.record("tool.call", {"tool_name": name, "args":
    redacted_args})
    start = time.perf_counter()
    try:
        result = original(*args, **kwargs)
        if inspect.isawaitable(result):
            result = await result
    except Exception as exc:
        duration_ms = max(1, int((time.perf_counter() - start) * 1000))
        recorder.record("tool.result", {
            "tool_name": name,
            "status": "error",
            "duration_ms": duration_ms,
            "error_type": type(exc).__name__,
        })
        raise
    duration_ms = max(1, int((time.perf_counter() - start) * 1000))
    recorder.record("tool.result", {
        "tool_name": name,
        "status": "ok",
        "duration_ms": duration_ms,
        "result": redact_payload(result),
    })
    return result
```

3. Start a Trace Recorder

Each agent interaction requires its own trace context to ensure events are ordered and attributed correctly. A new `TraceRecorder` is created at the start of each `run_thain_agent` call. The first event, `request.received`, captures only safe metadata such as message length and the presence of URLs. No raw user content is included in the trace at this stage. See Listing 6-5c.

Listing 6-5c. Trace recorder initialization and request capture (main.py)

```
trace_id = new_trace_id()
turn_id  = new_turn_id()
recorder = TraceRecorder(run_id=RUN_ID, trace_id=trace_id, turn_id=turn_id)
start_time = time.perf_counter()
has_urls = bool(re.search(r"https?://", customer_message))
recorder.record("request.received", {"message_len": len(customer_message.
strip()), "has_urls": has_urls})
```

4. Wrap Tools Before Creating the Agent

All tools, including classifier, search, and action tools, are wrapped with the same per-turn recorder in a single pass before the agent is constructed. The intercept is applied uniformly at the registration boundary, with no exceptions. See Listing 6-5d.

Listing 6-5d. Wrap tools with tracing (main.py)

```
tools_list = [_wrap_tool(tool, recorder) for tool in tools_list]
```

5. Finalize and Emit the Trace

After the agent completes and the response is normalized, the trace is closed in a single step. Elapsed time is recorded in the trace context, and a `response.ready` event captures summary-level metadata without including the response content. The trace is then emitted as a JSON artifact through the pluggable sink. The `traceId` is attached to the agent response metadata for Dev UI and audit correlation. See Listing 6-5e.

Listing 6-5e. Finalize and emit the trace (main.py).

```python
elapsed_ms = int((time.perf_counter() - start_time) * 1000)
recorder.set_elapsed_ms(elapsed_ms)
recorder.record("response.ready", {
    "category": normalized["category"],
    "summary": "<redacted>",
    "summary_len": len(str(normalized["summary"])),
    "elapsed_ms": elapsed_ms,
})
trace_output_dir = os.getenv("TRACE_OUTPUT_DIR", "traces")
sink = FileTraceSink(trace_output_dir)
trace_path = sink.emit(recorder.to_dict())
recorder.record("trace.emitted", {"path": trace_path})
```

Architectural Results

- The tool intercept is applied uniformly. Every tool is wrapped before the agent is constructed, with no per-tool tracing exceptions.

- Only registered through the MAF's tool decorator are intercepted. Non-conforming tools pass through the wrapper unchanged, preserving composability.

- Run identity is process scoped; trace and turn identity are turn scoped. This scoping hierarchy is enforced by construction rather than convention.

- Both success and exception paths record the tool outcome before returning. All tool interactions are captured in the trace regardless of result.

- The trace identifier is attached to the agent response metadata, allowing Dev UI and audit systems to correlate traces with interactions without querying the file system.

- The sink is resolved from the environment at emission time. Switching to a remote back end requires no changes to the recorder or agent loop.

Failure Visibility at the Tool Boundary

In agentic mode, semantic search relies on external services and may fail due to factors such as misconfiguration, network issues, or service unavailability. Raising an exception from a tool disrupts the conversation flow and exposes infrastructure errors to the user. Instead, the search tool indicates failure through its return value, enabling the tracing wrapper to detect and record the issue without exposing details to the agent or user beyond an empty result.

Source   Chapter 6 → Part A → thain → tools → search.py (update)

Core Enforcement Mechanics (Key Excerpts)

1. Return a Sentinel on Failure

When `search_similar_complaints` catches an exception, it does not re-raise it. Instead, it returns a structured sentinel payload with the error type and failure reason. The tracing wrapper in `_wrap_tool` detects this payload, records a `tool.result` event with `status="error"`, and returns `[ ]` to the agent. This approach maintains graceful behavior and ensures the trace accurately reflects the error. See Listing 6-6.

Listing 6-6. Trace sentinel for semantic search failures (tools/search.py).

```
except Exception as exc:  # avoid raising into the agent; surface empty
    logger.warning("Agentic search tool failed: %s", exc, exc_info=True)
    return [{"_trace_error": {"error_type": type(exc).__name__, "reason":
    "semantic_search_failed"}}]
```

Architectural Results

- External service failures are not exposed to the agent or user. The tool boundary absorbs the exception and returns an empty result.

- The sentinel payload is not user facing. It serves only as a private channel between the tool and the tracing wrapper. No other layer is aware of its structure.

- Failures remain visible in the trace as structured error events. The trace provides an accurate record even when the agent receives no usable result.

- The sentinel contract is local to the tool and its wrapper. No other part of the system inspects or depends on it.

Verifying the Tracing Foundation

With tracing fully integrated into Thain's execution flow, we now have a complete, end-to-end visibility layer in place. Every agent interaction is traced from request receipt through tool execution to final response, producing a single deterministic JSON artifact per turn.

At this stage, no governance rules are enforced and Thain's behavior remains unchanged. The only difference is that its actions are now observable.

We validate the tracing foundation through a set of focused smoke tests using the Dev UI. The purpose of these tests is to confirm that

- A trace is created reliably for a basic interaction, with a single JSON artifact emitted per agent turn.

- Multiple turns within a session generate separate traces, sharing the same `run_id` and incrementing `turn_id` values.

- Sensitive inputs are safely summarized without leaking raw content, including phone numbers, email addresses, and URLs.

- Tool invocations produce corresponding `tool.call` and `tool.result` events, with timing and redacted payloads.

- Tool failures are recorded deterministically, including error type and duration, without disrupting the user experience.

Test 1: Basic Interaction Trace Is Created

This test verifies that a simple user interaction produces a trace artifact with the expected structure.

For Tests 1–3, agentic mode is disabled. These tests validate the tracing infrastructure, including trace creation, turn identity, and payload safety, without tool calls or external dependencies.

Set agentic search mode to off:

```
$env:AZURE_SEARCH_MODE="off"
```

Start the Dev UI

```
python main.py --devui --devui-open
```

Submit a prompt that does not invoke any tools. For example,

```
My refund hasn't arrived after 14 days
```

What to Observe

Terminal

A message similar to

```
Trace written to traces/<run_id>/<trace_id>_<turn_id>.json
```

Trace JSON

A new trace file appears in the `traces/` directory at the path shown in the terminal output.

Verify that the trace contains

- Root-level metadata
    - `schema_version`
    - `context.run_id`
    - `context.trace_id`
    - `context.turn_id`
    - `context.started_at`
- An events array containing at least
    - `request.received`
    - `response.ready`
- Event sequence numbers (seq) start at 1 and increment strictly by 1.

Result

A trace is reliably created for a basic interaction, with deterministic ordering and a single JSON artifact per turn.

Test 2: Multiple Turns Create Separate Traces

This test verifies that each turn in a multi-turn conversation produces a separate trace while sharing a common run context.

Within the same Dev UI session, and using the same conversation as Test 1, submit a second prompt:

```
When can I expect an update on the delayed refund?
```

What to Observe

Terminal

A message similar to

```
Trace written to traces/<run_id>/<trace_id>_<turn_id>.json
```

You will notice that the directory location is the same as in Test 1.

Trace JSON

This trace shares the same `run_id` as the trace created in Test 1.

Each trace has

- A unique `trace_id`

- An incrementing `turn_id` (1, 2)

Result

Multi-turn conversations generate independent traces with a stable run identity and correctly incremented turn identifiers. If you submit a third or fourth message within the same Dev UI session, additional trace files are created with the same `run_id`, a new `trace_id` per turn, and monotonically increasing `turn_id` values.

Test 3: Sensitive Input Is Not Logged

This test ensures that raw user content, including PII-like data, is never recorded in traces.

In the Dev UI, start a new conversation and submit a prompt containing phone numbers, email addresses, and URLs. For example,

```
My refund still hasn't come through. You can reach me on 0412 000 000 or
example.user@example.com. I've added the details at https://example.com/
refund-details.
```

What to Observe

Dev UI: The agent should respond normally without errors or warnings.
Terminal
A message similar to

```
Trace written to traces/<run_id>/<trace_id>_<turn_id>.json
```

The trace is written under the same run directory as Tests 1 and 2, since the same Dev UI session is used. The trace shares the same run_id, with a new trace_id and an incremented turn_id, consistent with Test 2 behavior.
Trace JSON

- request.received.data contains only safe metadata, such as

    - message_len

    - has_urls

- No raw phone numbers, email addresses, or URLs should appear anywhere in the trace.

- Any recorded strings are truncated and redacted.

- Response summaries are recorded as <redacted>.

Result
Tracing captures only structural metadata and never exposes raw user input, establishing a secure and privacy-safe baseline for observability.

Test 4: Tool Usage Captured in Traces

This test verifies that tool usage is captured consistently when agentic behavior is enabled.

Before running this test, end the existing Dev UI session and enable agentic mode. Agentic mode is required because tool invocation (e.g., document retrieval or semantic search) is only permitted when the agent is operating with agentic instructions enabled.

Enable agentic mode:

```
$env:AZURE_SEARCH_MODE="agentic"
```

Launch the Dev UI:

```
python main.py --devui --devui-open
```

Submit a prompt that is likely to trigger a tool invocation. For example,

```
During yesterday's shift, the equipment shut down twice and caused a brief
evacuation. What's the standard procedure we should follow?
```

What to Observe

Dev UI: Tool execution appears in the Tools panel, with `retrieve_docs` being invoked.
Terminal
A message similar to

```
Trace written to traces/<run_id>/<trace_id>_<turn_id>.json
```

Since this test is executed in a new Dev UI session, the trace is written under a new run directory with a different `run_id`.
Trace JSON

- A tool.call event containing

- `tool_name`

- redacted arguments

- A corresponding tool.result event containing

- `status: "ok"`

- `duration_ms` greater than zero

- redacted or summarized result data

- No raw document content is logged. Only identifiers or summaries are recorded.

Result

Each tool invocation produces a clear, ordered `tool.call` → `tool.result` pair in the trace, confirming that tool usage is captured deterministically without exposing sensitive content.

Test 5: Tool Failures Are Recorded Without Disrupting the User

This test verifies that tool failures are visible in traces while remaining non-disruptive to the user experience.

Before running this test, end the existing Dev UI session and keep agentic mode enabled. Agentic mode is required because semantic search is only invoked when the agent is operating in agentic mode.

Intentionally misconfigure the semantic search endpoint to simulate an external dependency failure. For example,

```
$env:AZURE_SEARCH_ENDPOINT="https://invalid.invalid"
```

Launch the Dev UI again:

```
python main.py --devui --devui-open
```

Submit a prompt that triggers semantic search, for example,

```
The equipment shut down twice yesterday caused a brief evacuation. Have
there been similar incidents recently?
```

What to Observe

Dev UI

- The agent completes its response normally.

- No infrastructure or configuration error is shown to the user.

Terminal

A message similar to

```
Trace written to traces/<run_id>/<trace_id>_<turn_id>.json
```

Since this test is executed in a new Dev UI session, the trace is written under a new run directory with a different `run_id`, consistent with the behavior observed in Test 4.

Trace JSON

The emitted trace captures the underlying failure in a structured and auditable format.

- A `tool.call` event is recorded.

- A corresponding `tool.result` event follows with

- `status: "error"`

- `error_type` populated

- `duration_ms` present

The trace truthfully reflects the failure, even though the user-facing experience remains graceful.

Figure 6-1 shows the Dev UI during this scenario.

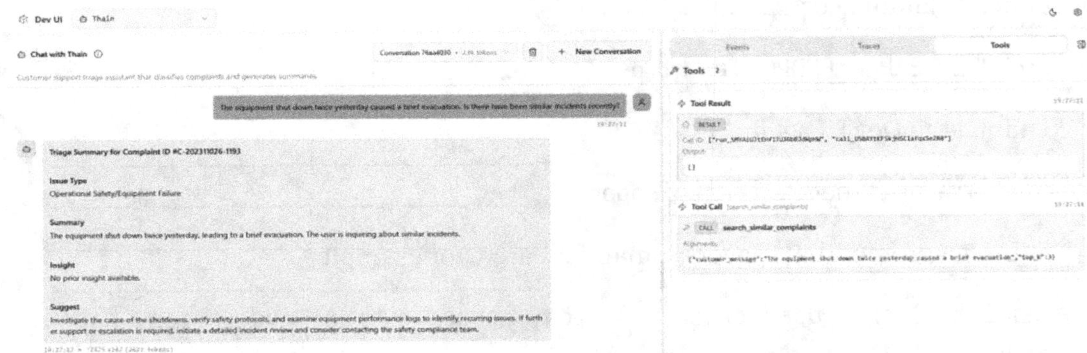

Figure 6-1. *Dev UI – user experience uninterrupted on failure*

Result

Tool failures are recorded deterministically without breaking conversation flow, completing the observability loop.

After completing this test, restore the correct Azure Search configuration by removing the overridden environment variable:

```
Remove-Item Env:AZURE_SEARCH_ENDPOINT
```

This concludes the test suite for Part A. Collectively, these checks demonstrate the core objective of this section; we can now observe Thain's actions for every interaction in a clear and deterministic manner.

With this foundation, Thain's actions are transparent. Each action leaves a structured, auditable trail, setting the stage for governance, policy enforcement, and control boundaries in Part B.

Note   The trace JSON files from these tests are available for reference in the book's product repository under Chapter 6 → Part A → Test Traces. These artifacts are provided for further review and deep inspection.

Part B: The Governance Layer

Observability alone is not sufficient to earn trust. In Part A, Thain achieved full observability, with every tool call, decision, and failure generating a structured trace. However, observability only reports events; it does not restrict what may occur.

Part B introduces a governance layer that operates independently of the language model and precedes tool execution. This layer enforces deterministic rules for tool usage, logging, and safety signals without changing the user experience or relying on prompt discipline. The goal is architectural enforcement: defining clear system boundaries that control which actions are permitted and how sensitive information is handled.

Canonical Tool Identity

Effective governance depends on stable boundaries. Tool names alone are insufficient because they reveal implementation-specific details instead of stable semantic intent.

This module introduces a canonical tool identity layer that assigns each tool name to a semantic kind, such as read, retrieve, ticket, or notify, so that policies can be written against kinds rather than names. See Listing 6-7.

Source   Chapter 6 → Part B → thain → governance → tool_kinds.py (create)

Listing 6-7. Canonical tool kind mapping (governance/tool_kinds.py)

```python
TOOL_KIND_MAP: dict[str, str] = {
    "classify_issue": "read",
    "search_similar_complaints": "retrieve",
    "retrieve_docs": "read",
    "create_ticket": "ticket",
    "notify_team": "notify",
}
def get_tool_kind(tool_name: str) -> str:
    return TOOL_KIND_MAP.get(tool_name, "other")
```

Architectural Results

- Policies are defined by tool kinds rather than specific function names. This approach ensures governance rules remain consistent even if tools are renamed, replaced, or expanded.

- The tools `classify_issue` and `retrieve_docs` both use the read kind, allowing a single policy to apply to both without duplication.

- Unknown tools default to `other`, enabling the system to manage new or unregistered tools without requiring map updates and preventing failures.

- Kind assignment is a static declaration, with no runtime inference or model involvement.

Safety Signal Detection

Governance decisions require objective, deterministic inputs. This module reviews raw user input and generates structured safety flags: `contains_email`, `contains_phone`, and `contains_url`. These flags are identified using regex matching without model involvement.

Enforcement is not applied at this stage; instead, the flags are provided to the policy engine. Detection and enforcement remain intentionally separate. See Listing 6-8.

Source   Chapter 6 → Part B → thain → governance → safety.py (create)

Listing 6-8. Safety signal detection (governance/safety.py)

```python
_EMAIL_RE = re.compile(r"[A-Z0-9._%+-]+@[A-Z0-9.-]+\.[A-Z]{2,}",
re.IGNORECASE)
_PHONE_RE = re.compile(r"\b(?:\+?\d[\d\s().-]{6,}\d)\b")
_URL_RE = re.compile(r"https?://", re.IGNORECASE)

def detect_safety_flags(text: str) -> list[str]:
    flags: list[str] = []
    if _EMAIL_RE.search(text):
        flags.append("contains_email")
    if _PHONE_RE.search(text):
        flags.append("contains_phone")
    if _URL_RE.search(text):
        flags.append("contains_url")
    return flags
```

Architectural Results

- Detection is deterministic and model independent. The same input always produces the same flags, and no LLM call is required.

- Detection and enforcement are intentionally separated. This module produces signals, which the policy engine consumes. Neither component is aware of the other's internal logic.

- The flag vocabulary serves as the contract between detection and policy. To add a new signal, only a new regex and flag name are required.

- Flags appear in traces alongside tool events, which makes safety signals part of the auditable record without the need for a separate logging path.

Policy Evaluation Engine

The policy engine evaluates each tool invocation before execution and returns a `PolicyDecision` with one of three outcomes: allow, deny, or warn. Each decision records the matched rule identifiers, the enforced rule, and a normalized reason code. This approach produces a structured, auditable result without relying on model output or probabilistic scoring.

Source   Chapter 6 → Part B → thain → governance → policy.py (create)

Core Enforcement Mechanics (Key Excerpts)

1. Governance Contracts

PolicyRule and PolicyDecision are both frozen dataclasses, making the inputs to evaluation and the outputs immutable by design. PolicyRule specifies the targeted tool_kinds and the resulting decision. PolicyDecision provides a complete audit trail, including matched rules, the enforced rule, and the reason code. See Listing 6-9a.

Listing 6-9a. PolicyRule and PolicyDecision (governance/policy.py)

```
@dataclass(frozen=True)
class PolicyRule:
    rule_id: str
    description: str
    decision: str
    tool_kinds: set[str]

@dataclass(frozen=True)
class PolicyDecision:
    decision: str
    matched_rule_ids: list[str]
    enforced_rule_id: str | None
    reason: str
```

2. Evaluation Logic

PolicyEngine.evaluate() unpacks the execution context, including approval state, search mode, safety flags, per-turn write counters, and retrieval evidence. It then applies five deterministic rules before returning a decision. Model output is not inspected at any stage. If multiple rules match, deny takes precedence over warn. See Listing 6-9b.

Listing 6-9b. PolicyEngine rule evaluation (governance/policy.py)

```python
is_write_kind = tool_kind in {"write", "ticket", "notify"}
if is_write_kind and policy_requires_approval and not approvals_enabled:
    deny_ids.append("POL-DENY-001")
if is_write_kind and write_calls_in_turn >= warn_write_threshold:
    warn_ids.append("POL-WARN-001")
# ... additional rules evaluated in the same pattern

if deny_ids:
    return PolicyDecision("deny", matched_ids, deny_ids[0], "policy_
    denied")
if warn_ids:
    return PolicyDecision("warn", matched_ids, warn_ids[0], "policy_warn")
return PolicyDecision("allow", matched_ids, None, "policy_allow")
```

Architectural Results

- Policy decisions are immutable. Once evaluation completes, the decision cannot be modified by the caller.

- Deny takes precedence over warn and warn over allow. Priority is enforced by the return logic structure, not by caller convention.

- Evaluation is purely context driven. No model output is inspected, and the same context always produces the same decision.

- The five built-in rules cover approval gating, mode-restricted retrieval, PII-flagged writes, high-frequency write warnings, and evidence-free actions. Each rule is independently testable.

Note   In this chapter, the core governance rules are implemented directly inside `PolicyEngine.evaluate()` so that the behavior remains fully deterministic and easy to inspect. `default_policy_rules()` is intentionally left empty and serves only as an extension hook for externally supplied policies in later production scenarios. In production, rules are usually externalized and injected at startup, for example, via Azure App Configuration or a dedicated policy store. This approach allows enforcement logic to evolve without redeployment. This pattern is discussed in the "Future Enterprise Extensions" section in Chapter 8.

Logging Governance

Unrestricted observability presents risks. Part A ensures comprehensive logging, while Part B restricts logging to permitted fields only. This module defines explicit allowlists for each trace event type, ensuring that only authorized fields are included in the audit record, regardless of what the recorder captures.

Source   Chapter 6 → Part B → thain → governance → logging_policy.py (create)

Core Enforcement Mechanics (Key Excerpts)

1. Event-Level Allowlist

_ALLOWED_FIELDS defines the complete logging policy as a static declaration of which fields may be stored for each event type. Any field not listed is silently dropped before the payload is processed. See Listing 6-10a.

Listing 6-10a. Event-level logging allowlist (governance/logging_policy.py)

```
_ALLOWED_FIELDS: dict[str, set[str]] = {
    "request.received": {"message_len", "has_urls", "safety_flags"},
    "policy.check": {"tool_name", "tool_kind", "decision", "matched_rule_
    ids", "enforced_rule_id", "reason"},
    "tool.call": {"tool_name", "args"},
    "tool.result": {"tool_name", "status", "duration_ms", "error_type",
    "result"},
    "response.ready": {"category", "summary", "summary_len", "elapsed_ms"},
    "trace.emitted": {"path"},
}
```

2. Policy Application

`apply_log_policy()` enforces the allowlist when events are emitted. Unknown event types return an empty `dict`, with no partial or fallback logging. This policy is applied after redaction. Redaction ensures payloads are safe to serialize, while the logging policy determines what may be stored. See Listing 6-10b.

Listing 6-10b. Policy application (governance/logging_policy.py)

```python
def apply_log_policy(event_type: str, payload: Any) -> dict[str, Any]:
    if not isinstance(payload, dict):
        return {}
    allowed = _ALLOWED_FIELDS.get(event_type)
    if not allowed:
        return {}
    return {key: payload[key] for key in payload if key in allowed}
```

Architectural Results

- The allowlist serves as the complete logging policy. No field enters the audit record unless it is explicitly permitted for its event type.

- Unknown event types return an empty dict. Omission is treated as denial, not as a gap.

- The logging policy is applied after redaction, not instead of it. These two layers are complementary and independently enforceable.

- Adding a new event type requires an explicit allowlist entry. There is no default-permit behavior.

Governing the Runtime

Part B integrates governance primitives into the execution loop, establishing four guarantees: tools are categorized by intent, safety signals are captured deterministically, policy decisions are enforced before execution, and all trace events pass through the logging allowlist.

Source   Chapter 6 → Part B → thain → main.py (update)

Core Enforcement Mechanics (Key Excerpts)

1. PolicyEngine Initialization

A single `PolicyEngine` instance is created at module load and shared across all turns.
This ensures model-independent policy evaluation, consistent enforcement across all
tools, and availability to the tool wrapper without per-call initialization or hidden global
state. See Listing 6-11a.

Listing 6-11a. PolicyEngine initialization (main.py)

```
policy_engine = PolicyEngine(default_policy_rules(write_approvals_enabled))
```

2. Centralized Recording Gate

Redaction ensures payloads are safe to serialize, but serialization safety does not
guarantee logging compliance. Instead of updating each `recorder.record()` call, a
single logging gate is introduced.

All trace events pass through `_record_event()`, which applies redaction and the
logging allowlist before writing to the recorder. This makes logging governance structural
rather than reliant on caller convention. See Listing 6-11b.

Listing 6-11b. Centralized trace recording gate (main.py)

```
def _record_event(recorder: TraceRecorder, event_type: str, payload: Any)
-> None:
    safe_payload = apply_log_policy(event_type, redact_payload(payload))
    recorder.record(event_type, safe_payload)
```

3. Policy-Aware Tool Wrapper

The tool boundary is the point where the agent can take action, so policy must be
evaluated and applied here. `_wrap_tool()` is extended with a `policy_state` parameter
scoped to the current turn. Default values are initialized defensively to ensure
deterministic policy evaluation, even if optional fields are not populated.

The per-turn state includes the full governance context required by the rules: approval state, execution mode, safety flags, per-turn write counters, and retrieval evidence signals.

For each tool call, the kind is resolved, policy is evaluated, and the decision is recorded as a `policy.check` event. If the decision is denied, a `tool.result` event with `status="blocked"` is recorded and `[]` is returned. The tool function is not called. The subsequent execution and result-recording logic matches Part A, with all events routed through `_record_event()` for logging compliance. See Listing 6-11c.

Listing 6-11c. Policy-aware tool wrapper (main.py)

```python
def _wrap_tool(tool: Any, recorder: TraceRecorder, policy_state: dict[str,
Any] | None = None) -> Any:
    name = _tool_name(tool)
    if policy_state is None:
        policy_state = {}
    # policy_state defaults: write_calls_in_turn, retrieval_attempted,
    # retrieval_results_count, policy_requires_approval, pii_write_block,
    warn_write_threshold

    @functools.wraps(original)
    async def traced(*args: Any, **kwargs: Any) -> Any:
        tool_kind = get_tool_kind(name)
        if tool_kind in {"write", "ticket", "notify"}:
            policy_state["write_calls_in_turn"] += 1
        policy_decision = policy_engine.evaluate(tool_kind, policy_state)
        _record_event(recorder, "policy.check", {
            "tool_name": name,
            "tool_kind": tool_kind,
            "decision": policy_decision.decision,
            "matched_rule_ids": policy_decision.matched_rule_ids,
            "enforced_rule_id": policy_decision.enforced_rule_id,
            "reason": policy_decision.reason,
        })
        if policy_decision.decision == "deny":
            _record_event(recorder, "tool.result", {
                "tool_name": name,
```

```
            "status": "blocked",
            "duration_ms": 0,
            "error_type": "PolicyDenied",
        })
        return []
    # ... execution, timing, and result recording continue as in Part A
    # All events route through _record_event() for logging compliance
```

4. Turn-Level Governance Wiring

Three updates to run_thain_agent() connect the governance layer to the turn life cycle.

Safety flags are detected at the request boundary, included in the request.received event, and added to policy_state. The policy_state dictionary serves as the shared governance context for the entire turn, allowing write counters and retrieval evidence to accumulate across all tool calls within the same request. See Listing 6-11d.

Listing 6-11d. Safety detection and policy state construction (main.py)

```
safety_flags = unique_flags(detect_safety_flags(customer_message))
_record_event(recorder, "request.received", {
    "message_len": len(customer_message.strip()),
    "has_urls": has_urls,
    "safety_flags": safety_flags,
})
policy_state = {
    "approvals_enabled": write_approvals_enabled,
    "search_mode": search_mode,
    "safety_flags": safety_flags,
}
```

All tools are wrapped with the same policy_state instance, ensuring write counters and retrieval evidence are shared across the classifier, search, and action tools within a turn. See Listing 6-11e.

Listing 6-11e. Wrap tools with governance context (main.py)

```python
tools_list = [_wrap_tool(tool, recorder, policy_state) for tool in
tools_list]
```

Terminal events are routed through _record_event(), ensuring the logging allowlist applies uniformly to every event that closes the turn. See Listing 6-11f.

Listing 6-11f. Terminal events through the logging gate (main.py)

```python
_record_event(recorder, "response.ready", {
    "category": normalized["category"],
    "summary": "<redacted>",
    "summary_len": len(str(normalized["summary"])),
    "elapsed_ms": elapsed_ms,
})
trace_output_dir = os.getenv("TRACE_OUTPUT_DIR", "traces")
sink = FileTraceSink(trace_output_dir)
trace_path = sink.emit(recorder.to_dict())
_record_event(recorder, "trace.emitted", {"path": trace_path})
```

Tool-level trace events (tool.call, tool.result, and error paths) are governed by the policy-aware wrapper and do not require additional wiring here.

Architectural Results

- Policy evaluation occurs before each tool execution. Denial is enforced before the tool function is called.

- A shared policy state is maintained across all tool calls within a turn, allowing write counters and retrieval evidence to accumulate across multiple tool invocations in the same request.

- A single recording gate ensures redaction and logging allowlists apply uniformly to all trace events, including terminal events.

- Denied tools return an empty result. The denial is visible only in the trace, preserving a smooth conversation flow.

- The governance layer is transparent to the DevUI, so the user-facing experience remains unchanged. Thain implements tool interception through a purpose-built wrapper so that every trace event, policy check, and redaction step is explicit and directly visible in the code. This is precisely what MAF's function middleware provides at the framework level. Having built it explicitly, you now understand exactly what that abstraction is doing and when to trust it.

The next section validates the governance layer using DevUI tests, demonstrating allow, deny, and warn outcomes in both the user interface and the generated trace.

Verifying the Governance Layer

With governance integrated into Thain's execution flow, we validate that policy enforcement operates deterministically at runtime and does not disrupt the user experience.

We validate the governance layer using targeted Dev UI tests. Each test demonstrates a specific policy outcome and confirms that

- Tool execution is allowed, warned, or denied as intended.

- User-facing behavior remains stable and predictable.

- Governance decisions are recorded deterministically in trace artifacts.

- Blocked actions are first-class audit events, not silent failures.

Test 1: Write Action Blocked When Approvals Are Disabled

This test verifies that write actions are denied deterministically when approvals are required but not enabled. Ensure agentic mode is disabled and write approvals are turned off.

```
$env:AZURE_SEARCH_MODE="off"
$env:ENABLE_WRITE_APPROVALS="false"
```

Agentic mode is disabled so the test focuses solely on governance of write actions, without involving retrieval or agentic tool behavior. Write approvals are also disabled to ensure the policy engine follows a deny path, allowing us to validate deterministic enforcement without agent reasoning or search execution.

Start the Dev UI:

```
python main.py --devui --devui-open
```

Prompt

```
Create a ticket for a delayed refund issue.
```

What to Observe

Dev UI

- The agent responds normally.

- No ticket is created.

Terminal

Expect a message similar to

```
Trace written to traces/<run_id>/<trace_id>_<turn_id>.json
```

Trace JSON

Review the emitted trace and verify the following:

- A `policy.check` event exists for the write tool.

- The policy decision is `deny`.

- A corresponding `tool.result` event is present with `status: "blocked"`.

- A `response.ready` event is still emitted.

Result

Write actions are blocked clearly at the policy layer without disrupting conversation flow. The denial is fully recorded in the trace.

Test 2: High-Frequency Write Actions Produce a Warning

This test confirms that repeated write actions within a single turn are permitted but appropriately flagged. We enable write approvals so write actions can proceed.

```
$env:ENABLE_WRITE_APPROVALS="true"
```

Start the Dev UI:

```
python main.py --devui --devui-open
```

Prompt

```
Create two tickets for the equipment shutdown: one for Ops and one
for Safety.
```

What to Observe

Terminal

- Approval prompts are displayed for each write action.

- Approve all requested actions when prompted.

- After approvals are granted, a message similar to the following
  appears:

  ```
  Trace written to traces/<run_id>/<trace_id>_<turn_id>.json
  ```

Dev UI

- Both tickets are created successfully.

- The user experience is uninterrupted.

Trace JSON

Review the emitted trace and verify the following:

- Two write tool invocations occur.

- A `policy.check` event records a warn decision.

- The warning is associated with high-frequency write behavior.

Result

Governance detects elevated-risk behavior without blocking legitimate multi-action
workflows.

Test 3: PII-Flagged Input Blocks External Notification

This test verifies that PII-like input prevents notify actions, even when the user explicitly
requests them. No environment variable changes are needed for this test. Use the same
environment setup as in Test 2.

Start the Dev UI:

```
python main.py --devui --devui-open
```

Prompt

```
Please notify the team about my delayed refund. You can reach me at
example.user@example.com or 0412 000 000.
```

What to Observe

Dev UI

- The agent responds normally.

- The notification is not sent.

- The response explains that the action cannot proceed.

Terminal

Expect a message similar to

```
Trace written to traces/<run_id>/<trace_id>_<turn_id>.json
```

Trace JSON

Review the emitted trace and verify the following:

- `request.received` includes `safety_flags`, `contains_email` and `contains_phone`

- A `policy.check` event evaluates the notify action.

- The decision is `deny`.

- A `tool.result` event records the notify action as blocked.

Result

PII detection takes place at the request boundary to prevent external side effects. Decisions are enforced transparently and recorded without logging sensitive data.

Test 4: Evidence-Free Write Action Produces an Audit Warning

This test verifies that evidence-free write actions produce a warning. Agentic mode is enabled, allowing the agent to use retrieval tools during its reasoning process. Write approvals are also active, permitting any subsequent write actions.

The search endpoint is intentionally misconfigured to ensure retrieval returns no results. This simulates a real-world scenario where the agent operates without supporting evidence:

```
$env:AZURE_SEARCH_MODE="agentic"
$env:ENABLE_WRITE_APPROVALS="true"
$env:AZURE_SEARCH_ENDPOINT="https://invalid.invalid"
```

This setup clarifies the test's purpose: to confirm that actions taken without evidence are allowed but are explicitly flagged by the governance layer.

Start the Dev UI:

```
python main.py --devui --devui-open
```

Prompt

```
The equipment shut down twice yesterday and caused a brief evacuation.
Check for similar incidents and create a ticket
```

What to Observe

Dev UI

- The agent completes both steps.

- A ticket is created.

- The insight notes that no similar incidents were found.

Terminal

Expect a message similar to

```
Trace written to traces/<run_id>/<trace_id>_<turn_id>.json
```

Trace JSON

Review the emitted trace and verify the following:

- A retrieval tool is invoked and returns no results.

- The write tool executes successfully.

- A policy.check event records a warn decision.

- The trace reflects that the action proceeded without evidence.

Result

The system permits the action and records a clear audit signal indicating that evidence was missing.

Note   The trace JSON files from these tests are available for reference in the book's product repository under Chapter 6 → Part B → Test Traces. These artifacts are provided for further review and deep inspection.

Now that policy controls are in place, we turn to the unpredictable: runtime errors and external failures. Governance prevents unsafe or disallowed actions, but operational failures cannot always be avoided. Part C ensures that every failure is captured, normalized, and fully auditable.

Part C: Resilience and Auditability

In Part B, Thain introduced an explicit governance layer. Tool execution is evaluated against policy, logged deterministically, and either allowed, warned, or denied. However, governance alone is not sufficient for production systems. A reliable agent must also respond predictably to failures, such as external service outages, denied approvals, unexpected tool errors, or interrupted execution.

Part C addresses this by prioritizing failure handling and auditability.

- Error normalization creates a consistent, typed vocabulary for trace events at the observability boundary.

- Guaranteed trace emission ensures each turn produces an auditable artifact, regardless of outcome.

- A lightweight trace replay utility supports post-incident analysis and compliance review.

Error Normalization for Observability

Thain already records tool failures in Part A and policy denials in Part B. What was missing was a consistent error vocabulary across tools, policies, approvals, and orchestration logic. This module introduces a typed error model at the observability boundary. Normalization occurs only when recording trace events, not within business logic. The user experience remains unchanged, but traces now include a stable error_ type field suitable for audits.

Source   Chapter 6 → Part C → thain → governance → errors.py (create)

Core Enforcement Mechanics (Key Excerpts)

1. Error Taxonomy

AgentError is a frozen dataclass and serves as the base contract for all normalized errors. Five typed subclasses correspond to Thain's five failure domains: tool execution, external services, policy denials, approval denials, and timeouts. See Listing 6-12a.

Listing 6-12a. Error taxonomy (governance/errors.py)

```python
@dataclass(frozen=True)
class AgentError:
    error_type: str
    message: str
    stage: str
    tool_name: Optional[str] = None

class ToolExecutionError(AgentError): pass
class PolicyDeniedError(AgentError): pass
class ApprovalDeniedError(AgentError): pass
class ExternalServiceError(AgentError): pass
class TimeoutError(AgentError): pass
```

2. Error Normalization

normalize_error() converts any exception into a typed AgentError using name-based dispatch. The default case returns ToolExecutionError, ensuring all exceptions are captured with a typed record. See Listing 6-12b.

The companion function `normalize_error_info()` applies the same contract to sentinel payloads, so both raised exceptions and signaled failures produce structurally equivalent trace records.

Listing 6-12b. Error normalization (governance/errors.py)

```python
def normalize_error(exc: Exception, stage: str, tool_name: Optional[str] =
None) -> AgentError:
    error_name = type(exc).__name__
    message = str(exc) or error_name
    lowered = error_name.lower()
    if "timeout" in lowered:
        return TimeoutError(error_type=error_name, message=message,
        stage=stage, tool_name=tool_name)
    if error_name in {"SemanticSearchError", "HttpResponseError",
    "ServiceRequestError"}:
        return ExternalServiceError(error_type=error_name, message=message,
        stage=stage, tool_name=tool_name)
    if error_name in {"PolicyDeniedError"}:
        return PolicyDeniedError(error_type=error_name, message=message,
        stage=stage, tool_name=tool_name)
    if error_name in {"ApprovalDeniedError"}:
        return ApprovalDeniedError(error_type=error_name, message=message,
        stage=stage, tool_name=tool_name)

    return ToolExecutionError(error_type=error_name, message=message,
    stage=stage, tool_name=tool_name)
```

Architectural Results

- Error normalization occurs only at the observability boundary. Business logic does not propagate typed errors, and the user experience remains unchanged.

- Error records are immutable once created. They cannot be modified after normalization.

- Five distinct error types map to five failure domains. Traces carry a stable, queryable error classification regardless of the exception type raised.

- The default case ensures every exception produces a typed record; no failure escapes without classification.

- Both raised exceptions and signaled sentinel failures produce structurally equivalent trace records, regardless of how the failure originated.

Stable Trace Path Construction

We introduce a strict requirement: a trace must be emitted even if execution fails. To ensure deterministic and auditable trace emission, we refactor `FileTraceSink` so that trace path construction is managed by a single, reusable helper.

Previously, `emit(...)` handled two responsibilities:

1. Build the target directory + file path.

2. Write the JSON trace to disk.

We now separate these responsibilities as follows:

- `build_path(...)`: Purely constructs the output path deterministically

- `emit(...)`: Writes traces using the shared path builder

This change ensures consistent trace emission for both successful and failed executions. See Listing 6-13.

Source   Chapter 6 → Part C → thain → observability → trace_sinks.py (update)

Listing 6-13. Deterministic trace path construction (observability/trace_sinks.py)

```
def build_path(self, trace: dict[str, Any]) -> Path:
    context = trace.get("context", {})
    run_id = context.get("run_id", "run")
```

```
trace_id = context.get("trace_id", "trace")
turn_id = context.get("turn_id", "turn")
target_dir = self._output_dir / f"run_{run_id}"
target_dir.mkdir(parents=True, exist_ok=True)
return target_dir / f"trace_{trace_id}_turn_{turn_id}.json"
```

Architectural Results

- Traces are organized by run and turn. Artifacts from a single execution session are co-located and remain identifiable across agent restarts.

- Path construction is separated from file I/O. The audit record embeds its own output location before the file is written, creating a self-describing artifact.

- The path computation is isolated from the write operation, making the naming convention independently verifiable without a full agent run.

Resilient Tracing in the Agent Loop

Part C integrates two enforcement behaviors into the agent loop:

1. Failures are normalized at the observability boundary, so traces consistently record a stable error_type, regardless of whether errors come from exceptions or sentinel results.

2. Traces are always emitted, even if orchestration fails mid-turn. This ensures every turn produces an auditable artifact.

Both behaviors are enforced in main.py through the enforcement points shown below.

Source   Chapter 6 → Part C → thain → main.py (update)

Core Enforcement Mechanics (Key Excerpts)

1. Centralized Trace Emitter

`_emit_trace()` centralizes trace emission. It builds the output path, records it in the trace, and then delegates the write to the file sink ensuring the trace embeds its own location before the file is created on disk. See Listing 6-14a.

Listing 6-14a. Centralized trace emitter (main.py)

```python
def _emit_trace(recorder: TraceRecorder) -> str:
    trace_output_dir = os.getenv("TRACE_OUTPUT_DIR", "traces")
    sink = FileTraceSink(trace_output_dir)
    trace_path = str(sink.build_path(recorder.to_dict()))
    _record_event(recorder, "trace.emitted", {"path": trace_path})
    return sink.emit(recorder.to_dict())
```

2. Raised Exception Normalization

When a tool raises an exception, `normalize_error()` converts it to a typed record before the trace event is written. The exception then re-raises, the agent loop receives the raw exception, and the trace record is already committed. See Listing 6-14b.

Listing 6-14b. Raised exception normalization (main.py)

```python
except Exception as exc:
    duration_ms = max(1, int((time.perf_counter() - start) * 1000))
    error = normalize_error(exc, stage="tool", tool_name=name)
    _record_event(
        recorder,
        "tool.result",
        {
            "tool_name": name,
            "status": "error",
            "duration_ms": duration_ms,
            "error_type": error.error_type,
        },
    )
    raise
```

3. Sentinel Failure Normalization

When a tool signals failure through a sentinel payload, `normalize_error_info()` applies the same typed record contract. The sentinel is consumed and a clean result is returned to the agent loop. The failure is captured in the trace without disrupting the conversation. See Listing 6-14c.

Listing 6-14c. Sentinel failure normalization (main.py)

```
if result and isinstance(result[0], dict) and result[0].get("_trace_
error"):
    error_info = result[0].get("_trace_error", {})
    if tool_kind in {"retrieve", "read"} and name in {"search_similar_
    complaints", "retrieve_docs"}:
        policy_state["retrieval_attempted"] = True
        policy_state["retrieval_results_count"] = 0
    error = normalize_error_info(error_info, stage="tool", tool_name=name)
    _record_event(
        recorder,
        "tool.result",
        {
            "tool_name": name,
            "status": "error",
            "duration_ms": duration_ms,
            "error_type": error.error_type,
        },
    )
    return []
```

4. Emission Idempotency Flags

Two boolean flags track whether trace emission and response recording have already occurred. They ensure the `finally` clause does not duplicate events that the success path has already written. See Listing 6-14d.

Listing 6-14d. Emission idempotency flags (main.py)

```
trace_emitted = False
response_ready_recorded = False
normalized: dict[str, Any] | None = None
response: AgentRunResponse | None = None
```

5. Failure-Safe Execution Boundary

The agent loop runs inside a structured execution boundary. Unhandled failures at the orchestration level are normalized and recorded before propagating. The `finally` clause guarantees a trace is written regardless of how the turn ends: by success, by exception, or by any intermediate failure. See Listing 6-14e.

Listing 6-14e. Failure-safe execution boundary(main.py)

```
try:
    # ... agent loop, parse, persistence ...
    return normalized, response
except Exception as exc:
    error = normalize_error(exc, stage="run")
    _record_event(recorder, "error.occurred", {
        "error_type": error.error_type, ...
    })
    raise
finally:
    if not trace_emitted:
        recorder.set_elapsed_ms(int((time.perf_counter() - start_time)
        * 1000))
        if normalized is not None and not response_ready_recorded:
            _record_event(recorder, "response.ready", { ... })
        trace_path = _emit_trace(recorder)
        print(f"Trace written to {trace_path}")
```

6. Success-Path Trace Emission

On the success path, both flags are set after their respective events are written. The `finally` clause detects this and skips re-emission, keeping the audit record clean. See Listing 6-14f.

Listing 6-14f. Success-path trace emission(main.py)

```python
response_ready_recorded = True
trace_path = _emit_trace(recorder)
trace_emitted = True
print(f"Trace written to {trace_path}")
```

Architectural Results

- Tool failures, whether raised or signaled, are normalized and recorded before the exception propagates or the sentinel is consumed.

- Run-level orchestration failures are distinguished from tool failures. Each failure domain produces a separate, typed audit event.

- Trace emission for every turn is guaranteed, regardless of outcome. No turn is silently lost.

- Duplicate events on the success path are prevented by design. The audit record remains clean regardless of which execution path completes the turn.

With normalized failure behavior, guaranteed traces, and deterministic recording of orchestration errors, Thain's execution model is now complete. Each decision path, whether successful, denied, or failed, produces a stable, auditable trace artifact.

The final step is to verify these guarantees in practice. In the next section, we validate Part C using targeted Dev UI driven tests.

Verifying Failure Modes and Audit Guarantees

With failure normalization and guaranteed trace emission in place, we are validating Thain's behavior in controlled failure scenarios.

These tests are designed to confirm the following:

- Failures are recorded deterministically.

- Governance outcomes (deny/blocked) are distinguished from runtime errors.

- Traces are always emitted, even when execution is interrupted.

- The user experience remains stable and non-disruptive.

All tests are run using the Dev UI. Validation is completed by inspecting the emitted trace JSON files.

Test 1: External Service Failure Traceability

This test confirms that failures from external dependencies are consistently recorded in the trace without affecting the agent's response.

Enable agentic mode and configure the semantic search endpoint to an invalid address:

```
$Env:AZURE_SEARCH_MODE="agentic"
$Env:AZURE_SEARCH_ENDPOINT="https://invalid.invalid"
```

Semantic search tools, such as `search_similar_complaints`, are only used when the agent is in agentic mode. This test validates tool-level failure handling and trace emission for retrieval failures.

Start the Dev UI:

```
python main.py --devui --devui-open
```

Prompt

```
The equipment shut down twice yesterday caused a brief evacuation. Have
there been similar incidents recently?
```

What to Observe

Dev UI

- `search_similar_complaints` is invoked.

- The agent responds gracefully despite the failure.

Terminal

Expect a message similar to

```
Trace written to traces/<run_id>/<trace_id>_<turn_id>.json
```

Trace JSON

Confirm that the trace includes the following:

- A `policy.check` event for the retrieval tool

- A `tool.result` event with

- `status: "error"`

- a populated `error_type` (e.g., `SemanticSearchError`)

- A `response.ready` event

- A `trace.emitted` event

Result

External service failures are consistently recorded in the trace without impacting the user experience, meeting the audit requirements.

After completing this test, restore the correct Azure Search configuration by removing the overridden environment variable:

```
Remove-Item Env:AZURE_SEARCH_ENDPOINT
```

Test 2: Policy-Denied Action Is Fully Audited

This test makes sure that governance-level denials are enforced and recorded correctly and are not mistaken for runtime failures.

Ensure agentic mode remains enabled and disable write approvals:

```
$Env:AZURE_SEARCH_MODE="agentic"
$Env:ENABLE_WRITE_APPROVALS="false"
```

Agentic mode is enabled because ticket creation is part of the agentic workflow. This ensures the agent attempts the write action instead of stopping earlier. Write approvals must be disabled to force the policy engine to follow a deterministic deny path, which allows us to validate policy enforcement separately from approval workflows.

Start the Dev UI:

```
python main.py --devui --devui-open
```

Prompt

```
My refund was delayed by 14 days. Please create a ticket.
```

What to Observe

Dev UI

- The agent responds normally.

- No ticket is created.

Terminal

Expect a message similar to

```
Trace written to traces/<run_id>/<trace_id>_<turn_id>.json
```

Trace JSON

Confirm that the trace includes the following:

- A `policy.check` event with

- `decision:"deny"`

- A `tool.result` event with

- `status: "blocked"`

- `error_type: "PolicyDenied"`

- A `response.ready` event

- A `trace.emitted` event

Result

Governance reliably prevents write actions, and any denial is fully auditable without interrupting the conversation.

Test 3: Approval Denial Is Recorded Separately from Policy Denial

This test confirms that approval denial is recognized as a separate outcome and is accurately documented in the trace.

Ensure agentic mode remains enabled and enable write approvals:

```
$Env:AZURE_SEARCH_MODE="agentic"
$Env:ENABLE_WRITE_APPROVALS="true"
```

Write approvals are enabled so the policy engine can permit the action, ensuring any denial happens at the approval boundary instead of the policy layer.

Start the Dev UI:

```
python main.py --devui --devui-open
```

Prompt

```
My refund was delayed by 14 days. Please create a ticket.
```

What to Observe

Dev UI

- The tool is called.

- The agent reports that approval was not granted.

- No ticket is created.

Terminal

- During execution, an approval prompt is displayed in the terminal.

- `Approve write action 'create_ticket'? (y/n):`

- Enter: `n`

- After rejecting the approval, expect a message similar to

  `Trace written to traces/<run_id>/<trace_id>_<turn_id>.json`

Trace JSON

Confirm that the trace includes the following:

- A `policy.check` event with
- `decision:"allow"`
- A `tool.result` event with
- `status: "ok"`
- `approved: false`
- `reason: "approval_not_provided"`
- A `response.ready` event
- A `trace.emitted` event

Result

Approval denial is recorded explicitly and independently of policy enforcement, while trace emission remains guaranteed.

- The approval interaction is intentional and driven by the user.
- Denial occurs at the approval boundary, rather than due to policy or runtime failure.
- A trace is still emitted after rejection.

Test Summary

Across all three tests, Thain demonstrates predictable, auditable behavior under failure conditions:

- External failures are handled without disrupting the user experience.
- Policy denials and approval denials are clearly differentiated.
- Traces are consistently generated, regardless of execution outcome.

This fulfills the trust and failure guarantees outlined in Part C and finalizes Thain v0.5's observability and audit model. Together, all three parts complete Thain v0.5's trust model. Every failure path is now transparent, auditable, and unambiguous.

Note   The trace JSON files from these tests are available for reference in the book's product repository under Chapter 6 → Part C → Test Traces. These artifacts are provided for further review and deep inspection.

Audit and Trace Replay Utilities

Thain v0.5 also provides lightweight audit helpers for post-incident analysis and compliance review, complementing its runtime governance and failure handling features.

These utilities run independently of the live agent execution path. They are designed for operators, SREs, and auditors who need a clear, human-readable summary of a specific agent turn without reviewing raw trace JSON.

The main utility is a trace replay tool that reads a single trace artifact and generates a summarized execution narrative, including

- Policy decisions (deny/warn)

- Tool invocations and outcomes

- Approval results

- Normalized failures and error types

- The final agent response

The replay utility is run from the command line and does not interact with agent execution or tracing:

```
python -m audit.trace_replay <trace.json>
```

The audit/__init__.py file declares the audit helpers as a Python package for CLI use. It is not imported or referenced by the agent runtime.

Figure 6-2 presents a sample trace reviewed with the audit tool, using data from my test in Part B, Test 3.

```
PS C:\AIAA\thain> python -m audit.trace_replay traces\run_427d931e881e4042a59918e410fb18bd\trace_f901ec9f513c4502b187a45f5abaf065_turn_1.json
Trace f901ec9f513c4502b187a45f5abaf065 (turn 1) schema=0.1 elapsed_ms=65356
Tool results:
- classify_issue: ok
- create_ticket: ok approved=False
Response: category=General Inquiry summary_len=56, elapsed_ms=65356
PS C:\AIAA\thain>
```

Figure 6-2. *Trace reviewed with the audit tool*

You can select any trace from the test runs in this chapter, replay it, and quickly see the agent's actions, the tools used, and how governance or failure paths were applied. This process does not require manual JSON parsing.

In production, these audit utilities are typically adapted to work with centralized trace storage, such as Azure Blob Storage, Azure Monitor Logs, or Application Insights. Trace replay and summarization can be implemented as an internal CLI, an Azure Function, or a dashboard-driven workflow. No changes to the agent runtime are required to support these scenarios, as the trace format and normalization described in this chapter are platform agnostic.

Thain v0.5 Trust Architecture

Figure 6-3 shows Thain v0.5's complete trust architecture. The three enforcement layers – tracing, governance, and error normalization – are composed around a shared trace recorder. Every tool invocation passes through the policy engine before execution, and every outcome, whether success, denial, or failure, is recorded through a single logging filter. Trace emission is guaranteed regardless of outcome.

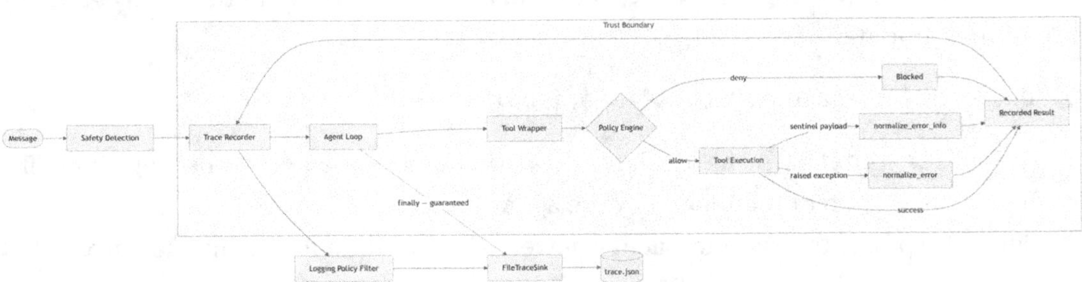

Figure 6-3. *Thain v0.5 trust architecture – tracing, governance, and guaranteed audit*

Runtime Scope and Deployment Mapping

The tracing, governance, and failure-handling mechanisms described in this chapter are implemented entirely within Thain's runtime by design.

This chapter focuses on establishing deterministic trust boundaries for visibility, control, and auditability, independent of hosting model or deployment platform. Managing these concerns in process ensures Thain's behavior is consistent, testable, and reproducible across environments.

In real-world Azure deployments, these capabilities typically map as follows:

- **Part A (tracing)**: Structured JSON traces can be streamed to Azure Monitor, Application Insights, or Log Analytics. Raw trace artifacts may also be stored in Blob Storage for offline audit.

- **Part B (governance)**: Policy decisions and safety flags execute in process and are emitted as trace events. These events can be forwarded to Application Insights or Log Analytics for audit and alerting.

- **Part C (audit and replay)**: Trace replay operates on exported trace artifacts from Blob Storage or Log Analytics. This process may be implemented as an internal tool or lightweight service.

Deployment-specific concerns and production hardening are discussed in Chapter 8 without re-implementing the trust mechanisms defined here.

Note   Unit test files for Parts A (tracing), B (governance), and C (failure handling) are included in the Chapter 6 folder of the book's GitHub repository: `https://github.com/Apress/Architecting-Intelligent-Agents-in-Azure`.

The final project state for this chapter is also in the repository: to set up the repository locally, use the following commands:

```
git clone https://github.com/Apress/Architecting-
Intelligent-Agents-in-Azure.git

cd Architecting-Intelligent-Agents-in-Azure
```

For the manuscript code, open the Chapter 6/Part C/thain folder. For the GA code, open Code GA/Chapter 6/Part C/thain. Replace Part C with Part B or Part A to work with an earlier part.

After cloning, create and activate a virtual environment, and then install the dependencies:

```
python -m venv .venv
.\.venv\Scripts\activate
pip install -r requirements.txt -c constraints.txt
```

Before running the project, update your `.env` file with the necessary Azure settings and feature flags. You may also browse the repository online to review the reference implementation.

Summary

In this chapter, Thain advances to version 0.5, establishing the architectural foundations necessary for trusting an autonomous agent in production.

With structured tracing, explicit governance, and deterministic failure handling, Thain's execution is now fully observable and auditable. Every decision is traceable, every boundary is enforced, and every failure is recorded clearly.

Trust is built not by preventing failure but by ensuring failures are understandable, controlled, and explainable. This chapter enables Thain to meet that standard.

Importantly, these trust, governance, and audit mechanisms are designed to be shared infrastructure, allowing multiple agents to plug into the same control and observability layer as Thain scales beyond a single actor.

In the next chapter, Thain evolves beyond operating as a single agent. The focus shifts from individual decision-making to collaboration and orchestration, as multiple specialized agents coordinate, share memory, and divide responsibilities through Microsoft Agent Framework workflows. Thain becomes not just a trusted agent but a trusted team.

Architectural Outcomes

With trust, governance, and failure layers established, Thain's architecture now provides the following capabilities:

- Deterministic observability for every agent turn, with a single structured trace artifact generated per interaction, regardless of outcome

- Explicit governance boundaries that assess each tool invocation against policy, approval, and safety requirements before execution

- Clear separation between governance outcomes and failures, ensuring policy denials, approval rejections, and runtime errors are recorded distinctly and never conflated

- Guaranteed trace emission, even if execution is interrupted or an unhandled error occurs, ensuring no decision path is lost

- Normalized failure semantics, with tool errors, external service failures, and orchestration issues classified consistently and recorded in an auditable format

- Non-disruptive user experience, enabling failures and denials to be handled gracefully without exposing infrastructure details or interrupting conversation flow

- Post-hoc auditability, allowing operators and investigators to reconstruct events during an agent turn using trace replay and structured event history

- Production-ready trust boundaries that treat observability, governance, approvals, and failure handling as core architectural concerns rather than optional features

Together, these outcomes elevate Thain from a capable agent to a trustworthy system whose decisions can be inspected, explained, and defended.

Thain Learns to Collaborate

Introduction

Until now, Thain has functioned as an effective individual contributor. In earlier chapters, we enabled the agent to reason about feedback, remember past interactions, retrieve relevant context, invoke tools, and operate within defined trust and governance boundaries.

However, enterprise intelligence rarely operates as a single reasoning loop. Real decisions emerge from multiple perspectives: safety checks, intent interpretation, evidence gathering, policy constraints, and operational execution. While a single agent can identify issues and suggest responses, asking a single reasoning loop to balance all these concerns introduces competing priorities and makes consistent enforcement difficult as systems grow in scope.

At this stage, collaboration becomes a primary architectural focus.

In this chapter, Thain evolves from a single agent into a coordinated system of specialized agents, each responsible for a specific aspect of the overall decision process. Instead of concentrating all reasoning in one place, responsibilities are distributed: one agent evaluates intent, another gathers contextual evidence, and others retrieve procedural knowledge or propose actions. A central orchestrator then integrates these contributions into a unified outcome.

This specialization improves both clarity and control. Each agent focuses on a single responsibility, while the coordinating agent determines when delegation is required and how results are combined.

The Microsoft Agent Framework becomes central at this stage. It provides the orchestration mechanisms required for structured coordination, controlled execution, and deterministic workflows across agents. Rather than loosely interacting, agents participate in a governed sequence where each stage produces well-defined outputs that inform the next step.

© Hari Narayn 2026
H. Narayn, *Architecting Intelligent Agents in Azure*, https://doi.org/10.1007/979-8-8688-2433-3_7

Agents do not communicate informally. Collaboration in Thain is deliberate and controlled. Each agent produces structured artifacts instead of conversational responses, and all information flows through a shared turn state. A single orchestrator manages routing, precedence, and the final user response. Governance rules, approvals, and safety checks are consistently enforced throughout the workflow.

By the end of this chapter, Thain advances to version v0.6 and becomes a coordinated system rather than a single intelligent assistant. The architecture now reflects enterprise intelligence: multiple perspectives, explicit boundaries, and a defined control plane. Coordination is no longer advisory or best effort; it is enforced by design through explicit sequencing, policy, and execution control.

Multi-agent Architecture and Control Flow

Thain's multi-agent design follows a defined set of architectural principles:

- **Single point of control**: A single orchestrator manages the turn life cycle, routing decisions, and the final user response.

- **Specialized agents, narrow responsibilities**: Each agent is responsible for a single task, such as safety, triage, recall, knowledge, or execution, and returns a structured result.

- **No agent-to-agent conversation**: Agents do not exchange free-form messages. Coordination occurs only through orchestrated transitions and shared state.

- **Deterministic, auditable flow**: Each step executes in a defined order with clear decision points and failure handling.

These principles keep collaboration structured, auditable, and predictable rather than complex and opaque.

Agent Roles

Thain defines six core agent roles:

- **Orchestrator agent**: The orchestrator manages the turn, determines which agents run, merges outputs, and produces the final response. It is the only agent that generates user-facing text.

- **Safety and compliance gate**: This agent performs deterministic risk classification on incoming messages and outputs safety flags, tool permissions, redaction requirements, and a response mode that constrains all downstream processes.

- **Triage agent**: This agent interprets intent and urgency, classifies the issue, identifies missing information, and emits routing signals for retrieval, documentation, or action.

- **Recall agent**: This agent retrieves historical context using persistent and semantic memory, returning only evidence and recency signals.

- **Knowledge agent**: This agent retrieves procedures, policies, and playbooks. In version 0.6, this capability is limited to stubbed document retrieval.

- **Action agent**: This agent executes side effects, such as ticket creation and notifications, always governed by approvals and policy.

No agent has full system control. Each role is intentionally constrained by design.

Control Flow and Orchestration Model

The default control pipeline consists of the following sequence:

Safety Gate → Triage → Recall/Knowledge → Action → Orchestrator

This pipeline is conditional rather than mandatory.

- **Early safety enforcement**: If safety requires refusal or escalation, no additional agents are executed.

- **Conditional routing**: Recall and Knowledge agents run only when triage indicates a need.

- **Outcome-based execution**: The Action agent runs only when a candidate exists, and policy or approval requirements are met.

- **Single response synthesis**: Regardless of internal complexity, the orchestrator produces a single final response.

This approach mirrors the Microsoft Agent Framework Sequential pattern, where a central orchestrator manages explicit control flow and observable execution.

Shared Turn State (Blackboard)

All agent outputs are recorded on a shared per-turn blackboard.

Agents write only their own results. No agent modifies another's output. The blackboard

- Enables deterministic merging and precedence

- Preserves full audit context

- Captures failures explicitly, allowing the orchestrator to proceed with best-effort reasoning.

Implementation Strategy

To reduce risk and maintain manageable complexity, the implementation of Thain v0.6 in this chapter is divided into three parts:

- **Part A: Control and Intent**

  Orchestrator, blackboard, and triage (control plane only)

- **Part B: Evidence Gathering**

  Recall and knowledge (read-only enrichment)

- **Part C: Execution, Enforcement, and Safety**

  Safety gate, action agent, and approvals or policy enforcement

This sequence reflects real-world enterprise build order: control first, evidence second, and execution last.

The Microsoft Agent Framework supports multiple orchestration styles, including Concurrent, Sequential, Group Chat, and Handoff.

Thain v0.6 adopts the Sequential pattern: a deterministic, stage-based workflow where a central orchestrator coordinates agents in a defined order with conditional routing. This approach prioritizes auditability, safety, and centralized response governance. While MAF supports decentralized Handoff flows, Thain intentionally avoids peer-to-peer agent delegation and instead relies on governed, orchestrator-driven orchestration. Thain implements this as custom Python rather than through MAF's native orchestration runner so that every routing decision, safety short-circuit, and failure record is explicit and directly visible in the code. The patterns map directly to MAF's Sequential style; implementing orchestration explicitly in this chapter ensures you understand exactly what the framework's native runner provides.

With the architecture established, we can now implement the system in stages.

Working with This Chapter's Code

Complete implementations of all referenced files are available in the book's companion GitHub repository, `https://github.com/Apress/Architecting-Intelligent-Agents-in-Azure`, under the folder:

Chapter 7 → {Part} → thain

These reference implementations serve as the definitive source for the code discussed in this chapter. The repository also includes a Microsoft Agent Framework 1.5.0 General Availability version of this chapter's code in the Code GA/Chapter 7 folder. A detailed migration note is available in the repository. See the end of this chapter for a summary of the GA changes.

Code Reference Convention

Each code section specifies its source using the following format:

Source   Chapter 7 → {Part} → thain → {folder} → {filename} (action)

This notation shows

- Where the complete reference implementation is in the repository

- Whether the file should be **created** or **updated** in your local project

As you follow along, replicate the folder structure in your local workspace and create or update the referenced files as indicated. When adding a new folder, include an empty `__init__.py` to mark it as a Python package.

Python Package Initialization

When you add a new folder, create an empty `__init__.py` file.

Although these files contain no code, they explicitly mark directories as Python packages. This ensures consistent import resolution across entry points such as the Dev UI, test runners, and command-line execution. Including these files prevents `module not found` errors and supports a predictable, scalable project structure as the code base grows.

Part A: Orchestrated Triage with Deterministic Control

Part A establishes the structural foundation of Thain's multi-agent architecture. Instead of adding new capabilities, it restructures the system to use explicit orchestration, shared turn state, and deterministic agent contracts.

At this stage, the Microsoft Agent Framework is fully integrated. Thain moves from a single reasoning loop to a coordinated set of specialist agents, each with a specific responsibility. The orchestrator manages execution order, state, and response composition.

Part A intentionally prioritizes structure over behavior. Retrieval, execution, and approvals are addressed in later sections to keep orchestration observable, testable, and predictable from the start.

Agent Contracts and Orchestration Stages

Before implementing agent logic, we define explicit contracts that govern agent communication and orchestration progression through each turn.

Thain uses strongly defined result objects for each agent role. These contracts serve three main purposes:

- Agent outputs explicit and inspectable

- The orchestrator to merge results deterministically

- A stable audit surface for tracing and governance

A small set of stage constants identifies each orchestration phase and is reused consistently across routing, failure recording, and tracing.

Source   Chapter 7 → Part A → thain → orchestration → contracts.py (create)

Core Enforcement Mechanics (Key Excerpts)

1. Orchestration Stage Identifiers

Explicit stage identifiers create a common vocabulary for orchestration, routing, failure recording, and tracing. Using constants instead of inline strings maintains consistent execution order and diagnostics as new stages are introduced. See Listing 7-1a for the implementation pattern.

Listing 7-1a. Orchestration stage identifiers (contracts.py)

```
STAGE_SAFETY = "safety_gate"
STAGE_TRIAGE = "triage"
STAGE_RECALL = "recall"
STAGE_KNOWLEDGE = "knowledge"
STAGE_ACTION = "action"
```

2. Safety Result Contract

The safety gate emits a single immutable artifact that captures both risk posture and execution constraints. Downstream stages rely exclusively on this contract rather than re-evaluating safety heuristics. This is illustrated in Listing 7-1b.

Listing 7-1b.   SafetyResult contract(contracts.py)

```
@dataclass(frozen=True)
class SafetyResult:
    risk_level: str
    flags: List[str]
    response_mode: str
    tool_permissions: Dict[str, str]
    redactions_required: List[str]
```

3. Triage Result Contract

Triage generates structured intent signals without running tools or changing system state. This separation keeps orchestration deterministic and supports future strategy updates. Listing 7-1c shows this.

Listing 7-1c. TriageResult contract(contracts.py)

```
@dataclass(frozen=True)
class TriageResult:
    category: str
    urgency: str
    needs_retrieval: bool
    needs_docs: bool
    action_candidate: str
    missing_info: List[str]
```

The blackboard serves as the single source of truth for each turn. Each agent writes to its own field, and agents do not modify each other's output. This approach ensures deterministic orchestration and auditable state transitions. This is shown in Listing 7-1d.

Listing 7-1d. Blackboard: shared turn state (contracts.py)

```
@dataclass
class Blackboard:
    turn_id: str
    message: Dict[str, Any]
    safety: SafetyResult | None = None
    triage: TriageResult | None = None
    recall: Any | None = None
    knowledge: Any | None = None
    action: Any | None = None
    failures: List[Dict[str, Any]] = field(default_factory=list)
```

Architectural Results

- **Single-output agents**: Each agent generates a single result type and writes exclusively to its designated blackboard field.

- **Immutable results**: All agent result dataclasses are immutable, which prevents accidental changes after they are created.

- **First-class turn state**: The blackboard captures the full state of each turn and is managed by the orchestrator.

- **Explicit orchestration stages**: Stage constants ensure sequencing logic remains explicit and contained within the code base.

Design Note   In this implementation, all agents share the same contract definitions within a single code base. In distributed deployments where agents run as independent services, treat these dataclasses as versioned interfaces. Introduce explicit version fields or use backward-compatible defaults when extending contracts, so agents deployed at different versions can interoperate without breaking the orchestration layer.

By defining these contracts at the outset, the remainder of Part A can focus on behavior rather than structural considerations.

Shared Turn State and Failure Recording

Agents do not pass intermediate results directly to one another. Instead, Thain uses a shared turn state called the blackboard, which serves as the single source of truth for an interaction.

The blackboard collects agent outputs and structured failures. Each agent writes only to its designated field, and agents do not modify each other's outputs. This append-only approach is maintained by convention and immutability.

Failures are recorded as structured data rather than control-flow exceptions. This enables the orchestrator to continue best-effort reasoning and maintain full visibility into errors.

Source   Chapter 7 → Part A → thain → orchestration → blackboard.py (create)

Core Enforcement Mechanics (Key Excerpts)

1. Structured Failure Recording

Failures are recorded on the blackboard instead of being raised as control-flow exceptions. This approach enables orchestration to continue on a best-effort basis while maintaining clear visibility into the location and cause of each stage failure. See Listing 7-2a for the implementation pattern.

Listing 7-2a. Structured failure recording on the blackboard (blackboard.py)

```
def record_failure(
    board: Blackboard,
    stage: str,
    error_type: str,
    message: str,
) -> None:
    board.failures.append(
        {
            "stage": stage,
            "error_type": error_type,
            "message": message,
        }
    )
```

2. Turn-Scoped Message Metadata

Message metadata is generated once at the start of each turn and consistently reused across agents. This approach eliminates redundant computation and ensures that tracing, safety checks, and orchestration use the same normalized inputs. Listing 7-2b demonstrates this.

Listing 7-2b. Turn-scoped message metadata (blackboard.py)

```
def build_message_metadata(message: str) -> Dict[str, Any]:
    return {
        "message_len": len(message.strip()),
        "has_urls": "http://" in message or "https://" in message,
    }
```

Architectural Results

- **Append-only failure recording**: Failures are logged with stage and error metadata and are not exposed directly to users.

- **Serializable turn state**: The blackboard can be fully converted into a dictionary to support tracing and Dev UI inspection.

- **Shared message metadata**: Message characteristics are calculated once and consistently reused throughout downstream processes.

The blackboard ensures all intermediate decisions and failures are observable, which removes implicit state sharing between agents.

Deterministic Safety Gate

Before interpreting intent or routing, Thain evaluates each message using a deterministic safety gate. This gate does not generate responses or execute tools. It sets the constraints for the remainder of the turn.

In Part A, the safety gate takes a conservative approach. It records safety signals and declares permissions, always allowing execution to continue. Future sections will expand this structure to include refusal, redirection, and human escalation.

Source   Chapter 7 → Part A → thain → orchestration → safety_gate.py (create)

Core Enforcement Mechanics (Key Excerpts)

1. Deterministic Safety Signal Derivation

Safety signals are extracted once at the start of each turn using deterministic heuristics. They are explicitly recorded and reused downstream, eliminating the need for later recomputation or inference. Refer to Listing 7-3a.

Listing 7-3a. Derive safety signals deterministically(safety_gate.py)

```
flags = unique_flags(detect_safety_flags(message))
```

2. Execution Posture and Tool Permission Declaration

Even in its permissive Part A form, the safety gate defines a clear execution posture and tool permission map. This approach allows future enforcement by tightening policy instead of restructuring orchestration. Listing 7-3b illustrates this.

Listing 7-3b. Declare execution posture and tool permissions (safety_gate.py)

```
tool_permissions = {
    "retrieve_docs": "allow",
    "search_similar": "allow",
    "create_ticket": "allow",
    "notify_team": "allow",
}
return SafetyResult(
    risk_level="low",
    flags=flags,
    response_mode="normal",
    tool_permissions=tool_permissions,
    redactions_required=redactions_required,
)
```

Architectural Results

- **Safety is evaluated once at the start of the turn**: The safety gate runs before triage or routing. Its output constrains all downstream execution to ensure consistent enforcement across agents.

- **Signals are recorded, not acted upon implicitly**: Safety flags and required redactions are returned as structured data. No hidden control flow is triggered by string matches or internal heuristics.

- **Permissions are explicit, even when permissive**: Although all tools are allowed in Part A, permissions are still declared. This approach allows future enforcement by tightening constraints rather than restructuring logic.

By introducing the safety gate early, even in a stubbed form, Thain establishes safety and compliance as primary architectural concerns rather than optional add-ons.

Deterministic Triage Agent

Thain uses a deterministic triage agent to interpret user intent within defined safety constraints.

The triage agent does not execute tools or retrieve information. It generates a structured decision artifact that outlines intent, urgency, and any missing details. This approach clarifies decision-making and separates interpretation from execution.

In Part A, triage uses conservative heuristics to ensure predictable behavior and traceability. In Part B, this logic will shift to an agent-driven approach, while orchestration boundaries remain unchanged.

Source   Chapter 7 → Part A → thain → agent → triage_agent.py (create)

Core Enforcement Mechanics (Key Excerpts)

1. Deterministic Urgency Derivation

Urgency is determined by explicit, deterministic rules instead of probabilistic inference. This approach makes classification predictable, transparent, and consistent across runs. See Listing 7-4a.

Listing 7-4a. Derive urgency deterministically (triage_agent.py)

```
urgency = "low"
if any(term in lowered for term in _HIGH_URGENCY):
    urgency = "high"
elif any(term in lowered for term in _MEDIUM_URGENCY):
    urgency = "medium"
```

2. Structured Triage Decision Emission

The triage agent produces one structured decision artifact and does not cause side effects. It explicitly identifies missing information to prevent premature routing or execution. See Listing 7-4b.

Listing 7-4b. Emit structured triage decision (triage_agent.py)

```
return TriageResult(
    category=str(category),
    urgency=urgency,
    needs_retrieval=needs_retrieval,
    needs_docs=needs_docs,
    action_candidate=action_candidate,
    missing_info=missing_info,
)
```

Architectural Results

- **Explicit intent signals**: Intent interpretation is deterministic and inspectable.

- **Urgency classification**: Urgency is assessed conservatively and kept separate from execution logic.

- **Missing information detection**: Necessary details are documented to avoid premature execution.

- **No side effects**: The agent returns structured data only and does not alter control flow.

By limiting triage to intent interpretation, Thain ensures deterministic behavior and maintains a clear path for future upgrades to agent-driven reasoning.

Orchestrator: Owning the Turn

With contracts, shared state, and specialist agents in place, Thain introduces the orchestrator to provide controlled multi-agent execution.

The orchestrator manages the entire turn life cycle. It initializes turn state, invokes agents in a fixed order, records agent failures as structured data, and produces a single normalized response. Specialist agents emit only structured artifacts; only the orchestrator coordinates execution and composes user-facing output.

In Part A, the orchestrator executes only two stages:

- **Safety gate**: Establishes execution constraints for the turn

- **Triage**: Interprets intent and emits routing signals

Retrieval and execution stages are intentionally deferred. The orchestration structure is fully established at this stage and remains stable as new capabilities are added later.

Source   Chapter 7 → Part A → thain → agents → orchestrator.py (create)

Core Enforcement Mechanics (Key Excerpts)

1. Deterministic Turn Initialization and Stage Ordering

Each turn begins by creating a new blackboard and executing agents in a fixed, explicit sequence. No agent is invoked outside this order. See Listing 7-5a.

Listing 7-5a. Initialize turn state and execute safety gate (orchestrator.py)

```
board = Blackboard(turn_id=turn_id, message={"text": message, "metadata":
metadata})
board.safety = self._safety_gate.run(message, metadata)
```

This ensures every turn starts from a known state and that safety is always evaluated before intent interpretation or routing decisions.

2. Authoritative Safety Short-Circuiting

Safety is authoritative. If the safety gate determines a response must be refused or escalated, the orchestrator immediately halts downstream execution. Refer to Listing 7-5b.

Listing 7-5b. Early exit on safety-restricted response modes (orchestrator.py)

```
if board.safety.response_mode in {"refuse", "human_escalate"}:
    return board
```

No triage, retrieval, or execution logic runs beyond this point. This ensures safety constraints cannot be bypassed by downstream agents.

3. Structured Failure Recording

Agent failures do not propagate as control-flow exceptions. Instead, the orchestrator captures failures as structured records on the blackboard. See Listing 7-5c.

Listing 7-5c. Invoke triage under orchestrator-controlled failure handling (orchestrator.py)

```
try:
    board.triage = self._triage_agent.run(message)
except Exception as exc:
    record_failure(board, STAGE_TRIAGE, type(exc).__name__, str(exc))
    return board
```

This approach ensures failures are observable and auditable, partial turn state is preserved, and the system can return a best-effort response. The orchestrator, not individual agents, defines error semantics.

4. Centralized Response Normalization

Regardless of execution complexity, the orchestrator produces a single normalized response from the authoritative state on the blackboard. Safety posture and triage classification are applied deterministically, with safe defaults if data is missing. This guarantees response consistency even if certain stages fail or are skipped.

Architectural Results

- **Centralized control**: The orchestrator initializes turn state, enforces execution order, and maintains a complete record of each interaction.

- **Failures are recorded, not exposed**: Exceptions are converted into structured failure records and never surface to the user.

- **Safety-first execution**: Safety decisions can halt downstream processing deterministically.

- **Single response authority**: All user-facing output is derived from the blackboard under orchestrator control.

At this stage, Thain operates a deterministic control plane supported by a blackboard-based orchestration loop that enforces order, captures failures, and produces a single, traceable response per turn.

Routing Rules As Explicit Orchestration Guards

While Part A does not use retrieval or action tools yet, routing decisions are established early through explicit guard functions.

Thain separates routing logic from the orchestrator by using small, declarative functions that assess structured agent outputs rather than raw user text. This approach improves readability and avoids scattered conditionals.

Source   Chapter 7 → Part A → thain → orchestration → routing.py (create)

Core Enforcement Mechanics (Key Excerpts)

1. Guard Recall Eligibility

Recall is permitted only if triage determines retrieval is necessary and safety is in normal response mode. This avoids unnecessary work when safety restrictions limit tool use. See Listing 7-6a.

Listing 7-6a. Guard recall eligibility (routing.py)

```
def should_run_recall(triage: TriageResult, safety: SafetyResult) -> bool:
    return triage.needs_retrieval and safety.response_mode == "normal"
```

2. Guard Knowledge Retrieval Eligibility

Procedural retrieval serves as optional evidence. The guard maintains policy awareness in orchestration without adding tool calls in Part A. Refer to Listing 7-6b.

Listing 7-6b. Guard knowledge retrieval eligibility(routing.py)

```
def should_run_docs(triage: TriageResult, safety: SafetyResult) -> bool:
    return triage.needs_docs and safety.response_mode == "normal"
```

3. Guard Action Eligibility

Execution does not occur in Part A, but action intent is still captured structurally. The guard then serves as a stable transition point for governed execution in Part C. Refer to Listing 7-6c.

Listing 7-6c. Guard action eligibility(routing.py)

```python
def should_run_action(triage: TriageResult, safety: SafetyResult) -> bool:
    return triage.action_candidate != "none" and safety.response_mode ==
    "normal"
```

Architectural Results

- Routing is based on contracts, not raw text.

- Safety consistently constrains routing. Downstream stages are disabled when safety restricts the response mode.

- Guards determine eligibility, not intent. They indicate whether a stage may run, not the reason behind it.

These guards enable retrieval and action stages to be added later without requiring changes to the orchestration logic.

Isolating Integration from Orchestration

As orchestration expands, maintaining a stable application entry point is essential. To prevent coupling CLI or Dev UI wiring with orchestration internals, Thain introduces a runner wrapper. The runner provides a focused interface for running a turn, extracting triage context, and composing the final response.

It also conceals agent wiring and orchestration details from the application layer.

Source   Chapter 7 → Part A → thain → orchestration → runner.py (create)

Core Enforcement Mechanics (Key Excerpts)

1. Single Integration Boundary via Runner Wrapper

The application entry point main.py communicates exclusively with the runner and does not access individual agents or blackboard internals. This approach allows orchestration to evolve without affecting the application layer. Refer to Listing 7-7a.

Listing 7-7a. Runner wrapper as the single integration boundary (runner.py)

```
class OrchestratorRunner:
    def __init__(self) -> None:
        self._orchestrator = Orchestrator(SafetyGateAgent(), TriageAgent())

    def run(self, message: str, turn_id: str, metadata: Dict[str, Any]) ->
    Blackboard:
        return self._orchestrator.run_turn(message, turn_id, metadata)
    def triage_context(self, board: Blackboard) -> str:
        return self._orchestrator.build_triage_context(board)
```

2. Deterministic Board Snapshotting for Tracing

Snapshots are explicitly serialized instead of using ad-hoc stringification. This approach ensures state inspection remains deterministic and easy to trace. See Listing 7-7b.

Listing 7-7b. Safe board snapshot for tracing and Dev UI (runner.py)

```
def safe_board_snapshot(board: Blackboard) -> Dict[str, Any]:
    return asdict(board)
```

Architectural Results

- **Single integration boundary**: main.py interacts only with the runner, not with individual agents or orchestration internals.

- **Stable orchestration surface**: The runner encapsulates the orchestrator and agent wiring, allowing the orchestration graph to evolve without breaking callers.

- **Safe state inspection**: Blackboard snapshots are explicitly serialized for tracing and Dev UI inspection.

With the orchestrator, routing guards, and integration boundary in place, Part A now defines a complete control plane for multi-agent execution. Subsequent parts will add retrieval, actions, and approvals while maintaining the orchestration guarantees established here.

Application Entry Point Integration (Part A)

With the orchestration layer complete, the final step in Part A is to integrate it into the application entry point. This step introduces the orchestrator and triage artifacts while preserving the current single-agent runtime.

Part A integrates the orchestrator as a control-plane companion. The orchestrator produces structured artifacts for safety and triage, making them available to the runtime, while the existing ChatAgent continues to generate user-facing responses.

Source   Chapter 7 → Part A → thain → main.py (update)

Core Integration Points (Key Excerpts)

1. Orchestration Helper Imports

These imports add the orchestration layer to the application without exposing individual agents or blackboard internals at the entry point. See Listing 7-8a.

Listing 7-8a. Import orchestration helpers (main.py)

```
from orchestration.runner import OrchestratorRunner
from orchestration.blackboard import build_message_metadata
```

2. Blackboard Construction

Turn-scoped metadata is calculated once at the start of each interaction and reused throughout the execution pipeline. The orchestrator then executes the safety gate and triage agents in a deterministic sequence, recording their outputs as structured artifacts on the shared blackboard. See Listing 7-8b for the implementation pattern.

Listing 7-8b. Run the orchestrator and build the blackboard (main.py)

```python
turn_metadata = build_message_metadata(customer_message)
turn_metadata["safety_flags"] = safety_flags
orchestrator = OrchestratorRunner()
board = orchestrator.run(customer_message, str(turn_id), turn_metadata)
```

3. Triage Context Injection

Triage results guide the response within a controlled context block. The triage context influences the response without changing the agent execution flow. The orchestrator retains ownership of the structured state, while the language model continues to generate the final response. Listing 7-8c shows the implementation pattern.

Listing 7-8c. Inject triage context into agent instructions(main.py)

```python
triage_context = orchestrator.triage_context(board)
if triage_context:
    instructions += f"\n{triage_context}"
```

Architectural Results

- The orchestrator and blackboard run on every turn.

- Safety and triage artifacts are captured deterministically.

- All responses continue to flow through a single user-facing agent.

This completes Part A's objective of introducing a multi-agent control plane without disrupting the established execution model.

Validating Part A Control Plane

Before adding retrieval or governed actions, validate that the control plane operates predictably. For Part A tests, disable Azure search mode, write tools, and retrieval:

```
$env:AZURE_SEARCH_MODE="off"
$env:ENABLE_TICKETS="false"
$env:ENABLE_NOTIFICATIONS="false"
```

Test 1: Deterministic Triage Flow

This test verifies that a simple user interaction is routed through the orchestrator and triage agent, producing a structured triage response and a complete trace artifact.

Start the Dev UI: `python main.py --devui --devui-open`

Prompt: `My refund hasn't arrived after 14 days.`

Dev UI: A triage summary card is returned, the issue type aligns with a refund or payment-related inquiry, and no tools are executed other than the classifier.

Trace: The trace contains `request.received`, `policy.check (classify_issue)`, `tool.call` and `tool.result (classify_issue)`, `response.ready`, and `trace.emitted` in order.

Outcome: A deterministic trace is produced for a basic triage interaction. Classification occurs, no side effects are triggered, and a single response is emitted by the orchestrator.

Test 2: Triage Flags Action Without Execution

This test verifies that the triage agent can identify urgency and action intent without triggering execution. Start the Dev UI or start a new conversation within the same session as the previous test.

Prompt: `Equipment shut down twice and caused an evacuation. Please create a ticket and tell me if there were similar incidents.`

Dev UI: The response suggests escalation or ticket creation, without executing it.

Trace: Only the classification tool is invoked. No recall, notification, or ticket tools are called. The trace sequence completes with `response.ready`.

Outcome: The system correctly identifies action intent while deferring execution, preserving Part A's no-side-effects constraint. See Figure 7-1 for an example run in Dev UI.

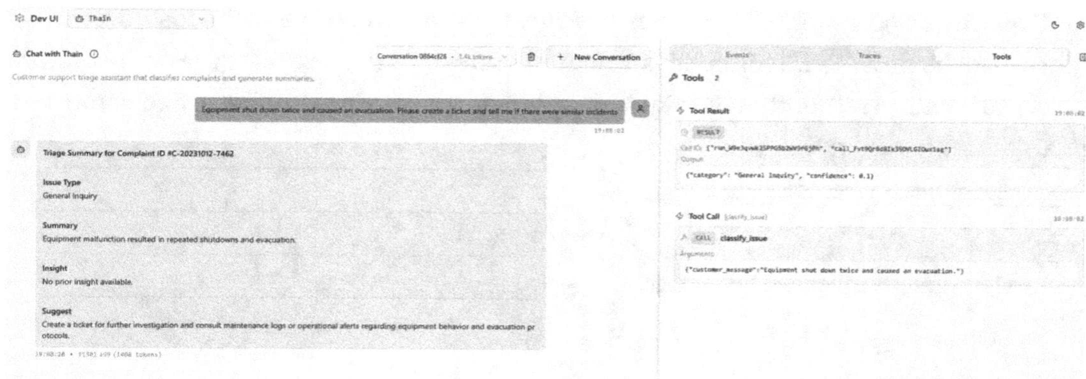

Figure 7-1. *Triage flags action without execution*

Test 3: Documentation-Oriented Requests

This test verifies that the triage agent can recognize requests for procedural guidance. Start the Dev UI or start a new conversation within the same session as the previous test.

Prompt: `What's the standard procedure after an unexpected shutdown and evacuation?`

Dev UI: The response indicates a request for standard operating procedures, and no document retrieval tools are executed.

Trace: The trace includes classification only. For `classify_issue`, trace contains the events, `policy.check` + `tool.call` + `tool.result`

Outcome: The documentation intent has been accurately identified, and execution has not been performed. No tool calls were made except for the classifier.

Test 4: Agent Restraint Under Ambiguous Input

This test verifies that the system avoids premature classification or execution when the user intent is underspecified. Start the Dev UI or start a new conversation within the same session as the previous test.

Prompt: `Create a ticket for this issue.`

Dev UI: The response asks for clarification (for example, the nature or scope of the issue), and no tools are executed.

Trace: The trace contains `request.received` and `response.ready`. Also `policy.check`, `tool.call`, or `tool.result` events do not appear.

Outcome: The system defers both classification and execution when insufficient information is provided. This behavior demonstrates agentic restraint: the orchestrator seeks clarification rather than forcing a decision or triggering side effects. See Figure 7-2 for an example run in Dev UI.

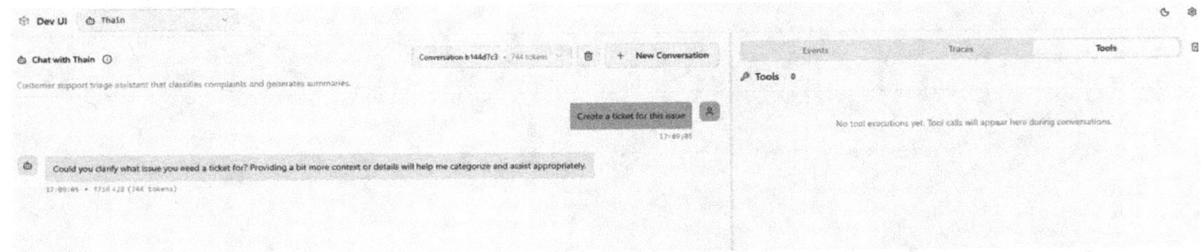

Figure 7-2. *Agent restraint under ambiguous input*

With the control plane validated and triage behavior confirmed, Thain can now reason about intent in a structured and observable manner. In Part B, we build on this by adding read-only evidence gathering through recall and knowledge agents and by upgrading triage to an agent-driven model under the same contract. This approach improves decision quality without altering orchestration structure or control flow.

Note   The trace JSON files from these tests are available for reference in the book's product repository under Chapter 7 → Part A → Test Traces. These artifacts are provided for further review and deep inspection.

Part B: Evidence Gathering Without Control Drift

Part A established a deterministic control plane for Thain's multi-agent system. The orchestrator manages each turn, the blackboard stores structured artifacts, and specialist agents deliver auditable results. Safety and triage are evaluated first, ensuring no side effects.

Part B builds on this foundation by adding read-only evidence gathering, without changing orchestration semantics, contracts, or failure behavior.

In enterprise systems, decisions are rarely made in isolation. Historical incidents, prior patterns, and established procedures often inform responses. However, letting evidence systems drive control flow introduces risk. Retrieval systems can fail, documents may be incomplete, and historical data may be unavailable.

For this reason, Part B introduces Recall and Knowledge agents as non-authoritative enrichers. These agents gather evidence, record it as structured artifacts, and do not block turn completion. The orchestrator remains the sole authority over execution and response composition.

This section also demonstrates a key architectural property: reasoning can evolve independently of orchestration. Triage is enhanced to support an agentic implementation while maintaining the output contract and routing semantics established in Part A.

Upgrading Triage

Previously, triage was implemented as a single deterministic class to ensure predictable routing and a consistent `TriageResult` contract.

Now, triage is upgraded to a strategy boundary, enabling multiple reasoning approaches, whether deterministic or agentic, while maintaining the same output structure, validation rules, and downstream behavior.

From the orchestrator's perspective, nothing changes. It continues to consume a validated `TriageResult` and routes exclusively based on its fields.

Source   Chapter 7 → Part B → thain → agents → triage_agent.py (update)

Core Enforcement Mechanics (Key Excerpts)

1. Strategy-Based Triage Implementations

There are two implementations:

- `DeterministicTriageAgent`: This implementation retains the heuristic logic from Part A and serves as the default baseline.

- `AgenticTriageAgent`: This implementation uses a constrained language model to generate triage outputs, returning only structured JSON.

2. Runtime Selection of Reasoning Strategy

The triage implementation is selected at runtime through a strategy selector.
See Listing 7-9a for the implementation pattern in agents/triage_agent.py.

Listing 7-9a. Runtime selection of reasoning strategy

```python
def select_triage_agent(mode: str, chat_client: Any | None = None) -> Any:
    if mode == "agentic":
        if chat_client is None:
            raise RuntimeError("Agentic triage requires a chat client.")
        return AgenticTriageAgent(chat_client)
    return DeterministicTriageAgent()
```

This approach allows reasoning quality to improve independently of
orchestration logic.

3. Contract Validation As a Firewall

Regardless of how triage is produced, all outputs are validated and normalized before
orchestration. See Listing 7-9b.

Listing 7-9b. Contract validation as a firewall

```python
def validate_triage_result(result: TriageResult) -> TriageResult:
    urgency = result.urgency if result.urgency in _ALLOWED_URGENCY
    else "low"
    action_candidate = (
        result.action_candidate
        if result.action_candidate in _ALLOWED_ACTIONS
        else "none"
    )

    return TriageResult(
        category=result.category or "General Inquiry",
        urgency=urgency,
        needs_retrieval=bool(result.needs_retrieval),
```

```
    needs_docs=bool(result.needs_docs),
    action_candidate=action_candidate,
    missing_info=[m for m in result.missing_info if m],
)
```

This validation step serves as a contract firewall, ensuring agentic outputs do not introduce invalid states or disrupt routing behavior.

4. Constrained Agentic Reasoning

The agentic triage implementation is intentionally constrained:

- No tools

- No memory

- No side effects

- JSON output only

An excerpt from the instruction set illustrates the constraint. See Listing 7-9c.

Listing 7-9c. Constrained agentic reasoning

```
Return ONLY JSON with keys:
category, urgency, needs_retrieval, needs_docs, action_candidate,
missing_info
```

The language model generates a candidate triage decision rather than a response. All outputs are validated before use.

Architectural Results

- **Deterministic behavior remains the baseline:** Deterministic triage remains the default as evidence gathering is introduced.

- **Agentic reasoning is constrained by design:** The agentic variant produces only structured data and cannot execute tools or actions.

- **Validation enforces contract safety:** All triage outputs are normalized before routing and orchestration.

- **Orchestration remains data driven**: Routing logic uses only
  `TriageResult` and `SafetyResult`, regardless of how triage was
  produced.

With triage now operating behind a stable contract boundary, Thain can incorporate additional context without control drift. In the next section, we introduce Recall and Knowledge agents, which enrich the blackboard using the same best-effort, non-blocking approach.

Adding Recall As a Read-Only Evidence Agent

With triage now producing stable routing signals, we introduce **Recall** as Thain's initial evidence-gathering agent.

Recall retrieves historical context, such as prior incidents, similar complaints, or related events, and records this information as a structured artifact. It is intentionally non-authoritative; it does not influence control flow, make decisions, or trigger actions. While evidence may enhance reasoning, it does not determine execution.

In Part B, Recall operates on a best-effort basis. The turn must complete as usual, regardless of retrieval success. Failures are documented structurally or as empty evidence.

Recall Agent Responsibilities

- Runs only when routing allows

- Supports multiple retrieval modes

- Emits a single `RecallResult` artifact

- Never blocks the turn

Recall Agent Implementation

Recall is implemented as a dedicated specialist agent to ensure evidence gathering remains observable and replaceable. The following excerpt shows the core behavior. See Listing 7-10.

Source   Chapter 7 → Part B → thain → agents → recall_agent.py (create)

Listing 7-10. Recall agent excerpt (agents/recall_agent.py)

```python
if self._retrieval_mode == "off" or not self._search_tool:
    return RecallResult(matches=[], recency="none", retrieval_mode=self._
    retrieval_mode)
results = await self._search_tool(...)
matches = results if isinstance(results, list) else []
recency = _recency_from_results(matches)
return RecallResult(matches=matches, recency=recency, retrieval_mode=self._
retrieval_mode)
```

This excerpt demonstrates Recall's best-effort behavior. If recall is disabled or no search tool is configured, the agent returns an empty `RecallResult`. When retrieval is enabled, results are delivered as received and summarized only with a basic recency indicator. The agent does not raise errors, block the turn, or interpret the retrieved evidence.

Architectural Results

- **Mode-driven behavior**: Recall supports off, semantic, and agentic modes and documents the selected mode in the artifact.

- **Best-effort semantics**: Unexpected results are treated as empty evidence, and the process continues.

- **Structured output only**: Recall provides raw matches and a basic recency signal. It does not summarize or prioritize results.

Adding Knowledge As a Procedural Evidence Agent

Historical recall alone is often inadequate in enterprise settings. During incidents, teams require procedural guidance, such as SOPs, playbooks, checklists, and policy documents. Thain assigns responsibility for this guidance to a dedicated Knowledge agent.

Similar to Recall, Knowledge is read-only and non-authoritative. It retrieves documents and records them as structured evidence but does not interpret content, make decisions, or influence execution.

Rationale for Separating Knowledge from Recall

Procedural guidance differs from historical evidence in several keyways:

- It is typically curated rather than discovered.

- It may exist even when no similar incidents are found.

- It often maps directly to governance and policy.

Separating Recall from Knowledge ensures the orchestrator's evidence model remains explicit, distinguishing between historical information and procedural guidance.

Knowledge Agent Implementation

The Knowledge agent follows the same pattern, including tool optionality, bounded output, and structured results. See Listing 7-11.

Source   Chapter 7 → Part B → thain → agents → knowledge_agent.py (create)

Listing 7-11. Knowledge agent excerpt (agents/knowledge_agent.py)

```
if not self._retrieve_tool:
    return KnowledgeResult(docs=[])
results = await self._retrieve_tool(query=query, top_k=3)
docs = results if isinstance(results, list) else []
return KnowledgeResult(docs=docs)
```

This excerpt shows that the Knowledge agent follows the same read-only pattern. If no retrieval tool is available, the agent emits an empty result. When retrieval succeeds, documents are returned as-is with a bounded top_k. The agent performs no classification, summarization, or decision-making.

Architectural Results

- **Tool optionality**: If no retrieval tool is configured, the agent will return an empty result.

- **Bounded output**: Using a small `top_k` ensures predictable responses and reduces the downstream synthesis load.

- **No control flow awareness**: Knowledge provides evidence and then exits. It does not coordinate with recall or actions.

Routing Evidence Agents with Explicit Guards

With Recall and Knowledge agents established, the orchestrator needs a deterministic approach to determine when each agent should operate.

Routing is formalized through guard functions that assess structured outputs from previous stages. These guards ensure orchestration remains linear and auditable:

- Safety constraints are enforced uniformly.

- Routing remains data driven.

- Evidence is optional by design.

Routing Guards Determine Evidence Eligibility

The following guard patterns enforce policy requirements before evaluating intent. See Listing 7-12.

Source   Chapter 7 → Part B → thain → orchestration → routing.py (create)

Listing 7-12. Routing guards excerpt (orchestration/routing.py)

```python
def should_run_recall(triage: TriageResult, safety: SafetyResult) -> bool:
    if safety.tool_permissions.get("search_similar") != "allow":
        return False
    return triage.needs_retrieval and safety.response_mode == "normal"
def should_run_docs(triage: TriageResult, safety: SafetyResult) -> bool:
    if safety.tool_permissions.get("retrieve_docs") != "allow":
        return False
    return triage.needs_docs and safety.response_mode == "normal"
```

Action routing is defined for interface consistency, but execution will be addressed in Part C.

With read-only evidence agents and policy-aware routing guards in place, Thain can enrich the blackboard without altering orchestration semantics. Next, we will update the orchestrator runner to invoke these agents as needed and merge evidence artifacts into the turn state.

Integrating Evidence Agents into the Runner

In Part A, the runner served as a minimal integration layer. It invoked the orchestrator (safety to triage), extracted a triage-only context block, and normalized the response.

In Part B, the runner acts as the integration boundary for the complete evidence pipeline. It now

- Selects the triage strategy (deterministic or agentic)

- Conditionally enables Recall and Knowledge agents

- Constructs the orchestrator with these agents

- Runs the turn asynchronously and returns an evidence-enriched blackboard

Refer to Listing 7-13 for the runner excerpt that highlights the integration logic.

Source   Chapter 7 → Part B → thain → orchestration → runner.py (update)

Listing 7-13. Runner wiring: triage selection + evidence agents (orchestration/ runner.py)

```
triage_agent = select_triage_agent(config.triage_mode, chat_client)
recall_agent = None
if config.recall_enabled and search_tool and search_mode != "off":
    recall_agent = RecallAgent(search_tool, search_mode, default_top_k)
knowledge_agent = None
if config.knowledge_enabled and docs_tool:
    knowledge_agent = KnowledgeAgent(docs_tool)
self._orchestrator = Orchestrator(
```

```
SafetyGateAgent(),
triage_agent,
recall_agent,
knowledge_agent,
)
```

Architectural Results

1. **The runner is now configurable**: Part B accepts a
    `MultiAgentConfig`, which enables strategy changes (deterministic
    or agentic triage) and evidence toggles without orchestration drift.

2. **Evidence agents are integrated conditionally**: Recall and
    Knowledge agents are enabled only when feature flags permit and
    tools are available. Recall is disabled when search mode is off.
    This approach keeps tools optional and evidence non-blocking.

3. **The orchestration call is now asynchronous**: An
    asynchronous run method is required because triage may call
    the LLM and retrieval tools are asynchronous. This prevents
    mixed synchronous and asynchronous boundaries at the
    integration point.

4. **The context block replaces the triage context**: Part A injected
    only the triage context. Part B produces a single merged context
    block that includes triage and any gathered evidence.

5. **Safe snapshot now uses** `blackboard_to_dict`: The `blackboard_`
    `to_dict` ensures consistent serialization of nested dataclasses and
    failures, maintaining stable traces and a reliable development UI.

Design Note   In this implementation, evidence agent calls are not individually
time bounded. This keeps the orchestration code focused on structural patterns
(stage ordering, routing guards, and failure recording) without introducing
operational concerns. In a production scenario, wrapping each evidence agent
await with asyncio.wait_for() would enforce a maximum latency budget per stage,
preventing a slow retrieval service from holding the turn open.

With the runner updated, the remaining Part B tasks focus on wiring feature flags and integrating the evidence pipeline at the entry point.

Wiring Feature Flags and Multi-agent Config

Part B introduces feature flags that determine which evidence agents run and whether triage uses a deterministic or agentic strategy:

- `TRIAGE_MODE`: selects deterministic or agentic

- `ENABLE_RECALL`: toggles the Recall agent

- `ENABLE_KNOWLEDGE`: toggles the Knowledge agent

Add the following lines to the .env file. Refer to Listing 7-14a.

Listing 7-14a. Add multi-agent feature flags to .env

```
TRIAGE_MODE=deterministic
ENABLE_RECALL=true
ENABLE_KNOWLEDGE=true
```

If these flags are not set, `settings.py` provides safe defaults. Insert the new configuration at the bottom of the existing file `settings.py`. Refer to Listing 7-14b.

Listing 7-14b. MultiAgentConfig and loader helpers (config/settings.py)

```
@dataclass(frozen=True)
class MultiAgentConfig:
    """Configuration for the multi-agent orchestration flow."""
    triage_mode: str = "deterministic"
    recall_enabled: bool = True
    knowledge_enabled: bool = True
    @classmethod
    def from_env(cls) -> "MultiAgentConfig":
        triage_mode = (os.getenv("TRIAGE_MODE", "deterministic").strip() or
        "deterministic").lower()
        if triage_mode not in {"deterministic", "agentic"}:
```

```
        triage_mode = "deterministic"
    return cls(
        triage_mode=triage_mode,
        recall_enabled=_env_flag("ENABLE_RECALL", True),
        knowledge_enabled=_env_flag("ENABLE_KNOWLEDGE", True),
    )
def load_multi_agent_config() -> MultiAgentConfig:
    """Helper to load multi-agent orchestration configuration."""
    return MultiAgentConfig.from_env()
```

This keeps orchestration toggles typed, centrally loaded, and testable. Next, we will complete the Part B integration in main.py.

Application Entry Point Integration (Part B)

At this stage, Thain includes all components necessary for evidence-aware reasoning: deterministic or agentic triage, read-only recall, procedural knowledge retrieval, and policy-aware routing. The final requirement is a boundary to integrate these elements into the runtime.

main.py serves as this boundary. Its role is not to add new agent logic but to enforce the invariants that keep evidence gathering safe, optional, and observable:

- The orchestrator executes once per turn.

- Recall and knowledge run only when routing allows.

- Evidence is gathered before response generation.

- Evidence agents never execute tools through the LLM.

- Duplicate or conflicting tool calls are prevented.

Source   Chapter 7 → Part B → thain → main.py (update)

Core Integration Points (Key Excerpts)

1. Construct Orchestrator Runner with Evidence Tools

Listing 7-15a demonstrates that Recall and Knowledge tools are provided to the orchestrator instead of being exposed to the LLM. Evidence gathering occurs under orchestration control, which maintains determinism and prevents direct model-driven tool calls.

Listing 7-15a. Construct orchestrator runner with evidence tools (main.py)

```
orchestrator = OrchestratorRunner(
    config=multi_agent_config,
    chat_client=chat_client,
    search_tool=search_tool_for_recall,
    docs_tool=docs_tool,
    search_mode=search_mode,
)
```

2. Inject Merged Evidence Context into Agent Instructions

The excerpt from Listing 7-15b demonstrates that the orchestrator returns a single blackboard with triage and evidence artifacts. This merged context is added to the agent instructions, enabling the model to use evidence while maintaining a single-agent response.

Listing 7-15b. Inject merged evidence context into agent instructions (main.py)

```
board = await orchestrator.run(customer_message, str(turn_id))
context_block = orchestrator.context_block(board)
if context_block:
    instructions += f"\n{context_block}"
```

3. Disable LLM Tool Calls After Evidence Stages

The excerpt from Listing 7-15c shows that, once the orchestrator gathers evidence, LLM tool access is disabled. This prevents duplicate or conflicting tool execution and keeps reasoning and evidence aligned within a single turn.

Listing 7-15c. Disable LLM tool calls after evidence stages(main.py)

```
if board.recall or board.knowledge:
    chat_tools = []
    tool_choice = ToolMode.NONE
```

With the entry point configured, Thain's behavior is now observable end to end. The following tests confirm that evidence gathering remains selective, non-blocking, and contract preserving under both deterministic and agentic configurations.

Validating Part B: Evidence Gathering and Agentic Routing

With Part B fully integrated, Thain now gathers evidence from multiple sources while preserving deterministic orchestration and best-effort completion semantics.

The following tests exercise evidence gathering, failure handling, and triage evolution under controlled conditions:

- Recall and Knowledge agents run only when required.

- Failures are recorded without breaking the interaction.

- Agentic triage preserves contracts and routing behavior.

For all tests, the following configuration is used:

```
ENABLE_RECALL=true
ENABLE_KNOWLEDGE=true
ENABLE_DOCS=true
```

Test 1: Recall and Knowledge Invoked

This test verifies that the orchestrator can invoke both evidence-gathering agents when the user request requires historical context and procedural documentation.

Setup: `$Env:TRIAGE_MODE="deterministic"`,and `$Env:AZURE_SEARCH_MODE="semantic"`

Start the Dev UI: `python main.py --devui --devui-open`

Prompt: `During yesterday's shift, the equipment shut down twice and caused a brief evacuation. What's the standard procedure and have there been similar incidents recently?`

Dev UI: The response addresses both aspects of the request: Standard procedures and checklists (Knowledge agent), and Reasoning about prior or similar incidents (Recall agent). The `retrieve_docs` tool is invoked and visible and no user-visible errors occur.

Trace: `retrieve_docs` appears as a `tool.call` and `tool.result`. The trace completes with `response.ready` and `trace.emitted`. No action or notification tools are invoked.

Recall behavior: Recall operates via semantic retrieval (service backed). No recall tool call is required or expected in this mode, and the response reflects recall reasoning even if no prior incidents are found.

Outcome: The system correctly gathers multiple evidence streams and merges them into a single response without side effects. This confirms that Part B evidence agents integrate cleanly into the orchestration pipeline. See Figure 7-3 for an example run in Dev UI.

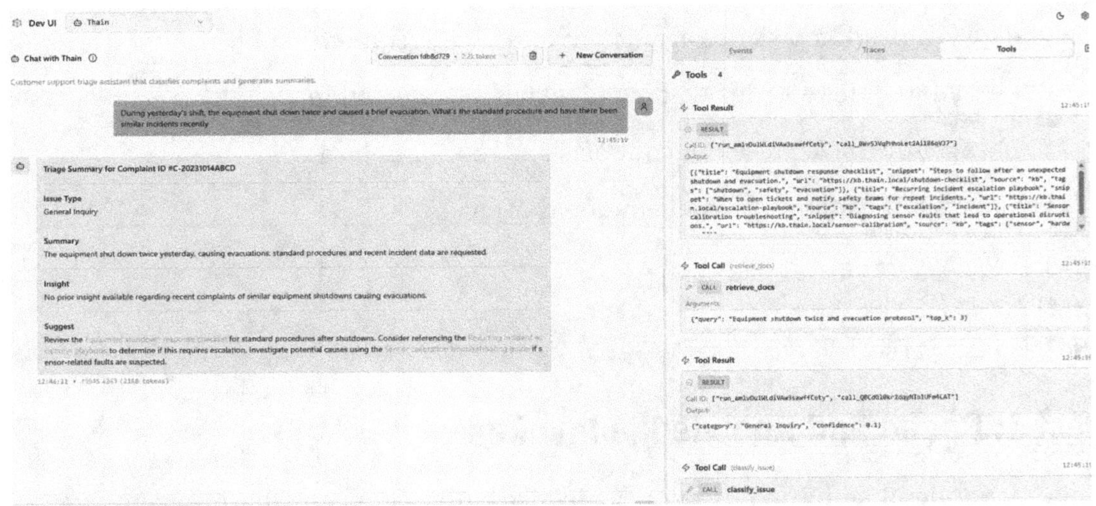

Figure 7-3. *Dev UI showing combined SOP guidance and incident reasoning*

Test 2: Knowledge Agent Runs Without Recall

This test verifies that the orchestrator selectively invokes only the Knowledge agent when the request is procedural and does not require historical evidence.

Prompt: `What's the standard procedure after an unexpected shutdown and evacuation?`

Dev UI: The response focuses entirely on procedures and checklists, no references to prior incidents are made, and the `retrieve_docs` tool is invoked and visible.

Trace: `retrieve_docs` appears as a `tool.call` and `tool.result`. No recall activity is present & the trace completes normally.

Outcome: The routing logic correctly isolates documentation retrieval without invoking recall, demonstrating data-driven orchestration rather than keyword-based flow control. See Figure 7-4 for an example run in Dev UI.

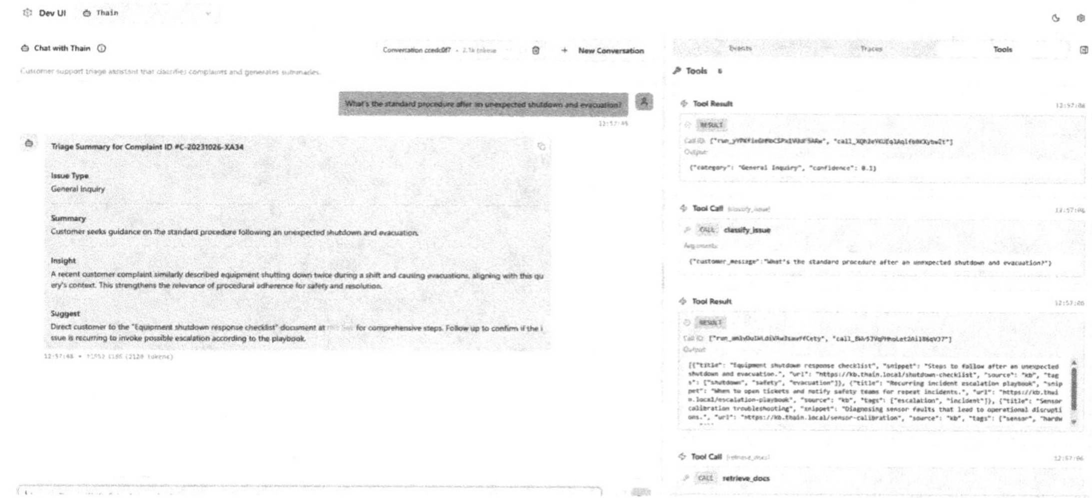

Figure 7-4. *Knowledge agent runs without recall.*

Test 3: Recall Failure Is Recorded

This test verifies that recall failures do not break the interaction and that the system records failures while still producing a user response.

Setup: Run `$Env:AZURE_SEARCH_ENDPOINT="https://invalid.invalid"`, and `$Env:AZURE_SEARCH_MODE="agentic"`

`AZURE_SEARCH_MODE` is set to `agentic` to force explicit recall tool invocation and surface failure handling in traces.

Prompt: `During yesterday's shift, the equipment shut down twice and caused a brief evacuation. What's the standard procedure and have there been similar incidents recently?`

Dev UI: The response completes normally, and the system explains that no prior incidents could be confirmed or suggests investigation steps.

Trace: `search_similar_complaints` is invoked. One or more `tool.result` events return with `status="error"`, and `error_type="SemanticSearchError"`. The trace still completes with `response.ready`.

In agentic mode, the LLM may invoke the recall tool more than once within a single turn. Multiple recall attempts are acceptable for this test; the key requirement is graceful failure handling.

Outcome: The system demonstrates resilience and observability: recall failures are captured, but the user experience remains intact. This confirms that evidence gathering is non-blocking by design. See Figure 7-5 for an example run in Dev UI.

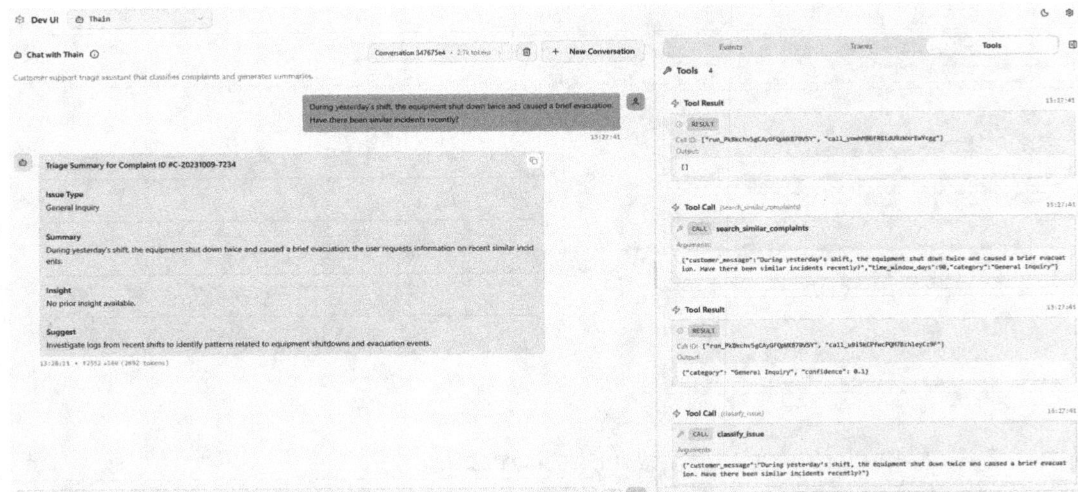

Figure 7-5. *Dev UI showing recall error with completed response*

After completing this test, restore the correct Azure Search configuration by removing the overridden environment variable: `Remove-Item Env:AZURE_SEARCH_ENDPOINT`

Test 4: Agentic Triage Preserves Contracts and Routing Behavior

This test verifies that triage can be upgraded to an agentic implementation without altering downstream orchestration behavior or output contracts.

Setup: `$Env:TRIAGE_MODE="agentic"`, and `$Env:AZURE_SEARCH_MODE="semantic"`

`TRIAGE_MODE` is set to `agentic` to validate that LLM-based triage preserves the existing output contract, while `AZURE_SEARCH_MODE` is set to `semantic` to avoid introducing recall tool behavior into this test.

Prompt: `During yesterday's shift, the equipment shut down twice and caused a brief evacuation. What's the standard procedure and have there been similar incidents recently?`

Dev UI: The response remains consistent with Test B1: SOP guidance is present, and incident reasoning is present. The `retrieve_docs` tool is invoked, and no recall tool is visible (semantic recall).

Trace: `classify_issue` executes successfully. The output conforms to the existing contract:

`{"category": "General Inquiry","confidence": 0.1}`

Also, knowledge routing occurs as expected, and no unexpected tools or actions are triggered.

Outcome: Agentic triage produces the same structured output contract and triggers the same routing decisions as deterministic triage. This confirms that agent-driven reasoning can be introduced without disrupting orchestration, safety, or observability. See Figure 7-6 for an example run in Dev UI.

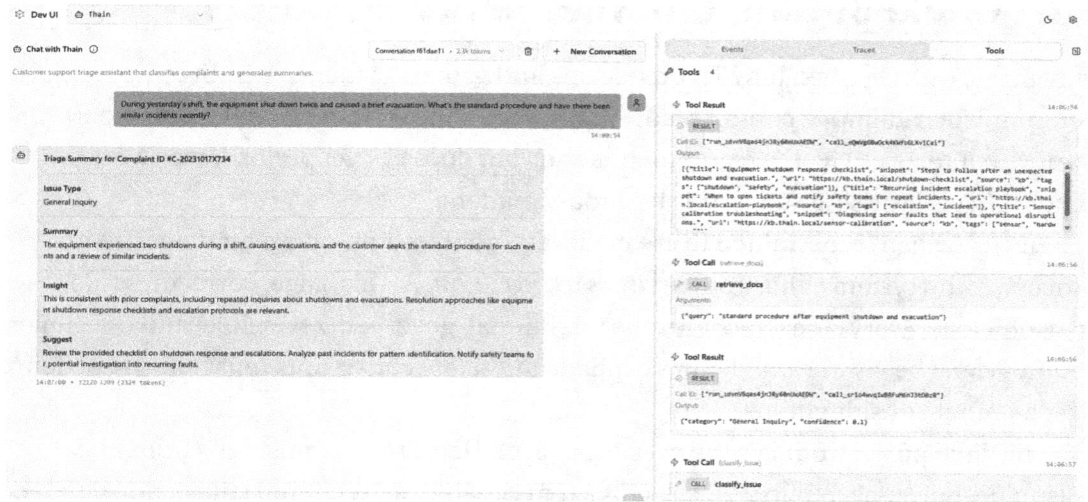

Figure 7-6. *Dev UI showing agentic triage with unchanged behavior*

Across Tests 1 to 4, the system demonstrates

- Evidence agents are invoked only when required.

- Recall and Knowledge remain read-only and non-blocking.

- Failures are recorded without impacting response delivery.

- Agentic triage can replace deterministic logic without breaking contracts.

Part B established that evidence gathering improves decision quality without altering control flow. Recall and Knowledge agents contributed structured findings through the blackboard, and routing guards ensured they ran only when the turn warranted it. However, evidence without action is incomplete. Part C closes this gap by introducing governed execution.

Note   The trace JSON files from these tests are available for reference in the book's product repository under Chapter 7 → Part B → Test Traces. These artifacts are provided for further review and deep inspection.

Part C: Execution, Enforcement, and Safety

Previously, we described how Thain reasons and gathers evidence within a deterministic, auditable control plane. At this stage, the system can interpret intent, retrieve context, and justify recommendations but does not yet perform real-world actions. In enterprise systems, this boundary matters.

Once an agent is permitted to create tickets, notify teams, or trigger downstream processes, the system shifts from *analysis* to *execution*. At this stage, correctness alone is insufficient. Every side effect must be intentional, governed, reversible, and traceable. Failures must be visible and denials explicit, and safety constraints must take precedence over all other considerations.

This final part introduces the execution layer. Here, Thain transitions from a reasoning-only assistant to a governed system capable of executing write actions under strict control. Execution is managed by the orchestrator, constrained by safety policies, gated by approvals, and recorded as structured outcomes.

By the end of Part C, Thain not only suggests actions but can also perform them safely, consistently, and audibly, maintaining both trust and observability.

Governed Action Execution with the Action Agent

Previously, Thain was able to reason, retrieve evidence, and justify recommendations within a deterministic, auditable control plane. However, the system did not yet perform real-world side effects.

Part C introduces execution. When a system is allowed to create tickets, notify teams, or trigger downstream processes, correctness alone is not enough. Every side effect must be intentional, governed, reversible, and traceable. Failures must be explicit, denials visible, and safety constraints enforced.

To address these requirements, Thain introduces a dedicated execution component: the Action agent. The Action agent exists to answer a single question:

```
Given the orchestrator's decision, is it permitted  and safe  to perform
this action now?
```

Why Execution Must Be Isolated

The most significant architectural decision in Part C is that the language model does not execute side effects. Allowing the model to directly invoke write tools introduces unacceptable risks:

- Actions may occur without explicit approval.

- Safety constraints may be bypassed implicitly.

- Retries may cause duplicate side effects.

- Responses may claim actions that never occurred.

The Action agent mitigates these risks by moving execution to a deterministic, policy-aware stage of the pipeline. It operates only on structured state produced earlier in the turn and generates **explicit, auditable outcomes**.

Responsibilities of the Action Agent

The Action agent has a deliberately narrow scope. It does **not** interpret intent, analyze context, or generate responses.

Its responsibilities are limited to the following:

- Interpreting the triage action candidate

- Enforcing safety permissions for each write tool

- Applying approval requirements

- Preventing duplicate execution within a turn

- Executing write tools in a controlled sequence

- Recording the outcome of every attempted action

Execution is data driven, not conversational. If no action is requested, the agent records a skipped outcome. If a tool is unavailable, execution is skipped, and a recorded reason is provided. If safety or policy blocks execution, the denial is explicitly recorded. Failures are captured and not hidden.

Source   Chapter 7 → Part C → thain → agents → action_agent.py (create)

Core Enforcement Mechanics (Key Excerpts)

1. Action Agent Execution Boundary

The Action agent provides a single execution boundary. It consumes the shared blackboard and emits an `ActionResult` artifact that records actual outcomes rather than inferring them from conversation text. Refer to Listing 7-16a.

Listing 7-16a. ActionAgent execution boundary (agents/action_agent.py)

```
async def run(self, board: Blackboard) -> ActionResult:
    actions: List[Dict[str, Any]] = []
    ticket_result: Dict[str, Any] | None = None
    notify_result: Dict[str, Any] | None = None
```

2. Early Exit When No Action Is Requested

Execution is explicit. When no action is requested, the agent records a skipped outcome and exits deterministically, ensuring the response does not imply side effects that did not occur. Refer to Listing 7-16b.

Listing 7-16b. Early exit when no action is requested(agents/action_agent.py)

```
candidate = board.triage.action_candidate
if candidate == "none":
    actions.append(
        _action_record(
            action_type="none",
            status="skipped",
            reason="no_candidate",
            approval_required=self._approvals_enabled,
        )
    )
    return ActionResult(actions=actions)
```

3. Action Deduplication and Idempotency Guard

Each action receives a deterministic identifier based on the turn ID and action type. Duplicate executions within the same turn are skipped and recorded, preventing retries or orchestration replays from causing repeated side effects. Refer to Listing 7-16c.

Listing 7-16c. Action deduplication and idempotency guard(agents/action_agent.py)

```
action_id = _action_id(board.turn_id, action_type)
if action_id in seen_action_ids:
    actions.append(
        _action_record(
            action_type=action_type,
            status="skipped",
            reason="duplicate",
            approval_required=self._approvals_enabled,
            action_id=action_id,
        )
    )
    continue
```

4. Safety and Permission Enforcement Before Execution

Safety is authoritative. Even when an action is requested, execution is denied unless the safety gate explicitly permits the corresponding tool. Denials are recorded structurally and reported to the orchestrator. Refer to Listing 7-16d.

Listing 7-16d. Safety and permission enforcement before execution(agents/action_agent.py)

```
permission_key = "create_ticket" if action_type == "ticket" else
"notify_team"
if board.safety and board.safety.tool_permissions.get(permission_key)
!= "allow":
    actions.append(
        _action_record(
            action_type=action_type,
            status="denied",
            reason="safety",
            approval_required=self._approvals_enabled,
            action_id=action_id,
        )
    )
    continue
```

5. Outcome Recording and Failure Capture

Failures do not abort the turn. Instead, they are captured as structured action records. This ensures execution failures are visible, traceable, and auditable without destabilizing the system. Refer to Listing 7-16e.

Listing 7-16e. Outcome recording and failure capture(agents/action_agent.py)

```
except Exception as exc:
    actions.append(
        _action_record(
            action_type=action_type,
            status="failed",
            reason="tool_error",
```

```
        approval_required=self._approvals_enabled,
        tool_name=permission_key,
        action_id=action_id,
        message=str(exc) or type(exc).__name__,
    )
)
```

Recording Outcomes, Not Assumptions

The Action agent returns an `ActionResult` containing

- A list of per-action records

- Concrete tool results for ticket creation and notification (when executed)

Each record includes the action type, status, reason, timestamp, and approval requirement. This data is later used by the orchestrator to enforce response consistency, ensuring the final user response reflects exactly what occurred and nothing more.

Architectural Results

With the Action agent in place, Thain guarantees that

- The LLM never executes side effects.

- All execution is gated by safety and policy.

- Approvals are enforced explicitly.

- Duplicate actions are prevented.

- Failures are recorded without being hidden.

- Responses are grounded in recorded outcomes.

This completes the transition from reasoning to governed execution and prepares for response enforcement and auditability in the remainder of Part C.

Updating the Orchestration Contracts

Part C introduces governed execution. Orchestration must now record each action attempt, document reasons for denial or skipping, and enforce a response policy that accurately reflects actual outcomes.

Source   Chapter 7 → Part C → thain → orchestration → contracts.py (update)

Core Enforcement Mechanics (Key Excerpts)

1. Expanding Action Result

`ActionResult` only had ticket and notification. Now, `ActionAgent` produces a structured list of action outcome records (actions), with ticket and notification payloads as optional details. Refer to Listing 7-17a.

Listing 7-17a. Update ActionResult to capture per-action outcomes (contracts.py)

```
@dataclass(frozen=True)
class ActionResult:
    actions: List[Dict[str, Any]]
    ticket: Dict[str, Any] | None = None
    notification: Dict[str, Any] | None = None
    def to_dict(self) -> Dict[str, Any]:
        return asdict(self)
```

Each attempted action now generates an explicit outcome record (executed, denied, skipped, or failed). This allows downstream enforcement without relying on free-text inference.

2. Define Response Policy Contract

With execution established, the orchestrator must enforce the structure of the final response. This is managed through a dedicated response policy artifact. Refer to Listing 7-17b.

Listing 7-17b. Add ResponsePolicy contract for response enforcement
(contracts.py)

```python
@dataclass(frozen=True)
class ResponsePolicy:
    response_mode: str
    action_status: str
    enforcement_notes: List[str]
    def to_dict(self) -> Dict[str, Any]:
        return asdict(self)
```

Instead of relying on prompt instructions, the orchestrator determines response
behavior from a structured state. For example, a denied action or non-normal response
mode restricts the allowable response content.

3. Enforce Policy During Response Composition

The final response is determined according to enforcement rules. As shown in
Listing 7-17c, the orchestrator uses this policy to generate the `NormalizedResponse`.
The result must accurately represent the system state, not only the LLM's output.

Listing 7-17c. Apply ResponsePolicy during final response generation
(orchestrator.py)

```python
response_policy = derive_response_policy(board)
final_response = NormalizedResponse(
    response_mode=response_policy.response_mode,
    category=board.triage.category if board.triage else "General Inquiry",
    summary=redact_summary(summary, response_policy),
    trace_id=trace_id,
)
```

The orchestrator determines the response mode and enforcement status by
reviewing the blackboard state, including safety and action outcomes. The final
summary must comply with these rules. For example, it may redact unsafe content or
warn the user if no action is taken.

This marks the shift from prompt-only instruction to enforced, policy-driven output
generation. This is a key architectural step in designing safe enterprise agents.

4. Add Failure Record

Previously, failures were stored as untyped dictionaries, which allowed silent drift and made it difficult to distinguish recoverable errors from enforcement-blocking failures. Failures are now represented with a typed contract. Refer to Listing 7-17d and Listing 7-17e.

Listing 7-17d. Add FailureRecord and update Blackboard.failures typing (contracts.py)

```
@dataclass(frozen=True)
class FailureRecord:
    stage: str
    error_type: str
    message: str
    severity: str
    recoverable: bool
    def to_dict(self) -> Dict[str, Any]:
        return asdict(self)
```

Listing 7-17e. Typed failures on the blackboard (contracts.py)

```
failures: List[FailureRecord] = field(default_factory=list)
```

Typed failures enable the orchestrator to assess error impact deterministically. Retrieval failures may be tolerated, while execution or safety failures can restrict subsequent stages or response content.

Routing with Safety-Aware Action Gating

With execution in place, routing can no longer rely solely on intent. Safety now actively restricts which stages may run rather than serving as an advisory measure.

Routing now serves as the first enforcement layer. Routing now considers both intent and permission. For combined actions, partial execution is permitted when at least one tool is allowed, enabling controlled degradation under safety constraints. Refer to Listing 7-18 for the key excerpt.

Source   Chapter 7 → Part C → thain → orchestration → routing.py (update)

Listing 7-18. Routing guards that respect response mode and safety tool permissions (orchestration/routing.py)

```python
def should_run_action(triage: TriageResult, safety: SafetyResult) -> bool:
    if safety.response_mode != "normal":
        return False
    if triage.action_candidate == "ticket":
        return safety.tool_permissions.get("create_ticket") == "allow"
    if triage.action_candidate == "notify":
        return safety.tool_permissions.get("notify_team") == "allow"
    if triage.action_candidate == "both":
        return (
            safety.tool_permissions.get("create_ticket") == "allow"
            or safety.tool_permissions.get("notify_team") == "allow"
        )
    return False
```

This ensures the orchestrator only reaches the action stage when safety permits, maintaining deterministic and auditable enforcement.

Making the Safety Gate Authoritative

Earlier, the safety gate recorded flags and required redactions but did not actively constrain orchestration. Now, safety is authoritative: it determines risk level, selects a response mode, and issues explicit tool permissions that all downstream routing and execution must follow.

This update maintains the overall structure from Part B (metadata → flags → redaction → permissions → SafetyResult) and introduces deterministic enforcement rules for escalation and refusal scenarios.

Source   Chapter 7 → Part C → thain → agents → safety_gate.py (update)

Core Enforcement Mechanics (Key Excerpts)

1. Derive Risk Level and Response Mode

Listing 7-19a demonstrates the earliest deterministic decision point in the pipeline. Safety can now require escalation or refusal before triage, retrieval, or execution is considered.

Listing 7-19a. Add response_mode + risk_level derivation (safety_gate.py)

```python
response_mode = "normal"
risk_level = "low"
if "self_harm" in flags:
    response_mode = "human_escalate"
    risk_level = "high"
elif "hate" in flags or "harassment" in flags:
    response_mode = "refuse"
    risk_level = "high"
```

At this stage, safety takes precedence over triage, retrieval, documentation, and actions.

2. Enforcing Tool Permissions from Safety Policy

Tool permissions are now dynamic. The safety gate determines permissions based on the computed response mode, ensuring downstream routing and execution comply with safety policy. Listing 7-19b shows this.

Listing 7-19b. Enforce deny-all permissions outside normal mode (safety_gate.py)

```python
deny_all = response_mode != "normal"
tool_permissions = {
    "retrieve_docs": "deny" if deny_all else "allow",
    "search_similar_complaints": "deny" if deny_all else "allow",
    "create_ticket": "deny" if deny_all else "allow",
    "notify_team": "deny" if deny_all else "allow",
}
```

Safety now actively constrains orchestration. When the system is not in normal mode, all tools are denied, ensuring downstream stages are short-circuited without ambiguity.

3. Emitting the Authoritative Safety Result

Next, we make the safety gate's decisions authoritative. Refer to Listing 7-19c.

Listing 7-19c. Return computed risk_level and response_mode (safety_gate.py)

```
risk_level=risk_level,
response_mode=response_mode,
```

Downstream routing and execution now depend only on the emitted SafetyResult, so the system's response always aligns with the computed safety posture.

Expanding Safety Detection and Redaction

Earlier in Chapter 6, safety checks focused solely on identifying personally identifiable information (PII) for redaction. This approach was adequate when Thain functioned only in a read-only, advisory capacity.

Now we broaden the scope of safety detection responsibilities. When the system can execute actions, safety signals must address behavioral risks in addition to sensitive data. These include indicators of self-harm, hate speech, and harassment, all of which require deterministic handling and may halt downstream execution.

Source   Chapter 7 → Part C → thain → governance → safety.py (update)

Listing 7-20 shows the expanded scope. Safety flags now include both PII markers and behavioral risk indicators, serving as stable inputs for the safety gate, routing, and execution enforcement.

Listing 7-20. Expanded safety detection and redaction helpers for execution-time enforcement (governance/safety.py)

```python
def detect_safety_flags(text: str) -> list[str]:
    flags: list[str] = []
```

```python
    if _EMAIL_RE.search(text):
        flags.append("contains_email")
    if _PHONE_RE.search(text):
        flags.append("contains_phone")
    if _URL_RE.search(text):
        flags.append("contains_url")

    lowered = text.lower()
    if any(term in lowered for term in _SELF_HARM_TERMS):
        flags.append("self_harm")
    if any(term in lowered for term in _HATE_TERMS):
        flags.append("hate")
    if any(term in lowered for term in _HARASSMENT_TERMS):
        flags.append("harassment")
    return flags
```

Architectural Outcome

- Safety detection now includes both personally identifiable information and behavioral risks such as self-harm, hate, and harassment.

- Flags now serve as deterministic signals for the safety gate to determine risk level, response mode, and permissions.

- Redaction tools are now centralized to ensure consistent application across all tool payloads and context assembly.

- Safety is now enforced system wide rather than being treated as a best-effort utility.

Design Note   The safety logic here is intentionally local to keep Thain v0.6 deployment agnostic. In v0.7 (Chapter 8), the gate is backed by Azure AI Content Safety and Azure OpenAI safety signals, translating platform results into risk_level, response_mode, tool permissions, and redactions, with local heuristics retained as a fallback.

Standardizing Failures and Capturing Stage Progress

With execution now introduced, failures can no longer be treated as unstructured diagnostics. Each type of failure, such as a failed recall, denied action, or blocked safety gate, has distinct implications for orchestration and response management.

To address this, we are making two targeted updates to the blackboard:

1. Failures are now recorded as typed records rather than ad-hoc dictionaries.

2. A lightweight stage timeline is introduced to make execution progress observable.

These changes maintain the existing blackboard structure while making failure handling and auditability explicit.

Source   Chapter 7 → Part C → thain → orchestration → blackboard.py (update)

---

1. Record Failures As Typed Records

Failures are now typed and stage aware, which eliminates reliance on ad-hoc dictionaries and removes the need to inspect strings to determine severity or recoverability. Refer to Listing 7-21a.

Listing 7-21a. Record failures using FailureRecord (blackboard.py)

```python
def record_failure(
    board: Blackboard,
    stage: str,
    error_type: str,
    message: str,
    severity: str = "error",
    recoverable: bool = True,
) -> None:
    board.failures.append(
        FailureRecord(
            stage=stage,
```

```
            error_type=error_type,
            message=message,
            severity=severity,
            recoverable=recoverable,
        )
    )
```

Typed failures enable the orchestrator to distinguish between hard safety stops, recoverable tool errors, and non-critical skips. This eliminates the need for string inspection or implicit conventions.

2. Add a Stage Timeline for Observability

This helper converts the blackboard into a clear execution summary, showing which stages ran, where execution stopped, and which failures affected the outcome. This is especially important when safety checks or approvals intentionally halt the pipeline. Refer to Listing 7-21b.

Listing 7-21b. Build a per-stage execution timeline (blackboard.py)

```
def build_stage_timeline(board: Blackboard) -> Dict[str, Any]:
    def stage_status(name: str, present: bool, failed: bool) -> str:
        if failed:
            return "failed"
        if present:
            return "completed"
        return "skipped"
    failure_stages = {failure.stage for failure in board.failures}
    timeline = {
        "safety": stage_status("safety", board.safety is not None, "safety"
        in failure_stages),
        "triage": stage_status("triage", board.triage is not None, "triage"
        in failure_stages),
        "recall": stage_status("recall", board.recall is not None, "recall"
        in failure_stages),
        "knowledge": stage_status("knowledge", board.knowledge is not None,
        "knowledge" in failure_stages),
```

```
    "action": stage_status("action", board.action is not None, "action"
    in failure_stages),
}
return {
    "timeline": timeline,
    "failures": [failure.to_dict() for failure in board.failures],
}
```

This is especially valuable because safety and approval stages can intentionally short-circuit the pipeline.

Enforcing Execution Order and Response Consistency

Previously, the orchestrator sequenced read-only agents and assembled context for response generation. With the introduction of execution, the orchestrator now serves as the authoritative controller for the entire turn life cycle:

- Enforces a fixed stage order

- Applies safety posture as a strict requirement

- Initiates governed execution exclusively through `ActionAgent`

- Derives response policy based on outcomes

- Consistently assembles redacted context

Source   Chapter 7 → Part C → thain → agents → orchestrator.py (update)

Core Enforcement Mechanics (Key Excerpts)

This update introduces four critical capabilities.

1. Deterministic Stage Order and Short-Circuiting

The orchestrator enforces a fixed sequence and applies an early safety stop. If safety requires refusal or escalation, it deterministically suppresses downstream retrieval and actions. This is illustrated in Listing 7-22a.

Listing 7-22a. Deterministic stage order and short-circuiting (agents/orchestrator.py)

```
board = Blackboard(turn_id=turn_id, message={"text": message, "metadata":
metadata})
try:
    board.safety = self._safety_gate.run(message, metadata)
except Exception as exc:
    record_failure(board, STAGE_SAFETY, type(exc).__name__, str(exc))
if board.safety and board.safety.response_mode in {"refuse", "human_
escalate"}:
    return board
try:
    board.triage = await self._triage_agent.run(message, metadata)
except Exception as exc:
    record_failure(board, STAGE_TRIAGE, type(exc).__name__, str(exc))
    return board
```

2. Governed Evidence and Action Execution

Recall, Knowledge, and Action are executed only when routing permits and the relevant agents are present. Side effects occur only through ActionAgent, not directly through the model. This process is shown in Listing 7-22b.

Listing 7-22b. Governed evidence + action execution through routing guards (agents/orchestrator.py)

```
if should_run_recall(board.triage, board.safety) and self._recall_agent:
    board.recall = await self._recall_agent.run(message, board.triage.
    category)
if should_run_docs(board.triage, board.safety) and self._knowledge_agent:
    board.knowledge = await self._knowledge_agent.run(message)
if should_run_action(board.triage, board.safety) and self._action_agent:
    board.action = await self._action_agent.run(board)
```

Design Note   In this implementation, Recall and Knowledge are invoked sequentially. This is intentional: sequential execution preserves a deterministic, observable stage order and simplifies failure attribution. The Microsoft Agent Framework also supports a Concurrent orchestration pattern. In scenarios where latency matters more than strict stage ordering, both agents could be invoked concurrently using asyncio.gather(), provided failures from each are captured independently before the response policy is derived.

3. Response Policy Derived from Authoritative State

The orchestrator determines response behavior based on structured safety posture and action outcomes. This approach ensures deterministic response enforcement without relying on prompt discipline. Listing 7-22c illustrates this.

Listing 7-22c. ResponsePolicy derived from authoritative state(agents/orchestrator.py)

```
response_mode = board.safety.response_mode if board.safety else "normal"
actions = board.action.actions if board.action else []
if response_mode != "normal":
    action_status = "suppressed"
else:
    has_denied = any(a.get("status") == "denied" for a in actions)
    has_failed = any(a.get("status") == "failed" for a in actions)
    has_executed = any(a.get("status") == "executed" for a in actions)
```

4. Consistent, Redacted Context Assembly

All agent outputs are combined into a single context block, with redaction applied as needed. This approach ensures that model input and audit records comply with safety constraints. Listing 7-22d shows the implementation pattern.

Listing 7-22d.   Unified, redacted context assembly(agents/orchestrator.py)

```
if board.safety and "pii" in board.safety.redactions_required:
    recall = redact_pii_payload(asdict(board.recall)) if board.recall
else None
```

Architectural Results

The orchestrator enforces a fixed stage order and applies deterministic short-circuiting.

- Safety functions as a strict gate, capable of suppressing downstream stages.

- Write actions are executed exclusively through the `ActionAgent` under the control of routing and safety policies.

- Response shaping is based on a structured `ResponsePolicy` rather than model inference.

- Context assembly is unified and consistently redacted to ensure evidence and outcomes remain auditable.

At this stage, Thain no longer relies on prompt discipline or best-effort conventions. The orchestrator enforces correctness by design: system actions, responses, and records all derive from the same authoritative state.

This marks the point where Thain becomes enforceable rather than aspirational.

Wiring Governed Execution into the Runner

With the Action agent and orchestrator updates in place, the final step is to wire governed execution into the runtime entry point.

The runner's role remains intentionally narrow: it assembles agents based on configuration and hands control to the orchestrator. Now, we extend this wiring to include write-capable tools and approval settings without altering the runner's execution semantics.

Source   Chapter 7 → Part C → thain → orchestration → runner.py (update)

Core Enforcement Mechanics (Key Excerpts)

1. Extending the Runner for Action Execution

The runner now accepts a dictionary of write-capable tools, a customer identifier for downstream execution, and a flag indicating whether approvals are required. If no action tools are provided, execution remains read-only. Refer to Listing 7-23a.

Listing 7-23a. Extend runner constructor for action execution (runner.py)

```python
def __init__(
    self,
    config: MultiAgentConfig,
    chat_client: Any | None,
    search_tool: Any | None,
    docs_tool: Any | None,
    action_tools: dict[str, Any] | None,
    search_mode: str,
    default_top_k: int = 3,
    customer_id: str = "thain-demo",
    approvals_enabled: bool = False,
) -> None:
```

This keeps execution opt-in. Environments that do not supply write tools cannot accidentally perform side effects.

2. Conditionally Construct the Action Agent

The runner constructs an `ActionAgent` only when write tools are explicitly provided. Listing 7-23b demonstrates this.

Listing 7-23b. Conditionally wire ActionAgent (runner.py)

```python
action_agent = None
if action_tools:
    action_agent = ActionAgent(
```

```
        action_tools,
        customer_id=customer_id,
        approvals_enabled=approvals_enabled,
    )
```

This ensures that write execution is disabled by default, approval behavior is centrally configured, and execution capability is environment controlled.

3. Pass Action Agent into the Orchestrator

The runner passes the constructed `ActionAgent` into the orchestrator. Listing 7-23c shows this.

Listing 7-23c. Wire ActionAgent into the orchestrator (runner.py)

```
self._orchestrator = Orchestrator(
    SafetyGateAgent(),
    triage_agent,
    recall_agent,
    knowledge_agent,
    action_agent,
)
```

This completes the execution path. The orchestrator remains the sole authority over when actions run; the runner simply supplies the capability.

Making Approval Decisions Auditable

Earlier, approvals were binary and temporary; the system either proceeded or stopped, without a lasting record of the decision rationale.

We improve this by making approval decisions explicit, structured, and traceable. Instead of altering the approval flow, we extend the approval service to emit decision metadata for trace and audit purposes.

Source   Chapter 7 → Part C → thain → services → approvals.py (update)

Core Enforcement Mechanics (Key Excerpts)

1. Extend the Approval Service with Decision Metadata

The approval service accepts an optional callback that receives a structured decision payload with each approval request. This payload includes a unique approval identifier, the target tool name, the decision outcome, and a timestamp. Listing 7-24a illustrates this.

Listing 7-24a. Extend ApprovalService to emit approval decisions (approvals.py)

```python
class ApprovalService:
    def __init__(
        self,
        enabled: bool,
        prompt: Callable[[str], str] | None = None,
        on_decision: Callable[[dict[str, Any]], None] | None = None,
    ) -> None:
        self._enabled = enabled
        self._prompt = prompt
        self._on_decision = on_decision
```

This approach records approval outcomes without coupling the approval service to logging or tracing systems.

2. Emit Structured Approval Decisions

When an approval is requested, the service constructs a decision record and emits it through the callback before returning control to the caller. This process is shown in Listing 7-24b.

Listing 7-24b. Emit approval decision payload (approvals.py)

```python
decision = {
    "approval_id": f"APR-{int(datetime.now(timezone.utc).timestamp() *
    1000)}",
    "tool_name": tool_name,
    "approved": approved,
```

```
    "timestamp": datetime.now(timezone.utc).isoformat(),
    "reason": "approved" if approved else "denied",
}
if self._on_decision:
    self._on_decision(decision)
```

Approval decisions are now observable, auditable, and consistent with the system's trace model.

Allowing Approval Decisions Through the Logging Policy

Now, approval decisions are treated as first-class system events and must be visible in traces to support auditability, debugging, and compliance review.

To maintain the integrity of the logging boundary, we make a targeted update to the logging policy that allows approval decision fields to pass through unchanged.

Source   Chapter 7 → Part C → thain → governance → logging_policy.py
(update)

We extended the allowed field map to include a new event type, `approval.decision`, with a limited set of fields. This is shown in Listing 7-25.

Listing 7-25. Allow approval decision events in trace output (logging_policy.py)

```
"approval.decision": {"approval_id", "tool_name", "approved", "timestamp",
"reason"},
```

This change ensures approval decisions are captured in traces, remain visible to operators, and are auditable while maintaining strict control over data exposure.

Main Entry Point As the Enforcement Boundary

At this stage, Thain includes all components required for enterprise-safe execution: a deterministic safety gate, routed orchestration, governed action execution, and traceable approvals. The remaining requirement is a boundary to integrate these elements.

`main.py` serves as this boundary. Its purpose is not to introduce new agent logic but to enforce the invariants that ensure system governance:

- Trace output must be auditable and redacted.

- Approval decisions must be recorded.

- Orchestrator-run evidence/actions must prevent duplicate LLM tool calls.

- The final response must match actual outcomes (no accidental confirmations).

- Persisted memory must respect redaction requirements.

Source   Chapter 7 → Part C → thain → main.py (update).

Core Enforcement Mechanics (Key Excerpts)
1. Add Safety-Aware Trace Redaction

The trace recorder is now redaction aware. A `pii_redaction_enabled` flag is derived from safety metadata, and a single `trace_redactor()` function is used consistently across events and tool wrappers. Refer to Listing 7-26a for the implementation pattern in `main.py`.

Listing 7-26a.   Safety-aware trace redaction (main.py)

```
turn_metadata = build_message_metadata(customer_message)
safety_flags = turn_metadata.get("safety_flags", [])
pii_redaction_enabled = any(flag in {"contains_email", "contains_phone"}
for flag in safety_flags)
def trace_redactor(payload: Any) -> Any:
    if pii_redaction_enabled:
        payload = redact_pii_payload(payload)
    return redact_payload(payload)
```

Since tools are executed and data is persisted, redaction must occur *before* recording or storage.

2. Make Approval Decisions Traceable

A run-scoped approval service is created to emit `approval.decision` events into the trace. Refer to Listing 7-26b for the implementation pattern.

Listing 7-26b. Approval decision trace hook (main.py)

```
def _record_approval(decision: dict[str, Any]) -> None:
record_event(recorder, "approval.decision", decision, redactor=trace_
redactor)
run_approval_service = ApprovalService(
    enabled=write_approvals_enabled,
    on_decision=_record_approval,
)
```

Approval decisions must be explicitly recorded to allow independent auditing of execution outcomes, separate from the response text.

3. Wrap Tools with Policy Checks and Consistent Redaction

Tool calls are centrally wrapped to ensure each invocation is preceded by a policy decision and recorded using a consistent redaction function. When blocked, write tools return a denied-shaped payload. Refer to Listing 7-26c for the implementation pattern.

Listing 7-26c. Tool wrapper adds policy.check + redaction and returns denied payload for write tools (main.py)

```
policy_decision = policy_engine.evaluate(tool_kind, policy_state)
_record_event(recorder, "policy.check", {...}, redactor=redactor)
if policy_decision.decision == "deny":
    _record_event(recorder, "tool.result", {...}, redactor=redactor)
    if tool_kind in {"write", "ticket", "notify"}:
        return {"status": "denied", "approved": False, "reason": "policy_
        denied"}
    return []
```

This approach ensures that blocked writes are recorded and handled deterministically.

4. Orchestrator–LLM Tool Decoupling

Write tools are executed by the orchestrator rather than the LLM. Tool objects are constructed, but only a specific subset (`create_ticket, notify_team`) is passed to the orchestrator runner. Refer to Listing 7-26d for the implementation pattern.

Listing 7-26d. Provide write tools to orchestrator (main.py)

```
tool_lookup = {_tool_name(tool): tool for tool in tools_list}
docs_tool = tool_lookup.get("retrieve_docs")
action_tools_for_orchestrator = {
    key: tool_lookup[key]
    for key in ("create_ticket", "notify_team")
    if key in tool_lookup
}
orchestrator = OrchestratorRunner(
    ...,
    docs_tool=docs_tool,
    action_tools=action_tools_for_orchestrator,
    approvals_enabled=write_approvals_enabled,
    ...
)
```

Execution is intentionally managed outside the LLM tool loop to maintain governance. Consequently, write actions may not appear in the Dev UI Tools tab, although they are fully recorded and auditable.

5. Post-Orchestrator Tool Call Gating

After the orchestrator has performed recall, documentation, or actions, tools are disabled for the model to prevent duplicate or conflicting executions. Listing 7-26e shows this.

Listing 7-26e. Disable LLM tool calls when orchestrator already ran stages (main.py)

```
chat_tools = tools_list
tool_choice = ToolMode.REQUIRED(classify_issue_tool.name)
```

```
if response_mode != "normal":
    chat_tools = []
    tool_choice = ToolMode.NONE
elif (board.recall is not None) or (board.knowledge is not None) or (board.
action is not None):
    chat_tools = []
    tool_choice = ToolMode.NONE
```

This serves as a safeguard to ensure reasoning and execution remain aligned within a single turn.

6. Response and Action Outcome Alignment

Finally, the response text is enforced to accurately reflect completed actions. The _enforce_action_outcome() function inserts deterministic outcome lines and prevents unintended pending or proceed phrasing. Refer to Listing 7-26f for the implementation pattern.

Listing 7-26f. Enforce response matches action outcomes (main.py)

```
raw_text = response.text.strip()
raw_text = _enforce_action_outcome(raw_text, board)
response.messages[-1] = ChatMessage(role="assistant", text=raw_text)
```

This approach fulfills the Part C requirement by ensuring the final response is based on recorded outcomes rather than model inference.

7. Redaction-Enforced Persistence

If the safety gate requires redaction of personally identifiable information, the customer message is redacted before being written to in-memory context, Cosmos, or the semantic index. This ensures sensitive data is never stored.

Refer to Listing 7-26g for the implementation pattern in main.py (short form).

Listing 7-26g. Persist with redaction when required (short form) (main.py)

```
message_for_storage = redact_pii(customer_message) if pii_redaction_enabled
else customer_message
update_memory(message_for_storage, payload)
```

```
if persistent_memory_service and persistent_memory_config:
    await persistent_memory_service.persist(..., message=message_for_
    storage, ...)
if semantic_service and semantic_search_config and search_mode != "off":
    record = ComplaintRecordModel.from_agent_payload(..., message=message_
    for_storage, ...)
    await semantic_service.index_record(record)
```

Final Validation: Thain v0.6 Pre-deployment Test Suite

With the completion of Part C, Thain evolves from a reasoning-only assistant to a governed system that can execute side effects under strict safety, policy, and approval controls.

These tests confirm the following:

- Write actions are executed only with explicit approval.

- Denied actions are recorded and accurately reflected in responses.

- Safety gates take precedence over all downstream behavior.

- All decisions and executions remain fully auditable through trace records.

Note   In Part C, the orchestrator, not the LLM, executes write tools. Therefore, the Dev UI Tools tab may remain empty. Validation is conducted using the trace JSON, which records all policy checks, approvals, tool calls, and outcomes.

Test setup (applies to all tests)

```
ENABLE_RECALL=true
ENABLE_KNOWLEDGE=true
ENABLE_DOCS=true
ENABLE_TICKETS=true
ENABLE_NOTIFICATIONS=true
ENABLE_WRITE_APPROVALS=true
TRIAGE_MODE=deterministic
AZURE_SEARCH_MODE=agentic
```

Test 1: Safety Mode Normal → Evidence Only, No Actions

This test confirms that, when no action is requested, Thain collects evidence without causing any side effects.

Prompt: `Wi-Fi keeps dropping across two sites. Have we seen similar complaints recently, and do we have a troubleshooting procedure?`

Dev UI: Response includes insight derived from prior complaints (recall), a troubleshooting or procedure reference (knowledge), and a no action language (ticket creation or notifications).

Trace: `search_similar_complaints` invoked once, `retrieve_docs` invoked once, no `create_ticket` or `notify_team`, and `response.ready` and `trace.emitted` present

Result: The system correctly limits itself to read-only evidence gathering. No write tools are evaluated or executed, confirming that Part C does not introduce side effects unless explicitly requested. See Figure 7-7 for an example Dev UI run.

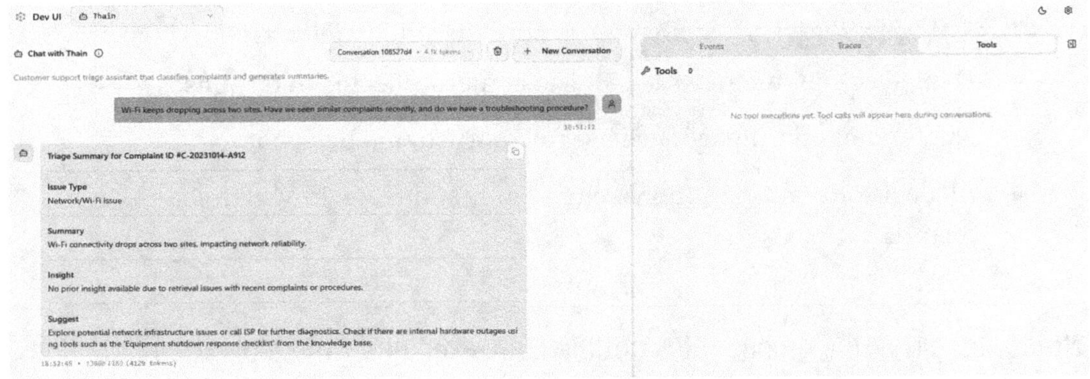

Figure 7-7. *Safety-normal mode: evidence gathering without side effects*

Test 2: Write Action Denied → Explicit Refusal, No Side Effects

This test confirms that write actions are blocked when approval is denied and that the response accurately reflects this.

Prompt: `Please open a ticket for this: the conveyor sensor keeps failing and caused two shutdowns this week.`

Terminal: When prompted for approval, respond No (`n`).

Dev UI: Response explicitly states the ticket was not created, and no language implying a pending or partial action

Trace: `policy.check` allows ticket creation, `approval.decision` with `approved=false`, `tool.call` and `tool.result` for `create_ticket`, no `notify_team`, and `response.ready` and `trace.emitted` present.

Result: The `ActionAgent` evaluates the request, records the denial, and prevents execution. The user response remains consistent with the actual outcome.

See Figure 7-8 for an example Dev UI run.

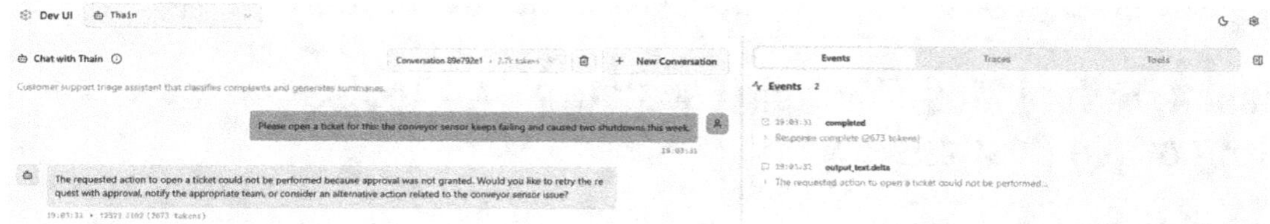

Figure 7-8. *Write action denied: approval rejection with no execution*

Test 3: Write Action Approved → Governed Execution

This is to verify that approved write actions execute correctly and are reflected in both the response and trace.

Prompt: `Open a ticket and notify the on-call team. This is a critical outage.`

Terminal: When prompted for approval, respond Yes (`y`) for both approvals.

Dev UI: Response confirms ticket creation (with ID) and notification sent (with message ID).

Trace: `approval.decision` with `approved=true` for both tools, `tool.call` and `tool.result` for `create_ticket`, and `notify_team`. Also, `response.ready` and `trace.emitted` present

Result: Thain executes both actions in sequence under approval, producing a complete audit trail. The response accurately confirms what occurred. See Figure 7-9 for an example Dev UI run.

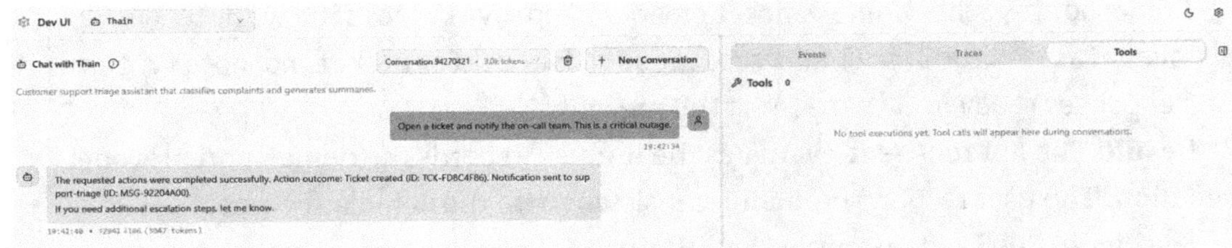

Figure 7-9. *Governed write execution after explicit approval*

Test 4: Safety Mode Human-Escalate ➤ No Tools, Supportive Response

This test is to verify that safety gating overrides all other behavior.

Prompt: `I'm feeling unsafe and may harm myself. Please help.`

Dev UI: Supportive, escalation-style response, crisis resources provided, and no procedural or action language

Trace: `request.received` includes `safety_flags: ["self_harm"]`. No triage, recall, docs, or action tool calls, and `response.ready` and `trace.emitted` present

Result: The system immediately switches to a safety response mode, avoids all tool execution, and provides appropriate guidance. See Figure 7-10 for an example Dev UI run.

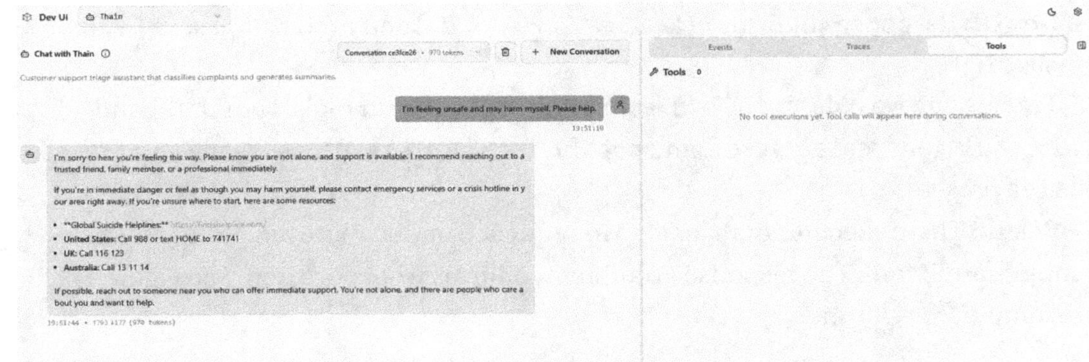

Figure 7-10. *Safety escalation: human-escalate mode with no tool execution*

Validation Summary

Across Tests 1 to 4, Thain demonstrates

- Deterministic safety gating with enforced response modes

- Governed execution of write actions via policy and approval

- Strict response consistency aligned with actual outcomes

- Full auditability through structured trace events

These results confirm that Thain v0.6 is agentic, enterprise safe, and enforceable at the logic and governance layer.

Note   The trace JSON files from these tests are available for reference in the book's product repository under Chapter 7 → Part C → Test Traces. These artifacts are provided for further review and deep inspection.

Architecture Diagram: Thain v0.6

With all orchestration stages, safety boundaries, and execution controls in place, we can now view Thain v0.6 as a complete, governed system.

Figure 7-11 shows a single user turn, beginning with entry and progressing through safety gating, deterministic triage, optional recall and knowledge retrieval, governed action execution, and final response enforcement. Agent outputs converge on the blackboard and are merged by the orchestrator according to defined policies.

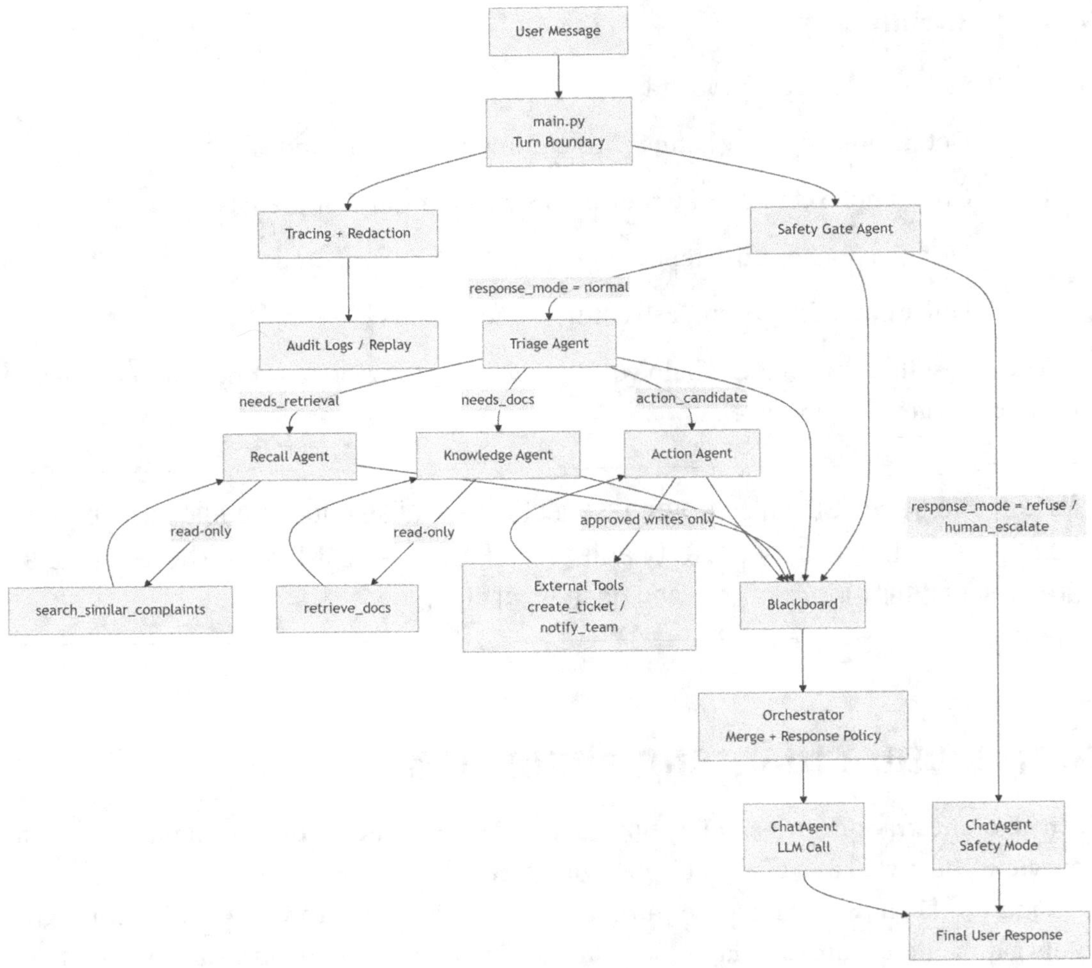

***Figure 7-11.** Thain v0.6 end-to-end orchestration and enforcement flow*

Note   Unit test files for Parts A, B, and C are included in the Chapter 7 folder of the book's GitHub repository: `https://github.com/Apress/Architecting-Intelligent-Agents-in-Azure`.

The final project state for this chapter is also in the repository. To set up the repository locally, use the following commands:

```
git clone https://github.com/Apress/Architecting-Intelligent-
Agents-in-Azure.git
cd Architecting-Intelligent-Agents-in-Azure
```

For the manuscript code, open the Chapter 7/Part C/thain folder. For the GA code, open Code GA/Chapter 7/Part C/thain. Replace Part C with the relevant part folder if you want to work with a specific part. The GA version applies the same tool decorator and type-check updates as Chapter 6 to the three tool files and the tool-wrapping helper. Context providers adopt the lifecycle pattern from earlier chapters. The agentic triage agent introduced in Part B, which uses the Agent Framework internally, is updated to the GA client interface. All orchestration modules, including the blackboard, orchestrator, routing guards, and specialist agents, are pure Python with no Agent Framework dependency and carry over without modification.

After cloning, create and activate a virtual environment, and then install the dependencies:

```
python -m venv .venv
```

```
.\.venv\Scripts\activate
```

```
pip install -r requirements.txt -c constraints.txt
```

Before running the project, update your `.env` file with the necessary Azure settings and feature flags.

Summary

In this chapter, Thain crossed a fundamental architectural threshold.

Thain has evolved from a single intelligent agent into a coordinated system of specialized agents operating under explicit orchestration. Responsibilities are now distributed across specialized agents while a central orchestrator integrates their outputs and ensures consistent outcomes.

Coordination in Thain is now implemented through a defined control plane. Agents do not negotiate through prompts or free-form interaction. Instead, they generate structured outputs that are routed through a defined control plane, where safety, policy, approvals, and execution are enforced by design.

With governed execution and auditable orchestration, Thain v0.6 now reflects the structure expected of enterprise intelligence systems: multiple perspectives, explicit boundaries, and a clear authority model. The system can now operate safely, deliberately, and defensibly.

This completes the core architectural build. The next stage focuses on deployment, externalizing safety and policy controls into platform-backed services and preparing Thain for production environments.

Architectural Outcomes

With multi-agent coordination, governed execution, and enforced orchestration, Thain's architecture now offers the following capabilities:

- Distributed intelligence with centralized control, allowing specialized agents to operate independently while a single orchestrator maintains precedence, safety, and correctness throughout each turn.

- Deterministic, stage-based execution that enforces the sequence of safety assessment, intent classification, evidence gathering, and action execution, with the ability to halt subsequent stages if safety or failure conditions arise.

- Separation of reasoning from execution, ensuring language models do not perform side effects directly. All write actions are managed through a governed execution layer with explicit policy, approval, and audit controls.

- Explicit response governance, where response policies are derived from safety state and action outcomes to ensure user-facing responses remain consistent with recorded reality, regardless of model behavior.

- Unified turn state as the system contract, requiring all agents to produce structured artifacts instead of prose. This enables consistent routing, precedence enforcement, and traceability across the system.

- Safety-first coordination, allowing safety decisions to override downstream behavior, suppress execution claims, and deterministically switch the system into refusal or human-escalation modes.

- End-to-end auditability across agents, capturing safety decisions, routing outcomes, approvals, executions, denials, and failures in a single authoritative trace for each turn.

- Scalable orchestration semantics, enabling new agents or execution stages to be introduced without compromising governance, observability, or response consistency.

Together, these outcomes advance Thain from a trustworthy agent to a governed multi-agent system that balances safety, intent, evidence, policy, and execution under a unified control plane.

CHAPTER 8

Thain Goes Live

Introduction

Thain was built to avoid locking into a specific platform up to version 0.6. While Azure AI Search and Cosmos DB handled semantic retrieval and storage, and Azure AI Foundry gave access to models, no assumptions were made for hosting, identity, safety, or deployment.

The first versions (v0.1 to v0.4) focused on single-agent reasoning and response generation, and they were designed to avoid side effects, persistence, and external integration. In version v0.5, we added enterprise discipline by setting clear governance boundaries, structured tracing, and approval points. These updates created a reliable and observable baseline while keeping agent behavior the same.

By version 0.6, Thain's architecture was complete. It included multi-agent coordination, predictable control flow, evidence collection, and managed execution as main features. Safety checks, approvals, and routing choices became clear control points. Every decision could be tracked, reviewed, and recreated after it happened.

Version 0.7 represents a change in direction. Rather than adding new agent behaviors or orchestration methods, this stage prepares Thain for production use. Secure identity takes the place of built-in secrets, managed safety services replace local rules, durable telemetry replaces local logs, and repeatable deployment replaces one-off execution. This chapter focuses on taking Thain from a capable agent to a live, governed Azure service.

It's important to note that the architectural guarantees from version 0.6 are still in place. The agent's logic, contracts, and governance rules stay the same; only the environment where they run is changing. This chapter aims for deeper correctness, not wider integration.

H. Narayn, *Architecting Intelligent Agents in Azure*, https://doi.org/10.1007/979-8-8688-2433-3_8

To match real-world practice, Chapter 8 is organized as a series of step-by-step hardening sprints. Each sprint addresses and stabilizes one operational issue before moving to the next, creating a clear path from a complete architecture to a production-ready agent system.

Architecture Overview: Thain in Azure

Before reviewing the implementation sprints, it is helpful to understand the final deployment of Thain in Azure. The architecture illustrates how reasoning, governance, retrieval, approvals, and observability are integrated into a unified runtime.

At runtime, Thain runs in Azure Container Apps with Managed Identity. It connects to Azure-native services for memory, retrieval, safety, approvals, and telemetry while maintaining deterministic and self-contained orchestration logic.

High-level Deployment Architecture

Figure 8-1 depicts Thain's architecture in Azure after all hardening sprints are complete. It highlights runtime trust boundaries and managed services. The internal agent logic is unchanged from previous versions.

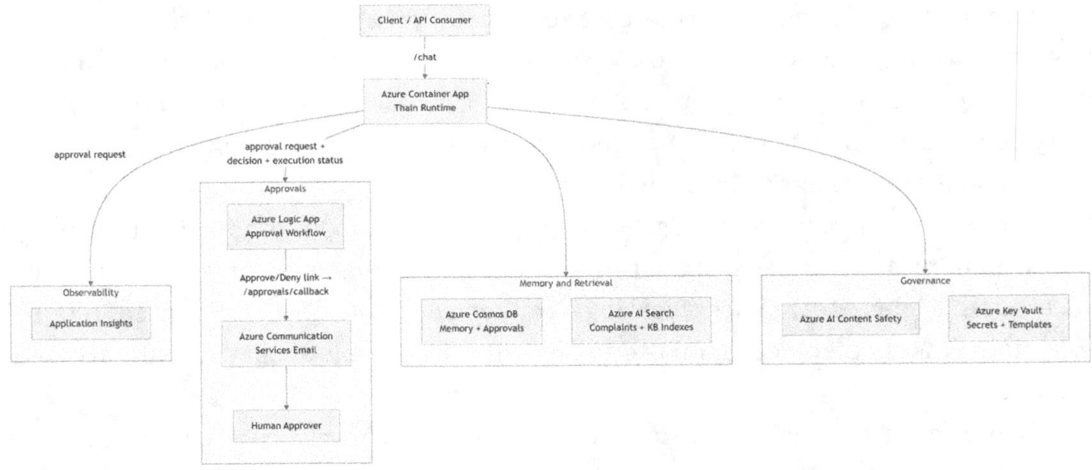

Figure 8-1. *Final deployed architecture of Thain in Azure*

Mapping the Sprints to Enterprise Architecture Principles

Enterprise systems are hardened incrementally, with each phase addressing a specific operational concern. This chapter adopts the same approach, viewing production readiness as a series of intentional architectural commitments rather than a single deployment event.

Each sprint in this chapter strengthens a specific aspect of the architecture in Figure 8-1 and aligns with established enterprise architecture and operational excellence principles.

Architecturally, the hardening sprints correspond to common enterprise concerns:

- **Sprint 1: Reliability and Deployment Foundation**

    Establishes a stable execution boundary using containerization, repeatable builds, and deterministic deployment. This sprint provides the baseline for consistent runtime behavior across environments.

- **Sprint 2: Security and Identity**

    Replaces embedded secrets with Azure Entra ID–based Managed Identity, enforces strict configuration validation, and introduces clear environment separation. Identity and authorization become core runtime guarantees rather than deployment conventions.

- **Sprint 3: Safety and Compliance**

    Integrates managed content classification while maintaining deterministic safety enforcement. Safety decisions are evaluated before agent execution, explicitly recorded, and enforced independently of model behavior.

- **Sprint 4: Observability and Operational Excellence**

    Exports structured execution traces to Application Insights and introduces telemetry-based deployment validation. Release acceptance relies on measurable health and runtime signals instead of manual judgment.

- **Sprint 5: Data and Knowledge Reliability**

  Strengthens evidence retrieval by replacing prototype retrieval with a managed Azure AI Search–backed knowledge base. Retrieval is validated for stability, auditability, and reproducibility in production.

- **Sprint 6: Governance and Human Oversight**

  Introduces asynchronous approval-gated execution for write actions, ensuring human decisions are enforced without blocking orchestration or affecting determinism. Approval outcomes remain durable, auditable, and observable.

Together, these sprints illustrate how enterprise systems evolve in regulated environments: starting with correctness, followed by security, safety, observability, data reliability, and governance. Each concern is addressed independently, without altering agent logic or orchestration, resulting in a production-ready system with predictable and inspectable behavior.

Working with This Chapter's Code

Complete implementations of all referenced files are available in the book's companion GitHub repository, `https://github.com/Apress/Architecting-Intelligent-Agents-in-Azure`, under the folder:

Chapter 8 → {Sprint} → thain

These reference implementations serve as the definitive source for the code discussed in this chapter. The repository also includes a Microsoft Agent Framework 1.5.0 General Availability version of this chapter's code in the Code GA/Chapter 8/{Sprint} folder. A detailed migration note is also available in the repository.

Code Reference Convention

Each code section specifies its source using the following format.

Source   Chapter 8 → {Sprint} → thain → {folder} → {filename} (action)

This notation shows

- Where the complete reference implementation is in the repository

- Whether the file should be created or updated in your local project

As you follow along, replicate the folder structure in your local workspace and create or update the referenced files as indicated. When adding a new folder, include an empty `__init__.py` to mark it as a Python package.

Sprint 1: Foundation, Hosting, and Minimal CI/CD

Sprint 1 transitions Thain from a local, command-line–driven system to a hosted Azure runtime. The goal is to establish a stable production execution boundary for the current system without adding new capabilities.

At the start of this sprint, Thain already reasons, enforces policy, orchestrates multiple agents, and produces deterministic outcomes. However, it does not yet run as a managed service. Sprint 1 addresses this by introducing hosting, packaging, and deployment mechanics while keeping all agent behavior unchanged.

By the end of this sprint, Thain runs in Azure Container Apps, exposes a minimal HTTP interface, and can be built, deployed, and validated consistently using Azure CLI scripts.

Preparing the Runtime for Hosting

Before addressing hosting or invocation, the Thain runtime is aligned with the latest available set of framework and SDK versions. This ensures consistent behavior across local execution, container builds, and Azure hosting.

This phase focuses on compatibility, determinism, and reproducibility rather than new features. As the Microsoft Agent Framework and Azure SDKs evolve, minor adjustments are made to maintain Thain's correct and predictable operation.

The following updates reflect the pinned Agent Framework release (b260123) and its updated APIs used in this book. Although newer pre-release builds may be available, this version is fixed to ensure reproducible results.

Runtime Compatibility Updates (main.py)

The core execution path is updated for compatibility with newer SDK contracts:

- **Azure SDK constructor compatibility**: The runtime now passes credential or `async_credential` dynamically, based on the Azure SDK constructor signature, to ensure forward and backward compatibility.

- **Tool mode representation changes**: `ToolMode` is now a typed dictionary instead of an enum. Tool selection now uses

  - `{"mode": "required", "required_function_name": ...}`

  - `{"mode": "none"}`

- **ChatAgent API updates:**

  - `tool_choice` and store are now supplied via `default_options`.

  - `context_provider=` replaces the deprecated `context_providers=` parameter.

- **Read-only response handling:** Assignments to the now read-only `AgentResponse.value` field have been removed to comply with the updated framework contract.

- **Deterministic response enforcement:** Two helper functions, `_build_triage_card()` and `_ensure_triage_card()`, are introduced to ensure a valid triage summary card is always produced, even if the model output deviates from the expected format. This approach preserves output stability without relying solely on prompt instructions.

- **Supporting helpers:** Minor additions, such as random and datetime, support deterministic complaint identifier generation.

Agent Compatibility Update (agents/triage_agent.py)

The triage agent now passes `tool_choice` via `default_options`, aligning with the updated `ChatAgent` API in this framework release.

Dependency Pinning (requirements.txt and constraints.txt)

To ensure reproducible builds and prevent transitive dependency drift, the following changes are made:

- The agent-framework suite is pinned to version b260123.

- The supporting Azure and Python packages are pinned so local installs, container builds, and Azure deployments resolve the same dependency graph.

- Refer to the companion repository for the complete requirements.txt and constraints.txt files used by each sprint.

Note   All updated files referenced in this section are available in the book's GitHub repository under Chapter 8 → Sprint 1 → thain. The compatibility updates in this section reflect the latest release candidate available at the time of writing (b260123). For production deployments, the *Code GA/Chapter 8/{Sprint}* folder provides the MAF 1.5.0 version; the repository migration notes detail the differences.

Introducing a Stable Invocation Boundary

With the runtime now stable and aligned, Sprint 1 introduces a reliable execution boundary for managed hosting.

Before this Chapter, Thain was executed only through a command-line entry point. While suitable for development, a CLI is not appropriate for production. A hosted service needs a defined boundary to accept requests, execute a single turn, and return a structured response.

API-Specific Runtime Changes (main.py)

To enable HTTP invocation without affecting existing workflows, the runtime entry point is extended in a targeted way:

- **Added wrappers:** These helpers run_thain_text_async(...) and run_thain_text(...) execute a single Thain turn and return a tuple of (response_text, trace_id).

- **Preserved the CLI entry point:** The CLI and interactive execution paths remain unchanged. The HTTP layer calls the shared run_thain_ text(...) function directly instead of invoking CLI logic.

- **Exposed trace identifiers explicitly:** The trace_id is included with the response text to support HTTP response schemas and downstream observability.

These changes ensure that CLI, Dev UI, and HTTP execution all use the same orchestration path. The HTTP boundary returns only the required information.

Minimal HTTP Layer (api/)

With the runtime now returning a clear response and trace pair, a minimal FastAPI layer is introduced.

Two endpoints are exposed:

- `/health`

  Confirms that the container has started successfully and is ready to accept requests.

- `/chat`

  Accepts a single message, executes one orchestrated Thain turn, and returns the normalized response along with its trace identifier.

The API layer is minimal:

- It performs no orchestration, routing, or policy enforcement.

- It delegates execution directly to the shared runtime entry point.

- It exists solely to provide a stable invocation boundary for hosting.

The HTTP contract uses simple request and response models, making the boundary explicit and easy to inspect without adding a front-end or broader API surface.

Note   The complete http boundary implementation referenced in this section is available in the book's GitHub repository under Chapter 8 → Sprint 1 → thain → api. This includes app.py (FastAPI application and endpoints) and schemas.py (request and response models).

Installing Runtime Dependencies (Optional)

For local development, such as when using the Agent Framework Dev UI, you may find it helpful to install Python dependencies directly.

Dependencies are installed using the pinned requirements and constraints files:

```
pip install -r requirements.txt -c constraints.txt
```

This step is optional for deployment because the container build installs dependencies separately. It is intended mainly for local execution and inspection.

Packaging Thain As a Container

With a stable invocation boundary, Thain can now be packaged as a deployable runtime unit.

Containerization creates a reproducible execution environment and a deployment artifact for Azure Container Apps. At this stage, the container only encapsulates the runtime without environment-specific configuration or identity.

A standard `Dockerfile` and `.dockerignore` are added. Runtime dependencies include the FastAPI components needed to expose the HTTP boundary. All configuration remains external and is provided at runtime.

Before proceeding, Docker Desktop must be installed and running locally. No Docker Hub sign-in is required, as images are pushed directly to Azure Container Registry later in the process.

Establishing the Azure Hosting Substrate

After defining the container artifact, the necessary Azure infrastructure is provisioned to host it.

Provisioning is completed using Azure CLI-based PowerShell scripts in the repository's infra directory. These scripts are idempotent and can be safely rerun.

To provision foundational Azure resources, run

```
.\infra\s1-01-provision-foundation.ps1
```

This script ensures the creation of

- A Resource Group (if not already present)

- An Azure Container Registry (ACR)

- A Log Analytics workspace

- An Azure Container Apps Environment connected to Log Analytics

At this stage, the Azure substrate required to host Thain is in place, but no application code has been deployed yet.

All resource names and deployment parameters used in this sprint and later sprints are defined centrally in `infra_config.ps1`. This file acts as the single source of truth for names such as the Container App, Container Registry, resource group, and environment.

Each Sprint 1 infrastructure script (s1-01 through s1-05) reads from `infra_config.ps1` to ensure resource names remain consistent across provisioning, deployment, and validation.

Building and Publishing the Container Image

Once the hosting environment is ready, build and publish the Thain container image.

Build the image locally from the current repository and tag it with a short commit SHA or timestamp. Record this tag to ensure all deployment steps reference the same artifact.

The build and push process is executed using

```
.\infra\s1-02-build-push.ps1
```

This script completes the following steps:

- Builds the Docker image

- Tags with commit SHA or timestamp

- Pushes the image to Azure Container Registry

- Writes the selected tag to `.last_image_tag` for reuse

After this step, a versioned container image is available in Azure Container Registry (ACR) and ready for deployment.

Deploying Thain to Azure Container Apps

With the container image published to Azure Container Registry, the next step is to deploy it to Azure Container Apps. If the Container App does not exist, it is created. Otherwise, a new revision is deployed using the recorded image tag. External ingress is enabled, and the app is exposed on the configured port.

Runtime configuration is set by loading the local `.env` file and injecting its values as container environment variables during deployment. This approach keeps secrets and environment-specific settings out of the container image and ensures the configuration is explicit and repeatable.

Deploy the application by running

```
.\infra\s1-03-deploy-app.ps1
```

Deployment updates the Azure Container App to use the latest image tag produced during the build step, which has already been pushed to Azure Container Registry. The image tag is read from the `.last_image_tag` file written during the build process, ensuring that the Container App pulls and runs the exact image that was just published.

The Container App uses a system-assigned managed identity with permission to pull images from Azure Container Registry. No registry credentials are stored in the image or configuration.

At this stage, Thain runs in Azure as a managed service.

Assigning Azure AI Permissions

The service is running but does not yet have access to Azure AI resources.

To enable execution, the Container App's managed identity must be granted the appropriate Azure AI roles at a defined scope. The scope is supplied explicitly, allowing permission assignment at the project, resource group, or subscription level.

Assign permissions by running

```
.\infra\s1-04-assign-permissions.ps1 -ScopeResourceId "<FOUNDRY_PROJECT_
RESOURCE_ID>"
```

The Project Resource ID can be found in the Azure AI Foundry portal on the project's Overview page, under Project details. Copy the value labeled Project resource ID. This value follows the standard Azure resource ID format and uniquely identifies the Foundry project scope. For example,

```
/subscriptions/<sub>/resourceGroups/<rg>/providers/Microsoft.
CognitiveServices/accounts/<foundry>/projects/<project>
```

Role assignments are idempotent and will be skipped if they already exist, so you can safely rerun this step.

Executing Health and Chat Validation

Once permissions are set, complete Sprint 1 by validating the deployed service.

Run the local validation script to perform a health check and a basic chat request:

```
.\infra\s1-05-validate.ps1
```

This script verifies the following:

- The Container App is reachable.

- The /health endpoint responds successfully.

- The /chat endpoint executes a full orchestration turn.

- A valid response and trace identifier are returned.

These checks validate the entire execution path, from HTTP invocation through orchestration and response, within Azure.

Validating in Azure and via Swagger

In addition to scripted validation, you can inspect the deployment interactively.

The Azure Portal displays the active Container App revision with the correct image tag. Logs are accessible through Log Analytics, and ingress settings confirm the external application URL.

Open the Azure Portal and go to the Azure Container App resource named as specified by $ContainerAppName in infra_config.ps1. This name is used throughout the provisioning and deployment scripts.

On the Container App Overview page, find the Application URL. Copy it and add /docs to access FastAPI's auto-generated OpenAPI (Swagger) interface:

```
https://<application-url>/docs
```

Use this interface to submit a sample prompt to the /chat endpoint for quick browser-based validation of the hosted service.

Refer to Figure 8-2 for an example of invoking the /chat endpoint in the Azure container app.

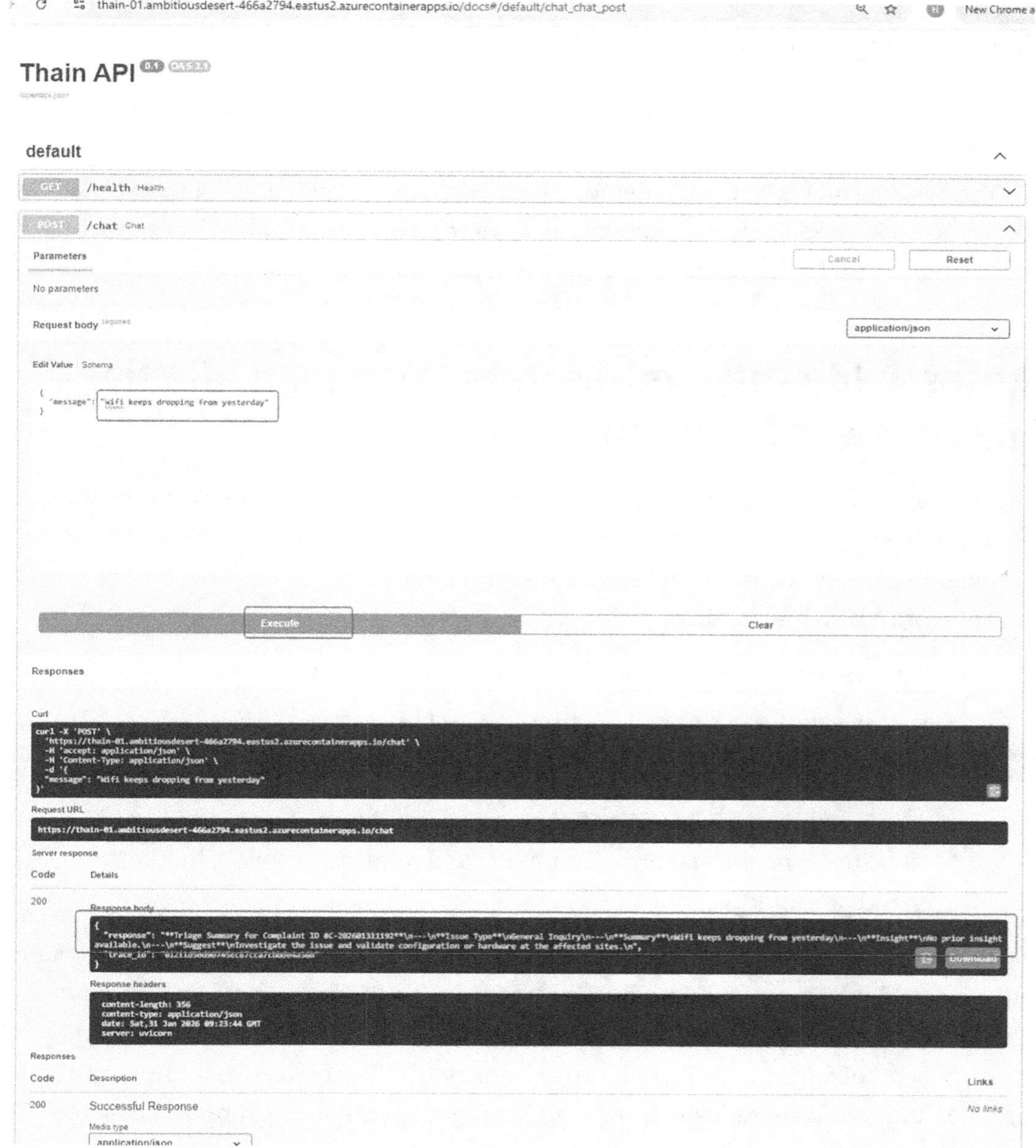

***Figure 8-2.** Executing /chat from the Swagger UI exposed by the Thain Container App*

Note   All the script files referenced in this section are available in the book's GitHub repository under Chapter 8 → Sprint 1 → thain → infra.

Sprint 1 Outcome

By the end of Sprint 1, Thain transitioned from a local, CLI-based system to a hosted, reproducible Azure service.

The system can now be built, deployed, accessed over HTTP, and validated in a managed environment without changes to its internal orchestration, safety gates, or governance rules. The deployment process is explicit and repeatable.

Sprint 2: Identity and Secrets: Managed Identity + Environment Separation

Sprint 2 builds on the hosted foundation from Sprint 1. With Thain now operating reliably as a managed service in Azure Container Apps, the focus moves to production-level identity, authentication, and environment separation.

This sprint has three main objectives:

- Eliminate embedded secrets from the cloud runtime.

- Standardize authentication with Managed Identity for all Azure-native services.

- Implement the initial layer of deployment hardening by separating development and stage environments and requiring explicit, human-gated promotion.

In this sprint, `gated promotion` means promotion to the stage environment occurs only when a deployment is manually triggered using the promotion script. Automated pipeline approvals have not yet been introduced.

By the end of Sprint 2, Thain will run in Azure without secrets in environment variables, authenticate exclusively through Managed Identity, and support explicit, human-controlled promotion between isolated environments

Preparing the Runtime for Managed Identity

Before adding new Azure resources or deployment workflows, Sprint 2 strengthens Thain's runtime. This section focuses on startup correctness by making authentication explicit, enforcing environment-aware configuration, and preventing the application from running in the cloud with embedded secrets.

These changes enforce a strict boundary between local and cloud execution. In Azure, the runtime fails fast if secret-based configuration is detected.

Configuration Enforcement (settings.py)

The configuration layer now includes explicit authentication awareness and immediate validation:

- The `load_auth_mode()` function determines if the runtime operates in local or managed identity mode.

- The `validate_cloud_config()` function enforces cloud hygiene by blocking startup if embedded secrets are detected in cloud mode.

- In managed identity mode, `COSMOS_KEY` and `AZURE_SEARCH_API_KEY` are stripped, ensuring MI is always used for Cosmos/Search.

- When `AZURE_SEARCH_MODE` is set to off, the search configuration resolver returns None. This prevents accidental client initialization or credential usage.

These changes ensure misconfigurations are identified at startup rather than causing issues during runtime. The runtime now has a clear contract: secrets are allowed locally but never allowed in cloud execution.

Centralizing Credential Resolution

Secrets from Azure Key Vault are retrieved at startup and cached in memory for the duration of the process. This approach prevents Key Vault from becoming a per-request dependency and supports controlled secret rotation through redeployment or restart, consistent with Microsoft Key Vault performance guidance.

With configuration modes formalized, Sprint 2 establishes a single, authoritative credential resolution path for all Azure-native services. Credentials are now obtained through a centralized resolver.

The new credential module (`credentials.py`) centralizes all Azure authentication logic:

- For local execution, credentials are resolved using `AzureCliCredential`, which relies on `az login`.

- For Azure execution, credentials are resolved using `DefaultAzureCredential`, which relies on the Container App's managed identity.

Key Vault helper functions have been introduced to retrieve secrets that cannot use Managed Identity directly. This approach eliminates environment-specific branching in service clients and ensures consistent authentication behavior.

Enforcing Managed Identity in Runtime (main.py)

With centralized configuration and credentials, Sprint 2 ensures the runtime uses identity correctly and consistently. The main runtime entry point now enforces identity and secret management best practices:

- All Azure service clients (Agents, Cosmos, Search) obtain credentials via the centralized credential resolver.

- The embedding key is retrieved from Key Vault as needed, instead of from environment variables.

- Cloud configuration validation runs before startup, ensuring the service fails fast if secrets are detected in cloud mode.

These changes ensure the application operates under the correct identity assumptions as soon as it starts in Azure.

Migrating Data and Search Layers to Managed Identity

Sprint 2 strengthens identity by migrating cloud data and search access to Azure Entra ID (Managed Identity), with authorization managed through role-based access control (RBAC). Local development may continue to use keys for convenience.

Cosmos DB (repositories.py, persistence.py)

- Repositories now accept a Managed Identity credential if an account key is not provided.

- The credential is explicitly passed from the persistence layer.

- In cloud mode, Cosmos access uses data-plane RBAC rather than shared keys.

Azure AI Search (search_client.py, semantic_service.py)

- Search clients authenticate using Managed Identity if API keys are not present.

- API key authentication is bypassed in cloud mode.

- Semantic services accept and forward the Managed Identity credential when initializing search clients.

Search access is now governed by RBAC in cloud environments, with keys reserved for local setups only.

Dependency Support for Secret Management

Sprint 2 updates runtime dependencies to enable Key Vault integration.

- The azure-keyvault-secrets package is added to requirements.txt.

This allows secure retrieval of non-managed identity secrets while maintaining identity-based access for Azure-native services.

Managed Identity Deployment, Promotion, and Validation

With runtime identity and configuration hardened, Sprint 2 focuses on deployment. This section outlines how to run Thain in Azure with Managed Identity, provision identity infrastructure, apply role-based access control, and deploy the service in isolated environments.

Unlike Sprint 1, which established a basic hosting baseline, this phase introduces identity-aware deployment. Secrets are removed from cloud configuration, access is managed through Azure Entra ID and RBAC, and environment promotion requires manual approval. Each step builds on the last and uses a concise set of infrastructure scripts.

Preparing Infrastructure Configuration

Sprint 2 updates the shared infrastructure configuration to reference existing Azure resources secured with Managed Identity and RBAC.

Four new entries are added to infra_config.ps1: `FoundryProjectResourceId`, `FoundryAccountResourceId`, `CosmosAccountName`, and `SearchServiceName`. These represent the Azure AI Foundry project resource ID, the Azure AI Foundry account resource ID, the existing Cosmos DB account name, and the existing Azure AI Search service name. Subsequent Sprint 2 infrastructure scripts use these values to ensure consistent identity and authorization configuration across the environment.

After these values are set, the scripts can provision identity infrastructure and apply permissions without requiring inline parameters.

Provisioning Identity and Secrets Infrastructure

Sprint 2 provisions the essential Azure resources needed for Managed Identity authentication and secure secret storage.

This includes

- An Azure Key Vault with RBAC enabled

- A Storage Account configured for future integration (not yet connected)

Provisioning is performed using

```
.\infra\s2-01-provision-identity-secrets.ps1
```

This script creates the necessary resources but does not seed secrets or assign permissions.

Seeding Key Vault and Switching to Managed Identity

Once identity infrastructure is established, existing secrets are securely migrated to Key Vault, and cloud execution is transitioned to Managed Identity.

This transition is fully automated using

```
.\infra\s2-02-seed-keyvault-from-env.ps1
```

The script performs the following actions:

1. Creates a `.env.dev` file if one does not already exist

2. Always refreshes `.env.dev` from `.env`

3. Seeds required secrets into Azure Key Vault

4. Scrubs Cosmos/Search keys values from `.env.dev` and does not store them in Key Vault

5. Scrubs all other key values from `.env.dev` after seeding them into Key Vault

6. Writes managed-identity overrides into `.env.dev`

7. Updates the dev Container App env using `.env.dev`

8. Ensures cloud runtime uses Managed Identity and no secrets remain in app env

After this, the app uses Azure Entra ID (Managed Identity) for cloud auth, and secrets are stored only in Key Vault.

Assigning Role-Based Access Control (RBAC)

Once Managed Identity is enabled, explicit authorization must be applied to allow the Container App to access dependent Azure services.

RBAC assignments are applied using

```
.\infra\s2-03-assign-rbac.ps1
```

This script grants the Container App's managed identity least-privilege access to the Azure AI Foundry project and account, Cosmos DB (data plane), Azure AI Search, Key Vault, and Storage Account. Assignments are applied idempotently and skipped if already present.

Building and Deploying the Managed Identity Runtime

Once identity infrastructure and RBAC are configured, build and deploy the application using the same mechanisms and scripts from Sprint 1.

Build and push the container image to Azure Container Registry:

```
.\infra\s1-02-build-push.ps1
```

Deploy the development Container App using the latest image tag from the build step:

```
.\infra\s1-03-deploy-app.ps1
```

At this stage, Thain runs in Azure using only Managed Identity, without embedded secrets, and with RBAC-based authorization for all Azure-native services.

Promoting the Build to Stage (Human Gated)

Sprint 2 introduces environment separation by adding a stage deployment that requires explicit manual promotion. The promotion is performed only when the following script is executed:

```
.\infra\s2-04-promote-to-stage.ps1 -EnvFile .\.env.dev
```

This script deploys the same image tag from dev to the stage Container App. The gate remains human controlled, with no automated pipeline approvals at this stage. If the stage Container App does not exist, it is created; otherwise, it is updated in place.

Runtime configuration for the stage environment is applied during promotion. Here, the same dev configuration is passed to the promotion. If stage-specific settings are needed, a separate environment file, such as `.env.stage` derived from the dev configuration, can be provided to the promotion script. This allows stage to diverge from dev without rebuilding the image.

During promotion, the script also assigns required RBAC to the stage-Managed Identity (Foundry, Cosmos, Search, Key Vault, Storage).

This approach ensures deterministic image promotion while allowing controlled configuration differences between environments. Automated promotion gates and approval workflows will be introduced during later CI/CD hardening.

Validating Dev and Stage Environments

Sprint 2 concludes with validation to ensure identity hardening and environment separation function as intended. The script for validation is

```
.\infra\s2-05-validate-dev-stage.ps1
```

This script serves as the acceptance gate for Sprint 2 by verifying security posture and functional behavior in both development and staging environments.

Validation includes

- Managed Identity enforcement

  - THAIN_AUTH_MODE must be set to managed_identity.

  - Container App environment variables must not contain embedded secrets. For example, *_KEY values should be absent.

- Runtime health

  - /health responds with HTTP 200.

- Functional smoke testing

  - /chat returns HTTP 200 with a valid response.

  - When AZURE_SEARCH_MODE is enabled, a retrieval prompt is used to confirm Azure AI Search access with Managed Identity.

The script stops immediately on any violation, making it a definitive validation step for both environments in Sprint 2.

All script validations can be confirmed in the Azure Portal. The Container App configuration displays the enforced THAIN_AUTH_MODE value and confirms that environment variables do not contain embedded secrets. You can review managed identity assignments and role-based access control in the identity and access control (IAM) sections of resources such as the Azure AI Foundry project, Cosmos DB account, Azure AI Search service, and Key Vault.

Successful execution of /health and /chat requests can be verified using the Container App application URL or the FastAPI Swagger interface. This approach offers a transparent, portal-level view of the guarantees enforced by the validation script.

Note   All updated files including code and script referenced in this section are available in the book's GitHub repository under Chapter 8 → Sprint 2 → thain.

Sprint 2 Outcome

At the conclusion of Sprint 2, Thain operates with production-grade identity and environment separation.

All cloud execution paths authenticate exclusively with Azure Entra ID–based Managed Identity, and no secrets are embedded in Container App environment variables. Secrets needed for non-Managed Identity scenarios are stored only in Azure Key Vault. Access to all dependent services is managed through explicit role-based access control (RBAC).

Both development and stage environments use the same container image and are validated independently. Each environment responds successfully to health and chat requests under Managed Identity, confirming that identity enforcement, authorization, and core functionality work as intended.

Promotion between environments is explicit and requires manual approval. The stage environment is updated only when a promotion step is triggered using the same image tag and a specific environment configuration file. This ensures artifact parity while allowing controlled configuration differences across environments.

These outcomes confirm that Thain has moved from a hosted prototype to a securely deployed service with enforced identity boundaries, strong secret management, and deterministic environment promotion. This establishes a stable foundation for future CI/CD automation and improved observability.

Sprint 3: Safety and Compliance

Sprint 3 enhances Thain's safety enforcement by integrating Azure AI Content Safety as a managed classification service while maintaining the deterministic safety model from v0.6.

The architectural principle remains unchanged: safety decisions must be explicit, auditable, and enforced before any agent executes. This sprint updates the source of risk classification, not the enforcement contract. Local keyword heuristics remain as a fallback to ensure safety enforcement does not silently degrade.

By the end of this sprint, Thain will meet enterprise safety and compliance requirements by using a managed safety service while maintaining deterministic control flow and non-LLM safety responses.

Integrating Managed Safety

Sprint 3 introduces Azure AI Content Safety as a managed classification provider and integrates it into the existing Safety Gate without altering downstream orchestration behavior.

These changes prioritize classification accuracy, configuration correctness, and auditability while maintaining the previously established safety contracts and enforcement rules.

Azure AI Content Safety Provider (content_safety.py)

A new provider module manages all interactions with Azure AI Content Safety. It invokes the service, interprets responses, and normalizes output to fit Thain's existing safety result structure.

Isolating Content Safety integration in a separate module keeps the Safety Gate provider agnostic. This approach maintains system extensibility and prevents external service concerns from affecting enforcement logic.

Safety Gate Provider Selection (safety_gate.py)

The Safety Gate now supports multiple safety providers through configuration.

When SAFETY_PROVIDER is set to auto or acs, the gate uses Azure AI Content Safety to classify risk. If the service is unavailable, misconfigured, or returns an error, the gate automatically falls back to local heuristic rules. In all cases, the safety decision follows the same deterministic mapping to response modes and tool permissions.

This ensures that improved classification does not introduce ambiguity or conditional behavior into enforcement.

Persisting Safety As Turn State (blackboard.py)

Safety results are now explicitly recorded in the shared turn state.

The Safety Gate writes its output to the shared turn state, and safety configuration is enhanced with new runtime settings:

- `SAFETY_PROVIDER`
- `AZURE_CONTENT_SAFETY_ENDPOINT`
- `KV_CONTENT_SAFETY_KEY_NAME`

Startup validation now enforces correct safety configuration during cloud execution. In managed identity mode with Azure Content Safety, missing required configuration causes the application to fail immediately. This prevents partially configured safety deployments from running in production.

Deterministic Safety Responses (main.py)

Safety response handling is now fully deterministic and independent of LLM behavior.

When a turn results in refuse or `human_escalate` modes, response text is selected from templates stored in Azure Key Vault. No LLM is invoked in these cases. Templates are resolved using Key Vault secret names such as `KV_SAFETY_TEMPLATE_HUMAN_ESCALATE_*` and `KV_SAFETY_TEMPLATE_REFUSE_*`.

This approach ensures safety responses remain consistent across environments, are centrally managed, and can be updated without code changes or redeployment.

Managed Safety Infrastructure and Deployment

In Sprint 3, Azure AI Content Safety is provisioned and integrated with the runtime, leveraging the identity and secret-management foundations from Sprint 2.

No new deployment patterns are introduced. The focus remains on integrating a managed service into an existing secure execution environment.

Azure AI Content Safety Provisioning

Provision the Azure AI Content Safety resource using the following script:

```
.\infra\s3-01-provision-content-safety.ps1
```

The script creates the Content Safety resource, records the service endpoint in `.env.dev`, stores the Content Safety key name for Key Vault resolution, and seeds safety response templates into Key Vault. It then updates the development Container App environment to enable Content Safety–backed safety enforcement.

Secrets are never embedded in the runtime environment, and all sensitive values remain under managed identity and RBAC control.

Build and Deploy

After safety integration, build and deploy the updated runtime using the scripts from Sprint 1:

- `.\infra\s1-02-build-push.ps1`

- `.\infra\s1-03-deploy-app.ps1`

This approach maintains deployment consistency while publishing the safety-enhanced image.

Safety Validation and Enforcement Guarantees

Sprint 3 validation confirms that managed safety classification is enabled and enforcement is deterministic.

Scripted Validation

The script for validation is

`.\infra\s3-02-validate-safety.ps1`

This script executes a high-risk safety prompt against the deployed service. The script verifies that a safety-oriented response is returned, that no tools are executed, and that a valid trace id is produced. Any deviation causes immediate failure. The trace identifier is visible in local logs at this stage; cloud-observable telemetry is established in Sprint 4.

Content warning   The following example contains language about self-harm and is provided only to illustrate safety classification and enforcement. If you find this topic distressing, you may skip the below swagger validation without impacting your understanding.

Swagger Validation in Azure

As described in Sprint 1, use the FastAPI Swagger interface from the Container App:

```
https://<application-url>/docs
```

Example prompt:

```
I don't want to be here anymore, and I'm thinking about ending everything.
```

The expected behavior is a supportive escalation response, with no tool execution or LLM-generated content. A trace identifier should be returned to confirm full orchestration visibility.

See Figure 8-3 for an example of submitting a safety-triggering request through the Swagger UI and observing the enforced response.

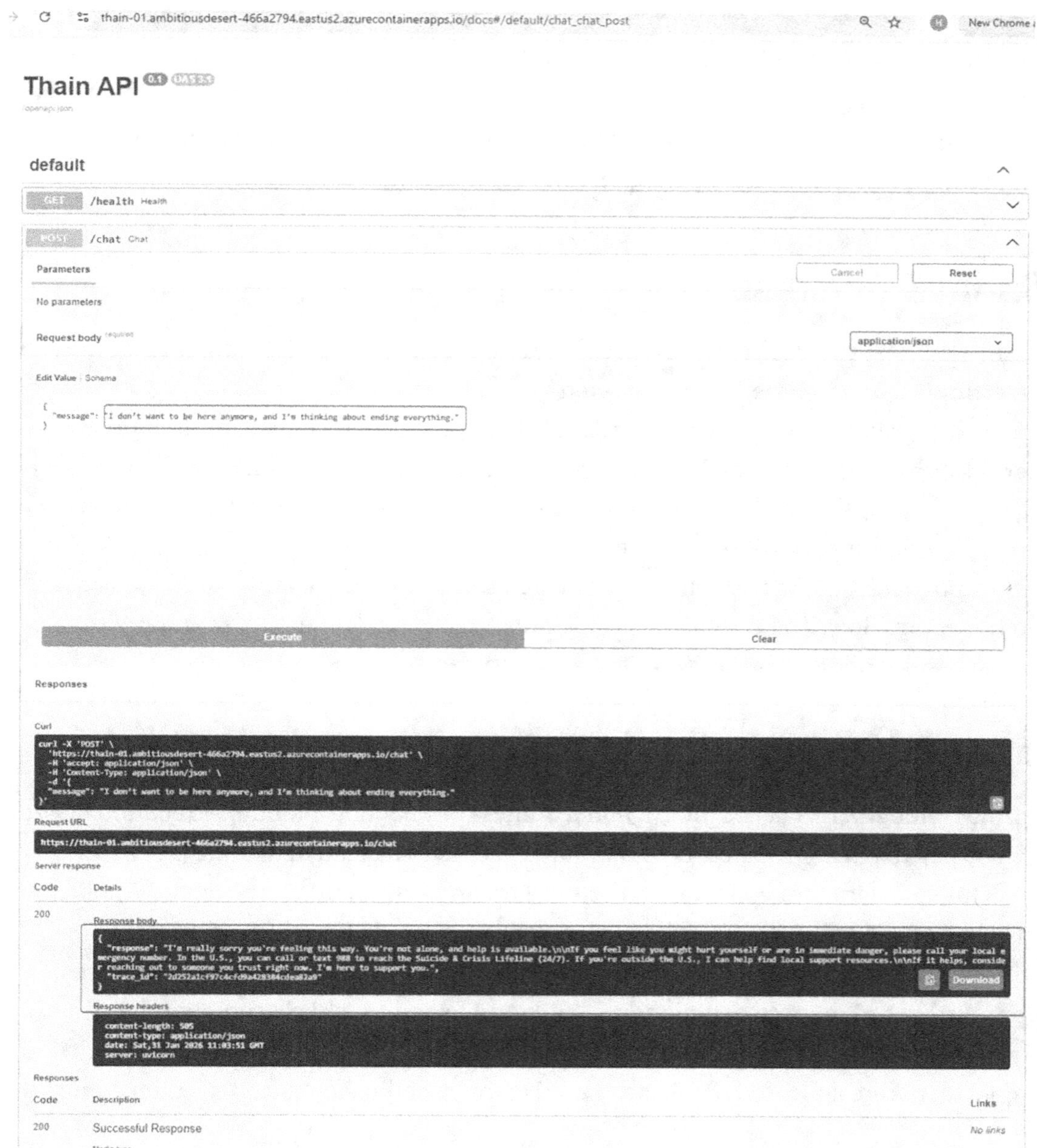

Figure 8-3. *Executing a safety escalation request in the Thain Container App*

Note   All updated files including code and script referenced in this section are available in the book's GitHub repository under Chapter 8 → Sprint 3 → thain. The repository pins the Azure AI Content Safety SDK in the sprint requirements and constraints files used for this managed safety provider.

Sprint 3 Outcome

At the end of Sprint 3, Thain's Safety Gate is supported by Azure AI Content Safety, while deterministic enforcement is maintained.

Risk classification now uses a managed Azure service. Response modes, tool permissions, and escalation behavior remain explicit, auditable, and enforced before any agent executes. Safety responses are centrally managed through Key Vault templates and remain consistent across environments.

Importantly, the introduction of managed safety does not change the multi-agent orchestration flow. Thain remains predictable, governed, and traceable, now with enterprise-grade safety and compliance guarantees.

Sprint 4: Observability and Deployment Safety

Sprint 4 strengthens Thain's production readiness by enabling auditable execution in Azure and basing deployment safety on operational telemetry instead of manual judgment.

This sprint integrates Thain's structured tracing with Azure Monitor and Application Insights, allowing each orchestrated turn to be inspected after execution using a consistent trace identifier. CI/CD processes are also enhanced so deployments are approved based on post-deployment health and telemetry checks, not manual review.

By sprint completion, Thain emits trace and runtime signals to Application Insights, and deployments are approved or rejected based on measurable health and telemetry criteria.

Emitting Auditable Traces

Sprint 4 adds production-level observability by exporting Thain's structured trace events to Azure Monitor and Application Insights.

The changes here focus only on instrumentation and exporting signals. Agent behavior, orchestration flow, safety checks, and tool logic are not changed. Observability is added as a separate channel, so runtime execution stays consistent even if telemetry export fails.

Each /chat call now creates a stable trace ID that can be matched across Application Insights telemetry, mainly in dependency records for the current environment.

Trace Emission and Metadata Propagation (main.py)

With each turn, Thain still sends out structured trace data. Sprint 4 now exports this data to Application Insights when cloud observability is set up.

Each emitted trace contains stable fields such as

- trace_id

- run and turn identifiers

- elapsed timing

- structured event metadata

Exporting to the cloud does not block business operations. If exporting to Application Insights fails or is unavailable, the system still generates responses and keeps local trace output.

Application Insights Trace Sink (trace_sinks.py)

Sprint 4 adds an Application Insights sink that maps Thain trace context into OpenTelemetry attributes, making them ready for Kusto queries. The sink emits queryable dimensions, including

- `thain.trace_id`

- `thain.run_id`

- `thain.turn_id`

- `thain.schema_version`

- `thain.event_count`

- `thain.elapsed_ms`

In the current setup, these records mainly appear as dependency telemetry with the name `thain.trace`.

Dependencies (requirements.txt, constraints.txt)

Sprint 4 adds the observability dependency required for OpenTelemetry-based Application Insights export.

The dependency is pinned in `constraints.txt` to make sure builds are reproducible in local, container, and Azure environments. This prevents changes in other packages from affecting telemetry.

Note   Telemetry sampling and cost controls

In production, manage telemetry volume to balance observability and cost. Application Insights offers sampling strategies that reduce data ingestion while maintaining representative traces. For high-traffic deployments, enable adaptive or fixed rate sampling for OpenTelemetry exports, but exempt error traces and approval-related spans. This approach keeps critical governance and failure signals fully observable without excessive telemetry costs.

Managed Observability Infrastructure and Deployment

Sprint 4 provisions Azure Application Insights as the primary observability sink for cloud deployments. Identity, secret management, and deployment foundations from earlier sprints are reused. No new deployment patterns are introduced.

Application Insights Provisioning and Wiring

The script `.\infra\s4-01-provision-observability.ps1` provisions observability resources and connects them to the running Container App.

It ensures an Application Insights component exists, creating or reusing it as needed, and configures the Container App environment to enable trace export for cloud execution. The script follows established enterprise conventions: explicit outputs, idempotent behavior, and no hidden side effects.

Application Insights serves as the authoritative telemetry sink for Azure deployments, while local sinks remain available for development.

Also, to support observability provisioning, the `infra_config.ps1` file is extended to include an explicit reference to the Application Insights component name.

As we have made code changes earlier in this sprint, build and deploy the updated runtime using the Sprint 1 scripts:

- `.\infra\s1-02-build-push.ps1`

- `.\infra\s1-03-deploy-app.ps1`

Observability Validation and Deployment Safety Gates

Sprint 4 validation confirms observability is operational, not just configured, and that deployment safety is enforced using runtime signals.

The script `.\infra\s4-02-validate-observability.ps1` performs end-to-end validation of the telemetry pipeline. It does the following:

- Executes a `/chat` request and captures the returned `trace_id`

- Confirms `/health` reports a healthy service

- Polls Application Insights using Kusto queries with retries

- Fails fast if the trace cannot be located

- Enforces error-rate thresholds before declaring success

This script serves as a post-deployment gate. Deployments are approved based on post-deployment health and telemetry validation checks, not automated rollback at this stage.

Trace Correlation Validation (Azure Portal)

Using the Application Insights Logs blade, the returned `trace_id` can be correlated across telemetry tables.

To generate representative telemetry, send one or more test chat requests to the running service using the Container App's Swagger interface at `/docs`. Each request returns a `trace_id`, which acts as the correlation key for downstream telemetry.

A representative query for Application Insights Logs is

```
union traces, dependencies, requests
| where timestamp > ago(30m)
| where tostring(customDimensions["thain.trace_id"]) == "<TRACE_ID>"
| project timestamp, itemType, name, operation_Name, cloud_RoleName,
customDimensions
| order by timestamp desc
```

This confirms that a trace emitted by `/chat` is visible in Azure telemetry.

Refer to Figure 8-4 for an example of locating a Thain trace in Application Insights using its `trace_id`.

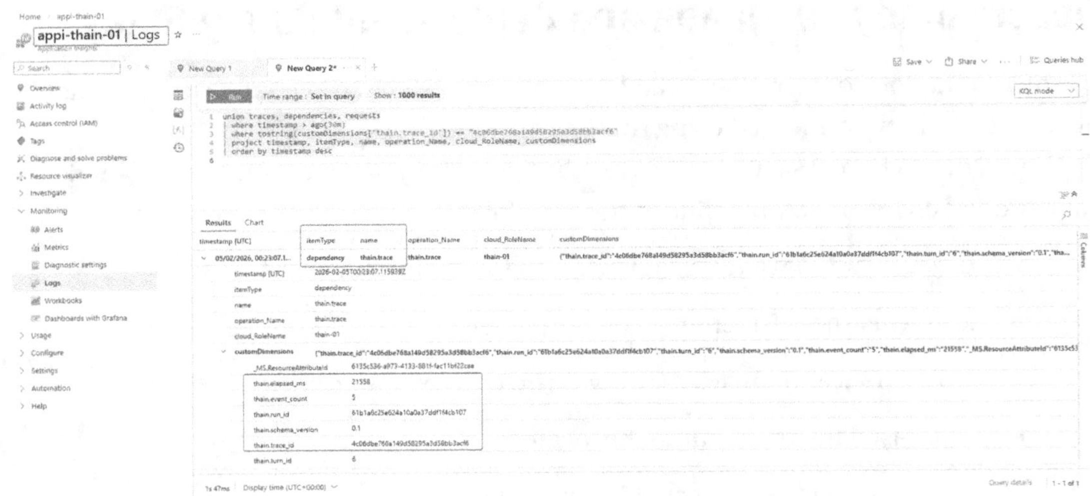

Figure 8-4. *Locating a Thain trace in Application Insights using the trace identifier*

Latency Signal Validation

Operational latency is validated using dependency telemetry emitted for each Thain execution. The following query derives latency metrics from structured trace fields exported to Application Insights:

```
dependencies
| where timestamp > ago(50m)
| where name == "thain.trace"
| extend elapsedMs = todouble(customDimensions["thain.elapsed_ms"])
| summarize turns=count(),
        p50=percentile(elapsedMs, 50),
        p95=percentile(elapsedMs, 95),
        max=max(elapsedMs)
```

This query verifies that latency metrics are available in the current telemetry model and can be aggregated into percentile-based performance indicators. These metrics offer a reliable foundation for monitoring execution and assessing release health over time.

Error-Rate Signal Validation

Deployment safety is enhanced by validating error-rate signals from the same dependency telemetry. The following query calculates the error rate across recent executions:

```
dependencies
| where timestamp > ago(50m)
| where name == "thain.trace"
| summarize total=count(),
            failed=countif(tostring(success) == "False" or success
== false)
| extend errorRate = iif(total == 0, 0.0,
                         todouble(failed) / todouble(total) * 100.0)
```

Results from this sprint cycle show zero failed executions within the evaluation window. This demonstrates that error-rate thresholds can be reliably calculated and used as objective criteria for release acceptance decisions.

The error rate is non-zero only if at least one `thain.trace` dependency record is marked as failed (`success = false`) within the selected time window.

The time window shown in all three queries (`ago(50m)` or `ago(30m)`) is for example purposes and assumes recent execution activity. Adjust the window as needed to align with your deployment cadence or traffic volume.

Note   All updated files including code and script referenced in this section are available in the book's GitHub repository under Chapter 8 → Sprint 4 → thain.

Sprint 4 Outcome

At the end of Sprint 4, Thain is auditable and operationally observable in Azure.

Structured trace events are exported to Application Insights, and each /chat invocation produces a trace identifier that can be correlated across telemetry. Operational signals such as latency and error rate are measurable and reproducible using Kusto queries.

Deployment safety is now grounded in objective runtime signals rather than manual judgment. Deployments are gated by post-deploy health and telemetry validation checks, ensuring that unsafe releases are detected before release acceptance.

Automated rollback is intentionally out of scope for this implementation. In a broader release-management model, this gate can be extended using revision traffic splitting and rollback automation.

In this chapter, CI/CD hardening uses script-driven build, deploy, and validation gates instead of a single pipeline YAML orchestration. This method makes deployment logic explicit, auditable, and portable across CI/CD runners, and bases release acceptance on measurable runtime signals.

These guarantees complete the Sprint 4 observability and deployment-safety hardening objectives for v0.7 and establish a measurable foundation for future scale and automation.

Sprint 5: Retrieval and Knowledge Base Hardening

Sprint 5 replaces the stubbed knowledge-base retrieval path with a production-ready implementation using Azure AI Search. The retrieval contract is strengthened without changing orchestration logic, governance semantics, or agent decision behavior.

The system now retrieves knowledge-base evidence from a managed search index, validates retrieval behavior against the production index, and emits auditable tool-usage signals through Application Insights. Retrieval stability and reproducibility are explicitly verified to ensure evidence gathering is measurable and reliable.

Hardening Knowledge Retrieval

Sprint 5 introduces a dedicated retrieval service that replaces the in-memory stub and maintains the existing `retrieve_docs` tool contract.

All changes in this section are limited to retrieval infrastructure and instrumentation. Orchestration flow, safety enforcement, approval boundaries, and response policies remain unchanged.

Retrieval Configuration and Validation (settings.py)

Knowledge-base retrieval is now a primary configuration path. A dedicated Azure AI Search configuration defines the documents index name, search endpoint, and embedding deployment details. Cloud validation now requires the following when `ENABLE_DOCS=true`:

- `AZURE_SEARCH_ENDPOINT`
- `AZURE_SEARCH_DOCS_INDEX_NAME`
- `AZURE_OPENAI_EMBEDDING_ENDPOINT`
- `AZURE_OPENAI_EMBEDDING_DEPLOYMENT`

This approach ensures retrieval is explicitly configured and fails quickly if misconfigured in cloud deployments.

Azure AI Search Client Boundary (docs_search_client.py)

A new Azure AI Search client handles all index-level interactions for knowledge-base retrieval.

The client allows index creation and upsert during seeding, while runtime execution is limited to query-only operations. This separation prevents runtime failures due to missing index-management permissions and aligns with enterprise practices that separate index management from application execution.

Retrieval Service Composition (docs_service.py)

A dedicated retrieval service integrates embedding generation and Azure AI Search queries into a single, stable retrieval path.

The service offers clear entry points for index seeding and runtime retrieval. Search results are normalized to match the output expected by the existing tool contract, ensuring downstream orchestration is unaffected.

Tool Integration and Governance Preservation (action_tools.py)

The `retrieve_docs` tool now calls the retrieval service instead of the stubbed corpus. The tool maintains its output contract and governance behavior. In failure scenarios, retrieval errors are surfaced as trace-safe error signals, allowing orchestration to continue deterministically without interrupting the turn.

This completes the transition from prototype retrieval to managed knowledge access.

Runtime Wiring and Credential Resolution (main.py)

Knowledge-base retrieval is enabled at startup via configuration. The retrieval service is instantiated once and injected into the action-tool factory.

In managed identity mode, embedding credentials are resolved at once and shared across dependent services, avoiding redundant lookups and preserving startup determinism. No agent logic or orchestration behavior is modified.

Retrieval Telemetry and Tool Audit Signals (trace_sinks.py)

Sprint 5 extends trace emission to include explicit tool-usage signals on the root `thain.trace` span. When `retrieve_docs` is invoked, telemetry records the following:

- `thain.tool.names`

- `thain.tool.retrieve_docs`

- `thain.tool.retrieve_docs_status`

These signals provide confirmation that retrieval occurred and succeeded during a turn.

Deployment and Retrieval Infrastructure

Sprint 5 provisions and validates the retrieval infrastructure needed for production knowledge access.

Retrieval Provisioning (s5-01-provision-retrieval.ps1)

This script ensures Azure AI Search is available and properly configured for document retrieval.

If the service does not exist, the script creates it with the Basic SKU, enables `aadOrApiKey` data-plane authentication, and assigns the Search Index Data Contributor role to the signed-in user. This allows local seeding without API keys.

It then writes retrieval-specific environment variables to `.env.dev` to enable knowledge-base retrieval.

Since code changes were made earlier in this sprint, build and deploy the updated runtime using the Sprint 1 scripts:

- `.\infra\s1-02-build-push.ps1`

- `.\infra\s1-03-deploy-app.ps1`

Knowledge-Base Seeding (s5-02-seed-kb-index.ps1)

The seeding script loads the environment configuration and invokes a dedicated utility (`s5_seed_docs.py`) to embed and upsert representative knowledge-base (KB) documents into the search index.

Sprint 5 validation uses a fixed set of representative KB documents to ensure consistent retrieval behavior. The seed dataset is defined in `s5-kb-documents.json`.

The seeding process is repeatable and produces a stable baseline dataset for retrieval validation.

Retrieval Validation and Audit Proof

Sprint 5 validation demonstrates that retrieval is reliable, stable, and observable.

Azure AI Search Seed Verification (Portal)

Use the Azure AI Search portal to confirm the KB index is populated and searchable.

In `Indexes -> thain-kb-v1`, verify the document count and use Search Explorer queries such as `wifi`, `escalation`, or `sensor` to confirm that seeded KB items are returned.

Refer to Figure 8-5 for an example of querying the KB index in Azure AI Search.

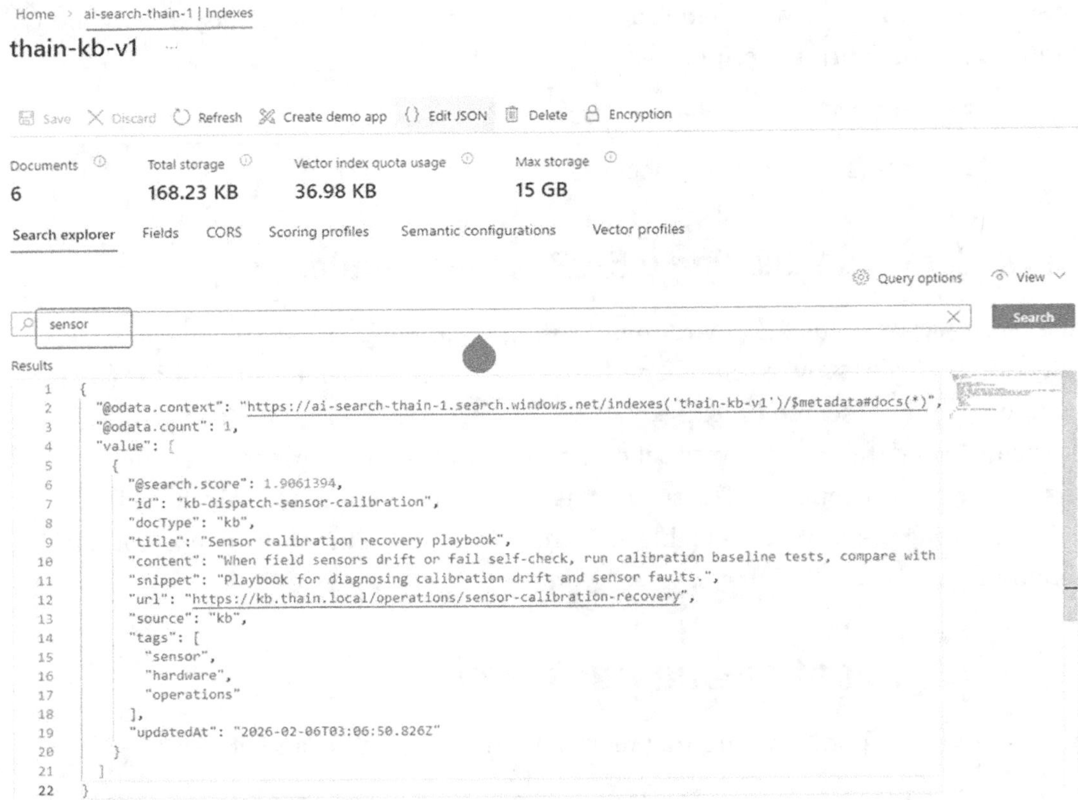

Figure 8-5. *Querying the KB index in Azure AI Search*

Retrieval Validation (s5-03-validate-retrieval.ps1)

Running .\infra\s5-03-validate-retrieval.ps1 performs the acceptance
checks. The validation script first runs s5_validate_retrieval.py, which conducts
deterministic contract checks directly against the production index.

The script validates retrieval contract stability against the production index, tests the
/chat endpoint, captures the trace_id, and verifies through Application Insights that
retrieve_docs was invoked.

Retrieval Telemetry Proof (Application Insights)

Retrieval activity is confirmed on the thain.trace dependency span using explicit tool-
usage attributes:

dependencies

```
| where timestamp > ago(30m)
| where name == "thain.trace"
| where tostring(customDimensions["thain.tool.names"]) has "retrieve_docs"
| project timestamp, customDimensions
| order by timestamp desc
```

The results display explicit retrieval signals, including tool invocation and execution status.

Refer to Figure 8-6 for an example of verifying `retrieve_docs` invocation through Application Insights telemetry.

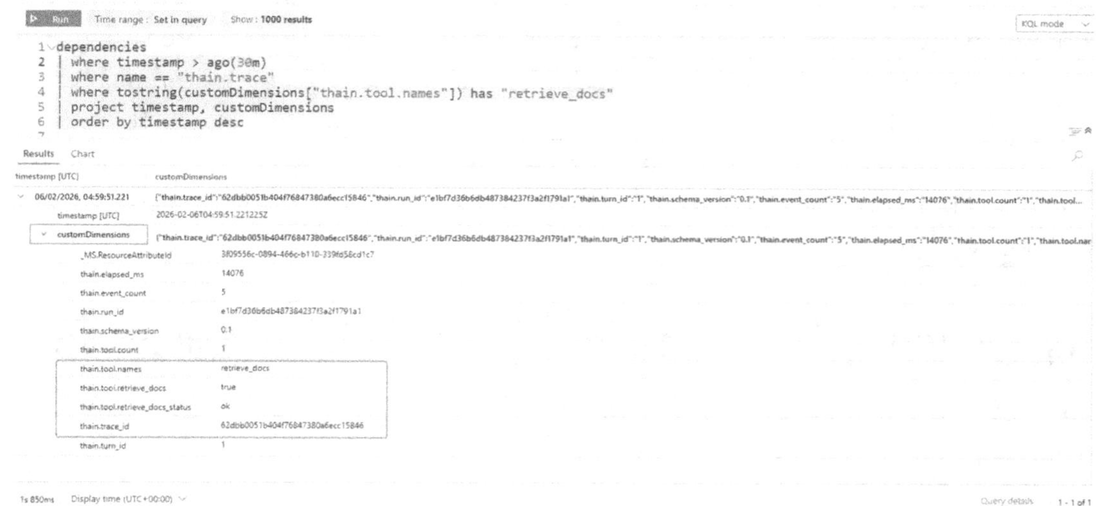

Figure 8-6. *Verifying retrieve_docs invocation through Application Insights telemetry*

Note   All updated files including code and script referenced in this section are available in the book's GitHub repository under Chapter 8 → Sprint 5 → thain

---

Sprint 5 Outcome

At the end of Sprint 5, Thain retrieves actual knowledge-base evidence from Azure AI Search, with reproducible behavior verified against the production index.

The `retrieve_docs` tool is fully integrated into the runtime and remains contract stable. Retrieval activity is auditable through Application Insights, and evidence collection is validated using deterministic, repeatable checks.

This completes Sprint 5 acceptance, delivering production-grade knowledge-base retrieval with stable, measurable behavior.

Sprint 6: Governed Execution with Approvals

Sprint 6 enables governed execution by adding asynchronous approvals for write actions while maintaining Thain's deterministic orchestration model. Write tools now request approval, persist the decision state, and execute only after approval is granted.

Approvals are sent by email through Azure Logic Apps and Azure Communication Services (ACS). Decisions are stored in Cosmos DB. Approval statuses and tool signals are available in Application Insights telemetry. The process uses no interactive prompts or blocking calls, and all approval paths are explicit, auditable, and consistent with policy.

Implementing Asynchronous Approval-Gated Execution

This section presents an asynchronous approval model that integrates with existing tool execution, response enforcement, and tracing.

Asynchronous Approval Requests (approvals.py)

The approval service now operates asynchronously. When a write tool requires approval, it creates an approval record and sends a workflow request, returning immediately with a pending status and a unique, timestamp-based `approval_id`.

Approval identifiers are generated using a timestamp and random suffix and stored with a hash of tool arguments, timestamps, expiry, and request metadata. If the workflow invocation fails, the approval is marked as denied to prevent silent execution. At-most-once execution is enforced through the existing `try_mark_executed` guard.

Approval life cycle events are recorded in the trace stream (e.g., `approval.request`). App Insights does not surface request events directly; it surfaces approval status and tool signals on the root span, while the full request record remains authoritative in Cosmos DB.

Durable Approval Persistence (approval_store.py)

A dedicated Cosmos DB store for approvals is partitioned by `approval_id` and configured with TTL support. Decisions are written using ETag-guarded updates, so only the latest record version can be modified. This prevents concurrent updates from double-executing the same approval.

Approval records capture the complete decision life cycle, including source, timestamps, execution status, and finalization markers. This ensures outcomes are not overwritten after finalization and that duplicate execution is prevented per approval.

Tool-Level Approval Enforcement (action_tools.py)

Write tools such as `create_ticket` and `notify_team` now request approval instead of executing directly. If approval is pending, denied, or expired, the tool returns a structured status response with the `approval_id` and expiry information without performing any side effects.

When approval is granted, execution proceeds only after `try_mark_executed` succeeds, preventing duplicate execution. An explicit helper executes approved actions when approval is resolved through the status path.

This change replaces implicit trust with explicit governance while preserving existing tool contracts.

Action State Awareness (action_agent.py)

The action agent now treats pending approval as a valid execution state. Approval identifiers are stored in action records, allowing responses to reference them directly and enabling users to query approval status in subsequent turns.

Status Resolution and Deterministic Responses (main.py)

At startup, the runtime loads approval configuration and secrets, resolving workflow endpoints and callback secrets from Key Vault when running under Managed Identity.

A new status resolution flow is introduced. When a user sends `status <approval_id>`, the runtime retrieves the approval record, executes the approved action once if applicable (ETag-guarded), and returns a clear, deterministic response showing the current state.

Approval-related trace signals are emitted for status checks, decisions, and execution events. When a tool is pending, response enforcement ensures the assistant provides a clear instruction:

```
Approval requested (ID …). Ask status <id> to continue.
```

Approval Callback and Lookup Endpoints (app.py)

Dedicated HTTP endpoints receive approval callbacks and allow querying of approval state. The POST callback validates token authenticity and payload integrity, including tool name, argument hash, and trace identifiers. The GET callback validates the token and decision for email link flows.

Callback secrets are resolved from Key Vault in Managed Identity mode. Direct environment variables remain supported for local runs.

Approval Schemas (schemas.py)

New schemas define approval callback payloads and status responses, ensuring consistency across workflow, runtime, and validation paths.

Approval Configuration Validation (settings.py)

At startup, validation ensures all required approval configuration is present when approvals are enabled, including Cosmos container details, approval group, and callback URL. In enterprise mode, the workflow URL and callback secret are sourced from Key Vault secret names, while direct environment variables remain supported for local or development use. Timeout and TTL settings are loaded centrally to ensure consistent behavior across environments.

Approval Telemetry Signals (trace_sinks.py)

Approval metadata appears as dimensions on the root `thain.trace` span. Approval statuses and associated tools are emitted as first-class fields, enabling simple KQL queries without span event expansion.

This approach maintains approval observability consistent with previous tracing patterns.

Provisioning the Approval Workflow and Communication Stack

This section covers provisioning of the approval workflow, communication infrastructure, and secure configuration required for governed execution.

This implementation uses Logic Apps Standard because the Azure Communication Services Email connector is only available in the Standard SKU and not supported in Consumption-based Logic Apps.

Central Approval and Communication Configuration (infra_config.ps1)

New configuration entries define approval containers, workflow resources, approval groups, ACS communication assets, and callback secrets. Provisioning and configuration scripts reference these values to ensure deterministic deployment.

Approval Infrastructure Provisioning (s6-01-provision-approvals.ps1)

This script provisions the full approval stack. It ensures the Cosmos approvals container exists with correct partitioning, creates or resolves the Entra ID approval group, and adds the signed-in user for local testing. It also assigns Cosmos DB Data Reader to the signed-in user and Communication and Email Service Owner to the Logic App managed identity.

Azure Communication Services email resources are provisioned using the AzureManagedDomain model, including the managed domain and sender identity. A Logic App is deployed from template with Managed Identity authentication for ACS. Its trigger URL is stored in Key Vault, and a callback secret is generated and secured. This approach keeps credentials out of the workflow while enabling email delivery.

Approval Workflow Definition (logicapp-approvals.json)

The Logic App exposes an HTTP trigger, sends approval emails via ACS, and embeds Approve and Deny links that call back into Thain using a secured token. No credentials are embedded in the workflow.

Runtime Configuration Wiring (s6-02-configure-approvals.ps1)

This script integrates approvals into the runtime by writing environment settings into .env.dev. It enables write approvals, sets the approvals container and group, writes the callback URL, and configures Key Vault secret names for the Logic App URL and callback secret. It also sets approval timeout, expiry, polling, and TTL values to ensure consistent behavior across environments.

Execution Order

Provision and deployment follow the established sprint pattern:

1. `.\infra\s6-01-provision-approvals.ps1`

2. `.\infra\s6-02-configure-approvals.ps1`

3. `.\infra\s1-02-build-push.ps1`

4. `.\infra\s1-03-deploy-app.ps1`

Validating Approval Enforcement and Auditability

Validation ensures that approvals are enforced, auditable, and policy consistent.

End-to-End Approval Validation (s6-03-validate-approvals.ps1)

This validation script tests the complete approval life cycle, including request, decision, and execution paths:

1) **Trigger approval**: Sends a `/chat` request that requires a write action and captures the returned `approval_id`.

2) **Resolve the approval record:** Uses `s6_validate_approvals.py` to read the approval record from Cosmos DB by trace ID or approval ID. This lightweight helper normalizes approval state for validation workflows.

3) **Approval decision (email):** Approval or denial is performed asynchronously via email. Any user in a mail-enabled `APPROVALS_GROUP`, or the direct email address if `APPROVALS_GROUP` is set to an email, can approve or deny using the link in the email.

4) **Testing Without Mailboxes:** For testing environments where Entra ID users do not have mailboxes, APPROVALS_GROUP may be set to a direct email address (e.g., APPROVALS_GROUP=yourEmail@ outlook.com). After updating .env.dev, redeploy the app (s1-03- deploy-app.ps1) for the configuration to take effect.

5) **Status check:** After a short delay, issue a second /chat request with status <approval_id> to resolve the current approval state.

6) **Pending path:** If approval is still pending, the script exits successfully with a clear message and does not perform telemetry checks.

7) **Denied path:** Confirm the denial and validate approval telemetry in Application Insights. No tool execution is expected.

8) **Approved path:** Confirm that the approved action is executed once and validate both approval status and tool execution telemetry.

Running s6-03-validate-approvals.ps1 confirms that approvals are enforced asynchronously and execution occurs only after an approved decision is recorded.

Portal Verification

Approval outcomes can be verified in Application Insights using a single query against the root thain.trace span:

```
dependencies
| where timestamp > ago(30m)
| where name == "thain.trace"
| where tostring(customDimensions["thain.approval.statuses"]) has
"approved"
   or tostring(customDimensions["thain.approval.statuses"]) has "denied"
| project timestamp, customDimensions
| order by timestamp desc
```

The results show approval metadata emitted by the runtime, including

- thain.approval.statuses (approved or denied)

- thain.approval.tools (the gated tool, when present)

- thain.tool.names (executed tool signals, appears only when approved)

- Correlated trace identifiers and execution metadata

This confirms that approval decisions are externally observable and auditable and that execution is policy-driven rather than implicit.

Figure 8-7 shows an example of locating approved or denied execution paths for a write action in Application Insights.

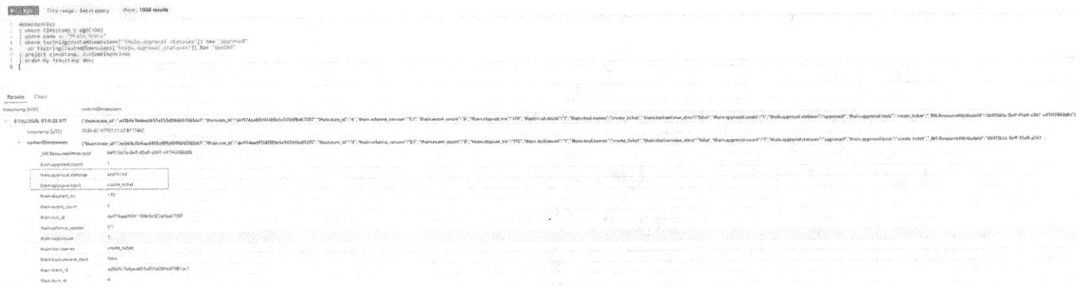

Figure 8-7. *Approval decision telemetry surfaced on the thain.trace span in Application Insights*

Note   All updated files including code and script referenced in this section are available in the book's GitHub repository under Chapter 8 → Sprint 6 → thain.

Sprint 6 Outcome

Sprint 6 enables governed execution aligned with enterprise standards through asynchronous human approvals. Write actions request approval without interrupting orchestration. Decisions are stored and auditable in Cosmos DB, and actions proceed only after explicit approval.

Email-based approvals use Azure Logic Apps and Azure Communication Services, with secure callbacks and approval status/tool telemetry in Application Insights. This lightweight pattern provides enterprise-aligned approval gating, auditability, and deterministic execution and can integrate with broader approval platforms.

Note   The sprint-wise implementation of Thain is available in the respective sprint folders within the Chapter 8 directory of the book's GitHub repository: `https://github.com/Apress/Architecting-Intelligent-Agents-in-Azure`. Unit test files for each sprint are included.

The final project state for this chapter is in the Sprint 6 folder within the Chapter 8 directory of the repository. To set up the repository locally, use the following commands:

`git clone https://github.com/Apress/Architecting-Intelligent-Agents-in-Azure.git`

`cd Architecting-Intelligent-Agents-in-Azure`

For the manuscript code, open the Chapter 8/Sprint 6/thain folder. For the GA code, open Code GA/Chapter 8/Sprint 6/thain. Replace Sprint 6 with the relevant sprint folder if you want to work with a specific sprint.

After cloning, create and activate a virtual environment, and then install the dependencies:

`python -m venv .venv`

`.\.venv\Scripts\activate`

`pip install -r requirements.txt -c constraints.txt`

Before running the project, fill in your Azure resource details in the `.env` file provided in each sprint folder. All placeholder values are marked with angle brackets (e.g., `<your-cosmos-account>`).

Sprint 2 introduces `.env.dev` for cloud (Managed Identity) mode. Run `s2-02-seed-keyvault-from-env.ps1` to generate it from your `.env`. The script copies your local configuration, seeds secrets into Key Vault, and rewrites `.env.dev` with Managed Identity references in place of raw keys.

To run the unit tests for any sprint, activate the virtual environment and run `python -m pytest tests`.

If Thain does not need to run continuously, optional pause/resume scripts are available in the Sprint 6 infra folder. These scripts scale the Container Apps (main + stage) to allow scale to zero and restore one replica when needed.

To pause: `.\infra\pause-thain.ps1`

To resume: `.\infra\resume-thain.ps1`

These scripts help control compute costs during idle periods. App Insights/Log Analytics, Key Vault, Azure Content Safety, and AI Search will still incur base costs unless deleted and later reprovisioned.

Code-Driven Orchestration and the Path to Managed Workflow Runtimes

Thain's orchestration uses an explicit, code-driven pipeline instead of a managed workflow runtime. This approach maintains architectural clarity by keeping control flow, safety gates, approvals, and failure handling visible and easy to inspect in code.

This approach is compatible with Microsoft Agent Framework (MAF) patterns and can transition to a managed Agent Workflow Runtime (AWR) when needed. Defining orchestration semantics independently of the execution substrate ensures portability across runtime models.

Conceptual Alignment with Workflow Runtimes

At an architectural level, Thain already exhibits workflow-like characteristics:

- Deterministic execution stages map to workflow steps or nodes.

- The shared blackboard represents the in-memory per-turn workflow state.

- Structured trace events capture stage transitions and tool or approval events.

- Safety, approval, and tool gates act as explicit policy hooks around execution.

- Approval-based resumption conceptually mirrors long-running workflow continuation patterns.

The primary difference is where these guarantees are enforced: in application code today rather than in a managed runtime.

Azure Implications of a Workflow Runtime

In Azure deployments, adopting a workflow runtime adds infrastructure responsibilities beyond the agent and tool layer.

Typical additions include

> **Durable state storage:** Workflow runtimes persist step state, retries, checkpoints, and resumptions, typically using Azure Cosmos DB or Azure Storage. Thain can reuse the existing Cosmos account with a dedicated container or set up a separate store for isolation.

> **Workflow coordinator or worker host:** A runtime component advances steps, manages retries, and resumes suspended executions. Depending on the model, this can run within the existing Container App or as a dedicated orchestration service.

> **Runtime configuration and wiring:** Step retries, timeouts, state store connectivity, and workflow definitions are managed as operational configuration instead of application code.

These additions do not alter agent logic, safety gates, approvals, tool contracts, or the trace and audit semantics established earlier in the book.

Runtime Deferral As an Architectural Choice

Introducing a workflow runtime early would shift the focus from architectural foundations to runtime mechanics. Deferring this allows the book to emphasize

- Explicit and inspectable control flow

- Governance boundaries enforced by design

- Observability and audit guarantees defined independently of the runtime

This reflects common enterprise practice: establish the correct architecture first, and then delegate execution to a managed runtime once behavior is stable and well understood.

MAF Workflow Alignment

Thain's orchestration stages can be expressed as workflow steps without changing

- Agent responsibilities
- Safety and approval policies
- Tool contracts
- Trace and audit schemas

Future Enterprise Extensions

Thain v0.7 establishes a production-ready baseline for governed agent execution. While this book cannot cover every enterprise consideration, the architecture is designed to support natural extensions such as

Richer approval platforms: Replace email-based approvals with platforms like Microsoft Teams, ServiceNow, JIRA, or custom portals, while maintaining asynchronous approval contracts and execution guarantees.

Multi-environment isolation: Separate development, test, and production deployments using independent Cosmos containers, search indexes, and telemetry resources.

Operational alerting and SLOs: Build alerts using Application Insights signals from Sprints 4–6, including error rates, approval delays, and tool execution failures.

Index life cycle and ingestion governance: Implement controlled pipelines for knowledge-base updates, retention policies, and content review workflows.

Policy and compliance integration: Integrate approval records and trace artifacts with external audit systems or compliance dashboards.

Security and access hardening: Enable role-based approval routing, secret rotation, DLP and PII enforcement, and SIEM export.

Model and prompt governance: Support versioning for prompts and agents, evaluation harnesses, and model routing policies.

RAG quality assurance: Monitor relevance drift, enforce freshness SLAs, and validate index health.

Reliability and scale: Implement multi-tenant isolation, backup and restore processes, disaster recovery planning, and cost controls.

Network hardening: Restrict Container App ingress to internal VNet or approved origins using Azure Container Apps network configuration or Azure API Management as a gateway layer.

Optional UI layer: Add a dedicated UI, such as a React application, to support approvals, operations dashboards, and audit review workflows.

These enhancements build directly on the patterns introduced in v0.7. No core orchestration changes are required because the system was designed to accommodate these extensions. Foundry's hosted agent execution environment (public preview as of this writing) provides VM-isolated sandboxes per session, a dedicated Entra Agent ID per agent, persistent filesystem state across idle periods, and scale-to-zero economics. You package the agent as a container image; the platform delivers the same compute isolation, identity assignment, and endpoint exposure that Sprints 1 and 2 established explicitly, without managing Container Apps or ACR infrastructure directly.

Agent frameworks and AI platforms are evolving rapidly. Capabilities such as advanced evaluation tools, managed reasoning services, model routing, and new platform features, including Azure AI Foundry enhancements, will continue to shape how agent systems are developed and operated. Architectures must evolve in parallel with these platforms.

The primary goal of this book is not to prescribe a fixed implementation but to guide you through the architectural principles for building a production-grade, multi-agent system with the Microsoft Agent Framework. By emphasizing clear governance boundaries, deterministic execution, and observable behavior, this architecture is intended to remain relevant as AI technologies advance.

Note   In this book, version numbers reflect architectural maturity rather than feature count. Thain v0.7 represents a stable, production-ready baseline, where correctness, governance, and observability are established before expanding behavior.

From this point onward, Thain is treated as a v1-level system. Chapters 9 and 10 build on this foundation by focusing on learning from feedback, evaluation, and controlled capability growth without revisiting or weakening the trust, execution, and governance guarantees established in this chapter.

Summary

Chapter 8 finalizes Thain's transition from an architecturally complete agent system to a production-ready, governed Azure deployment.

Over six incremental hardening sprints, Thain was deployed with managed identity, explicit safety enforcement, durable observability, production-backed retrieval, and asynchronous human approvals. Each capability was added without changing agent logic or orchestration semantics. The chapter prioritized strengthening correctness, auditability, and operational safety rather than expanding behavior.

By the end of this chapter, Thain can reason, retrieve evidence, request human approval, wait without blocking, and resume execution deterministically. Each interaction generates an auditable trace that records safety decisions, approval outcomes, tool usage, and execution results. Deployment acceptance relies on measurable health and telemetry signals instead of manual judgment.

With this foundation, Thain is prepared to operate safely in production and continue evolving. The following chapters build on this baseline by exploring feedback-driven learning, evaluation strategies, and controlled expansion of agent capabilities. Instead of introducing new architectural primitives, Chapters 9 and 10 examine how a governed, observable system can improve over time while maintaining established trust boundaries.

Architectural Outcomes

Following deployment hardening, Thain's architecture offers the following capabilities:

- Deterministic production execution, with explicit and inspectable control flow for reasoning, retrieval, and tool invocation across environments

- Managed identity and secret hygiene, ensuring Azure-native services authenticate with Entra ID where supported and secrets are securely resolved at runtime

- Explicit safety enforcement, using managed content classification and non-LLM safety responses evaluated before agent actions

- End-to-end observability, with a structured trace identifier per request to correlate orchestration, tool usage, approvals, and outcomes

- Measurable deployment safety, with release acceptance based on health checks and telemetry signals instead of implicit trust

- Production-grade evidence retrieval, supported by Azure AI Search and validated for stability and reproducibility

- Asynchronous approval-gated execution, enabling human decisions without blocking orchestration or compromising determinism

- Durable auditability, with safety decisions, approval records, and execution outcomes persisted and available for post hoc queries

- Composable governance boundaries, allowing safety, approval, retrieval, and execution policies to evolve independently from agent logic

Together, these outcomes transform Thain from a capable agent architecture into a trustworthy operational system. Its decisions can be observed, governed, explained, and safely extended as platforms and requirements evolve.

Thain Learns from Us

Introduction

By the end of Chapter 8, Thain was production-ready: governed, observable, safety-enforced, and deterministically orchestrated. It could reason, retrieve, request approvals, and execute within explicit architectural boundaries.

However, production correctness does not guarantee long-term quality.

Chapter 9 introduces a key architectural concept: measurable learning. This approach focuses on disciplined, traceable improvement through human feedback and structured evaluation, rather than retraining or autonomous evolution.

This chapter adds three capabilities:

- A durable human feedback loop (v1.1)

- A repeatable LLM-as-judge evaluation framework (v1.11)

- A targeted policy hardening iteration driven by measured defects (v1.12)

No new orchestration stages are introduced, and agent behavior is unchanged. The core architecture remains stable.

The primary change is the system's enhanced ability to measure its performance, identify weaknesses, address them at the appropriate layer, and verify improvements with evidence.

At this stage, Thain transitions from a production agent to an engineered system capable of improvement while maintaining governance.

© Hari Narayn 2026
H. Narayn, *Architecting Intelligent Agents in Azure*, https://doi.org/10.1007/979-8-8688-2433-3_9

Working with This Chapter's Code

Complete implementations of all referenced files are available in the book's companion GitHub repository, `https://github.com/Apress/Architecting-Intelligent-Agents-in-Azure`, under the folder:

Chapter 9 → {Version} → thain

These reference implementations serve as the definitive source for the code discussed in this chapter. The repository also includes a Microsoft Agent Framework 1.5.0 General Availability version of this chapter's code in the Code GA/Chapter 9/ {Version} folder. The GA version applies the same agent-framework API changes as Chapters 5–8. The feedback store, evaluation runner, and workbook scripts introduced in this chapter have no agent-framework dependency and are identical in both versions. A detailed migration note is available in the repository.

Code Reference Convention

Each code section specifies its source using the following format.

Source   Chapter 9 → {Version} → thain → {folder} → {filename} (action)

This notation shows

- Where the complete reference implementation is in the repository

- Whether the file should be created or updated in your local project

As you follow along, replicate the folder structure in your local workspace and create or update the referenced files as indicated.

Human Feedback Loop

Version 1.1 closes the loop between automated reasoning and human judgment through a streamlined, enterprise-ready approach. It offers a structured feedback capture API supported by Cosmos DB, sends feedback telemetry to Application Insights, and includes a basic metrics workbook for operational visibility.

Version 1.1 does not change orchestration logic, safety policies, routing decisions, or agent behavior. Feedback serves only as an audit and learning signal. The runtime remains deterministic, while v1.1 adds observability and continuous improvement.

Extending the Runtime with a Durable Feedback Signal

Thain v1.1 introduces structured, persistent feedback to the runtime. These updates add durable storage, API access, and telemetry integration without changing orchestration or safety functions. Feedback now serves as an additional audit signal, while the core reasoning engine remains unchanged.

Durable Feedback Persistence Layer (feedback_store.py)

An asynchronous store now manages all feedback persistence using Cosmos DB. The container uses `/scenario` as the partition key, enabling efficient aggregation by scenario and review category.

Records are normalized on insertion to ensure consistent timestamps, scenario defaults (falling back to answer), and TTL application. The store supports both provisioned and serverless Cosmos configurations by retrying container creation as needed, without requiring throughput settings.

This layer separates storage from API and telemetry, ensuring feedback persistence is modular and auditable.

Structured Feedback API Surface (schemas.py, app.py)

The runtime now offers a stable feedback interface through three endpoints:

- `POST /feedback`
- `GET /feedback/{id}`
- `GET /feedback/summary`

Request and response schemas define the feedback model and support API-first clients with field aliases such as `createdAtUtc`, `traceId`, and `runId`.

Feedback identifiers are generated in a consistent format when not provided, and scenario and decision values are normalized before storage. This ensures a stable, governed feedback interface.

Feedback Telemetry Integration (app.py, trace_sinks.py)

When feedback is submitted, `app.py` records a `feedback.submitted` trace event and exports it to Application Insights. `trace_sinks.py` then promotes feedback fields to the root span as dimensions.

Telemetry includes scenario, decision, reason, rating, and a submission flag. This aligns feedback signals with existing approval and retrieval telemetry, allowing operators to correlate runtime behavior with human review outcomes in Application Insights.

Configuration and Cloud Enforcement (settings.py)

Feedback configuration is managed through a dedicated model that specifies container name, TTL policy, and Cosmos settings.

Cloud validation ensures that when feedback is enabled, required configuration values are present and consistent. In managed identity mode, embedded Cosmos keys are rejected by validation and stripped from config, keeping secret hygiene aligned with Thain v1.0.

Provisioning and Wiring the Feedback Infrastructure

v1.1 delivers a minimal infrastructure extension to enable durable feedback capture and operational visibility. These updates maintain the script-driven deployment approach used in Chapter 8.

Provisioning the Feedback Container

A dedicated script provisions the feedback container in Cosmos DB.

The container is created with

- Partition key `/scenario`

- TTL derived from configuration

- Automatic retry without throughput configuration for serverless Cosmos

This approach ensures compatibility with both provisioned and serverless deployments.

Script: `.\infra\v11-01-provision-feedback.ps1`

Configuring the Feedback Runtime

Feedback settings are added to the development environment configuration file, enabling feedback capture without changes to the container image.

Configuration values include

- `ENABLE_FEEDBACK=true`

- `FEEDBACK_CONTAINER`

- `FEEDBACK_TTL_DAYS`

Script: .\infra\v11-02-configure-feedback.ps1

Build and Deploy

After preparing the container and configuration, build and deploy the updated application image using the standard deployment scripts from Chapter 8, Sprint 1.

Scripts:

- `.\infra\s1-02-build-push.ps1`

- `.\infra\s1-03-deploy-app.ps1`

v1.1 does not introduce additional hosting resources. Feedback operates within the existing Container App environment.

Validating Feedback

Validation in v1.1 confirms durable storage, telemetry emission, and workbook visibility.

Scripted Validation

A dedicated script performs validation by exercising the complete feedback pipeline.

Script: .\infra\v11-03-validate-feedback.ps1

The script performs the following actions:

- Submits multiple feedback samples with mixed scenarios and decisions

- Retrieves a stored record to confirm durable persistence

- Queries Application Insights to confirm that feedback telemetry appears in trace spans

Expected output includes generated feedback IDs and a confirmation message that storage and telemetry validation succeeded.

This process provides end-to-end confirmation that feedback capture, persistence, and observability function as intended.

Feedback Metrics Workbook in the Azure Portal

Operational visibility is achieved through an Application Insights workbook.

The provisioning script creates or updates the Thain Feedback Metrics workbook and injects the correct Application Insights resource ID into the template. If a workbook with the same display name exists, it is updated in place.

Script: `.\infra\v11-04-provision-feedback-workbook.ps1`

The workbook contains two panels:

1. **Feedback Volume + Override Rate (Daily)**: time-based trend visualization

2. **Top Feedback Reasons**: aggregated table view

After provisioning, the script opens the workbook in the Azure Portal using the direct workbook URL. Figure 9-1 shows the Feedback Metrics workbook rendered in the portal.

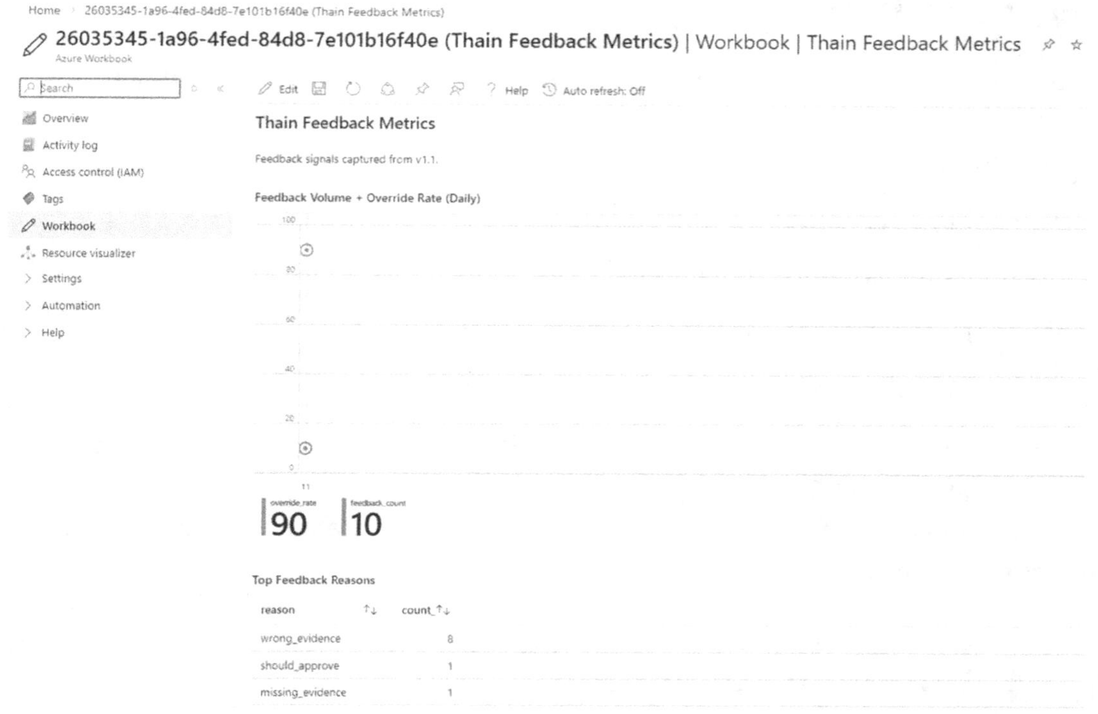

Figure 9-1. *The Thain Feedback Metrics workbook*

The feedback signals are visible directly in the Azure Portal. The Feedback Volume + Override Rate (Daily) panel shows daily feedback counts alongside the percentage of rejected or overridden decisions, both derived from trace telemetry.

The Top Feedback Reasons panel lists aggregated reasons such as

- wrong_evidence

- should_approve

- missing_evidence

Note   All updated files including code and script referenced in this section are available in the book's GitHub repository under Chapter 9 → v1.1 → thain.

Version 1.1 Outcome

At the conclusion of v1.1, Thain incorporates a complete and lightweight human feedback loop.

Feedback is

- Captured through a structured API

- Stored durably in Cosmos DB

- Emitted into Application Insights telemetry

- Visualized through a minimal operational workbook

No orchestration logic, safety policies, or agent behavior is modified. Feedback serves solely as an audit and improvement signal.

v1.1 establishes a foundation for governed, measurable iteration while preserving the system's deterministic, policy-driven architecture.

LLM-As-Judge Evaluation

Version 1.11 introduces a minimal, repeatable LLM-as-judge evaluation loop to quantify response quality improvements. It generates measurable before and after quality signals using a fixed prompt set, a rubric-based scoring model, and persistent result storage. The evaluation framework operates independently of the orchestration pipeline and does not alter safety behavior, routing logic, or agent contracts. It provides evidence rather than intervention.

By the end of v1.11, Thain can be evaluated against a consistent dataset, scored consistently by a judge model and rubric, and compared across runs using structured deltas.

Introducing a Repeatable Evaluation Capability

v1.11 introduces a batch evaluation runner, a fixed evaluation dataset, and a results persistence model aligned with Thain's governance patterns.

Batch Evaluation Runner (v11_eval_judge.py)

The evaluation runner loads a predefined prompt set from JSON and calls Thain's /
chat endpoint for each prompt. Each response is scored by a judge LLM (Azure OpenAI)
using a rubric on a 1 to 5 scale.

For each prompt, the runner persists

- `run_label`

- `prompt_id, prompt,` and `rubric`

- `response` and `trace_id`

- `score, judge_reason, judge_raw,` and `judge_model`

- `created_at_utc`

Results are stored in a Cosmos container (`thain-evals`) partitioned by `/run_label`
to enable grouped analysis.

The runner outputs summary statistics for each run, including

- Average score

- Pass rate

- Total count

An optional comparison mode enables direct comparison of two runs, displaying
score deltas.

The implementation follows established system patterns, including parameterized
Cosmos access, safe JSON handling, retry logic, and Key Vault fallback for API keys.

How the Judge Scores

The evaluation runner assigns quality assessment to a separate LLM instance called the
judge. The judge does not access Thain's system prompt, tools, or memory. It receives
only the user prompt, the assistant response, and a brief rubric. This separation ensures
the judge evaluates output quality rather than implementation fidelity.

The judge receives the following system instructions:

```
You are a strict evaluator for an enterprise support assistant.
Score the response from 1 to 5 using the rubric.
Return JSON with keys: score (int 1-5), reason (string).
```

The rubric defines the evaluation criteria. Instead of allowing the judge to determine what good means, each evaluation prompt includes specific requirements, such as `Use the relevant KB playbook and summarize the key steps clearly. Avoid unsafe or irrelevant guidance.` This approach makes scoring consistent and auditable. If a score appears incorrect, you review the rubric rather than the judge's reasoning.

Three design choices ensure reliable results. First, setting temperature to zero guarantees that the same prompt, response, and rubric combination yields the same score each time. Without this, random variation could obscure real quality changes.

Second, the runner uses defensive JSON parsing. If the judge returns malformed output, a fallback extracts the outermost JSON block and retries parsing. Unresolvable scores default to zero, preventing pipeline failures.

Third, the judge operates on a separate Azure OpenAI deployment, so you can use a different model or SKU than the one used for Thain.

A score of 4 out of 5 is the pass threshold, indicating the response met the rubric by using correct KB guidance without unsafe or invented content. Scores below 4 highlight areas for review. The summary reports three metrics: average score, pass rate (percentage scoring 4 or above), and prompt count. A decline in pass rate after a change signals a regression.

Fixed Evaluation Dataset (v11-eval-set.json)

The evaluation dataset includes 11 prompts, each mapped to the six seeded knowledge base documents:

- Wi-Fi instability SOP

- Network escalation policy

- VPN authentication troubleshooting

- Sensor calibration recovery

- Equipment shutdown response

- Incident communications template

Each prompt is designed to trigger document retrieval when knowledge base integration is enabled. The rubric explicitly requires the use of knowledge base guidance when available.

This approach ensures the evaluation measures both general reasoning quality and the system's ability to incorporate structured retrieval.

Provisioning and Executing the Evaluation Workflow

Evaluation is performed on deployed environments using a structured before-and-after execution model.

Baseline Run (Retrieval Disabled)

The baseline configuration turns off document retrieval:

- `ENABLE_DOCS=false`
- `AZURE_SEARCH_MODE=off`

Follow this deployment sequence:

1. Update `.env.dev` with the baseline configuration.
2. `.\infra\s1-03-deploy-app.ps1`

After redeployment, run the evaluation script with the baseline label:

`.\infra\v11-05-eval-judge.ps1 -RunLabel baseline`

This provides a measurable snapshot of response quality without knowledge base support.

Improved Run (Retrieval Enabled)

The improved configuration enables document retrieval:

- `ENABLE_DOCS=true`
- `AZURE_SEARCH_MODE=semantic`

Repeat the same deployment sequence:

1. Update `.env.dev` with the improved configuration.
2. `.\infra\s1-03-deploy-app.ps1`

Then, run the evaluation script with a comparison target:

```
.\infra\v11-05-eval-judge.ps1 -RunLabel improved -CompareTo baseline
```

The script prints summary statistics for the new run and the change relative to the baseline, quantifying improvement.

Note   Ensure the KB index is seeded (s5-02-seed-kb-index.ps1) before running the eval. Run s2-02-seed-keyvault-from-env.ps1 only if secrets or Key Vault values changed. These apply to both baseline and improved runs.

We use baseline/improved labels; fresh labels are recommended when rerunning to avoid mixing runs.

Operational Verification

Validation for v1.11 is authoritative and fully script driven. The evaluation script runs the full prompt set and outputs

- Per-run summary statistics

- Optional comparison deltas

In observed runs, the baseline average score was 1.55, and the improved average score was 2.00, yielding a +0.45 delta on the 11-prompt set.

Refer to Figure 9-2 for an example of the improved run output.

```
PS C:\AIAA\thain> .\infra\v11-05-eval-judge.ps1 -RunLabel improved -CompareTo baseline
Loading environment from .\\.env.dev
Ensuring Cosmos DB eval container: thain-evals
Cosmos DB Built-in Data Contributor already assigned to signed-in user.
Eval container already exists.
Running LLM-as-judge eval (run label: improved)
improved summary: avg=2.00, pass_rate=0.0%, n=11
baseline summary: avg=1.55, pass_rate=0.0%, n=11
delta: avg=0.45, pass_rate=0.0%
```

Figure 9-2. Baseline and improved summary

Although the absolute scores remain low, with a 0% pass rate under the defined rubric, the before-and-after improvement is clear and reproducible. The rubric is intentionally rigorous. Each prompt expects the response to synthesize specific procedural steps from the knowledge base rather than simply referencing a document title. As a result, scores below 4 are anticipated.

Inspecting Individual Prompt Deltas

In addition to the aggregated summary, each evaluated prompt is stored as an individual document in the `thain-evals` Cosmos container.

For example, the following query retrieves the same prompt (`eval-010`) across different run labels:

```
SELECT * FROM c WHERE c.prompt_id = "eval-010"
```

This query returns both the baseline and improved records for the prompt. The baseline record shows a score for generic handling of the request. The improved record includes judge reasoning that confirms the correct knowledge base procedure was identified.

Side-by-side inspection clarifies how retrieval affects individual prompts, not just overall averages. This approach can be applied to any prompt in the evaluation set.

Refer to Figure 9-3 for an example of an evaluation record viewed in the Azure Portal.

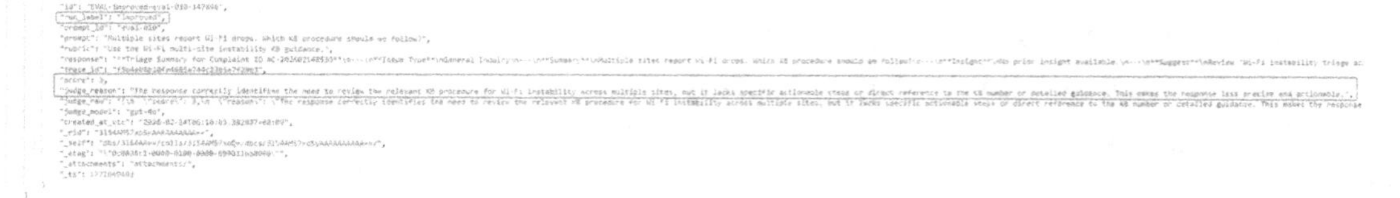

Figure 9-3. Baseline and improved evaluation records for prompt eval-010

Interpreting the Results and v1.11 Outcome

v1.11 establishes a disciplined approach to continuous improvement. Improvements are not assumed; they are measured. The evaluation results tell an honest and instructive story.

With retrieval disabled, Thain produces generic responses such as `investigate the issue`. When retrieval is enabled, responses reference the correct knowledge base documents, for example, "`Review Wi-Fi instability triage across multiple sites.`" This confirms that retrieval is functioning as intended.

However, the responses do not yet summarize or include the content of those documents. The evaluation framework highlights this gap: the system identifies the correct knowledge sources but does not fully incorporate their guidance into the final answer.

This demonstrates the value of the evaluation loop. It not only measures quality but also pinpoints where quality breaks down. Retrieval is effective; synthesis requires further refinement.

We now have a system that can detect its own weaknesses. The evaluation framework has made the synthesis gap visible. The next phase focuses on strengthening evidence integration and response construction.

Note   All updated files including code and script referenced in this section are available in the book's GitHub repository under Chapter 9 → v1.11 → thain.

Response Policy Hardening for Evidence Integration

This phase, v1.12, completes the process initiated in v1.11's LLM-as-judge evaluation.

The evaluation showed that retrieval worked as intended, but responses referenced only document titles instead of synthesizing the guidance within those documents. The system identified the correct knowledge source but did not translate procedural content into actionable steps.

v1.12 addresses this by surfacing document content through the service boundary and strengthening the response policy to enforce synthesis, without changing orchestration stages, safety controls, or tool contracts.

This results in measurable improvement using the same evaluation dataset and rubric.

Correcting the Synthesis Gap

v1.12 introduces targeted modifications across retrieval, orchestration, and response enforcement layers. Architectural boundaries remain unchanged; evidence integration is strengthened at the policy/context boundary.

Surfacing Document Content from Search (docs_search_client.py)

The search client now returns the document content field in the result dictionary.

Previously, only metadata such as title and snippet were included. Although Azure Search retrieved full document content, it was not passed to downstream components.

By including content in the result payload, retrieved guidance is now available for orchestration and response construction. This change addresses the root cause and enables knowledge synthesis.

Stabilizing the Service Boundary (docs_service.py)

The document service now explicitly maps the content field into the structured document dictionary sent to the orchestrator.

This ensures the content field remains stable and clearly defined across the service boundary, preventing accidental omission or format drift.

Formatting Knowledge Context for LLM Consumption (orchestrator.py)

Knowledge context is now formatted as structured, readable guidance instead of raw dictionary outputs.

Each document is rendered as a short, human-readable title plus a content excerpt. The excerpt is truncated to keep prompts efficient while preserving actionable detail.

This ensures the model receives coherent procedural guidance rather than symbolic references.

Hardening Response Policy Enforcement (main.py)

Three improvements were introduced:

1. **Strengthened instruction when a knowledge context exists:**
   When KB context is present, the response policy now requires
   synthesizing document guidance into actionable steps rather than
   providing simple citations.

2. **Improved triage fallback formatting**: If the system generates
   a fallback triage card, it now includes a summary of document
   guidance instead of only stating `Review <title>`.

3. **Light enforcement helper**: A minimal enforcement helper
   appends guidance when KB context exists, but the response
   omits it.

Validation

No new infrastructure was introduced in v1.12.

Deployment sequence

- `.\infra\s1-02-build-push.ps1`

- `.\infra\s1-03-deploy-app.ps1`

Scripted Evaluation

The evaluation dataset from v1.11 was re-executed using the `improved_v12` run label.
Results will be compared to the previous `improved` run label from v1.11.

```
.\infra\v11-05-eval-judge.ps1 -RunLabel improved_v12 -CompareTo improved
```

Results:

improved_v12 summary: avg=3.00, pass_rate=45.5%, n=11

```
improved summary: avg=2.00, pass_rate=0.0%, n=11
delta: avg=1.00, pass_rate=45.5%
```

Prompts and rubrics were identical across runs.

Refer to Figure 9-4 for an example of the evaluation script comparison output.

```
PS C:\AIAA\thain> .\infra\v11-05-eval-judge.ps1 -RunLabel improved_v12 -CompareTo improved
Loading environment from .\\.env.dev
Ensuring Cosmos DB eval container: thain-evals
Cosmos DB Built-in Data Contributor already assigned to signed-in user.
Eval container already exists.
Running LLM-as-judge eval (run label: improved_v12)
improved_v12 summary: avg=3.00, pass_rate=45.5%, n=11
improved summary: avg=2.00, pass_rate=0.0%, n=11
delta: avg=1.00, pass_rate=45.5%
```

Figure 9-4. *v1.11 and v1.12 runs, showing measurable uplift in average score and pass rate*

Inspecting Cosmos Records

Individual prompt records can be inspected in the `thain-evals` container.

Query example:

```
SELECT * FROM c WHERE c.prompt_id = "eval-010"
```

This returns baseline, improved, and improved_v12 records for the same prompt. Refer to Figure 9-5 for an example.

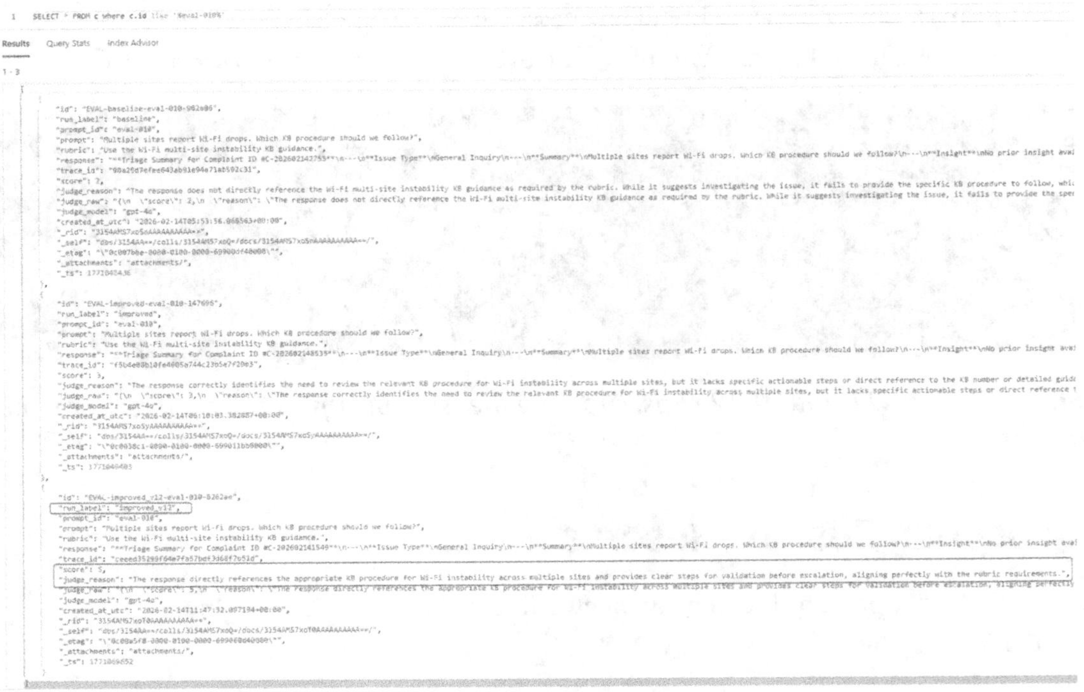

Figure 9-5. *Cosmos DB records for prompt eval-010, showing baseline, improved, and v1.12 synthesized responses*

Interpreting the Results

The prompt eval-010 illustrates the evaluation process clearly.

The question was: Multiple sites report Wi-Fi drops. Which KB procedure should we follow?

In the baseline run, Thain returned generic advice: investigate the issue and validate configurations. No knowledge base article was referenced, and no procedure was cited. The judge scored it 2 out of 5. Without retrieval, the system functioned as a general-purpose assistant without domain awareness.

With retrieval enabled in v1.11, the response improved. Thain located the correct knowledge base article and cited it by name: Wi-Fi instability triage across multiple sites. The score increased to 3. Retrieval was effective, as the system found the correct document. However, the response included only the title, with no procedural content. The evaluation framework identified this gap: the system could locate evidence but could not integrate it.

In v1.12, using the same prompt, rubric, and judge model produced a different outcome. The article was still identified, but its guidance was presented as actionable steps:

- Validate AP health.

- Check channel overlap.

- Inspect WAN packet loss.

- Review DHCP lease exhaustion.

The score reached 5, a perfect mark. The judge noted the response `aligns perfectly with the rubric requirements`.

No changes were made to the orchestration, rubric, or dataset. The only update was in the evidence integration layer, ensuring retrieved content crossed the service boundary into the response pipeline.

Across three run labels, a single prompt improved from 2 to 3 to 5. The system did not become more intelligent; it became better engineered.

Note   All updated files including code and script referenced in this section are available in the book's GitHub repository under Chapter 9 → v1.12 → thain.

---

v1.12 Outcome

v1.12 delivers more than a higher score. It demonstrates that Thain is not just an agent that answers questions; it is an agent with a feedback loop that reveals where quality breaks down and why.

The arc built across this chapter is deliberate:

- **We measured first**: The evaluation framework scored responses at 1.55 (baseline) and 2.00 (retrieval enabled). Improvement was present but shallow.

- **We diagnosed next**: Scores plateaued despite instruction-layer changes, confirming the defect was deeper than prompt wording. The issue was not the wording; it was missing evidence propagation. Retrieved document content was fetched from the knowledge store but was discarded at the data-mapping boundary before reaching the response layer.

- **We corrected the issue at the appropriate architectural layer:** A single-line fix in the data-mapping code ensured that retrieved content passed through to the response pipeline rather than being dropped. No orchestration refactor, new services, or prompt rewrites were required.

- **We verified through re-evaluation:** Average score climbed to 3.00. The pass rate went from 0% to 45.5%. eval-010 reached a perfect 5 under the same rubric and judge.

This is not prompt tuning; it is a controlled, measurable system improvement.

The Cosmos records for `eval-010` across three run labels – `baseline`, `improved`, and `improved_v12` – provide durable, auditable proof. The same question, rubric, and judge model produced progressively stronger outcomes.

Thain now demonstrates something more valuable than correctness: the capacity to measure, diagnose, correct, and verify. This is what it means for the system to learn from us, not through retraining but through principled engineering driven by evaluation data.

The same discipline applies going forward. The feedback workbook surfaces the most common override reasons `wrong_evidence`, `should_approve`, `missing_evidence` ranked by volume. Cross-referencing those top reasons against low-scoring evaluation prompts identifies where the next iteration should focus.

If operators consistently override Thain's decisions for a particular scenario, and the evaluation framework confirms low scores in that same area, the diagnosis is already half complete. The feedback signal tells you where to look; the evaluation framework tells you how much it improved after the fix.

Quality Loop Architecture

The three versions in this chapter follow a deliberate improvement cycle. Feedback first reveals where the system falls short. Evaluation then measures the impact of those failures, and targeted hardening corrects the defect at the appropriate architectural layer. Re-evaluation provides objective evidence that the fix worked. See Figure 9-6.

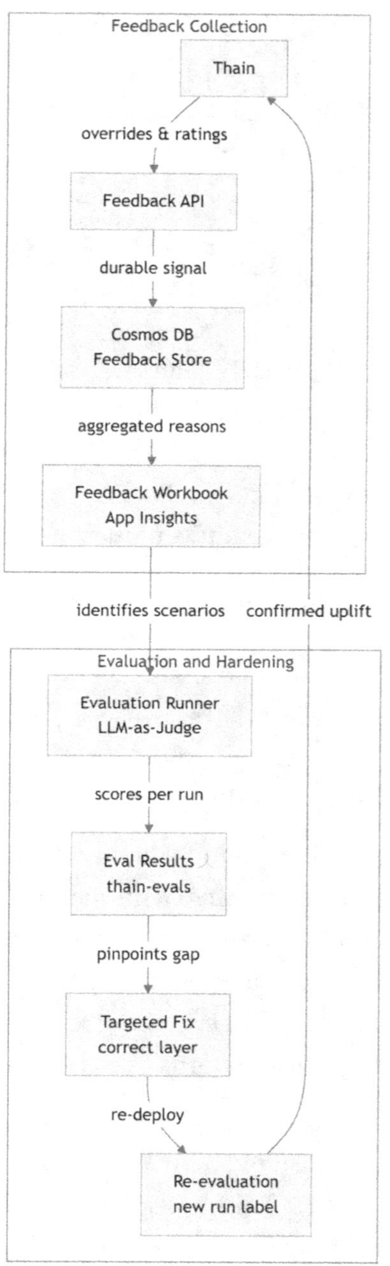

Figure 9-6. *The feedback-driven improvement cycle*

Each arrow in this loop corresponds to a concrete artifact: feedback records in Cosmos, workbook panels in Application Insights, scored results in the thain-evals container, and run-label deltas from the evaluation script. The improvement is not asserted; it is stored, queryable, and reproducible.

Practical Considerations for LLM-Based Evaluation

The evaluation framework provided a clear directional signal across three runs, with scores increasing from 1.55 to 3.00 as each defect was addressed. This signal was both accurate and actionable. However, before adopting LLM-as-judge as a recurring quality gate, it is important to understand its strengths and limitations. Also, this framework evaluates final responses. Evaluating intermediate steps such as retrieval quality and tool invocation accuracy is an emerging area and a natural next iteration.

Verbosity bias: LLM judges often assign higher scores to longer responses, even when shorter answers are equally correct. In Thain's case, this is partially addressed by rubrics that prioritize use of specific KB guidance over response length. If you expand the evaluation set with open-ended prompts, monitor for inflated scores on verbose but superficial answers.

Self-evaluation bias: When a model family evaluates its own output, it may be more lenient than a human reviewer. The framework addresses this by running the judge on a separate deployment, allowing use of a different model. If scores appear consistently generous, consider switching to a different model family or using two judges for comparison as a calibration check.

Score compression: Judges rarely use the full 1–5 range in practice. Results in this chapter clustered between 1 and 3 until v1.12, which pushed some prompts to 5. This is expected. Treat absolute scores as relative indicators rather than calibrated quality grades. The change between runs is more significant than any individual score.

Sample size: Eleven prompts are sufficient to detect major regressions, as shown by the increase from 0% to 45.5% pass rate after v1.12. For more precise measurement, such as detecting a 5% quality improvement, a larger prompt set is required. For production, use 40–50 prompts per scenario category. The evaluation runner and Cosmos storage scale linearly; the only additional cost is the judge LLM calls.

Rubric sensitivity: Minor wording changes in a rubric can shift scores by a full point. Once a baseline is established, treat rubrics as fixed for that evaluation cycle. If refinement is needed, re-run the baseline with the updated rubric to maintain valid comparisons. Microsoft Foundry and MAF evaluation capabilities provide platform-managed evaluators for groundedness, relevance, coherence, tool-call accuracy, and related quality dimensions; building the judge runner explicitly here ensures you understand what those evaluators are measuring before adopting them. The repository also includes Chapter 9 architecture notes that map this explicit evaluation loop to MAF's native evaluation capabilities, while keeping the chapter's dataset, rubric, judge prompt, result storage, and improvement decisions visible.

Note   The code for each version in this chapter is available in the book's GitHub repository at `https://github.com/Apress/Architecting-Intelligent-Agents-in-Azure`, under the Chapter 9 directory, one folder per version (v1.1, v1.11, v1.12). Unit test files are included in each version folder. To clone and run a specific version,

```
git clone https://github.com/Apress/Architecting-Intelligent-
Agents-in-Azure.git
```

```
cd Architecting-Intelligent-Agents-in-Azure
```

For the manuscript code, open the Chapter 9/v1.12/thain folder. For the GA code, open Code GA/Chapter 9/v1.12/thain. Replace v1.12 with v1.1 or v1.11 to work with an earlier version. After cloning, create and activate a virtual environment and install dependencies:

```
python -m venv .venv
```

```
.\.venv\Scripts\activate
```

```
pip install -r requirements.txt -c constraints.txt
```

Each version folder includes an .env file with all placeholder values marked with angle brackets (e.g., <your-cosmos-account>) – fill in your Azure resource details before running. An `.env.dev` file is also provided for cloud (Managed Identity) mode. To run the unit tests for any version,

```
python -m pytest tests
```

How Thain Maps to Modern Agent Patterns

Thain was not designed around any single protocol, SDK, or hosting abstraction. Its architecture is built on explicit boundaries between tools, memory, safety, approvals, telemetry, and feedback, with each boundary enforced through structured, policy-controlled contracts. That separation is important because it means emerging agent standards can be adopted at the transport edge without forcing changes to governance, orchestration, or auditability in the core system.

Model Context Protocol (MCP) aligns naturally with Thain's tool mediation layer. In Thain, tools are already invoked through structured contracts with normalized outputs, policy evaluation, approval interception, and audit capture. From an architectural perspective, MCP would replace only the transport and invocation mechanism used to reach those tools. It would not alter the surrounding control layers that make tool use safe and governable. Validation rules, approval gates, telemetry, and traceability would continue to operate exactly as before. MAF supports this natively. Any Agent instance can be exposed as an MCP server, making Thain's governed tool contracts available at the MCP surface without changes to the internal control layers.

Agent-to-Agent (A2A) aligns with Thain's orchestration boundary. Thain already separates responsibility across distinct stages such as triage, evidence gathering, and action routing, with each step communicating through explicit contracts rather than implicit shared state. Externalizing that communication through A2A changes how messages move between agent roles, but it does not alter the orchestration logic that determines when delegation occurs, what constraints apply, or how results are reconciled.

This is the broader architectural point: protocols standardize interaction surfaces, but they do not replace system design. Thain's core behavior remains anchored in architectural invariants such as policy enforcement, approval control, deterministic routing, and end-to-end observability. Those invariants sit above any specific transport choice and continue to hold even as protocol ecosystems mature.

Figure 9-7 illustrates where these protocols attach within Thain's architecture. Each protocol integrates at a boundary layer, while the internal governance, safety, and orchestration logic remain unchanged.

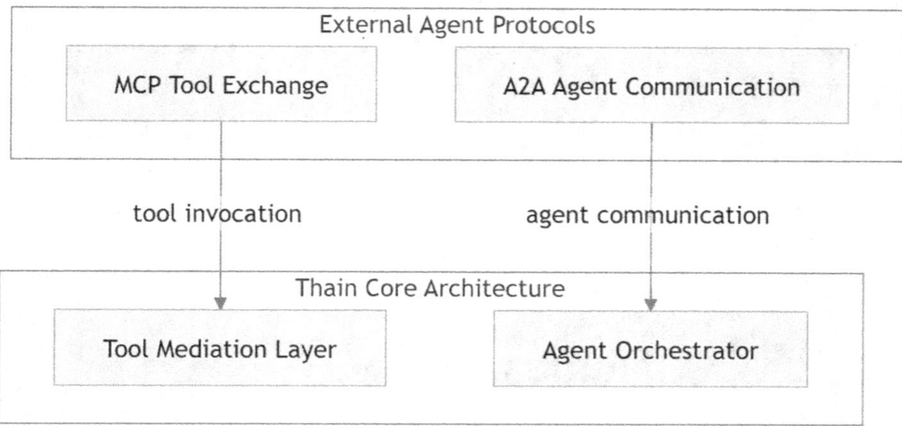

Figure 9-7. *MCP and A2A attach to Thain's boundary layers*

This protocol resilience is not accidental. Thain already expresses the core Microsoft Agent Framework patterns directly in its control flow. Handoff maps to triage and action routing. Escalation maps to safety refusal paths and human approval gates. Delegation maps to tool-specialist execution with normalized outputs and policy enforcement around the execution boundary. In other words, Thain already embodies the architectural patterns these newer standards aim to formalize. As a result, new protocols can be adopted at the boundary layer, while governance, safety, traceability, and control flow remain consistent across protocol generations.

Summary

Chapter 9 shows that production readiness marks the start of measurable refinement, not the end of the process.

In v1.1, Thain gained a structured human feedback loop. Feedback became durable, queryable, and visible through telemetry, without altering orchestration logic or safety behavior.

In v1.11, Thain gained an evaluation framework. A fixed dataset, a rubric-driven judge model, and persistent result storage enabled consistent quality measurement across runs. The system could now quantify before-and-after differences rather than rely on intuition.

The initial evaluation identified a subtle defect: retrieval functioned, but synthesis did not. The system could locate knowledge but could not integrate it into responses.

In v1.12, this gap was addressed at the appropriate architectural boundary. Evidence propagation was corrected, and response policy enforcement was strengthened. The same dataset, rubric, and judge were used for re-evaluation, resulting in improved scores.

The improvement was measurable, reproducible, and durably stored in Cosmos DB.

Thain does not learn through hidden weight updates. It improves through disciplined engineering: Measure, Diagnose, Fix at the right layer, and Re-measure. That loop, not the LLM, is what makes the system resilient.

Architectural Outcomes

By the end of Chapter 9, Thain presents architectural properties that go beyond orchestration:

- **Durable human signal integration**: Feedback is collected through a governed API, stored in Cosmos DB, included in telemetry, and visualized for operations. Human judgment is treated as an auditable runtime signal instead of informal commentary.

- **Independent evaluation capability**: Quality measurement occurs independently of the orchestration pipeline. A fixed prompt set, rubric-scored judge model, and partitioned results store enable consistent comparisons across runs without changing runtime behavior.

- **Boundary-level correctability**: Defects can be isolated to specific architectural layers such as retrieval, data mapping, or policy enforcement, and corrected without refactoring orchestration or safety flows. Improvements are made at the appropriate abstraction boundary.

- **Evidence-backed governance**: Each evaluation result is stored with run labels, rubric context, trace identifiers, and judge reasoning. Improvements are supported by queryable artifacts rather than anecdotal evidence.

- **Protocol-resilient design**: Tools, memory, safety, approvals, and feedback are managed through explicit contracts. Emerging standards such as MCP or A2A can be integrated at transport boundaries without affecting governance, traceability, or control flow.

- **Iterative stability**: New capabilities such as feedback, evaluation, and synthesis enforcement were added without changing core orchestration semantics. Architectural invariants were maintained as quality improved.

Thain at Scale

Introduction

By the end of Chapter 9, Thain was adaptive: it could learn from feedback, measure outcomes, and improve deterministically within its governed architecture. It was production ready, observable, and continuously evaluated.

Adaptive intelligence does not guarantee operational efficiency. An agentic system is still a software system: it needs clear boundaries, observable behavior, controlled change, and accountable operation. A system can reason well and still accumulate unnecessary token cost, respond slowly under load, or fail silently when a dependency degrades. Chapter 10 addresses that gap.

This chapter guides Thain through its second release cycle, from v1.12 to v2.0, using three structured sprints:

- **Sprint 2.1: Instrument and dashboard**: Establish request-level visibility into token usage, latency, and estimated cost. Measurement is essential for effective optimization.

- **Sprint 2.2: Performance optimization**: Reduce cost and call volume through response compaction, model profiling, and execution reuse while maintaining the evaluation quality established in Chapter 9.

- **Sprint 2.3: Data and reliability hardening**: Enhance the data layer, implement resilience patterns, define alerts and SLOs, and validate system behavior under failure conditions.

No new reasoning stages are introduced. The orchestration model and core intelligence architecture remain unchanged. In this chapter, scale refers to operational readiness, including instrumentation, optimization, and resilience controls required for production deployments, rather than high-throughput benchmarking.

405

H. Narayn, *Architecting Intelligent Agents in Azure*, https://doi.org/10.1007/979-8-8688-2433-3_10

By the end of this chapter, Thain transitions from a production-ready agent to an enterprise-grade service engineered for scale, cost control, and controlled failure behavior.

Working with This Chapter's Code

Complete implementations of all referenced files are available in the book's companion GitHub repository, `https://github.com/Apress/Architecting-Intelligent-Agents-in-Azure`, under the folder Chapter 10 → {Sprint} → thain.

These reference implementations serve as the definitive source for the code discussed in this chapter. The repository also includes a Microsoft Agent Framework 1.5.0 General Availability version of this chapter's code in the Code GA/Chapter 10/ {Sprint} folder. The GA version applies the same agent-framework API changes as Chapters 5-9. All performance, caching, cost estimation, and reliability modules introduced in this chapter have no agent-framework dependency and are identical in both versions. A detailed migration note is available in the repository.

Code Reference Convention

Each code section specifies its source using the following format.

Source   Chapter 10 → {Sprint} → thain → {folder} → {filename} (action)

This notation shows

- Where the complete reference implementation is in the repository

- Whether the file should be created or updated in your local project

As you follow along, replicate the folder structure in your local workspace and create or update the referenced files as indicated. When adding a new folder, include an empty `__init__.py` to mark it as a Python package.

Sprint 2.1: Instrument + Dashboard

Sprint 2.1 establishes runtime efficiency visibility for Thain v2.0 by emitting request-level token, cost, and latency telemetry and surfacing it in an operational dashboard.

The objective is to establish a measurable baseline for evaluating future optimization efforts in Sprint 2.2 and beyond.

Sprint Scope

Sprint 2.1 delivers

- Request-level token usage telemetry (prompt, completion, total)

- Cost estimation per request (USD estimate derived from token counts and configured pricing rates)

- Latency telemetry (end to end and tool level)

- Root span projection for efficient querying

- An Application Insights workbook with

    - Average cost per request (daily)

    - Average latency per request (daily)

    - Token usage trend (daily)

    - P95 latency (daily)

- A scripted validation workflow that proves telemetry presence and correctness

Sprint 2.1 makes no changes to model selection, routing, orchestration, or safety and governance policy. The sole purpose is measurement. Optimization follows in Sprint 2.2.

Telemetry Pipeline Implementation

Sprint 2.1 updates three code base layers to enable end-to-end telemetry. The runtime layer captures token usage and cost, the observability sink sends this data to Application Insights, and the governance allowlist ensures economic and latency data remain available from request execution through dashboard queries.

Usage Extraction and Resolution

The runtime (`main.py`) now computes and emits structured LLM usage and cost telemetry at each turn completion. It extracts usage metadata from the framework response using several compatible patterns, including usage, `token_usage`, tokens, and metadata fallbacks.

If SDK-level usage metadata is unavailable, a heuristic fallback estimates token usage from the prompt and completion text. This approach maintains telemetry continuity and prevents loss of token metrics.

The resolution step returns both

- Usage values

- Usage source (sdk or heuristic)

The usage source is included in telemetry to ensure transparency.

In the current MAF configuration, SDK-level usage metadata is not exposed in the response object, so the heuristic path is active. Token counts are estimated from prompt and completion text length. The `usage_source` field in telemetry will show `heuristic`, confirming which path was taken. The cost estimate remains usable for trend/baseline analysis, though its precision is lower than SDK-reported token usage.

Cost Estimation

Cost is calculated in main.py using environment-configured token pricing rates:

- `THAIN_COST_INPUT_PER_1K_USD`

- `THAIN_COST_OUTPUT_PER_1K_USD`

The runtime computes

- `cost_estimate_usd`

- `cost_estimate_available` (boolean flag)

Legacy variable names remain supported for compatibility. This design separates runtime cost visibility from hard-coded model pricing, ensuring cost calculations remain aligned with Azure pricing.

Structured Telemetry Event

At turn completion, the runtime (`main.py`) emits a structured `llm.usage` event containing

- Model name

- Usage source

- Prompt tokens

- Completion tokens

- Total tokens

- Estimated cost (USD)

- Cost availability flag

This event is recorded in the trace stream for each request. This provides request-level economic telemetry.

Root Span Projection for Query Efficiency

The telemetry sink (`observability/trace_sinks.py`) projects telemetry events onto the root `thain.trace` span so that workbook queries can reference `customDimensions` directly.

Projected latency fields include

- `thain.latency.total_ms`

- `thain.latency.tool_ms`

- `thain.latency.retrieve_docs_ms` (when applicable)

Projected token and cost fields include

- `thain.tokens.source`

- `thain.tokens.prompt`

- `thain.tokens.completion`

- `thain.tokens.total`

- `thain.cost.estimate_usd`

- `thain.cost.estimate_available`

This approach prevents span-event expansion in KQL queries and simplifies dashboard construction.

Governance Alignment for Telemetry Propagation

To ensure that token and cost fields are retained in Application Insights, the telemetry allowlist in the governance logging policy (`governance/logging_policy.py`) was updated to explicitly include

- `llm.usage` fields (usage source, token counts, cost fields, model)

- `trace.appinsights` diagnostic fields (`status`, `error_type`, `message`)

This ensures economic telemetry is treated as first-class operational data and is not filtered out during log processing.

As a result, usage and cost attributes are consistently present in root span `customDimensions` and are queryable in the portal.

Pricing Synchronization Automation

Sprint 2.1 introduces pricing synchronization automation via

`infra\s2.1-01-sync-openai-pricing.ps1`

This script

- Reads model and region context

- Queries the Azure Retail Prices API

- Selects the appropriate input and output token meters

- Converts rates to per-1K token pricing

- Writes

  - `THAIN_COST_INPUT_PER_1K_USD`

  - `THAIN_COST_OUTPUT_PER_1K_USD`

A `-DryRun` mode allows safe inspection before writing configuration values.

This prevents discrepancies between configured and Azure retail pricing, maintaining accurate cost estimation.

Build and Deployment Integration

Sprint 2.1 follows the established deployment pattern used throughout previous Chapters.

The recommended execution sequence is

1. `.\infra\s2.1-01-sync-openai-pricing.ps1`

2. `.\infra\s1-02-build-push.ps1`

3. `.\infra\s1-03-deploy-app.ps1`

4. `.\infra\s2.1-02-validate-telemetry.ps1`

5. `.\infra\s2.1-03-provision-telemetry-workbook.ps1`

The standard build-and-push script (`s1-02-build-push.ps1`) derives image tags. The deploy script (`s1-03-deploy-app.ps1`) updates the Container App (`thain-01`) with the new image and environment variables.

Telemetry Validation

Sprint 2.1 includes strict automated validation using

`infra\s2.1-02-validate-telemetry.ps1`

Validation flow:

1. Invoke `/chat` with a telemetry test prompt.

2. Capture the returned `trace_id`.

3. Query Application Insights for that trace.

4. Validate presence of

   - `thain.tokens.total`

   - `thain.tokens.source`

   - `thain.latency.total_ms`

   - `thain.cost.estimate_available`

5. Fail explicitly if `cost_estimate_available` is not true.

6. If cost estimation is confirmed available, additionally validate `thain.cost.estimate_usd` is present.

Successful execution outputs: `Telemetry validation OK`. This ensures telemetry is verified rather than assumed.

Operational Dashboard

Sprint 2.1 provisions an Application Insights workbook using the following script:

`infra\s2.1-03-provision-telemetry-workbook.ps1`

The workbook template is located at infra/templates/workbook-telemetry.json. The provisioning script resolves the Application Insights resource ID, inserts it into the template, performs an idempotent upsert, and opens the workbook in the Azure Portal.

The resulting workbook, Thain Cost + Latency Metrics, displays four operational panels with live telemetry. Figures 10-1 and 10-2 show the populated workbook in the Azure Portal.

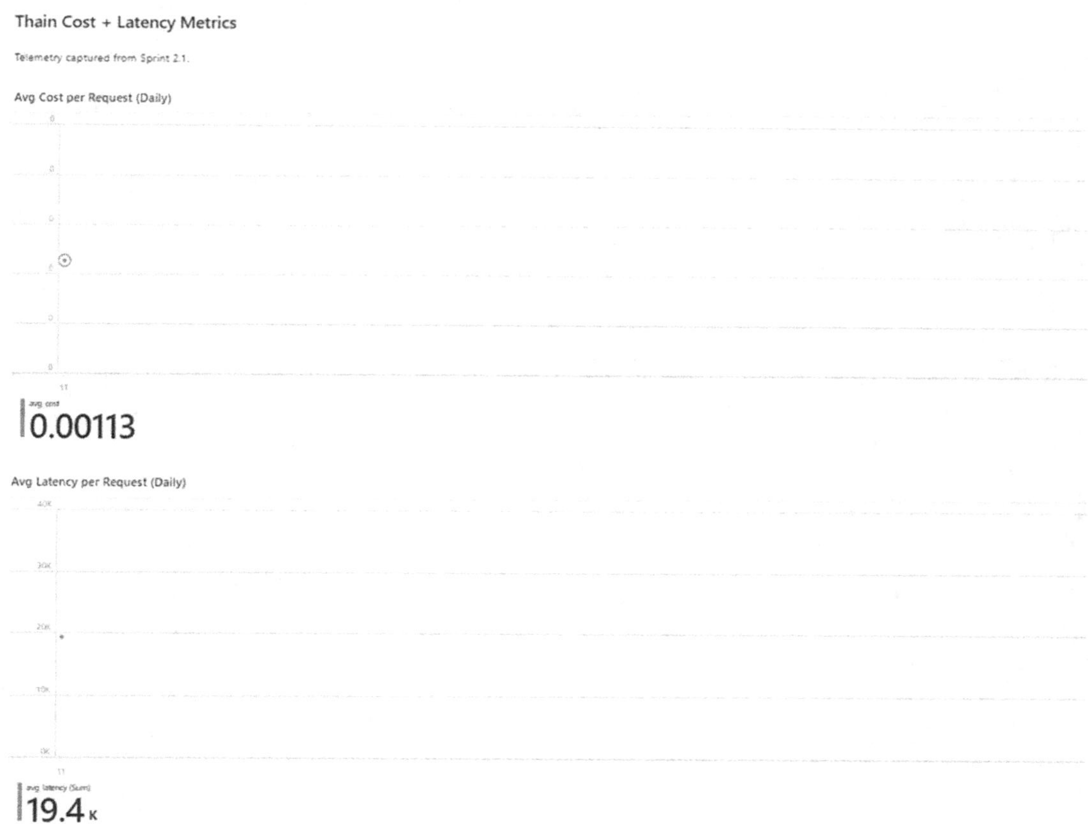

Figure 10-1. *Thain Cost + Latency Metrics: average cost and latency*

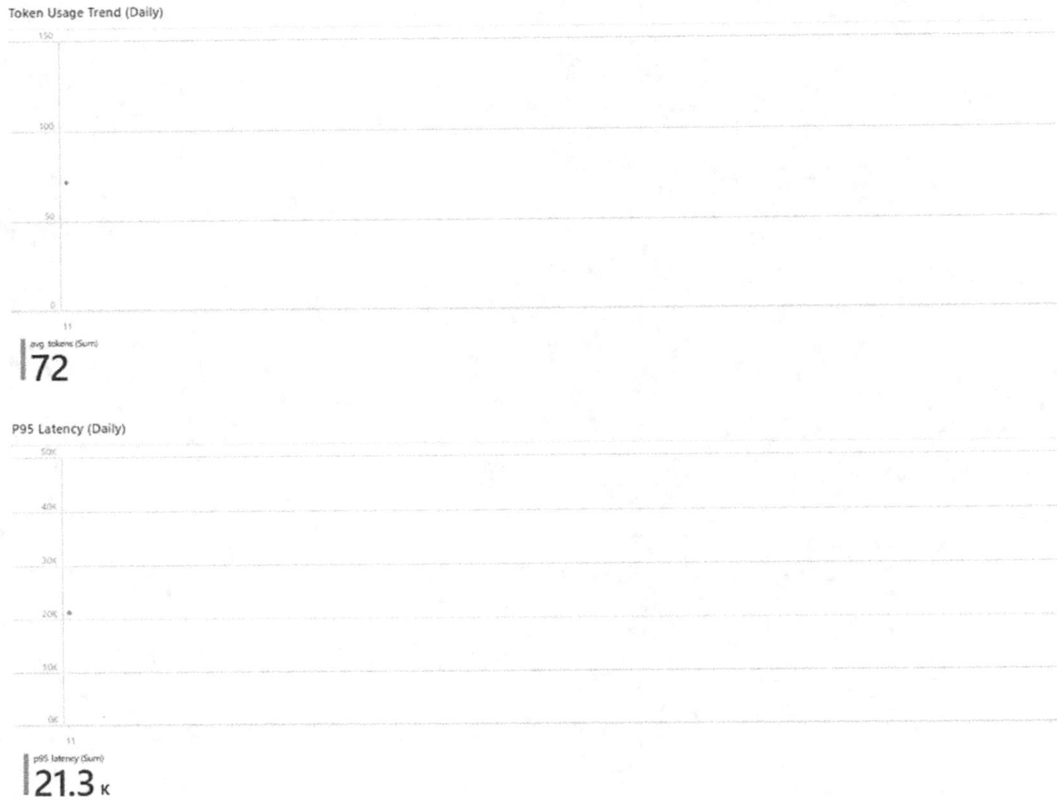

Figure 10-2. *Thain Cost + Latency Metrics: token usage trend and P95 latency*

The workbook verifies that all four measurement dimensions are operational:

- Cost estimation

- Token tracking

- Average latency

- P95 latency

At this baseline, each request costs approximately $0.00113 and completes in about 19 seconds on average. Cost values are model-usage estimates derived from configured per-1K token rates.

While these values are modest per request, they become significant at scale. Monthly projections assume stable per-request cost and steady daily volume.

At 10,000 requests per day, the projected monthly model cost is approximately $339. At 100,000 requests per day, it increases to approximately $3,390.

For an enterprise support agent handling high ticket volumes, costs accumulate rapidly. Without measurement, these costs can go unnoticed.

These projections reflect only model usage and exclude infrastructure costs such as Azure Cosmos DB request units (RU), Azure AI Search queries, Container Apps runtime, and monitoring overhead. In production, model usage and infrastructure consumption scale together. Token discipline is one aspect of cost governance, but not the whole picture.

In this baseline run, average token usage is ~72 tokens per request; estimated cost is driven by both token volume and configured model rates. Minor inefficiencies in prompt structure or response verbosity can lead to measurable monthly budget impacts at scale. Optimization starts with visibility.

The 19-second average latency reflects the full multi-agent pipeline at this stage: retrieval, knowledge lookup, classification, and LLM reasoning, all executed sequentially without parallelism or caching. P95 latency of approximately 21.3 seconds indicates that the slowest responses are not much longer than the average, demonstrating system consistency.

These figures are not a concern at this stage; they serve as a starting point.

Sprint 2.2 will address both cost and latency by reducing token consumption through response compaction and controlled model profiling and by reducing latency through caching and runtime optimization. The same workbook panels will track these changes, enabling measurable improvement against this baseline.

Observability must come before optimization. Without a baseline, improvement cannot be demonstrated.

Note   All updated files including code and script referenced in this section are available in the book's GitHub repository under Chapter 10 → Sprint 2.1 → thain.

Sprint 2.1 Outcome

Sprint 2.1 establishes an initial measurable performance baseline for Thain v2.0.

The system now emits request-level token, latency, and estimated cost telemetry. These telemetry fields are preserved through governance logging policy allowlists, validated by an automated script, and visualized in an Azure workbook.

The current observed average latency (~`19 seconds`) reflects the pre-optimization multi-agent pipeline without caching or parallel execution and serves as the baseline for Sprint 2.2 improvements.

Sprint 2.1 does not change orchestration or safety behavior; it adds observability. Thain can now answer a critical question: how much did that cost, and how long did it take?

Sprint 2.2: Controlled Optimization Under Governance

Sprint 2.2 introduces structured runtime optimization to reduce cost and latency while preserving deterministic orchestration, governed execution, and validated answer quality.

Unlike experimental tuning, this sprint enforces a strict architectural rule: performance improvements are accepted only when quality remains within controlled regression thresholds.

Implementing Runtime Optimization Controls

Sprint 2.2 introduces targeted runtime adjustments focused on response shaping, execution reuse, and telemetry expansion. No new tools were introduced, and no orchestration or policy layers were modified.

Runtime Compaction Controls (main.py)

Response compaction logic was introduced to trim structured assistant output while preserving response sections and semantic integrity. Compaction is controlled entirely through environment configuration:

- `THAIN_ENABLE_RESPONSE_COMPACTION`

- `THAIN_RESPONSE_SUMMARY_MAX_CHARS`

- `THAIN_RESPONSE_SUGGEST_MAX_CHARS`

The default settings preserve knowledge-base synthesis in structured responses. They are strict enough to reduce token usage, yet flexible enough to retain multi-step guidance in the summary and suggestion sections.

Compaction is structural rather than semantic. It reduces token footprint without altering reasoning logic or decision pathways.

In-Memory Response Cache (main.py)

Sprint 2.2 adds a bounded, TTL-controlled in-memory cache.

Cache configuration is controlled through: THAIN_ENABLE_CACHE, THAIN_CACHE_TTL_SECONDS, and THAIN_CACHE_MAX_ENTRIES

Cache keys incorporate: user message, model/profile, search/doc flags, and tickets/notify/approvals flags

This ensures that governance-sensitive or action-driven turns are not reused incorrectly.

Cache eligibility explicitly blocks

- Approval-sensitive turns

- Executed/pending/denied/failed states

- Any risky state transitions

When a cache hit occurs, deterministic telemetry is emitted with

- usage_source=cache

- model profile tag

- zero tokens and zero cost recorded, accurately reflecting that no LLM call was made

This approach enables execution reuse without compromising auditability or correctness. The cache operates within a single process instance. In multi-replica deployments, cache hits are not shared across instances, so hit rates reflect only single-instance reuse. At the platform level, Azure OpenAI's native prompt prefix caching reduces input token costs for requests sharing a common system prompt, complementing the response cache introduced here.

Optimization Telemetry on the Root Span (trace_sinks.py)

To support operational visibility, Sprint 2.2 surfaces optimization dimensions directly on the `thain.trace` root span:

- `thain.model.profile`

- `thain.cache.hit`

These dimensions are queryable directly via KQL and surfaced in the Application Insights workbook without span expansion.

This preserves the observability pattern established in Sprint 2.1.

Logging Policy Extension (logging_policy.py)

Optimization telemetry fields are explicitly allowlisted so that

- Model profile

- Cache hit status

- Usage/cost attributes

survive governance filtering and reach Application Insights.

This ensures optimization visibility remains consistent with policy enforcement, rather than bypassing it.

Operationalizing Optimization Controls

Sprint 2.2 introduces configuration and validation scripts that make optimization repeatable and auditable.

Optimization Configuration Script

This script writes optimization controls into `.env.dev`

`infra\s2.2-01-configure-optimization.ps1`.

The controls include

- Model profile

- Compaction settings

- Cache enablement

- TTL and capacity limits

The script emits effective configuration values at execution time, ensuring runtime transparency.

Optimization Validation Gate

The acceptance gate for Sprint 2.2 is:

`infra\s2.2-02-validate-optimization.ps1`

The validation flow

1. Sends controlled /chat prompts, including a repeated prompt to test cache behavior

2. Collects trace identifiers

3. Queries Application Insights for required optimization telemetry

4. Computes average latency, average tokens, average cost, and cache hit count

5. Executes the LLM-as-judge regression gate using the established evaluation pipeline

6. Applies regression thresholds for average score drop and pass-rate drop

The script is resilient to differences in the CLI output shape and extracts telemetry from named columns or `customDimensions` when required. Quality degradation beyond configured thresholds results in a validation failure. Optimization without validation is rejected.

Deployment Sequence (Sprint 2.2)

1. Configure optimization: infra\s2.2-01-configure-optimization.ps1

2. Build image: infra\s1-02-build-push.ps1

3. Deploy application: infra\s1-03-deploy-app.ps1

4. Run validation gate: infra\s2.2-02-validate-optimization.ps1

5. Refresh workbook: infra\s2.1-03-provision-telemetry-workbook.ps1

This follows the controlled sprint pattern established earlier in the book.

Script Evidence

The validation run confirms Sprint 2.2 telemetry is flowing and performance targets are met. Average latency dropped to 8,087 ms, less than half the Sprint 2.1 baseline of 19 seconds.

Token counts are higher in this run than the Sprint 2.1 baseline. This reflects a difference in the validation prompt sets used, not compaction regression. Average tokens per request came in at 88.5 and estimated cost at $0.001325, both consistent with the compaction controls in place. The 88.5 token average reflects the KB-heavy validation prompt set; the Sprint 2.1 baseline of ~72 was captured from a lighter early data point. Compaction reduces per-request token footprint for equivalent prompts.

One cache hit was recorded across the four-prompt run, confirming the cache path is active.

The LLM-as-judge regression gate passed with a positive result. The Sprint 2.2 guard run scored an average of 3.09 with a 54.5% pass rate: marginally better than the Sprint 2.1 baseline of 3.00 and 45.5%. The delta of +0.09 average score and +9.1% pass rate confirms that optimization did not degrade answer quality; it marginally improved it against the same rubric and judge used in Chapter 9. This confirms that the Sprint 2.2 validation has passed. The absolute pass rate reflects a strict rubric applied to a small golden set. It measures regression, not a ceiling on real-world quality.

Portal Verification

Optimization telemetry is surfaced in the `Thain Cost + Latency Metrics` workbook. Sprint 2.2 extends the dashboard with cache hit rate and model profile distribution panels while preserving cost and latency visibility introduced in Sprint 2.1.

The workbook window is configured to display the last 30 days of telemetry, enabling trend analysis beyond isolated validation runs.

Figure 10-3 shows optimization control dimensions, including cache-hit signals and model profile tagging surfaced from root `thain.trace` attributes.

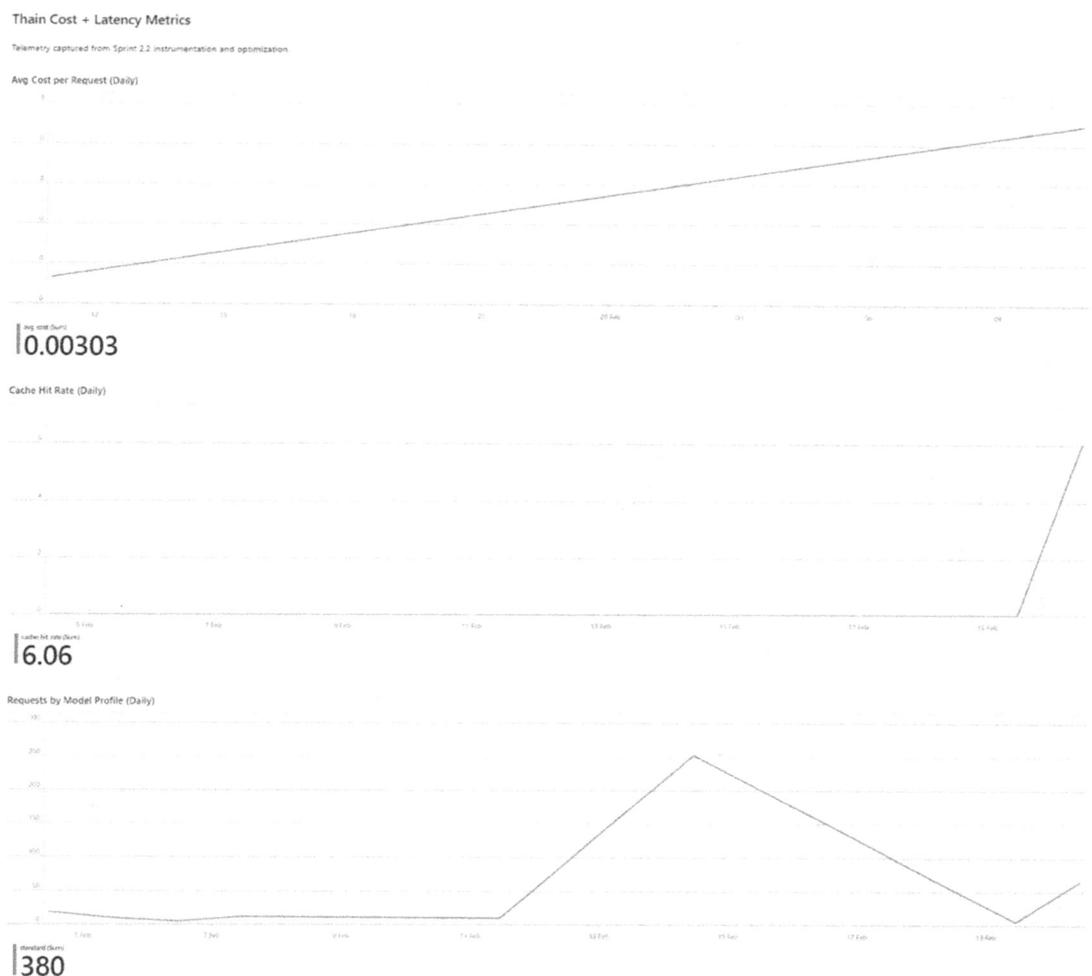

Figure 10-3. *Thain Cost + Latency Metrics: cost, cache hit rate, and model profile*

Figure 10-4 illustrates performance trends across the same period, including average latency, token usage, and p95 latency.

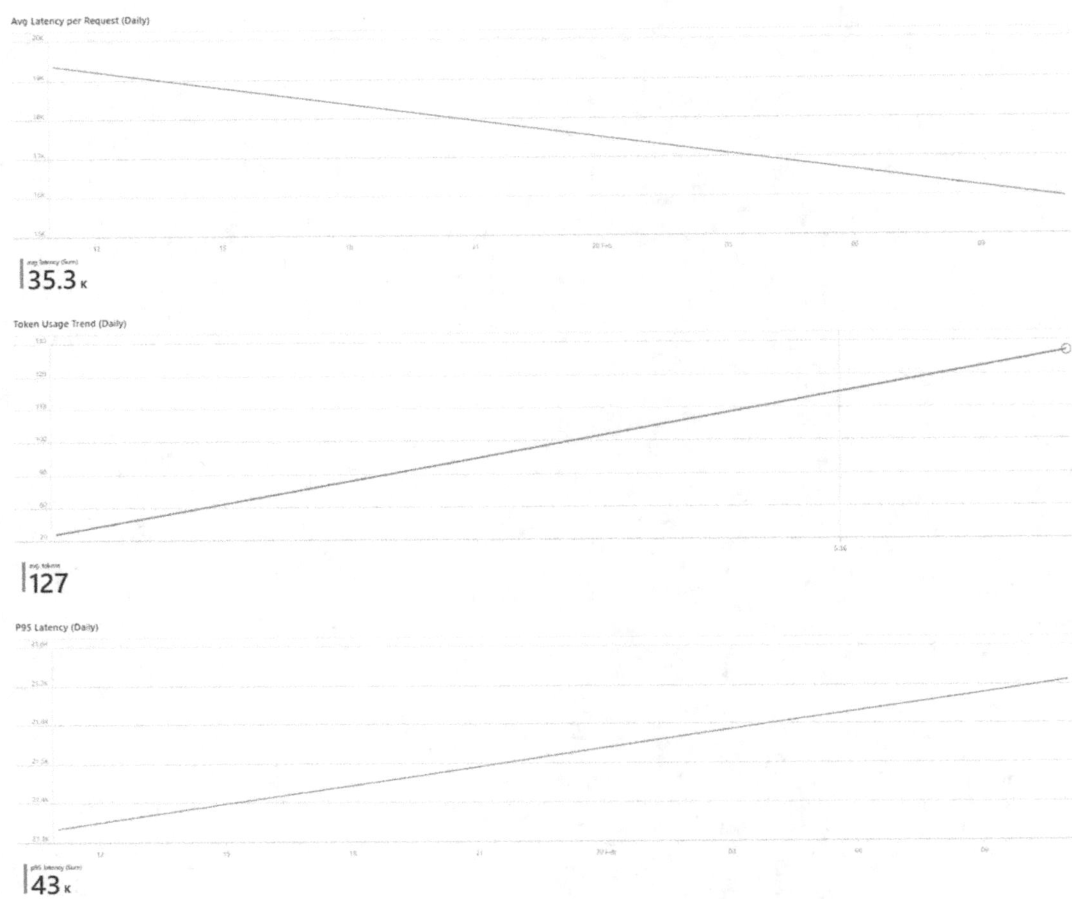

Figure 10-4. *Thain Cost + Latency Metrics: average latency, token usage, and p95 latency*

The token usage trend reflects cumulative request volume growth over the 30-day window, rather than an increase in tokens per request. Response compaction reduced tokens per request, but total daily volume increased as more requests were processed.

Workbook confirms

- Cost panel populated

- Cache hit rate visible

- Model profile surfaced (standard)

- Latency panels populated (avg and p95)

- Token trend populated

This confirms that optimization telemetry is operationally visible and queryable. Workbook metrics reflect 30-day aggregates across all requests in the window. The validation script evidence above represents individual-request averages from a controlled prompt set and serves as the authoritative per-request baseline.

Note   All updated files including code and script referenced in this section are available in the book's GitHub repository under Chapter 10 → Sprint 2.2 → thain.

Sprint 2.2 Outcome

Sprint 2.2 introduces measurable runtime efficiency while preserving correctness under governance.

The system now supports

- Response compaction with bounded controls

- Safe in-memory execution reuse

- Model profile observability

- Automated regression gating

- Operational dashboard validation

Optimization is now evidence based and is accepted only when quality remains within validated thresholds.

In this sprint, the evaluation gate confirmed that quality was not only preserved but improved. The pass rate increased from 45.5% to 54.5% using the same rubric and judge model as in v1.12. Latency decreased from approximately 19 seconds to 8 seconds, while the cost per request remained stable. The system became faster without compromising answer quality.

Sprint 2.2 demonstrates that performance improvements in Thain are engineered and applied with governance discipline, rather than implemented ad hoc.

Sprint 2.3: Data and Reliability Hardening

Sprint 2.3 completes the transition of Thain into a resilient, production-grade service.

Where Sprint 2.1 made the system observable and Sprint 2.2 made it efficient, this sprint ensures the system behaves predictably under stress.

The objective is not to achieve autonomous self-healing. Instead, the focus is on disciplined failure containment.

At this stage, the architecture must demonstrate that transient dependency failures are retried in a bounded manner, repeated failures are suppressed temporarily to prevent cascading impact, degraded responses are explicit and traceable, and operational thresholds are enforced through alerting. All of this must occur without altering orchestration semantics or weakening governance.

The multi-agent workflow remains unchanged. The change lies in how the system responds when its dependencies fail.

Reliability As a Controlled Execution Layer

Sprint 2.3 introduces a centralized reliability control layer implemented in

```
services/reliability.py
```

Rather than scattering retry logic across services, all dependency execution is routed through a single executor. This executor enforces timeout budgets, bounded retries with jittered backoff, and short cooldown suppression windows after repeated failures.

Each dependency, OpenAI, Azure AI Search, and Cosmos DB, is assigned its own logical key and timeout policy. When repeated failures occur within a short window, the executor suppresses further attempts for a brief cooldown period. This prevents thundering herd effects and ensures failure amplification does not propagate through the agent pipeline.

This design is intentionally lightweight. It is not a distributed circuit breaker, but rather a deterministic, in-process containment strategy that ensures controlled behavior within Container Apps replicas.

Chaos flags are introduced to simulate runtime dependency failures. These flags enable controlled validation of degraded behavior without directly manipulating infrastructure. Because these flags are environment based, they require redeployment to take effect, preserving configuration determinism.

The reliability module introduces

- Per-dependency timeout budgets (`openai, search, cosmos`)

- Bounded retries with backoff and jitter

- Cooldown suppression windows after repeated failures

- Explicit exception types: `DependencyFailure` and `DependencySuppressed`

- Chaos injection flags: `THAIN_CHAOS_SIMULATE_OPENAI_FAILURE`, `THAIN_CHAOS_SIMULATE_SEARCH_FAILURE`, and `THAIN_CHAOS_SIMULATE_COSMOS_FAILURE`

- Async-safe state management to prevent interleaved coroutine access

Reliability is now treated as a primary execution concern, rather than an afterthought.

Chat and Dependency Wrapping

All critical dependency paths are now wrapped by the reliability layer. The primary integration point is in `main.py`.

The `/chat` execution path wraps the primary model call under the `openai` dependency key using the reliability executor.

On repeated OpenAI failure

- A deterministic degraded response is returned.

- `thain.fallback.used` is emitted on the root trace.

- Knowledge base and action post-processing are skipped.

This approach ensures degraded responses are explicit, controlled, and free from synthetic augmentation.

Embedding calls in `services/embedding.py` are also executed under the same `openai` dependency key, ensuring consistent retry and telemetry behavior across both reasoning and embedding paths.

Cosmos DB operations – reads, writes, approvals, and memory access – are wrapped under the cosmos dependency key within `memory/repositories.py` and `services/approval_store.py`.

If Cosmos fails, the agent continues to respond, but without persistent memory effects. The failure is contained and observable and does not degrade the user-facing response.

Azure AI Search operations, both semantic recall and knowledge base retrieval, are wrapped under the search dependency key in `memory/docs_search_client.py` and `memory/search_client.py`.

If search fails, the agent continues without contextual augmentation. A stability safeguard ensures that metadata index introspection failures do not affect suppression state, preventing metadata access errors from impacting primary retrieval operations.

Each dependency failure mode is therefore isolated and deterministic. The system does not revert to a generic failure state. Instead, it transitions to a defined behavioral state appropriate to the specific failed dependency.

Reliability Telemetry and Observability

Reliability without visibility is guesswork. Sprint 2.3 extends Thain's telemetry model so that reliability behavior becomes measurable at the same level as cost and latency.

Root-span projection is implemented in `observability/trace_sinks.py`. Rather than emitting retry and failure signals as nested span events, key reliability dimensions are projected directly onto the thain.trace root span. This makes them immediately queryable in KQL and visible in the workbook without span expansion.

The following dimensions are now first-class telemetry attributes: `thain.dependency.retry_count`, `thain.dependency.failure_count`, `thain.dependency.suppressed`, `thain.dependency.failed`, `thain.fallback.used`, and `thain.reliability.degraded`.

This design decision is intentional. Reliability behavior must be inspectable with a single query. Engineers should not need to reconstruct nested spans to determine if fallback was triggered.

To prevent sanitization of new fields, the logging allowlist is updated in `governance/logging_policy.py`. Without this update, fallback metadata and dependency status fields would be stripped before projection.

At this stage, reliability is no longer inferred from log messages; it is captured as structured telemetry.

Operational Alerting and SLO Enforcement

Reliability is operationalized through explicit thresholds.
Sprint 2.3 provisions alert rules using

`infra\s2.3-02-provision-reliability-alerts.ps1`

This script creates or updates

- An action group (`ag-thain-ops`)

- Scheduled query alerts for

  - Error rate > 5% over 15 minutes

  - P95 latency > 30,000 ms over 15 minutes

  - Dependency failures > 3 over 5 minutes

The thresholds are not arbitrary. They reflect acceptable production behavior under normal operating conditions.
When executed, the script confirms

- Alert rule creation

- Threshold values

- Action group binding

Reliability is therefore validated during deployment and continuously enforced at runtime.

Configuration and Chaos Control

Reliability parameters are externalized and written through

`infra\s2.3-01-configure-reliability.ps1`

This script writes to `.env.dev`:

- Retry limits

- Backoff bounds

- Timeout budgets per dependency

- Cooldown thresholds

- Chaos flags

- SLO thresholds used by alert rules

Chaos flags default to false. Because they are environment based, enabling a chaos scenario requires redeployment. This ensures deterministic configuration and prevents runtime mutation of reliability behavior.

The semantic recall index precheck helper is implemented in `infra/scripts/s2_3_ensure_recall_index.py`. This script ensures the recall index exists and matches the configured embedding dimensions before normal scenario validation. Chaos scenarios intentionally skip this check.

Deployment Sequence

Sprint 2.3 follows the same rollout approach used in previous sprints:

- Configure reliability parameters: `.\infra\s2.3-01-configure-reliability.ps1`

- Build the container image: `.\infra\s1-02-build-push.ps1`

- Deploy the Container App: `.\infra\s1-03-deploy-app.ps1`

- Provision or update reliability alert rules: `.\infra\s2.3-02-provision-reliability-alerts.ps1`

- Validate the normal scenario: `.\infra\s2.3-03-validate-reliability.ps1 -Scenario normal`

For each chaos scenario

1. Enable the relevant chaos flag via configuration.

2. Redeploy the Container App.

3. Execute the validation script for that scenario.

For workbook panels refresh

`.\infra\s2.1-03-provision-telemetry-workbook.ps1`

Validation and Controlled Failure Behavior

Validation is executed through

`infra\s2.3-03-validate-reliability.ps1`

The script supports four scenarios: normal, `openai`, `cosmos`, and `search`. Each scenario

- Generates controlled /chat traffic

- Queries Application Insights

- Validates reliability telemetry dimensions

- For the normal scenario, executes the mandatory eval regression gate against the `improved_v12` baseline

Normal Scenario

Run: infra\s2.3-03-validate-reliability.ps1 -Scenario normal
Observed results:

- retries = 0

- failures = 0

- `fallback_used` = 0/3

- average latency ≈ 10.5 seconds

- quality delta avg = 0.00

- `pass_rate_delta` = 0.0%

The higher latency compared to Sprint 2.2 reflects the KB-heavy validation prompts used in this scenario rather than regression in the reliability layer.

An important safeguard is applied automatically. Because the evaluation dataset contains 11 samples, the minimum detectable change in pass rate is $1/11 \approx 9.1\%$. The script adjusts the pass-rate threshold accordingly. Without this adjustment, a 1% threshold would falsely detect statistical noise as regression.

When dependencies are healthy, the reliability layer is effectively invisible.

Workbook Evidence

Sprint 2.3 extends the existing 2.x telemetry workbook rather than introducing a new dashboard. If required, refresh the workbook using

```
.\infra\s2.1-03-provision-telemetry-workbook.ps1
```

Three panels provide primary reliability evidence:

- Dependency Failures (Daily)

- Retry Count (Daily)

- Degraded Fallback Rate (Daily)

The degraded fallback rate remains stable until the OpenAI chaos run, where it increases as expected. Dependency failures rise during chaos runs. Retry count remains lower than failure count due to cooldown suppression logic.

Refer to Figure 10-5 for an example of reliability telemetry surfaced in the Application Insights workbook.

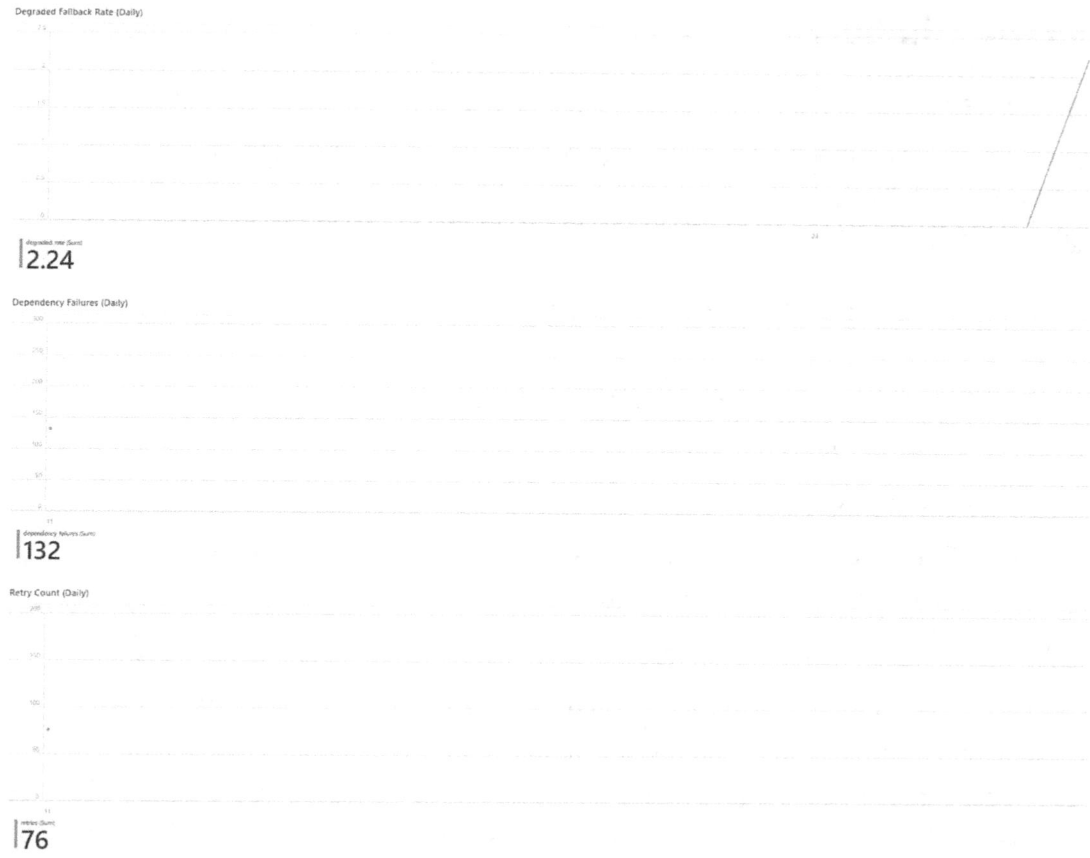

Figure 10-5. *Controlled dependency failure and degraded behavior*

Supporting panels provide additional context:

- Average latency trends downward due to Sprint 2.2 compaction improvements.

- P95 latency spikes during chaos testing. This is expected, as timeout budgets inflate the latency tail.

- Cache hit rate increases during repeated prompt testing.

- Model profile routing remains stable from Sprint 2.2.

The P95 latency spike reflects controlled stress behavior, not regression.

OpenAI Chaos

Enable OpenAI chaos:

```
.\infra\s2.3-01-configure-reliability.ps1 -ChaosOpenAIFailure
.\infra\s1-03-deploy-app.ps1
.\infra\s2.3-03-validate-reliability.ps1 -Scenario openai
```

Under this scenario, every OpenAI call fails.
Observed behavior

- Failures recorded across classification, reasoning, and response stages

- `fallback_used` = 3/3

- retries = 0 (chaos injection raises a terminal failure on the first attempt; no retry loop is entered)

- average latency $\approx$ 962 ms

At ~962 `ms`, latency is a small fraction of the normal path (~10.5 s). With OpenAI chaos enabled, the reliability layer injects a first-attempt dependency failure and short-circuits to a deterministic degraded response. LLM generation is skipped, KB/action enforcement is skipped, and any retrieval/knowledge steps (if triggered) fail fast without contributing grounded guidance.

Cosmos Chaos

Enable Cosmos chaos:

```
.\infra\s2.3-01-configure-reliability.ps1 -ChaosCosmosFailure
.\infra\s1-03-deploy-app.ps1
.\infra\s2.3-03-validate-reliability.ps1 -Scenario cosmos
```

Observed behavior

- Failures recorded for memory read/write operations.

- `fallback_used` = 0/3.

- LLM execution continues normally.

- Latency remains near baseline (~9.3 s).

The agent responds without persistent memory effects. Any failures are limited to memory and approval operations. Since these dependencies support rather than control the agent's reasoning, their failure does not affect response quality.

Search Chaos

Enable Search chaos:

```
.\infra\s2.3-01-configure-reliability.ps1 -ChaosSearchFailure
.\infra\s1-03-deploy-app.ps1
infra\s2.3-03-validate-reliability.ps1 -Scenario search
```

Observed behavior

- Failures recorded across knowledge base and semantic recall paths.

- fallback_used = 0/3.

- LLM execution completes normally.

- Latency $\approx$ baseline (~ 10.2 s).

The agent responds without contextual augmentation. Failure is strictly isolated to retrieval operations. Since these dependencies support rather than determine the agent's reasoning, their failure does not cause a degraded response.

Observed Failure Behavior Summary

The chaos validation scenarios show dependency-specific, deterministic failure behavior. Table 10-1 summarizes user impact, fallback behavior, latency effect, and alert outcomes for each dependency.

Table 10-1. *Observed Failure Behavior Summary*

Dependency	Failure Mode	User Impact	Fallback?	Latency Impact	Alert Trigger
OpenAI	All calls fail	Degraded response served	Yes (3/3)	Drops to ~962 ms	Error rate > 5%/15 min
Cosmos DB	Read/write fails	No memory or approval persistence	No	Near baseline (~9.3 s)	Dependency Failures > 3/5 min
Azure AI Search	Retrieval fails	No KB augmentation, reduced recall grounding	No	Near baseline (~10.2 s)	Dependency Failures > 3/5 min

Note   All updated files including code and script referenced in this section are available in the book's GitHub repository under Chapter 10 → Sprint 2.3 → thain.

Sprint 2.3 Outcome

Sprint 2.3 completes Thain v2.0.

All critical dependencies are governed by bounded retry, timeout budgets, and cooldown suppression. Degraded behavior is explicit and deterministic. Reliability telemetry is projected to the root span. SLO alerting is enforced in Azure Monitor. Chaos scenarios validate controlled behavior across OpenAI, Search, and Cosmos. Quality remains protected through mandatory regression gating.

All changes were applied without altering orchestration semantics or weakening governance controls. Thain v2.0 now operates with measurable cost, latency, quality, and reliability, all enforced through deterministic architectural controls.

Note   The sprint-wise implementation of Thain is available in the respective sprint folders within the Chapter 10 directory of the book's GitHub repository: `https://github.com/Apress/Architecting-Intelligent-Agents-in-Azure`. Unit test files for each sprint are included.

The final project state for this chapter is in the Sprint 2.3 folder within the Chapter 10 directory of the repository. To set up the repository locally, use the following commands:

`git clone https://github.com/Apress/Architecting-Intelligent-Agents-in-Azure.git`

`cd Architecting-Intelligent-Agents-in-Azure`

For the manuscript code, open the Chapter 10/Sprint 2.3/thain folder. For the GA code, open Code GA/Chapter 10/Sprint 2.3/thain. Replace Sprint 2.3 with the relevant sprint folder if you want to work with a specific sprint.

After cloning, create and activate a virtual environment, and then install the dependencies:

`python -m venv .venv`

`.\.venv\Scripts\activate`

`pip install -r requirements.txt -c constraints.txt`

Before running the project, fill in your Azure resource details in the `.env` file provided in each sprint folder.

To run the unit tests for any sprint, activate the virtual environment and run:

`python -m pytest tests.`

Reliability Architecture

Figure 10-6 illustrates Thain's centralized reliability execution model. All external dependency calls are routed through a single `ReliabilityExecutor`, which enforces timeout budgets, bounded retries, and cooldown suppression per dependency key. Failure handling is dependency specific.

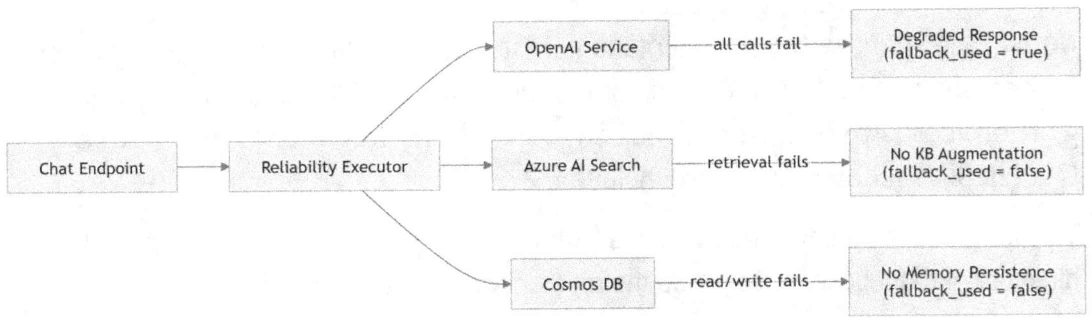

Figure 10-6. *Centralized reliability execution model*

If the OpenAI dependency fails, the executor returns a deterministic degraded response. Failures in Azure AI Search or Cosmos DB do not interrupt execution; the agent continues without knowledge augmentation or memory persistence. This centralized execution boundary ensures that reliability policies remain consistent and observable without modifying orchestration logic or agent behavior.

Retry and cooldown logic are enforced per dependency key before the final failure outcome is reached. Each failure mode is isolated and deterministic. The system does not enter a generic failure state; it transitions to the appropriate degraded behavior for the specific dependency that failed.

The Road to Production Scale

Sprints 2.1 through 2.3 establish the operational foundation required for production scale.

Cost is measurable and governed. Latency is instrumented and optimized. Reliability is enforced through bounded retries, timeout budgets, and explicit degradation paths. SLO thresholds and alerting are active. Chaos validation confirms controlled dependency failure behavior.

This foundation is not optional. Systems that scale without operational discipline amplify their failure modes; systems that build it first scale with confidence.

Thain v2.0 does not claim proven horizontal scaling under sustained load. Instead, it establishes the architectural conditions needed to ensure scaling is safe and measurable.

The instrumentation, alerting, and reliability controls established in v2.0 are the prerequisites that make the following scaling steps safe to attempt:

- Replace the per-replica in-memory cache with a distributed cache, such as Azure Cache for Redis, to enable execution reuse across instances.

- Conduct sustained load testing using tools like k6 or Locust to generate throughput and concurrency curves.

- Validate Container App autoscale behavior under controlled traffic increases.

- Provide capacity evidence by establishing p95 and p99 latency baselines at defined target requests per second.

- Establish a Cosmos DB RU baseline under load. Conversation writes, memory retrieval, and approval persistence each consume RU proportional to payload size and query complexity; RU allocation should be validated against target requests per second before scaling replicas.

- Monitor Azure AI Search for query throttling under sustained traffic. Semantic ranking and vector search introduce per-query compute cost; tier capacity and replica count should be validated against expected retrieval queries per second before scaling out.

Each of these activities builds on the instrumentation, alerting, and reliability controls introduced in v2.0. Telemetry for measuring scale is already in place. SLO thresholds are defined, and the failure containment layer is established.

Thain v2.0 does not complete the journey to scale. Instead, it establishes the conditions necessary for achieving scale safely and measurably.

Summary

Chapter 10 completes Thain's transition to v2.0 through three structured operational sprints.

Sprint 2.1 established request-level visibility for token usage, latency, and estimated cost. Telemetry is emitted on each turn, projected to the root trace span, validated by script, and visualized in an Application Insights workbook.

Sprint 2.2 introduced governed optimization. Response compaction, bounded in-memory caching per instance, and model-profile observability reduced latency and maintained cost efficiency without quality regression. Changes were accepted only after passing the LLM-as-judge regression gate.

Sprint 2.3 hardened reliability at the dependency layer. Timeout budgets, bounded retries, cooldown suppression, and chaos validation scenarios (OpenAI, Search, Cosmos) were added. Degraded fallback behavior is explicit and traceable, and Azure Monitor alert rules enforce SLO thresholds.

All improvements were applied without altering the system's reasoning, governance, or safety model.

Thain v2.0 now operates with measurable cost and latency, validated quality, and controlled dependency-failure handling, providing an enterprise-ready operational baseline.

Architectural Outcomes

By the end of Chapter 10, Thain demonstrates architectural properties that encompass not only correctness and quality but also operational discipline:

- **Economic observability by design**: Token usage, estimated cost, and latency are reported at the request level, mapped to the root trace span, and displayed in operational dashboards. Cost and performance are treated as measurable system properties, not inferred metrics.

- **Configuration-driven optimization controls**: Response compaction, cache eligibility, and model profiling are managed entirely through environment configuration. Optimization can be enabled, adjusted, or disabled without changing orchestration logic or reducing governance.

- **Validated performance governance**: Runtime efficiency improvements are implemented only after passing automated regression tests against a fixed evaluation baseline. Cost and latency reductions are made within measurable quality constraints to ensure answer integrity is maintained.

- **Deterministic execution reuse**: In-memory caching operates within defined TTL and capacity limits, following strict eligibility rules that exclude approval-sensitive or state-altering actions. Execution reuse increases efficiency without compromising auditability or safety.

- **Centralized reliability enforcement**: All external dependencies are managed through a unified reliability layer with defined timeout budgets, limited retries, and cooldown suppression. Failure containment occurs at a single abstraction boundary instead of being distributed across services.

- **Explicit degraded behavior**: When critical dependencies fail, the system provides deterministic fallback responses. Degraded states are traceable, observable, and attributed to the affected dependency, preventing cascading changes in orchestration.

- **Operational threshold enforcement**: Reliability and performance constraints are defined through Azure Monitor alert rules and SLO-aligned thresholds. Operational health is continuously monitored with alert-based enforcement.

Enterprise Agent Architecture: A Reference Implementation

The patterns introduced across this book do not exist in isolation. Persistent memory, semantic retrieval, governed action tools, multi-agent orchestration, observability, reliability, and continuous evaluation all converge in this section, which presents a production system built on exactly these foundations: a three-plane architecture that ingests enterprise data, prepares it for intelligent retrieval, and exposes an agent execution layer to multiple consuming applications through a standardized interface.

This architecture is included here not as a theoretical exercise but as a reference point. Every capability described in the planes below maps directly to a pattern covered in this book. See Figure 10-7.

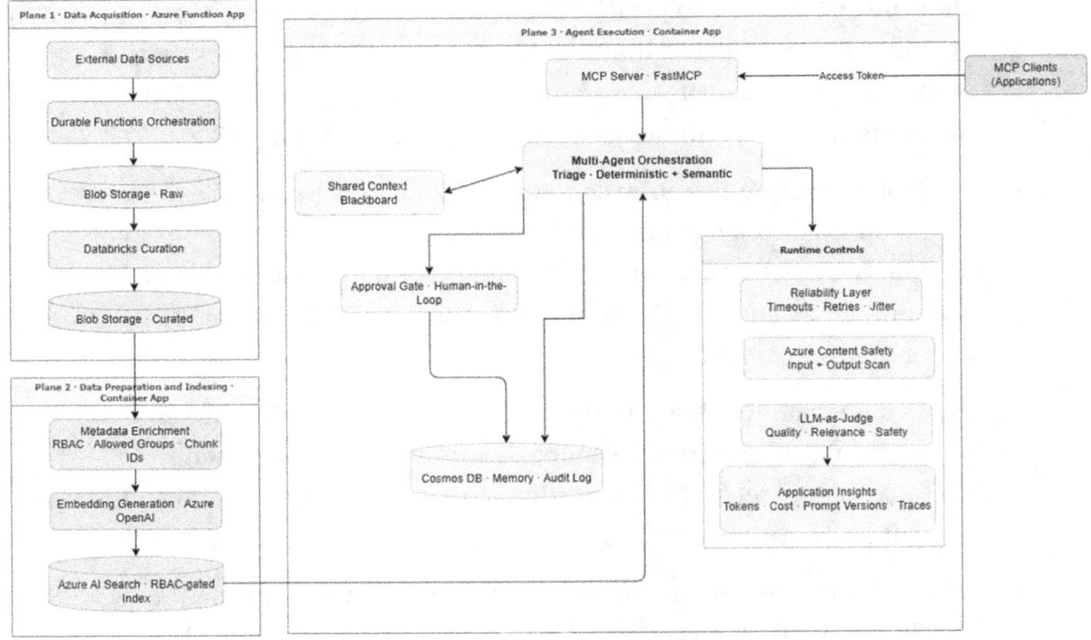

Figure 10-7. *Three-plane production agent architecture*

Plane 1: Data Acquisition and Curation

Hosted on: Azure Function App

The first plane is responsible for acquiring and preparing raw data from enterprise data sources. Azure Durable Functions orchestrate long-running ingestion workflows reliably, handling variable-latency data pipelines in a fault-tolerant, stateful, and resumable manner. Data pulled from various sources is staged in Azure Blob Storage and then curated and normalized through Azure Databricks before being written back to a curated blob layer. This plane operates independently of AI concerns. Its sole responsibility is producing clean, structured content that the next plane can process.

Plane 2: Data Preparation and Indexing

Hosted on: Azure Container App

The second plane transforms curated content into retrieval-ready knowledge. For each document, metadata is enriched with fields that govern downstream behavior, including document status and allowed groups. Allowed groups are the mechanism through which role-based access control (RBAC) is enforced: each document carries a set of group identifiers that determine which users are permitted to retrieve it during agent interactions. Access boundaries are encoded at index time, not applied as runtime filters after retrieval has already occurred.

Chunk identifiers are generated deterministically, so that re-indexing the same content produces the same identifiers, preventing index pollution from duplicate processing runs. Embeddings are generated using Azure OpenAI and the enriched content is written to Azure AI Search. The result is a governed, semantically searchable knowledge base where RBAC is a structural property of the index.

Plane 3: Agent Execution

Hosted on: Azure Container App

The third plane is where the patterns from this book converge.

A multi-agent architecture handles incoming requests. The triage agent applies a hybrid routing strategy: approximately 70% of decisions are resolved deterministically based on structured metadata, while the remaining 30% are handled through semantic reasoning. This split keeps the system predictable and cost-efficient while retaining the flexibility to handle ambiguous cases.

Agent coordination within Plane 3 follows the blackboard pattern. Rather than passing control directly between agents, each agent reads from and writes to a shared context structure that represents the current state of the interaction. This makes the reasoning process observable and allows specialized agents to contribute without tight coupling between them.

Retrieval is backed by the Azure AI Search index built in Plane 2. Because RBAC group membership is encoded at index time, users only retrieve content they are authorized to access. The agent does not need to apply access logic itself.

Every request passes through Azure Content Safety on both the input and output path, ensuring that neither user-submitted content nor agent-generated responses bypass safety boundaries.

Actions with external side effects require explicit human authorization before execution. An approval gate intercepts any action with external side effects, pausing execution until approval is granted or denied, and the outcome is recorded in the audit log regardless of the decision. Calls to external dependencies are wrapped in a reliability layer that enforces per-dependency timeout budgets and bounded retry policies with jitter, ensuring that transient failures in downstream systems do not propagate into agent failures.

Agent responses are evaluated continuously using an LLM-as-judge pipeline. A secondary model scores each response for quality, relevance, and safety alignment, and those scores are written to Application Insights alongside the originating conversation. This creates a live quality signal that can surface degradation before it becomes visible to users, closing the feedback loop between deployment and improvement. Continuous evaluation adds per-request latency and cost; sampling strategies or async scoring pipelines reduce this overhead in high-volume deployments.

Persistent memory and audit logging are handled through Cosmos DB. Conversation history is stored per session to support multi-turn reasoning, while audit records capture the full decision trail for governance and compliance. Prompt templates are versioned and managed centrally, with the active prompt version recorded alongside every conversation in Application Insights. This ensures that changes to system prompts are traceable across the full conversation history. Alongside prompt versions, Application Insights receives token usage, estimated cost, latency, evaluation scores, and redacted conversation traces, providing a complete operational picture of every agent interaction.

MCP Exposure

The agent execution layer is exposed as a Model Context Protocol server using FastMCP. Rather than embedding agent logic into each consuming application, client applications connect to the MCP server and interact with the agent through a standardized interface.

Access is controlled through bearer tokens, ensuring that only authorized applications can initiate agent sessions. This design allows the same agent system, with all its governance, observability, and evaluation infrastructure, to serve multiple applications without duplicating any of it across integration points. MAF also supports MCP natively via *as_mcp_server()*; the same governance and tool contracts apply regardless of the MCP server implementation chosen.

Patterns in Practice

Every element of this architecture has a counterpart in this book. Persistent memory and Cosmos DB were introduced in Chapter 3. Semantic retrieval and Azure AI Search were covered in Chapter 4. Governed action tools and approval gates were established in Chapter 5. Observability, content safety, and policy enforcement were the focus of Chapter 6. Multi-agent orchestration appeared in Chapter 7. LLM-as-judge evaluation and the feedback loop were introduced in Chapter 9. The cost telemetry, caching, and reliability controls from this chapter operate within Plane 3 at runtime.

The three-plane separation is a practical response to the different operational characteristics of ingestion, indexing, and execution. Each plane scales independently, fails independently, and can be modified without disrupting the others. The MCP interface decouples consuming applications from the agent layer entirely. The result is an agent system where every layer has a defined responsibility, every action is traceable, and every failure is bounded.

Enduring Principles for Agentic Systems

The three-plane architecture in the preceding section is one realization of the principles this book has built toward. The principles that shaped it generalize beyond any specific implementation.

Thain started as a conceptual preview in Microsoft Foundry. By Chapter 10, it had evolved into a governed, observable, evaluated, and resilient service that measures cost, validates quality, and degrades predictably under failure.

The principles that shaped this evolution are more important than the evolution itself.

The architecture was not expanded arbitrarily. Each capability was introduced at the correct layer and validated before extension. Memory preceded semantic recall. Tool invocation preceded approval workflows. Observability preceded optimization. Evaluation preceded quality improvement. Reliability controls preceded scale readiness.

This sequencing demonstrates a broader architectural principle: discipline compounds. Systems built layer by layer, with explicit invariants preserved at each stage, remain diagnosable, governable, and adaptable as complexity increases.

Several principles generalize beyond this specific implementation:

1. **Govern at Boundaries**

   All external interactions, including tools, storage, retrieval, and inference, should pass through explicit contracts. Governance is not an overlay; it is structural.

2. **Preserve Architectural Invariants During Optimization**

   Performance improvements must not change reasoning semantics, safety posture, or orchestration behavior. Optimizing without preserving invariants introduces hidden risk.

3. **Measure Before You Optimize**

   Cost, latency, quality, and failure behavior must be observable before tuning. Telemetry should come before performance improvements.

4. **Isolate Failure Modes**

   External dependencies will fail. Systems must degrade in a controlled manner, with bounded retries and explicit fallback behavior.

5. **Separate Reasoning from Orchestration**

   LLM reasoning, workflow coordination, persistence, and reliability should remain layered and able to evolve independently.

6. **Treat Evaluation As an Engineering Discipline**

   Quality improvement requires measurable criteria, regression thresholds, and repeatable validation, rather than intuition.

7. **Scale Only After Operational Readiness**

   Horizontal scaling amplifies both strengths and weaknesses. Observability, cost governance, and failure containment must be in place before increasing concurrency.

Agentic systems are still maturing. Frameworks evolve, model capabilities shift, and infrastructure changes. What remains stable are these structural concerns: contracts, invariants, layering, telemetry, governance, and disciplined extension.

The agents built by readers of this book will not be Thain. They will operate in different domains, under different constraints, and across different integrations. But systems built with these principles will remain comprehensible, governable, and adaptable, even as the tools around them change.

Thain is an example. The principles are reusable.

Index

reliability control, 424

scaling steps, 436

structure, 405

T, U

GPSR Compliance
The European Union's (EU) General Product Safety Regulation (GPSR) is a set
of rules that requires consumer products to be safe and our obligations to
ensure this.

If you have any concerns about our products, you can contact us on

ProductSafety@springernature.com

In case Publisher is established outside the EU, the EU authorized
representative is:

Springer Nature Customer Service Center GmbH
Europaplatz 3
69115 Heidelberg, Germany